E-Supply Chain Technologies and Management

Qingyu Zhang
Arkansas State University, USA

Information Science REFERENCE
INFORMATION SCIENCE REFERENCE
Hershey · London · Melbourne · Singapore

Acquisitions Editor:	Kristin Klinger
Development Editor:	Kristin Roth
Senior Managing Editor:	Jennifer Neidig
Managing Editor:	Sara Reed
Assistant Managing Editor:	Sharon Berger
Copy Editor:	Maria Boyer
Typesetter:	Michael Brehm
Cover Design:	Lisa Tosheff
Printed at:	Yurchak Printing Inc.

Published in the United States of America by
Information Science Reference (an imprint of IGI Global)
701 E. Chocolate Avenue, Suite 200
Hershey PA 17033
Tel: 717-533-8845
Fax: 717-533-8661
E-mail: cust@idea-group.com
Web site: http://www.idea-group-ref.com

and in the United Kingdom by
Information Science Reference (an imprint of IGI Global)
3 Henrietta Street
Covent Garden
London WC2E 8LU
Tel: 44 20 7240 0856
Fax: 44 20 7379 0609
Web site: http://www.eurospanonline.com

Library of Congress Cataloging-in-Publication Data

E-supply chain technologies and management / Qingyu Zhang, editor.

p. cm.

Summary: "This book explores concepts, models, and IT infrastructures of the e-supply chain, and develops a broad understanding of issues pertaining to the use of emerging technologies and their impact on supply chain flexibility and management. It provides key ideas, concepts and applications suited to guide efforts in transforming current business processes to adapt to the digital age"--Provided by publisher.

Includes bibliographical references and index.

ISBN 978-1-59904-255-8 (hardcover) -- ISBN 978-1-59904-257-2 (ebook)

1. Business logistics--Technological innovations. 2. Information technology. I. Zhang, Qingyu, 1970-

HD38.5.E18 2007

658.70285'4678--dc22

2006033760

British Cataloguing in Publication Data
A Cataloguing in Publication record for this book is available from the British Library.

Table of Contents

Detailed Table of Contents

Section I
Concepts and Modeling of E-Supply Chain

The chapter develops a procedure, eSCM-I, to improve the supply chain business process. It is based on the supply chain operations reference (SCOR) model and IDEF0 technique. A four-step procedure is proposed: (1) process standardization, (2) business process modeling, (3) benchmarking of best practices, and (4) gap determination. The procedure identifies process interdependencies and coordinates supply chain activities.

The chapter models transshipments in the supply chain and particularly explores the shipments among distribution centers in a geographically dispersed network. The authors investigate transshipment strategies in a continuous review system under dynamic demand. They propose three heuristic decision rules for making transshipment decisions. By using numerical experiments and simulation analysis, the authors identify a best heuristic rule to determine effective transshipment policies.

The chapter deals with the issues for small and medium-sized enterprises (SMEs) in supply chains. It provides an overview of literature on the role of SMEs in economy, supply chain management (SCM), information and communication technologies (ICTs), and e-business. The author discusses both opportunities and challenges for supply chains in general and also SMEs in particular.

The chapter addresses supply chain integration by the use of collaboration tools. The author explains the concept of collaboration tools and its importance in the supply chain integration, evaluates the requirements for supply chain management, and emphasizes the collaborative problem areas within the supply chain. A case study for an application of collaboration tools is presented. The author argues that supply chain collaboration is effective only if the collaboration tools are integrated and used jointly by supply chain partners.

The chapter introduces the concept of experience management in multi-agent systems for supply chain management. The authors argue that agents in the supply chain must be capable of dynamically adapting their behavior. The chapter discusses issues in agent negotiation and cooperation, and provides an example of multi-agent architecture. The role of trust and deception in supply chains for real-time enterprises is also discussed.

The chapter proposes an infrastructure for modeling and coordinating e-business processes using e-coalitions (i.e., support for collaborations with supply chain partners over the Internet). It discusses traditional EDI systems and modern EDI systems over the Internet. It also describes a typical scenario where e-coalitions involve a travel agency and its partners for supplying flight tickets. The open software infrastructure for supporting supply chain and e-commerce includes CORBA, DCOM, and JVM.

The chapter presents a case study on a leading Chinese manufacturer of industrial valves that successfully integrated ERP and SCM systems. The integration of ERP and SCM improved the company's operations and resulted in many benefits. The process of implementation and integration also poses many challenges, some of which are unique to a Chinese manufacturing organization. The authors conclude with several lessons learned from the company's experience.

Preface

As information and communication technologies (ICTs) radically facilitate the convergence of data, voice, and video; support real-time transactions and interactivity; and enhance access and connectivity, we are confronted with new challenges for designing and building an e-supply chain. An e-supply chain is the use of information technology (IT), electronic means, or cyberspace to bring together widely dispersed suppliers and buyers, to enhance coordination and knowledge sharing, and to manage upstream and downstream value chain channels spanning from the supplier's supplier to the customer's customer. E-supply chain enables firms to improve flexibility and move toward real-time operations by sharing information and collaborating dynamically among partners.

E-supply chain activities include plan, source, make, deliver, and return. IT links the separated supply chain activities into an integrated, coordinated system that is fast, responsive, flexible, and efficient. For example, EDI, teleconferencing, and e-mail systems reduce the cycle time in communication. Bar coding, radio frequency identification, and material handling technologies are used for efficient distribution and inventory management. E-supply chain portals and ERP systems enable real-time end-to-end information sharing and real-time decision making. Supply chain technologies will ultimately enable more flexible and agile business practices. They will help companies come together and form virtual organizations to co-create value.

However, issues related to technologies, standards, costs, and management have hindered the creation of a true e-supply chain that seamlessly incorporates all partners. Many challenges need to be addressed to gain a deeper understanding of how to effectively apply and manage these technologies.

The objective of the book is to explore the concepts, modeling, technologies, IT infrastructures, and performance management of the e-supply chain and develop a broad understanding of issues pertaining to the use of emerging information technologies and their impacts on e-supply chain management. The book aims to highlight e-supply chain technologies and their effective management and guide efforts in transforming current business processes to adapt to the digital age.

This book is designed to cover a broad range of topics in the field of e-supply chains in 14 chapters. It is primarily intended for professionals, researchers, and practitioners who want to explore/understand the concepts and principles of the e-supply chain and want to apply various e-supply chain models and systems to solve business problems. Each chapter is designed to be stand-alone, and thus readers can focus on their interested topics.

SECTION I

Section I consists of five chapters on the concepts and modeling of e-supply chain. Chapters I and II deal with the modeling of e-supply chain management. Chapter III discusses the concepts of e-supply chain and SME. Chapters IV and V present the concepts of e-services and service value network.

Chapter I

Procedure for Modeling and Improving E-SCM Processes by Patcharee Boonyathan and Latif Al-Hakim, develops a procedure referred to as eSCM-I to improve the supply chain business processes, taking into consideration the Internet and e-business communication technologies. It is based on the supply chain operations reference (SCOR) model for process standardization and the IDEF0 technique (i.e., a graphical method designed to model the activities, actions, and decisions of an organization or system) for process mapping. The four-step procedure is proposed to improve competitive advantage and customer satisfaction: process standardization, business process modeling, benchmarking and identification of best practices, and gap determination. The procedure identifies process interdependencies and manages supply chain coordination.

Chapter II

Dynamic Transshipment in the Digital Age by Shilei Yang, Bintong Chen, and Charles L. Munson, explores how to handle transshipment among distribution centers in a geographically dispersed network. They investigate transshipment strategies in a continuous review system with dynamic demand and present a dynamic program that identifies the optimal transshipment rule. Since the dynamic program presented is time consuming and difficult for practitioners to implement, they propose three distinct heuristic decision rules for making transshipment decisions. After numerical experiments and simulation analysis based on various combinations of demand rates and delivery costs, they identify a good heuristic rule, which can be conveniently implemented in practice to determine effective transshipment policies.

Chapter III

E-Com Supply Chain and SMEs by Ron Craig, takes the perspective of small and medium-sized enterprises (SMEs) in supply chains. It reviews the important role of SMEs in national and world economies. The chapter provides an extensive overview of literature on supply chain management (SCM), information and communication technologies (ICTs), and e-business. Both opportunities and challenges for supply chains in general and SMEs in particular are considered. The future direction for researchers and practitioners are pointed out.

Chapter IV

Building and Managing Modern E-Services by John Hamilton, addresses the development cycle of an e-services model. Services as a value creation process progress from supply and demand chains, to value chains, to service value chains, and finally to service value networks. This progression pathway develops over time and enables service businesses to develop competitive business solutions. Service value networks, as an advanced value creation structure, house fully integrated e-demand and e-supply chains, working in harmony to deliver flexible business solutions to customer requests. This chapter also offers managers a balanced scorecard structural mechanism through which management controls e-services.

Chapter V

Service Value Networks: Delivering Competitive E-Services by John Hamilton, addresses service value networks as a key pathway to establishing and likely retaining future strong competitive positioning within a service industry sector. He defines service value network as the flexible delivery of a service, and/or product, by a business and its networked, coordinated value chains such that a value-adding and target-specific service and/or product solution is effectively and efficiently delivered to the individual customer. The procedure to research and develop a service value network is described.

SECTION II

Section II consists of five chapters on e-supply chain technologies and IT infrastructure such as radio frequency identification (RFID), security, collaboration tools, software agents, and EDI. Chapter VI deals with automated data capture technologies—RFID. Chapter VII discusses infrastructure security. Chapter VIII handles collaboration tools. Chapter IX presents software agents in the supply chain. Chapter X deals with EDI and e-coalition.

Chapter VI

Automated Data Capture Technologies: RFID by Vidyasagar Potdar, Chen Wu, and Elizabeth Chang, provides an introduction to RFID technology. The authors discuss the main components of the RFID technology, which includes RFID transponders, RFID readers, RFID middleware, and RFID labels. A detailed classification and explanation of these components is provided, followed by the benefits and applications that can be achieved by adopting this technology. They also depict the adoption challenges such as security, privacy, cost, scalability, resilience, and deployment. They describe some successful RFID deployment case studies on the adoption of RFID technology. For business executives and consultants, they provide a comprehensive list of RFID vendors across the globe. For researchers, they list some open issues on adoption challenges. For advanced users, in-depth technical details are provided about security and privacy enhancing protocols.

Chapter VII

Information Security Risk in the E-Supply Chain by Wade H. Baker, Gregory E. Smith, and Kevin James Watson, identifies the sources of IT threats in the supply chain, categorizes those threats, and validates them through a survey of 188 companies representing a range of supply chain functions. They argue that the integration of information flows facilitate collaboration between supply chain partners; however, the interconnectivity also increases supply chain risks. The increased use of information technology has removed an organization's internal and external protective barriers, and thus supply chains are more vulnerable to IT-specific risks. Through analysis, they suggest that supply chain risk is affected by IT threats, and thus the benefits of collaboration facilitated by IT integration must exceed the increase in risk.

Chapter VIII

The Use of Collaboration Tools in Supply Chain: Implications and Challenges by Ozlem Bak, addresses supply chain integration by the use of collaboration tools, including inter- and intra-enterprise applications such as customer relationship management, supplier relationship management, e-business and employee-business integration, e-supply chain management, Web-enabled services, wireless applications, and software applications. The chapter explains the concept of collaboration tools and its importance in the supply chain integration, evaluates the requirements for supply chain management (SCM), and emphasizes the collaborative problem areas within supplier and SCM relations. A case study of an application of collaboration tools is presented. He argues that collaboration in supply chain is effective only if the collaboration tools are integrated or used jointly by supply chain partners.

Chapter IX

Negotiation, Trust, and Experience Management in E-Supply Chains by Gavin Finnie and Zhaohao Sun, introduces the concept of experience management in multi-agent systems for supply chain management and develops a unified model for cooperation, negotiation, trust, and deception. They argue that agents in the supply chain must be capable of dynamically adapting their behavior, and the experience management paradigm offers a new approach to automated learning. The chapter discusses issues in agent negotiation and cooperation, and provides an example of multi-agent architecture. The role of trust and deception in supply chains for real-time enterprises is also discussed. Some new areas of research are highlighted.

Chapter X

Trading E-Coalition Modeling for Supply Chain by Pierre F. Tiako, proposes an appropriate infrastructure for modeling and coordinating e-business processes using e-coalitions (i.e., support for collaborations with supply chain partners over the Internet). It discusses EDI systems and EDI over the Internet. It also describes a typical scenario where e-coalitions involve a travel agency and its partners for supplying flight tickets. The idea combines support for modeling and coordinating relationships among e-coalition components located in different places with an architecture for their distribution. The open software infrastructure for supporting supply chain and e-commerce includes CORBA, distributed component object model (DCOM), and Java Virtual Machine (JVM).

SECTION III

Section III consists of four chapters on best practices and performance management of e-supply chain. Chapter XI deals with practices of ERP and SCM integration. Chapter XII discusses satisficing performance targets. Chapter XIII presents an information feedback approach to maintaining service quality. Chapter XIV deals with performance management.

Chapter XI

E-Supply Chain System at Valvex and Its Integration with ERP Systems by Raktim Pal, Indranil Bose, and Alex Ye, presents a case study on a leading Chinese manufacturer of industrial valves that successfully integrated the ERP systems from Entreplan and an SCM system from Excelvision. This chapter describes the implementation of the e-SCM system at Valvex and its integration with the existing ERP system. The integration of ERP and SCM improved the operations at Valvex and resulted in many benefits. The authors point out that the process of implementation and integration poses many challenges, and some of them are unique to a Chinese manufacturing organization. They conclude with several lessons learned from the experience of Valvex that may be useful for organizations that plan to undertake similar projects.

Chapter XII

Coordination of a Supply Chain with Satisficing Objectives Using Contracts by Chunming (Victor) Shi and Bintong Chen, studies a decentralized supply chain consisting of a supplier and a retailer, both with the satisficing objective or performance targets. They examine the supply chain under three types of commonly used contracts: wholesale price, buy back, and quantity flexibility contracts. They identify the Pareto-optimal contract(s) for each contractual form and the contractual forms, which are capable of supply chain coordination with the satisficing objectives. They show that wholesale price contracts can coordinate the supply chain with the satisficing objectives, whereas buy back contracts cannot. Furthermore, quantity flexibility contracts must degenerate into wholesale price contracts to coordinate the supply chain. This provides an important justification for the popularity of wholesale price contracts. The authors also discuss possible extensions to their model.

Chapter XIII

Information Feedback Approach for Maintaining Service Quality in Supply Chain Management by R. Manjunath, considers a feedback mechanism that conveys the status of the supply chain, starting from the tail end with the pre-specified service quality as seen by the end user of the supply chain. Maintaining the service quality in a supply chain has become a challenging task with increased complexity and number of players down the chain. The chapter highlights the advantages of using a predicted and shifted slippage or loss rate as the feedback signal. Based on the feedback, the source is expected to change the rate of transfer of the commodity over the supply chain. Thus the resources would get utilized effectively, reducing the stranded time of the commodity down the chain and the service quality gets improved.

Chapter XIV

Performance Management by Srikanth Srinivas, designs a performance management framework that helps firms choose, implement, and get significant benefits from e-supply chain technologies. The framework combines critical variables, balanced scorecard, and capability maturity. He organizes the framework using a balanced scorecard revolving around five critical variables of value, variety, velocity, variability. and visibility. The maturity level of each of these critical variables is classified using a six-level capability maturity continuum—ignorance, awareness, understanding, approach, action, and culture. The framework helps managers identify where the gaps are and thus leverage technologies to bridge those gaps.

All chapters have gone through a rigorous, double-blind review process before acceptance. It is hoped that the readers will find these chapters informative, enlightening, and helpful.

Acknowledgments

Publishing a scholarly book is a collective effort and involves many people. I wish to thank all involved in the collation and review process of the book, without whose support the book could not have been completed.

Special appreciation and gratitude go to the publishing team at IGI, in particular to Kristin Roth, Jan Travers, and Medhi Khosrow-Pour, whose contributions throughout the process of the book publication have been invaluable.

I want to thank all the authors for their excellent contributions to this book. I'm also grateful to all the reviewers, including most of the contributing authors, who served as referees for chapters written by other authors, and provided constructive and comprehensive reviews in the double-blind review process.

Last but not least, I thank my wife, Mei, and my parents for their love, encouragement, and unfailing support throughout this project.

Qingyu Zhang, PhD, CFPIM, MCSD, MCSE, MCDBA
Arkansas State University, USA
August 2006

Section I
Concepts and Modeling of E-Supply Chain

Chapter I
Procedure for Modeling and Improving E-SCM Processes

Patcharee Boonyathan
University of Melbourne, Australia

Latif Al-Hakim
University of Southern Queensland, Australia

ABSTRACT

Today's managers are turning to the functions of the supply chain to improve margins and gain competitive advantage. The explosion of the Internet and other e-business technologies has made real-time, online communication throughout the entire supply chain a reality. Electronic supply chain management (e-SCM) is a reference to the supply chain that is structured via electronic technology-enabled relationships. This chapter concentrates on the development of a procedure referred to as eSCM-I for e-SCM process improvement. The procedure focuses on process mapping and relies on principles of coordination theory. It is based on SCOR to standardize the process and take advantage of this technique of benchmarking/best practices potential. The procedure employs IDEF0 technique for mapping the processes.

INTRODUCTION

Supply chain management (SCM) is a network of entities that encompasses every effort involved in producing and delivering a final product, from the supplier's supplier to the customer's customer (Supply Chain Council, 1997, in Lummus & Vokurka, 1999). A key principle is that all strategies, decisions, and measurements are made considering their effect on the entire supply chain, not just individual functions or organizations (Towill, 1996).

The association of supply chain management with e-business offers new challenges for marketing. The explosion of the Internet and other telecommunication technology has made real-time, online communication throughout the entire supply chain a reality. The Internet allows companies to interact with customers, and collect enormous volumes of data and manipulate it in many different ways to bring out otherwise unforeseen areas of knowledge (Abbott, 2001). Poirier and Bauer (2000) refer to the term 'electronic supply chain management' as a reference for the "natural combining of supply chain and e-commerce." Electronic supply chain management (e-SCM) is a concept introduced to the need of adaptability and flexibility in a highly dynamic e-business environment which focuses on network integration. E-SCM refers to the supply chain that is built via electronic linkages and structurally based on technology-enabled relationships (Williams, Esper, & Ozment, 2002).

Poirier and Bauer (2000) highlight three constituents in the preparation and execution of e-SCM:

1. **E-network:** Business networks should satisfy customer demands through a seamless (fully connected end-to-end) supply chain to serve the end consumer (see also Towill, 1997).
2. **Responses:** Customer responses form the central theme of the supply chain strategy. The market value of the supply chain can be dramatically enhanced by jointly creating profitable revenue growth through integrated inter-enterprise solutions and responses.
3. **Technology:** Each of the above constituents can achieve the purposes and goal of the supply chain by being supported with leading-edge technology, particularly e-commerce.

The three constituents—e-network, customer responses, and technology—could be seen as the "input" into e-SCM working together to achieve the ultimate aim (output) of the supply chain—that is, customer satisfaction. In synergy with the model developed by Goldman, Nagel, and Preiss (1995) and Meade and Sarkis (1999) for agile manufacturing, Figure 1 models the dimensions of an e-SCM environment within the context of the IDEF0 process mapping modeling technique.

Murillo (2001) and Helms, Ettkin, and Chapman (2000) indicate that the problem in pursuing supply chain construction efforts is not a lack of ideas about what to do, but instead about how to coordinate the efforts throughout the supply network. It was drawn by Peppard (1995) that a business process approach can act as a catalyst for bringing together the various things that have been occurring in the organization and management areas over the past decade. He further suggests that a process focus can provide an integrative mechanism. Process management involves planning and administering the activities necessary to achieve a high level of performance in a process, and identifying opportunities for improving quality and operational performance. Ultimately it includes translating customer requirements into product and service design requirements (Evans & Lindsay, 2002).

Goldman et al. (1995) recognize the significance of employees as a company asset and emphasize the importance of leveraging the impact of people and information for an agile enterprise. Evans and Lindsay (2002) show direct correlation between employees' (people) satisfaction and customer satisfaction, and argue that 'people' are the only organization asset that "competitors cannot copy; and the only one that can synergize, that is, produce output whose value is greater than the sum of its parts." Evans and Lindsay (2002) also emphasize that the two key components of service system quality are employees and information technology. Meade and Sarkis (1999) state that people and information are the most valued resources. It follows that the mechanism that converts the input of the e-SCM environment to its output (i.e., customer satisfaction) includes three constituents: process, people, and information sharing. In an analogy with agile enterprise dimensions (Goldman et al., 1995; Meade &

Figure 1. E-SCM general representation: Input, output, mechanism, and control

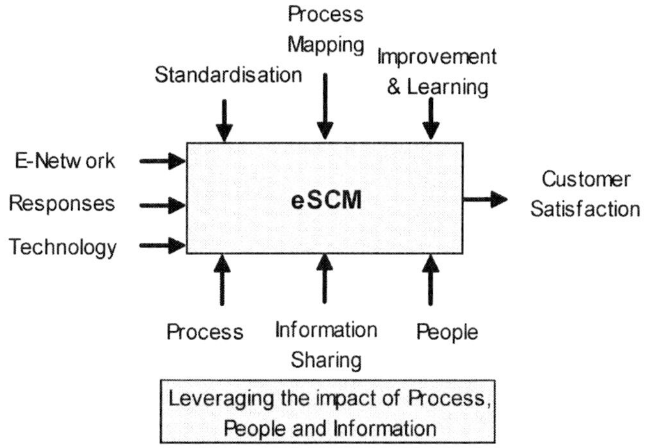

Sarkis, 1999), the leading mechanism for e-SCM is leveraging the impact of process, people, and information for the entire supply chain.

A key factor for the successful construction of e-network is that each organization in the supply chain looks beyond the basic function within the business and synchronizes its processes with the entire supply chain. Based on this concept, the network construction may not achieve the required result without mapping the process and considering the capacities of the other processes of the entire chain (Al-Hakim, 2003). Standardization of business processes is necessary to allow the communication and integration between business partners of the supply network since the complexity of processes in the supply chain has grown exponentially (Gunasekaran, Patel, & Tirtiroglu, 2001).

The SCOR process reference model was established by the Supply Chain Council (SCC) in 1996 for standardization purposes. The model describes, characterizes, and evaluates a complex management process. Such a model builds on the concepts of business process reengineering (BPR), benchmarking, and process measurement by integrating these techniques into a cross-functional framework.

In an agile environment, employees' skill, knowledge, and information are no longer enough for achieving or enhancing competitiveness without "the ability to convert the knowledge, skills, and information embodied in its personnel into solution products for the individual customers" (Meade & Sarkis, 1999, p. 243). "Ability to convert" is what e-SCM is really relying on to achieve customer satisfaction (Al-Hakim, 2003). The mechanism of e-SCM—that is, leveraging processes, information, and people—cannot be achieved without the improvement of the processes and enhancing the learning of employees throughout the entire supply chain. This in turn requires process mapping and standardizing the supply chain processes. These three elements—process mapping, standardization, and improvement and learning—form the control part of e-SCM that is capable of leveraging the supply chain process, information, and people in order to convert the input into e-SCM ultimate output: the customer satisfaction, as shown in Figure 1.

This research concentrates on the development of a procedure for e-SCM process improvement. The procedure focuses on process mapping and relies on principles of coordination theory. It is based on SCOR to standardize the process and take advantage of this technique of benchmarking/best practices potential. The procedure employs IDEF0 technique for mapping the processes.

PROCESS MAPPING

Process mapping is a technique used to detail business processes by focusing on the important elements that influence their behavior (Soliman, 1998). It consists of constructing a model that shows the relationships between activities, people, information, and objects involved in the production of a specified output (Biazzo, 2002). The fundamental concept of business process mapping is based on the depiction of the relationships among its elements: activities, resources, information, and objects involved in the production of a specified output (Biazzo, 2002; Hunt, 1996). The concept is focusing on the important elements that influence their actual behaviors. The level of mapping varies from an overview map "macro-map" to a very detailed map "micro-map" (Soliman, 1998). Soliman (1998) argues that the more levels of mapping (micro-levels), the more useful the information, but also more cost occurs. However, the fewer levels of process mapping could result in a poorly designed process, and hence higher skilled operators would be required to understand and operate it. So, the number of process mapping level depends on how much information is needed. The key idea to business process mapping is that the representative must be able to facilitate the process analysis when the conditions and sequence of activities change (El Sawy, 2001; Hunt, 1996). For e-SCM, the business process mapping for the supply chain should take full advantage and be managed via e-network. Entities of e-network are linked by Internet-based technologies, and accordingly, any developed procedure for the process mapping of e-SCM processes should be realized by the same technology. The process mapping realized by Internet technology is referred to as e-process mapping. The e-process mapping procedure for e-SCM should satisfy five necessary conditions:

1. Standardization of processes throughout the network
2. Reengineering processes and benchmarking practices
3. Realization of mechanism and the control activities by which each process converts input into output
4. Coordination of the supply chain interdependencies throughout the entire e-network
5. Achievement of the level of security designated by the elements of e-network

The first two conditions can be achieved by employing the SCOR reference model. IDEF0 technique is an ideal technique for the third condition. By integrating SCOR with IDEF0, it is possible to model the interdependencies between activities of e-SCM. The procedure developed by Al-Hakim (2003) can be used to accommodate the level of security required by e-network entities. The following two sections outline the SCOR model and IDEF0 techniques.

SCOR Reference Model

The supply chain operations reference (SCOR) model is an industry standard approach to define, design, and improve supply chains (Stewart, 1997). The Supply Chain Council has developed and endorsed the SCOR model as the cross-industry standard for supply chain management.

The latest version of the SCOR model, version 6.0, is the sixth major revision since the model was introduced in 1996. Revisions of the model are made when it is determined by council members that changes should be made to facilitate the use of the model in practice. Version 4.0 of SCOR had a focus on physical product, while version 5.0 was expanded to incorporate both service transaction and post-delivery customer support. In version 6.0, there is the expansion of

Figure 2. Integrated concepts for process reference model (Source: Supply Chain Council, 2003)

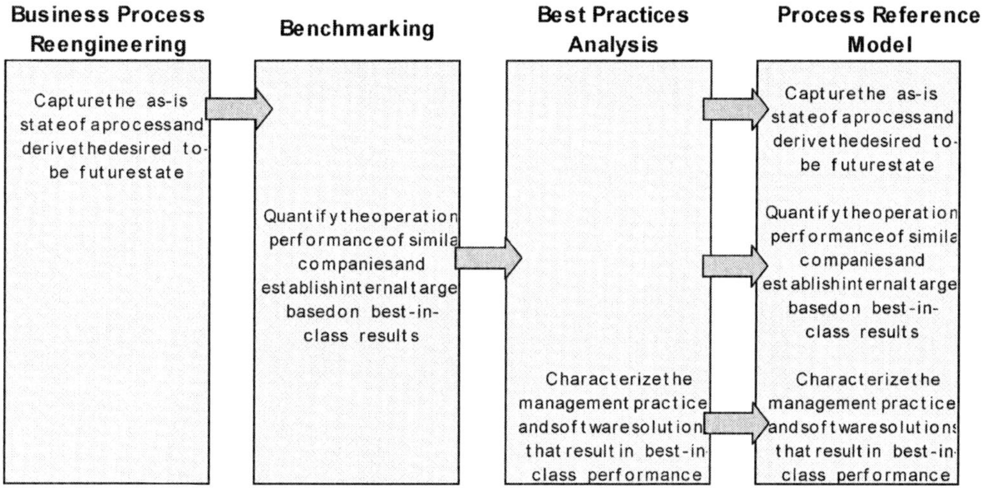

delivery and return process. The update of best practices for e-business has been included in the model (Supply Chain Council, 2003). This updated feature of version 6.0 makes SCOR suitable for modeling e-SCM.

The SCOR model tries to capture end-to-end business operation processes, including (Supply Chain Council, 2003):

- All customer interactions, from order entry through paid invoice
- All product (physical material and service) transactions, from your supplier's supplier to your customer's customer, including equipment, suppliers, spare parts, bulk product, software, and so forth
- All market interactions, from the understanding of aggregate demand to the fulfillment of each order

However, SCOR does not attempt to describe every business process or activity, including: sales and marketing (demand generation), research and technology development, product development, and some elements of post-delivery customer support.

The model is built on the concepts of BPR, benchmarking, and process measurement. It integrates these techniques into a cross-functional framework as shown in Figure 2. Once a complex management process has been captured in a process reference model, it can be described unambiguously, communicated consistently, and redesigned to achieve competitive advantage. In addition, given the use of standard measurement for process elements and activities, the process itself can be measured, managed, and controlled, and it may be refined to meet a specific purpose.

SCOR focuses on five basic management processes in the supply chain as illustrated in Figure 3. These processes are plan, source, make, deliver, and return.

There are four levels of details in SCOR (Figure 4).

- **Level 1:** Provides a broad definition of the plan, source, make, delivery, and return process types, and is the point at which a company establishes its supply chain competitive objectives.
- **Level 2:** Defines 26 core process categories that are possible components of a supply chain. A company can configure both its actual and ideal supply chain by selecting from these core processes.
- **Level 3:** Provides a company with the information it needs to plan and set goals

Figure 3. SCOR generic framework

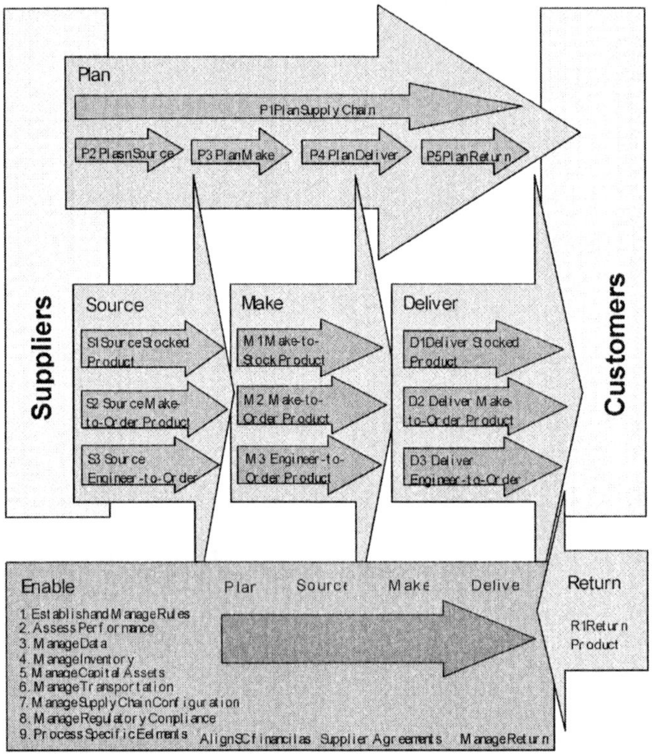

Figure 4. Four levels of SCOR business process (Source: Supply Chain Council, 2003)

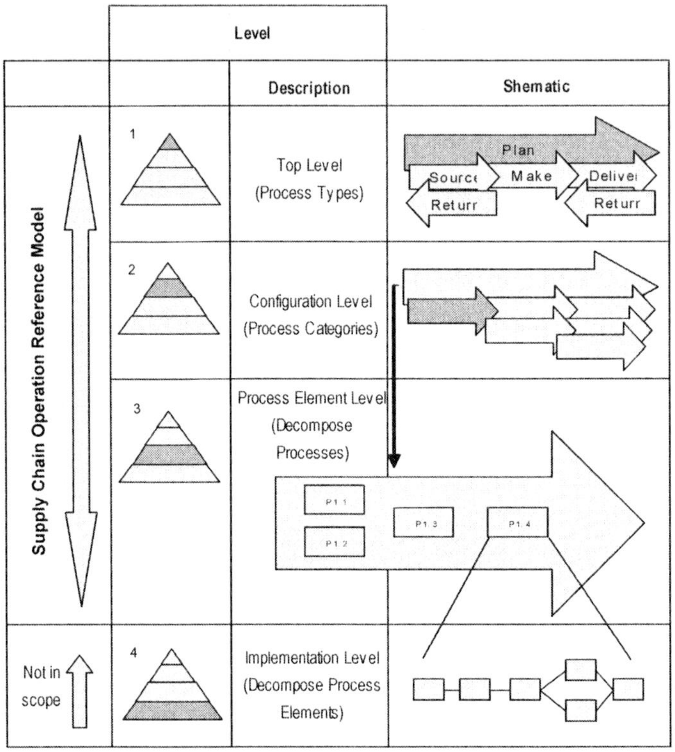

successfully for its supply chain improvements through detailed practices, and system software capabilities to enable best practices.

- **Level 4:** Focuses on implementation, when companies put specific supply chain improvements into play. Since changes at level 4 are unique to each company, the specific elements of the level are not defined within the industry standard model.

IDEF0

IDEF0 is one of the most widely known tools for process mapping. It was originally developed to describe, specify, and model manufacturing systems in a structured graphical form for the United States Air Force, Department of Defense (DOD) organizations as part of the Corporate Information Management Initiative (Fulscher & Powell, 1999; Lin, Yang, & Pai, 2002; Plaia & Carrie, 1995). IDEF0 is designed to model the decisions, actions, and activities of an organization or system (Lin et al., 2002). IDEF0 models contain information describing how an organization executes its business processes. The purpose of IDEF0 models is to enable process analysis and identification of business process improvement opportunities (Kappes, 1997). IDEF0 methods are centered on the concept of mapping the functional processes of an organization.

The IDEF0 technique follows a rigorous methodology with definite rules that must be followed to generate a valid model (Kappes, 1997). IDEF0 describes a business process as a series of linked *activities;* each activity is specified by four elements: inputs, controls, outputs, and mechanisms. These elements are referred to as ICOMs (Fulscher & Powell, 1999; Lin et al., 2002). Figure 5 illustrates generically how IDEF0 is used to depict activities, inputs, outputs, controls, and mechanisms.

A brief description of each ICOM follows:

Figure 5. IDEF0 elements: Inputs, outputs, controls, and mechanisms

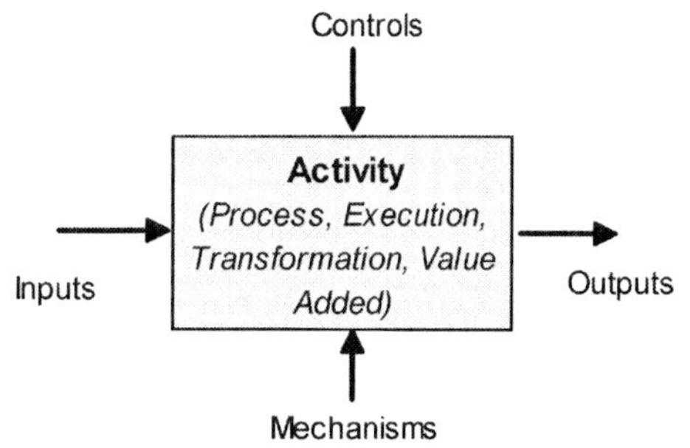

- **Input:** Data or materials that are consumed to produce an output of an activity.
- **Control:** Data that constrain or regulate the activity and hence the transformation of inputs into outputs.
- **Output***:* Data or materials produced by or resulting from the activity. It must include the input data in some form.
- **Mechanism:** Resources (usually people, machines, or systems) that provide energy to, or carry out, the activity.

If we call both the information and the objects involved in the description "data," then we can say that input arrows show the data needed to perform the activity, while output arrows show the data created when the activity is performed. Control arrows describe the conditions or circumstances which govern the transformation, while mechanism arrows represent people or devices that carry out the activity (Fulscher & Powell, 1999; Plaia & Carrie, 1995).

IDEF0 Mapping Procedure

In the mapping procedure, IDEF0 allows a hierarchical or top-down decomposition approach to analyze processes at multiple levels of abstraction (Fulscher & Powell, 1999; Kappes, 1997; Plaia & Carrie, 1995). The essence of hierarchical decomposition approaches to business process mapping, in which a basic, single-activity description of the process is

Table 1. Type of interdependencies within and between organizations

Author	Focus	Types of Interdependency
Svensson, 2002	Company business activities in marketing channels	• Time dependency • Relationship dependency • Functional dependency
Crowston, 1997	Process redesign	• Activities (input/output) • Resources (actors, equipment, time)
Nassimbeni, 1998	Inter-organizational relationship	• Flow interdependencies • Process interdependencies • Scale interdependencies • Social relationship interdependencies
Li et al., 2002	Supply chain complexities	• Task/task interdependency o Order prerequisite interdependency o Demand interdependency • Task/resource interdependency o Order/organization interdependency o Order/inventory interdependency o Order/capacity interdependency • Resource/resource interdependency o Supply interdependency o Inventory interdependency o Capacity/capacity interdependency
Medcof, 2001	R&D (technology)	• Resource dependency
Mattsson, 2000 (see Svensson, 2002)	Operationalization	• Market dependence • IT dependence

decomposed step-by-step into its constituent activities to whatever level of detail, is appropriate for the mapping purposes (Fulscher & Powell, 1999). This hierarchical decomposition of activities helps to organize the development of IDEF0 models and proved critical in keeping the group focused on its task of abstracting the essence of the process itself from the details of current practice (Fulscher & Powell, 1999; Plaia & Carrie, 1995).

Kappes (1997) explained that the IDEF0 decomposition first breaks the highest level activity into lesser level activities. Then each of these activities is broken into one or more activities until the required level of detail is obtained. Each activity is given a unique node number depending on its level in the model. The top-level activity which represents the subject of the model is always given the number A0. The IDEF0 hierarchical decomposition fits exactly the hierarchical decomposition of the SCOR model. IDEF0 is an ideal technique for mapping supply chain processes based on the SCOR environment. In addition, IDEF0 allows users to describe what an organization does, but it does not specify the logic in sequencing activities (Lin et al., 2002; Plaia & Carrie, 1995). SCOR can be used to fill this gap.

Table 2. Supply chain coordination mechanism

Author	Focus	Coordination Mechanism
Lummus & Vokurka, 1999; Tracey & Smith-Doerflein, 2001; Kerrin, 2002	Interdependency in supply chain	• SC integration/collaboration • SC inter-organization collaboration
Lewis, 2000	Interdependency in supply chain	• E-business solution—standard business process model using XML language to SC optimization
Forza & Venelli, 1997	Interdependency of activities/works in supply chain	• Quick response/ integration requirement
Crowston, 1997	Process dependencies	• Coordination approach to process description, analysis, and redesign using two general heuristics rule for identifying dependencies
Li et al., 2002	Interdependency in supply chain	• Representing the interdependencies using supply chain modeling mathematical approach
Neuman & Samuel, 1996; Hoek, 1998; Hoek et al., 2001	Interdependency in supply chain	• Integration across and between interfaces using performance measurement approach to control SC
Nassimbeni, 1998	Process interdependencies	• Input/output standardization, process standardization and skill standardization

Supply Chain Interdependencies

Supply chain is seen as a complex network of organizations with complex activities. SCM comprises different kinds of dependencies in, between, and across organizations (Li, Kumar, & Lim, 2002; Svensson, 2002). Inside a network, firms enter into a complex set of interdependencies with other firms, both vertical and horizontal. Vertical inter-dependencies arise among collaborating partners who complement each other in producing or commercializing the product (Svensson, 2002). Horizontal inter-dependencies arise between partners who exchange knowledge or resources to develop new products or new technologies, or to promote and distribute their products (Nassimbeni, 1998). These interdependencies within and between organizations are identified in a number of literatures shown in Table 1. In order to achieve efficient network, interdependencies require effective coordination efforts (Li et al., 2002; Nassimbeni, 1998; Svensson, 2002).

The dependency between business activities in supply chains leads to the necessity for cooperation and coordination between companies in order to achieve the ultimate goals of business operations (Crowston, 1997; Svensson, 2002). Malone and Crowston (1994) initiate the coordination theory and define the coordination as a process for managing interdependencies between activities. Identifying the relationships between the interdependencies is a vital process for achieving the coordination. It is stated that the success of SCM depends on the management of coordination processes (Biazzo, 2002; Li et al., 2002).

Several studies have dealt with coordination aspects in recent years. A number of supply chain coordination mechanisms have been proposed by many researchers to manage the supply chain interdependencies; these are illustrated in Table 2.

To deal with identifying interdependencies in the supply chain, Li et al. (2002) proposed the supply chain modeling approach to describe the complexities of supply chains. The approach aims to capture the complexities and interdependencies in the supply chain by representing the interdependency of task and resource using a mathematical model. The work of Li et al. (2002) contributes to the identification of supply chain interdependencies, however they mainly focus on using a mathematical approach to capture these interdependencies, which have a very limited use where the high-complexities level of relationships exist.

Nassimbeni (1998) nominates the use of input/output standardization, process standardization, and skills standardization as the coordination mechanism to process interdependencies by focusing on the type of inter-organization network structures in the existing literature and analyzing the main forms of interdependency in the networks. Four types of interdependencies are defined, including flow interdependencies, scale interdependencies, process interdependencies, and social relationship interdependencies. Nassimbeni (1998) applies the main coordination mechanism concepts to these interdependencies. Even so, rationale for the use of the mechanism is not yet provided.

Crowston (1997) proposed two general heuristics for identifying dependencies. These are (1) dependency-focused analysis and (2) activity-focused analysis.

Dependency-focused analysis identifies dependencies, then searches for coordination mechanisms. It examines the activities and the resources they use, and determines possible dependencies by considering which resources are used by more than one activity. By asking the questions such as what are the inputs, outputs, and resources of process, and checking whether these are used by other processes, the interdependencies can be identified.

The activity-focused analysis identifies coordination mechanisms, then searches for dependencies. Activity-focused analysis searches directly for coordination activities and for actors or resources that coordinate with them.

Despite the fact that these methods provide advantages in identifying interdependencies in process networks, they mainly focus on a common-sense approach. They do not address the typical problem with a very highly complex set of business processes. Hence it gives limited emphasis to identification of supply chain interdependencies and supply chain network integration for the purpose of supply chain improvement.

Because of the size and complexity of the supply chain network structure, the representations of inter-organization relationships and interdependencies between them are necessary. As the patterns between partners might be different, the process of producing comprehensive maps of the network to identify the interdependencies is essentially required. The next section outlines a business process improvement procedure for e-SCM and identifies some interdependencies existing between supply chain processes.

Figure 6. Overview of eSCM-I procedure

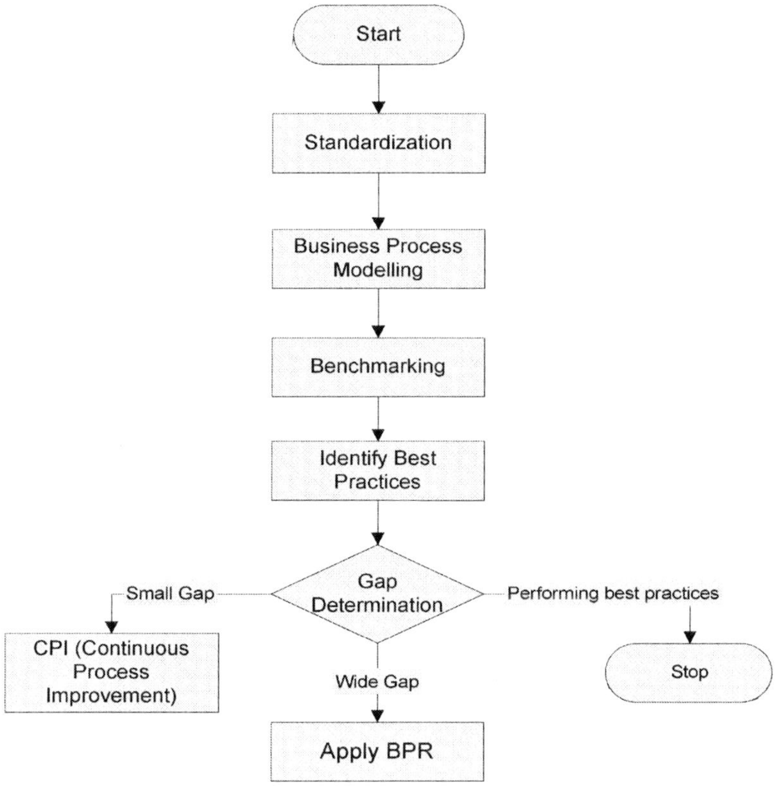

E-SCM IMPROVEMENT PROCEDURE

This research develops an e-SCM business processes improvement (eSCM-I) procedure of four steps (see Figure 6):

- **Step 1:** Standardization
- **Step 2:** Business Process Modeling
- **Step 3:** Benchmarking and Identification of Best Practices
- **Step 4:** Gap Determination

The eSCM-I procedure adopts the concept of standardization by using the SCOR model at the first step of the procedure presented in step 1. The second step is the use of the IDEF0 technique for business process modeling. Benchmarking and selecting best practices based on SCOR make up the next step of the new procedure. The final step is gap determination and selecting BPR or CPI approach for improvement.

Step 1: Standardization of Business Process

The first step of the eSCM-I procedure is the standardization of business process using the SCOR model. Mintzberg (1983) suggests the use of standardization as the coordination mechanism for managing interdependencies in business processes. Standardization is the use of standard procedures, processes, materials, and/or parts for designing, manufacturing, and distributing a product. Nassimbeni (1998) claims that standardization can involve inputs, outputs, processes, and skills.

This step proposes the use of the SCOR model for standardization. The SCOR model provides standardization of three key categories: Process Types, Basic Management Processes, and Process Level in the process reference model format. The model also contributes standard definitions for processes and sub-processes. This standardization allows organizations to capture the complexities, describe unambiguously, communicate consistently, and redesign to achieve competitive advantage in relation to supply chain processes. In addition, given the standard measurement metrics for process elements and activities, the process itself can be measured, managed, and controlled, and ultimately it may be refined to meet a specific purpose for improvement.

In summary, the primary purpose of using the SCOR model in the first step of the SC_BPI procedure is to take advantage of process standardization. When all supply chain participants standardize their processes using SCOR, they can manage the communication between them which leads to improved coordination of the entire chain.

However, level 1-3 SCOR processes are still generic for all types of industries (Al-Hakim, 2003). Implementing the model, as we discuss in the following sections, involves conceptually linking or mapping it to all product and information flows for all enterprise-specific supply chain processes (step 2), collecting and evaluating performance data for gap analysis (step 3), and launching process improvement approaches (step 4).

Step 2: Business Process Modeling

Mapping the processes for the supply chain is proposed as the second step of the eSCM-I procedure after standardization because companies have an overwhelming number of processes that require integration. The purpose of business process modeling is also to analyze processes, manage supply chain interdependencies, and define the functionality and behavior of supply chain processes to the level of detail required by business users (Li et al., 2002). The approach to modeling in this step has been based on a structured graphical presentation of the IDEF0 technique.

Considering the principal idea of coordination and management of interdependencies in supply chain business process, the use of the IDEF0 structured process modeling method to SCOR is proposed in this step of the SC_BPI procedure. This step of implementing IDEF0 in SCOR provides five main contributions to supply chain improvement, including structured presentation of processes, identification of organizational interdependencies, decomposition structure of organizational interdependencies, identification of inter-organizational interdependencies, and decomposition structure of inter-organizational interdependencies.

Structured Presentation of Processes

As its first contribution, IDEF0 provides a good overview of the input, output, control, and mechanism objects within the supply chain operation aspect (see Figure 7). Using IDEF0, a process is presented to show what data or materials are consumed, what data or materials are produced, data that constrain or regulate the process, and also the resources (people, machines or systems) that carry out the process.

Figure 7. IDEF0 structured presentation of process

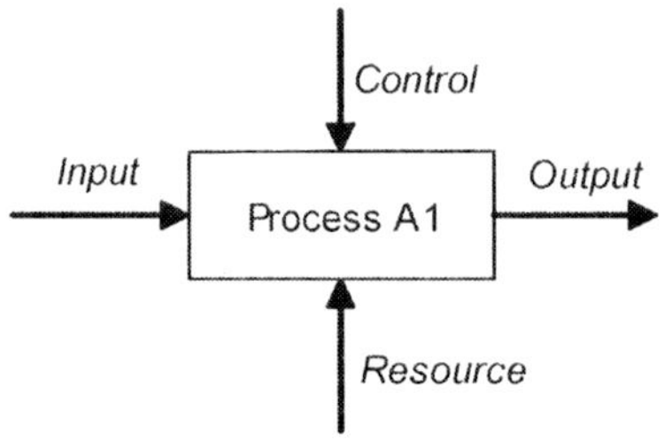

Figure 8. Interdependencies from the relationship linked by inputs

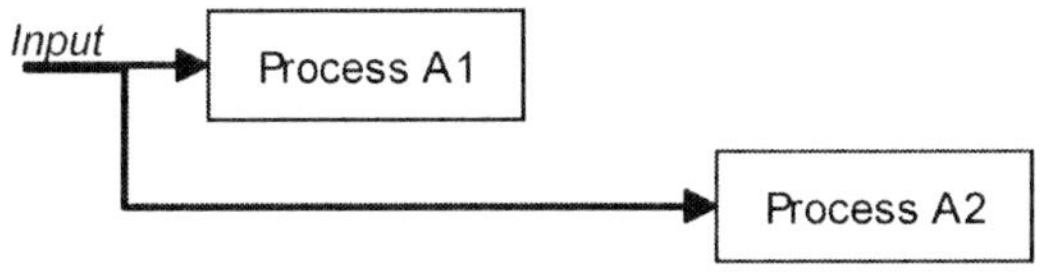

Identification of Organizational Interdependencies

IDEF0 technique gives not only a good overview of input, output, control, and mechanism for each entity of the process, but also overviews the relationship between each entity linked by these objects. The relationships created by these links assist companies in identifying four types of interdependencies, which are listed below.

Interdependencies from the Relationship Linked by Inputs
These interdependencies occur when the same data, materials, or any other inputs that are consumed to produce an output of a process are needed by different processes (see Figure 8).

Interdependencies from the Relationship Linked by Input and Output Objects
Once the data or materials are consumed to a process, they transform into outputs. These outputs are needed by another process, which causes the interdependencies in a range of ways, as presented in Figure 9.

Interdependencies from the Relationship Linked by Output and Control
Data and information that form an output of a process can also become a constraint or control of other processes. These transformations of outputs into control factors result in the output-control interdependencies between processes, as shown in Figure 10.

Figure 10. Interdependencies from the relationship linked by output and control

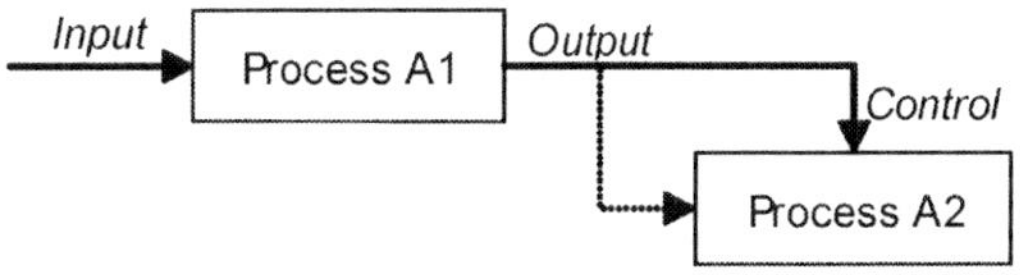

Figure 9. Interdependencies from the relationship linked by input and output

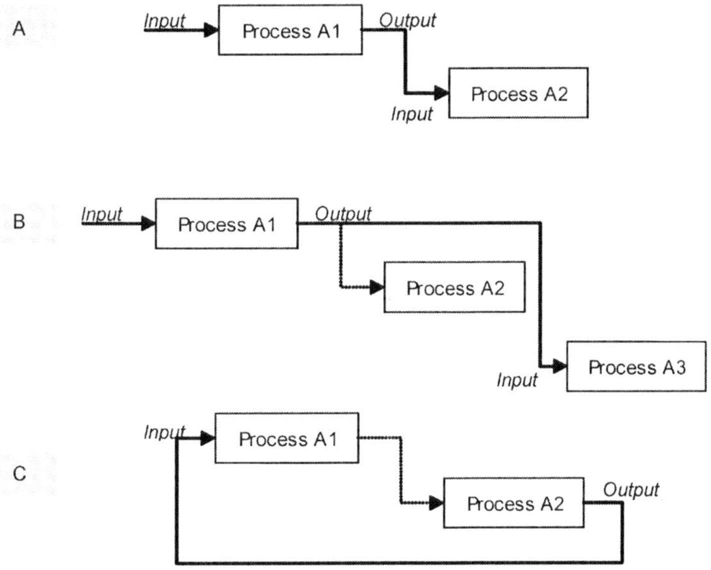

Figure 11. Interdependencies from the relationship linked by resources

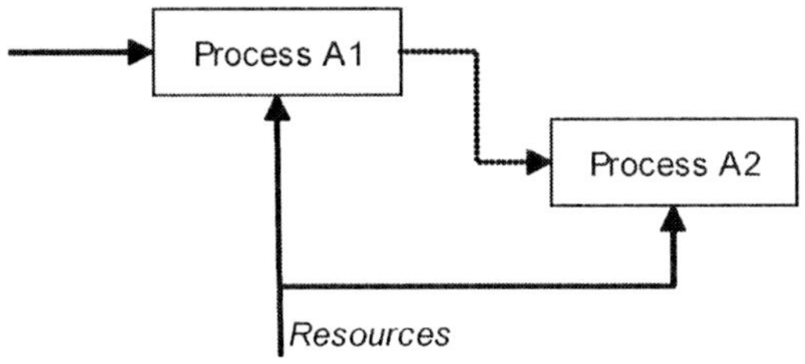

Figure 12. Organizational interdependencies using IDEF0

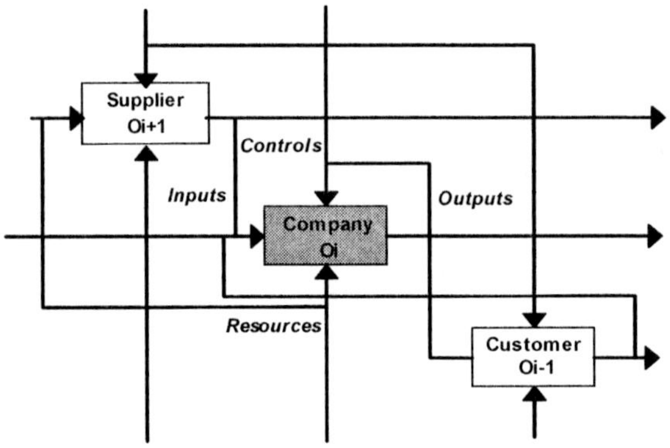

Interdependencies from the Relationship Linked by Resources

Organization entities in the supply chain network are interconnected to exchange critical resources, such as raw materials, labor, access to markets, specialized skills, and knowledge (Tillquist, 2002). The resource interdependencies in the supply chain process occur when different processes need to use or share the same resources (including information), as shown in Figure 11. Managing these inter-organizational dependencies requires the use of information technology (IT) to tightly integrate partner relations by binding operational functions, processes, strategic plans, and knowledge (Tillquist, 2002).

An example of organizational process interdependencies including input, input-output, output-control, and resources interdependencies is exhibited in Figure 12. The company (denoted as organization Oi in Figure 11) performs the top-level supply chain processes based on the SCOR model divided into: *plan*, *source*, *make*, *deliver*, and *return*. Each of these processes has its own input, output, control, and mechanism involved in the processes. The relationships linked by connection of the input, output, control, and mechanism create the interdependencies within the entity of the supply chain.

The identification of these organizational interdependencies helps companies to avoid and reduce dependencies when they analyze and design processes. Companies can also manage those interdependencies that cannot be avoided for better coordination in their organization.

Decomposition Structure of Organizational Interdependencies

The third contribution of IDEF0 is based on the decomposition structure of IDEF0. IDEF0 allows the decomposition of process into various hierarchical detailed levels. This feature makes IDEF0 an ideal technique for modeling processes based on the SCOR four-level procedure.

Figure 13 shows the decomposition of organization Oi from organization level to top level and level 1, respectively. From this decomposition, the detail of interdependencies can be more specifically observed at the extended level; for example, level 1 extends to level 2, and level 2 extends to level 3 of the SCOR model.

Identification of Inter-Organizational Interdependencies

Identification of inter-organizational interdependencies is the extended scope of the second contribution of IDEF0 (identification of organizational interdependencies). At the organizational level, IDEF0 identifies the relationship of input, output, control, and resources between processes within the company. Utilizing a combination of SCOR and IDEF0 at the inter-organizational level helps organizations identify and manage interde-

Figure 13. Decomposition of organizational business process

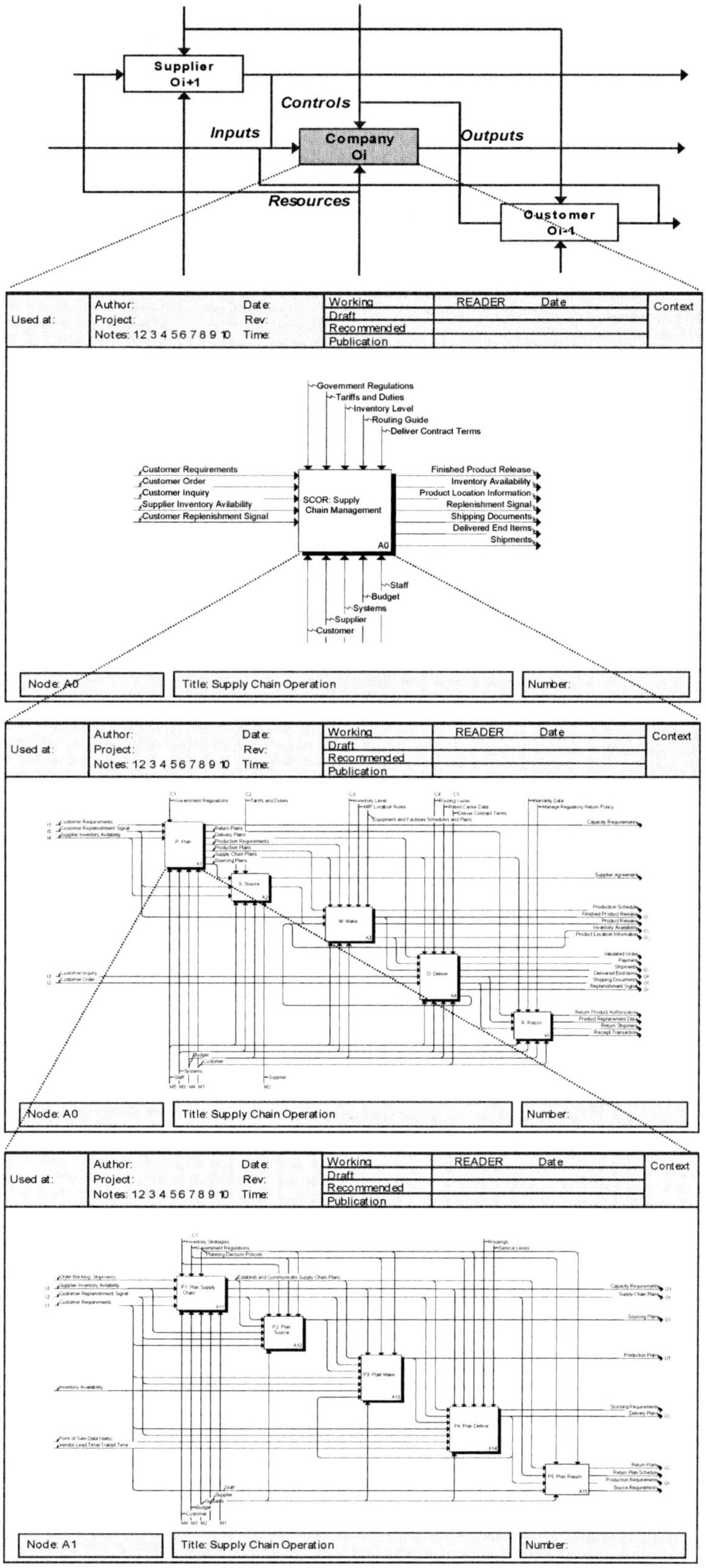

pendencies occurring in and between processes. This ultimately leads to coordination of the entire supply chain. The example of identifying interdependencies between organizations based on SCOR and IDEF0 is exhibited in Figure 14.

Organizational interdependencies identification results in the recognition of interdependencies within organizations. Inter-organizational interdependencies identification, in advance, helps companies to recognize the links and relationships between organizations. This eventually constitutes supply chain integration and coordination.

Decomposition Structure of Inter-Organizational Interdependencies

The fifth contribution of IDEF0, decomposition of structure of inter-organizational interdependencies, is based on the combination of process decomposition and inter-organization interdependencies relationship presentation. The decomposition of process to the detailed level between organizations allows companies to enter into the consideration level of interdependencies identification between them. This will also facilitate companies to keep

Figure 14. Detailed inter-organization using IDEF0 technique

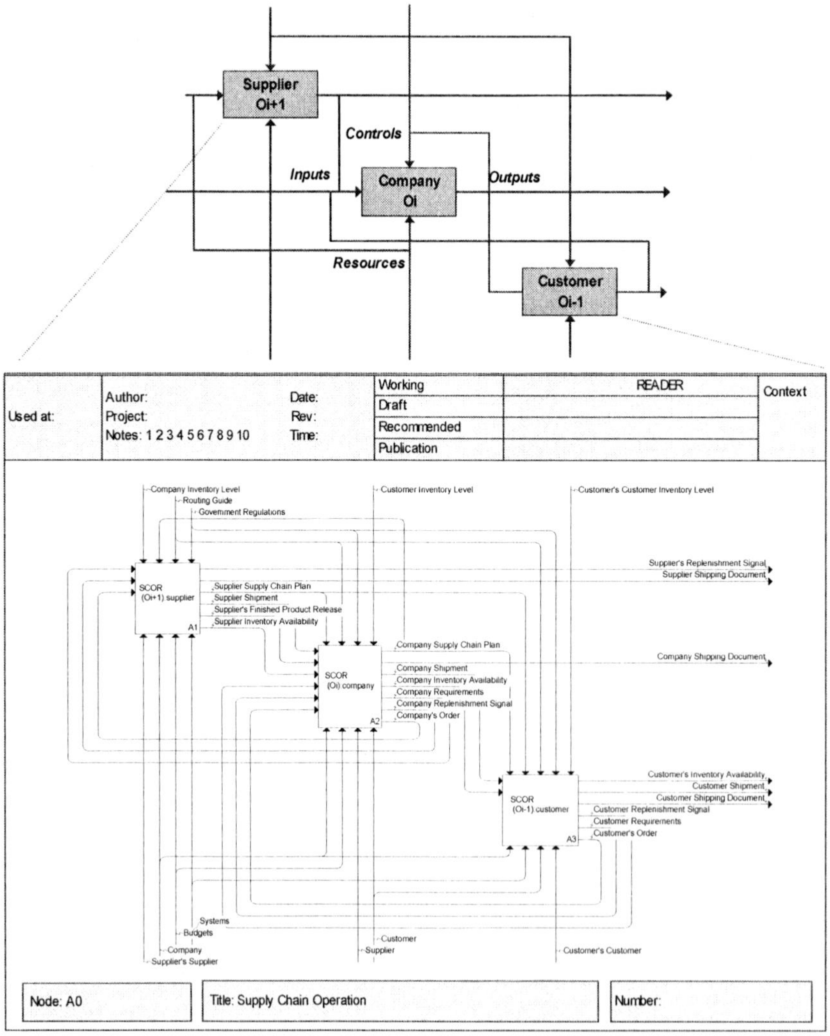

Figure 15. Decomposition structure of inter-organizational interdependencies

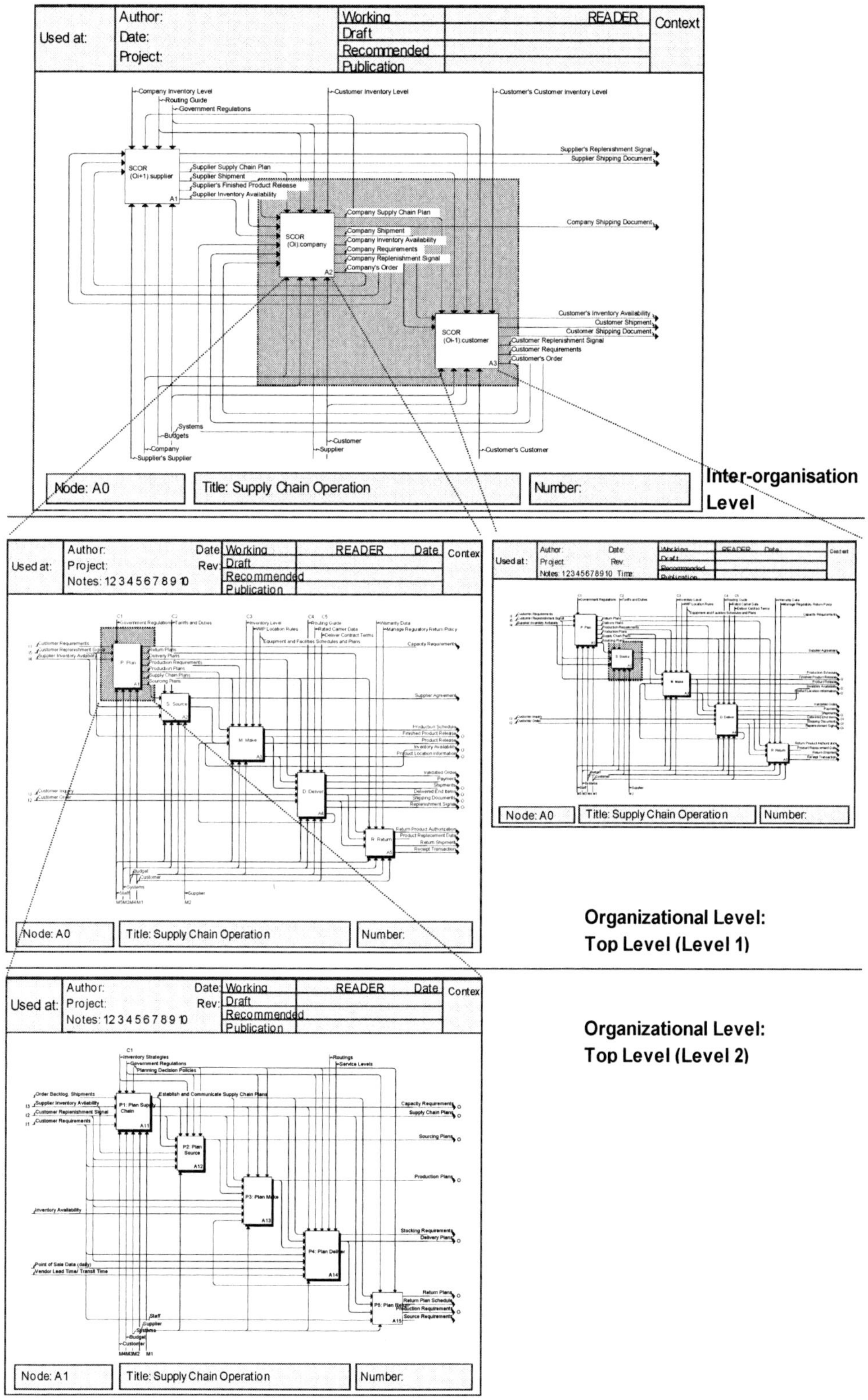

Figure 16. Gap determination for selecting BPI approaches

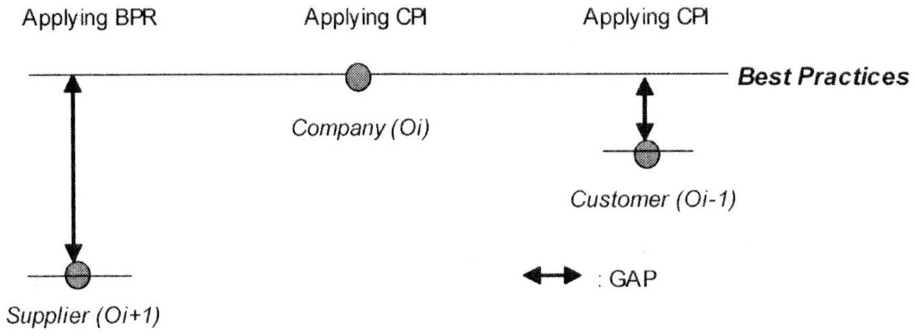

these interdependencies at a manageable level for the goals of supply chain improvement.

Figure 15 displays the example of decomposition at two organizations, a company (Oi) and its customer (Oi-1). The figure illustrates that, at the inter-organizational level, there are many interdependencies occurring. One is caused by the input-output relationship. The figure shows that one input *customer replenishment signal* of company (Oi) is derived from the output that was created by customer (Oi-1). With decomposition to level 1, it can be found that the *customer replenishment signal* is actually produced from *deliver* process in customer organization, and it goes to *plan* process in the company organization. If the company further decomposes its *plan* process to level 2, it can be found that this *customer replenishment signal* is needed as an input to all processes in the level including: *plan supply chain, plan source, plan make, plan deliver,* and *plan return.*

Step 3: Benchmarking and Identifying Best Practices

Business process benchmarking and the selection of best practices are identified as the tools for supply chain improvement. The SCOR model provides a list of best-in-class practices for each process element. However, SCOR best-in-class practices are generic lists. A best practice that has a significant effect on the performance of a certain stage and certain process in an organization may not necessarily have the same effect on other processes of the supply chain. Thus, in selecting a best practice to improve the entire supply chain, the entire flow of process linked to the partners should be considered. For this purpose, the first level of the Web-based system introduced by Al-Hakim (2003) plays a major role.

The first level of the Web-based system allows an individual partner of an e-network to analyze, compare, and evaluate their practices with the practices of other partners of the e-network. The feature allows e-network partners or e-SCM experts to simulate the effect of practices along the supply chain and to select practices that achieve the best flow of material along the supply chain.

Step 4: Gap Determination

After selection of best practices which need to be applied from the previous step, a gap analysis is used to measure the current performance of each e-network partner with those targets desired to be achieved and then to define the change that is needed to be made to the process. Applying the alternative business improvement approaches with the aim of improving supply chain in this procedure is based on performance strategies. The business process reengineering (BPR) approach primarily aims to gain dramatic improvements, while the continuous process improvement (CPI) approach comprises improvements that are individually small, confined within functional boundaries. The CPI approach therefore focuses on improving the existing system by closing small performance gaps.

Therefore, as depicted in Figure 16, if the performance gap is wide, substantial improvement and a high degree of change is needed at a specific stage. Dramatic process transformation is required for breakthrough performance change. In contrast, if the performance gap and degrees of change are small, incremental improvement is needed to achieve small but meaningful improvement in business results. Again, the Web-based system (in Al-Hakim, 2003) allows e-SCM experts to evaluate the action required for each e-network partner to take.

CONCLUSION

This research attempts to develop a procedure referred to as eSCM-I to improve supply chain business processes, taking into consideration the Internet and e-business communication technologies. The procedure identifies process interdependencies and managing supply chain coordination.

The eSCM-I procedure uses the SCOR model for purposes of process standardization. This standardization step plays an essential role as a coordination mechanism to manage interdependencies within a supply chain network.

IDEF0 was selected to model SCOR business processes. The IDEF0 technique has been found suitable for the purpose of describing SCOR processes in general when the flow of information and the independency relationships are to be considered. The IDEF0 method has the potential to contribute additional aspects that are not represented in the current SCOR models, resulting in a more comprehensive representation of supply chain processes. IDEF0 identifies the interdependency relationships in terms of input, output, control, and mechanism. This identification is very useful for effective modeling and management of the supply chain coordination.

The SCOR model provides a list of best-in-class practices and features for each process element which allows individual trading partners to analyze, compare, and apply the best practices. However, there is no indication of how to select and apply the various alternative best practices at the microanalysis level. This research suggests the suitability of using the traditional flowcharting method for selecting best practices in the SCOR environment using a "gap analysis" approach.

By identifying the gap between existing practices and best practice, the final step of the eSCM-I procedure provides an introduction to improvement approaches such as business process reengineering (BPR) or continuous process improvement (CPI) from the holistic viewpoint. Ultimately, the SCOR-based eSCM-I procedure introduced in this chapter provided five main contributions to supply chain improvement, including structured presentation of processes, identification of organizational interdependencies, decomposition structure of organizational interdependencies, identification of inter-organizational interdependencies, and decomposition structure of inter-organizational interdependencies.

REFERENCES

Abbott, J. (2001). Data data everywhere—and not a byte of use? *Qualitative Market Research: An International Journal, 4*(3), 182-192.

Al-Hakim, L. (2003). Web-based supply chain integration model. In J. Mariga (Ed.), *Managing e-commerce and mobile computing technologies* (pp. 183-207). Melbourne: IRM Press.

Biazzo, S. (2002). Process mapping techniques and organizational analysis: Lessons from sociotechnical system theory. *Business Process Management Journal, 8*(1), 42-52.

Crowston, K. (1997). A coordination theory approach to organizational process design. *Organization Science, 8*(2), 157-175.

El Sawy, O.A. (2001). *Redesigning enterprise processes for e-business*. Sydney: McGraw-Hill.

Evans, J.R., & Lindsay, W.M. (2002). *The management and control of quality* (5th ed.). Mason, Oh: South-Western.

Fulscher, J., & Powell, S.G. (1999). Anatomy of a process mapping workshop. *Business Process Management Journal, 5*(3), 208-237.

Goldman, S.L., Nagel, R.N., & Preiss, K. (1995). *Agile competitors and virtual organizations: Strategies for enriching the customer.* New York: Van Nostrand Reinhold.

Gunasekaran, A., Patel, C., & Tirtiroglu, E. (2001). Performance measures and metrics in a supply chain environment. *International Journal of Operations & Production Management, 21*(1/2), 71-87.

Helms, M.M., Ettkin, L.P., & Chapman., S. (2000). Supply chain forecasting—collaborative forecasting supports supply chain management. *Business Process Management Journal, 6*(5), 392-407.

Hunt, D.V. (1996). *Process mapping: How to reengineer your business processes.* Brisbane: John Wiley & Sons.

Kappes, S. (1997). Putting your IDEF0 model to work. *Business Process Management Journal, 3*(2), 151-161.

Li, Z., Kumar, A., & Lim, Y.G. (2002). Supply chain modeling—a coordination approach. *Integrated Manufacturing Systems, 13*(8), 551-561.

Lin, F., Yang, M., & Pai, Y. (2002). A generic structure for business process modeling. *Business Process Management Journal, 8*(1), 19-41.

Lummus, R.R., & Vokurka, R.J. (1999). Defining supply chain management: A historical perspective and practical guidelines. *Industrial Management & Data Systems Journal, 99*(1), 11-17.

Malone, T.W., & Crowston, K. (1994). Interdisciplinary study of coordination. *ACM Computing Survey, 26*(1), 87-119.

Meade, L.M., & Sarkis, J. (1999). Analyzing organizational project alternatives for agile manufacturing processes: An analytical network approach. *International Journal of Production Research, 37*(2), 241-261.

Medcof, J.W. (2001). Resource-based strategy and managerial power in networks of internationally dispersed technology units. *Strategic Management Journal, 22*(11), 999-1012.

Murillo, L. (2001). Supply chain management and the international dissemination of e-commerce. *Industrial Management & Data Systems, 101*(7), 370-377.

Nassimbeni, G. (1998). Network structures and coordination mechanisms: A taxonomy. *International Journal of Operations & Production Management, 18*(6), 538-554.

Peppard, J. (1995). Broadening visions of BPR: The imperative of strategic integration. In *Working Paper Series 11/95.* Cranfield UK: Cranfield School of Management.

Plaia, A., & Carrie, A. (1995). Application and assessment of IDEF3—process flow description capture method. *International Journal of Operations & Production Management, 15*(1), 63-73.

Poirier, C.C., & Bauer, M.J. (2000). *E-supply chain: Using the Internet to revolutionize you business.* San Francisco: Berrett-Koehler.

Soliman, F. (1998). Optimum level of process mapping and least-cost business process re-engineering. *International Journal of Operations & Production Management, 18*(9/10), 810-816.

Stewart, G. (1997). Supply-chain operations reference model (SCOR): The first cross-industry framework for integrated supply-chain management. *Logistics Information Management Journal, 10*(2), 62-67.

Supply Chain Council. (2003). *Supply-chain operations reference model version 6.0.* Retrieved August 8, 2003, from http://www.supply-chain.org

Svensson, G. (2002). A typology of vulnerability scenarios towards suppliers and customers in supply chains based upon perceived time and relationship dependencies. *International Journal of Physical Distribution & Logistics Management, 32*(3/4), 168-187.

Tillquist, J. (2002). Strategic connectivity in extended enterprise networks. *Journal of Electronic Commerce Research, 3*(2), 77-85.

Towill, D.R. (1996). Industrial dynamics modeling of supply chains. *International Journal of Physical Distribution & Logistics Management.*

Towill, D.R. (1997). The seamless supply chain: The predator's strategic advantage. *International Journal of Technology Management, 13*(1), 37-56.

Williams, L.R., Esper, T.L., & Ozment, J. (2002). The electronic supply chain: Its impact on the current and future structure of strategic alliances, partnerships and logistics leadership. *International Journal of Physical Distribution & Logistics Management, 32*(8), 703-719.

Chapter II
Dynamic Transshipment in the Digital Age

Shilei Yang
Washington State University, USA

Bintong Chen
Washington State University, USA

Charles L. Munson
Washington State University, USA

ABSTRACT

In recent years, e-retailing has become the growth engine for the retailing industry. A large online retailer usually has multiple distribution centers serving different geographical regions. This chapter explores how to handle transshipment among distribution centers in a geographically dispersed network. We investigate transshipment strategies in a continuous review system with dynamic demand. We present a dynamic program that identifies the optimal transshipment rule. However, the dynamic program is time consuming and might be difficult for practitioners to implement. Therefore, we propose three distinct heuristic decision rules for making transshipment decisions. By employing numerical experiments, we analyze simulated results through various combinations of demand rates and delivery costs. We provide comments and suggestions based on the comparative results generated from different decision rules. As a result, we identify a good heuristic rule, which can be conveniently implemented and used in practice to determine effective transshipment policies.

INTRODUCTION

Nearly two-thirds of all North American households have purchased online. Although the majority of retail sales still take place at traditional brick-and-mortar stores, online sales over the next five years are expected to grow at a compounded annual growth rate of 14% (Forrester, 2005). The fast growth rate of Internet retailing provides new challenges for management.

Online customers need not to care from where their orders are physically shipped. Consequently, many Internet retailers can improve service and reduce expected delivery cost by transshipping between distribution centers. Especially for large online retailers with extensively dispersed networks, the use of transshipments has a significant benefit by redistributing inventories among multiple distribution centers (DCs) (Maltz, Rabinovich, & Sinha, 2004). However, such a practice will incur additional transportation cost in comparison to shipping from its local DC. On the other hand, issuing transshipment will also reduce the ability of the source DC to meet its own local customer demand. In the following, we will use Amazon.com to illustrate a transshipment scenario.

Amazon.com, one of the most successful pure Internet retailers, has grown from a book reseller to a retailing giant on the Internet. Amazon.com reported its net profit in 2005 as $359 million on $8.49 billion in net sales (Finfacts Team, 2006). From its humble beginnings using one distribution center in Seattle, Amazon.com has expanded to seven distribution centers across the United States as listed in Table 1.

Although there are a total of seven DCs, two of them are located in the same state. So according to their physical locations, we can roughly divide the continental U.S. into six different service regions (Figure 1).

Suppose that a customer from Atlanta places an order at Amazon.com; however, the local DC at McDonough, Georgia, is already out of stock. Apparently, this customer demand cannot be directly satisfied from the local DC. Now the question arises: how should the Amazon.com DC operations manager transship the product—ship it out from Kansas, Kentucky, or even from Seattle? The naive solution adopted by most practitioners would be to transship that item from the nearest DC. However, our analysis shows that under some circumstances, this frequently used technique

Table 1. Physical location of Amazon's DCs

DC Locations	DC Targeting Region	Market Number
(1) Seattle, Washington	Northwestern U.S.	1
(2) New Castle, Delaware	Northeastern U.S.	2
(3) Fernley, Nevada	Western U.S.	3
(4) Coffeyville, Kansas	Midwest and Southwest U.S.	4
(5) Campbellsville, Kentucky	Midwestern U.S.	5
(6) Lexington, Kentucky	Midwestern U.S.	5
(7) McDonough, Georgia	Southeastern U.S.	6

Figure 1. The Amazon distribution network

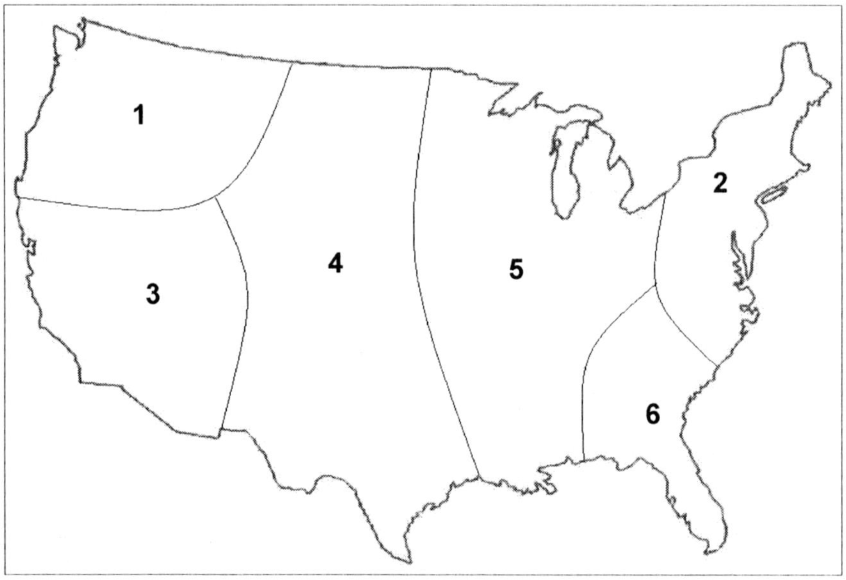

may not be the most efficient way to reduce the overall delivery cost.

The rest of this chapter is organized as follows. In the next section, we provide the relevant literature review. We then outline the notation and basic assumptions of our model and develop a dynamic program with the aim of minimizing the total expected delivery cost. Next, we propose three heuristic decision rules, which we evaluate by numerical simulation. We wrap up the chapter with a summary of our main results and some ideas for future research.

LITERATURE REVIEW

Literature examining transshipment models can be classified by several major characteristics: emergency situations or non-emergency situations, one-period or multiple-period, two-location or multiple-location, periodic review system or continuous review system, and static demand or dynamic demand.

Many earlier papers focusing on transshipment deal with emergency lateral transshipment. Such papers (Lee, 1987; Axsater, 1990; Alfredsson & Verrijdt, 1999) tend to study low-demand service parts or repairable items in continuous review systems. They all assume that demand will first be filled from stock on hand and any remaining will be supplied by an emergency lateral transshipment. In contrast, some researchers (Das, 1975; Robinson, 1990; Archibald, Sassen, & Thomas, 1997) extend the emergency transshipment to non-emergency transshipment. Instead of a continuous review system, they use a periodic one, in which transshipments can occur regularly. Both papers assume zero lead times for ordering and transshipment. Tagaras and Cohen (1992) evaluate different pooling rules for lateral transshipment, but with non-negligible lead times. Herer and Tzur (2001) use a shortest path network method to search for optimal transshipment solutions. Grahovac and Chakravarty (2001) use a triggering level to differentiate the regular order and emergency order—that is, emergency transshipments will only occur if the inventory level reaches a predetermined level.

Two recent papers (Minner, Silver, & Robb, 2003; Axsater, 2003) relax most of the restrictions described previously. Under a special assumption that no further transshipments will take place, they use a decision technique based on full system information that maximizes the savings via a single one-time transshipment. This heuristic rule can be used repeatedly as an approximation. Rudi, Kapor, and Pyke (2001) take a new approach, which analyzes the transshipments under a decentralized system rather than using traditional centralized coordination. With the localized setting, they use a Nash equilibrium to coordinate transshipment prices that lead to joint profit maximization. Related models studying dynamic environment with transshipment can be found in Herer and Rashit (1999), Robinson (1996), and Lin et al. (2004).

In the digital age, communications between different DCs are almost instantaneous, and thus inventory sharing is relatively easier. Transshipment occurs more often with online stores than with traditional brick-and-mortar stores because customers do not need to take actual possession of the product at the virtual stores (Harrington, 1999). In this chapter we specifically target this prominent issue faced by e-retailers serving geographically dispersed markets. In a complex decision situation, it is mathematically difficult to find theoretical results for transshipment. Heuristic decision rules with predefined conditions represent the most common technique to approach the transshipment problem. By comparing different heuristic rules based on expected optimal cost, we illustrate that a commonly used practice is not cost efficient and then identify an appropriate one that can be implemented easily by practitioners.

MODEL DESCRIPTION

We model a single-product system for one-period analysis. We consider a centralized e-retailer with a large geographic market divided into a number of regional markets according to the locations of its DCs. We first assume that the arrival rates of order requests from each market are independently Poisson distributed. At the start of the period, we assume that all DCs are replenished at the same time (from a supplier whose concerns are exogenous to this model). No replenishment is allowed within the period, implying that only within-DC transshipment is allowed for satisfying demand when stocks run out at any DCs. The inventory position of each DC is reviewed continuously for the purpose of regular transshipment. Customers can place orders online as long as the system has stock remaining. However, once the system inventory reaches zero, the current selling period ends and no more online ordering is allowed.

When a demand is realized online from a market, an order fulfillment request is generated. If the product is available at the local DC, the item is shipped out from the local DC to the customer. If there are no units available at the local DC, transshipment is requested to other DCs with stock on hand. Unlike the traditional inventory-sharing of offline stores, the transshipped item is shipped out directly to the customer from the selected DC. Our goal is to minimize the total expected delivery cost in this uncertain demand environment.

Box 1 describes the model notation. For simplicity, we aggregate all customers from one regional market into one customer located at the DC in that market, which implies no distance difference among customers in the same market. Thus, we can assume a zero local shipment cost—that is, $C_{ii} = 0$. The delivery cost matrix should be symmetric as seen in Figure 2. For any given symmetric delivery cost matrix, we introduce a new term. If delivery costs follow the basic geometric axiom—that is, $C_{ij} + C_{jk} \geq C_{ik}$ for any i, j, and k, we refer to this type of delivery cost matrix as a realistic matrix, otherwise we call it a nonrealistic matrix.

Box 1. Notation

n = number of distribution centers in the system
S_i = current inventory position at DC i (i=1, 2,…, n)
λ_j = expected periodic demand rate at market j (j=1, 2,…, n)
C_{ij} = unit transshipment cost from DC i to market j
D_j = expected remaining demand within the current period from market j

Figure 2. Symmetrical delivery cost matrix

$$\begin{bmatrix} 0 & C_{12} & \cdots & C_{1n} \\ C_{12} & 0 & \cdots & C_{2n} \\ \vdots & \vdots & & \vdots \\ C_{1n} & C_{2n} & \cdots & 0 \end{bmatrix}$$

It is easy to show that when operating under conditions of a realistic cost matrix, customer demand should be fulfilled by its local DC whenever possible. Indeed, without loss of generality, we suppose that there are only two units in system inventory (one in DC i and the other in DC j). Now when a demand is realized at market j, we transship one unit from DC i to market j, which incurs a delivery cost C_{ij}. Next demand can be from any market k(k = *1, 2,..., n*), then the delivery cost must be C_{jk}. So the total cost is $C_{ij}+C_{jk}$ in this scenario. If transshipment only happens when the local DC is out of stock, the total cost should be $C_{jj}+C_{ik}=0+C_{ik}=C_{ik}$. We know $C_{ij}+C_{jk}\geq C_{ik}$, so our observation is always true under a realistic cost matrix.

We shall state the following additional assumptions:

1. The initial inventory position of each DC at the beginning of the period is known.
2. The delivery cost already considers the issue of delivery time—that is, longer delivery time requires higher delivery cost.
3. The DCs located at the same regional market are considered as one, which implies that the number of DCs is the same as the number of markets.
4. Orders are filled on a first-come, first-served basis.

OPTIMAL TRANSSHIPMENT RULE

In this section we present a dynamic program to find the optimal dynamic transshipment strategy.

For any given inventory positions $S_1, S_2, \ldots, S_n$, let $T(S_1, S_2, \ldots, S_n)$ denote the minimum cost to deliver all units until the selling period ends. Although the market demand is dynamic and uncertain, it follows a Poisson distribution with rate $\lambda=\sum_{i=1}^{n}\lambda_j$. So the probability that the next unit demand comes from market j is λ_j/λ. Hence, we can build the following dynamic program (Figure 3).

The boundary conditions are $T(0, 0,..., 0)=0$ and $T(S_1, S_2,..., S_n)=\infty$ if any $S_j<0$. The complexity is approximately $n^2\cdot S_1\cdot S_2\cdot\ldots\cdot S_n$. With this dynamic program, we can recursively solve any $T(S_1, S_2, \ldots, S_n)$. Suppose when a demand is realized in market k, $S_k=0$ and $S_p>0$ for any $p\in P$, where P is the set of all DCs with stock on hand. Based on the dynamic programming results, the optimal strategy would be transshipment from DC p with $\min_{p\in P}\{C_{pk}+T(S_1,..., S_p-1,..., S_n)\}$. In the rest of the chapter, we will refer to this optimal strategy as the *optimal rule*.

For example, consider a simple case with three DCs, where $\lambda_1=1$, $\lambda_2=2$, $\lambda_3=3$ and a triangular delivery cost matrix (Figure 4).

Figure 4. Triangular delivery cost matrix

$$\begin{bmatrix} C_{11} & C_{12} & C_{13} \\ C_{21} & C_{22} & C_{23} \\ C_{31} & C_{32} & C_{33} \end{bmatrix} = \begin{bmatrix} 0 & 1 & 1 \\ 1 & 0 & 1 \\ 1 & 1 & 0 \end{bmatrix}$$

Figure 3. Dynamic program

$$T(S_1, S_2,\ldots, S_n)=$$

$$\frac{\lambda_1}{\lambda} \min\{C_{11} + T(S_1 - 1, S_2,\ldots, S_n), C_{21} + T(S_1, S_2 - 1,\ldots, S_n),\ldots, C_{n1} = T(S_1, S_2,\ldots, S_n -1)\}$$

$$+ \frac{\lambda_2}{\lambda} \min\{C_{12} + T(S_1 - 1, S_2,\ldots, S_n), C_{22} + T(S_1, S_2 - 1,\ldots, S_n),\ldots, C_{n2} = T(S_1, S_2,\ldots, S_n -1)\}$$

$$+ \ldots$$

$$+ \frac{\lambda_n}{\lambda} \min\{C_{1n} + T(S_1 - 1, S_2,\ldots, S_n), C_{2n} + T(S_1, S_2 - 1,\ldots, S_n),\ldots, C_{nn} = T(S_1, S_2,\ldots, S_n -1)\}$$

Table 2 shows the results using initial inventory positions (3, 3, 3). Suppose that current inventory positions are (3, 3, 0), and a customer from market 3 places an order. From Table 2, since $c_{13} + T(2,3,0) = 1 + 2.78 < c_{23} + T(3,2,0) = 1 + 2.88$, we need to make a transshipment from DC 1 to market 3. We will illustrate how to compute $T(S_1, S_2, S_3)$ after describing heuristic rule 3.

Even though the results from Table 2 were derived from a simple setting, some observations become evident. The optimal system cost does not necessarily decrease with the reduction of inventory positions, which seems counter-intuitive. It is explainable because we assume that the local shipment cost is zero. Thus, the more balanced the inventory positions, the lower the probability of a transshipment—hence the smaller the optimal cost.

We can attain the optimal transshipment policy using the dynamic program. However, the calculation of dynamic program is time costly and difficult to implement. Since the transshipment decision has to be decided upon frequently in the digital age, in the next section we propose three heuristic decision rules that can be easily implemented by practitioners.

Table 2. Optimal costs under a triangular matrix

S_1	S_2	S_3	$T(S_1,S_2,S_3)$
3	3	3	2.33
3	3	2	2.57
3	3	1	2.90
3	3	0	3.32
3	2	3	2.21
3	2	2	2.33
3	2	1	2.56
3	2	0	2.88
3	1	3	2.30
3	1	2	2.28
3	1	1	2.37
3	1	0	2.58
3	0	3	2.61
3	0	2	2.46
3	0	1	2.42
3	0	0	2.50
2	3	3	1.84
2	3	2	2.03
2	3	1	2.36
2	3	0	2.78
2	2	3	1.67
2	2	2	1.73
2	2	1	1.94
2	2	0	2.28
…			
0	0	1	0.5
0	0	0	0

Figure 6. Ratio rule

$$\min_{p\in P}\left\{\frac{D_p}{S_p}C_{pk}\right\}=\min_{p\in P}\left\{\left(\frac{\lambda_p}{\lambda}\times\sum_{i=1}^{n}S_i\right)\times\frac{C_{pk}}{S_p}\right\}=\left(\frac{\sum_{i=1}^{n}S_i}{\lambda}\right)\min_{p\in P}\left\{\frac{\lambda_p}{S_p}C_{pk}\right\}$$

HEURISTIC TRANSSHIPMENT RULES

To the extent that shipping cost is roughly proportional to distance, it appears reasonable to transship from the closest DC with stock on hand. This intuitive approach is widely adopted in practice. We name the first decision rule as *the Nearest Rule.*

Nearest Rule

Transshipment should be from the DC with the minimum unit transshipment cost: $\min_{p\in P}\{C_{pk}\}$, *where k is the DC already out of stock and P is the set of all DCs with stock on hand.*

Now, consider a online retailer with three DCs, given $\lambda_1 = 1$, $\lambda_2 = 2$, $\lambda_3 = 3$, and a triangular delivery cost matrix (Figure 5).

Suppose that current inventory positions are (2, 0, 3), and a customer from market 2 places an order. According to the Nearest Rule, the retailer needs to make a transshipment from DC 3 since $C_{12} > C_{32}$.

Unfortunately, this myopic Nearest Rule only considers the one-time delivery cost. It does not take into account that transshipment will reduce the source DC's ability to meet its own future demand. A higher future demand rate implies a higher probability of stocking out. So transshipping from a DC with a high market demand may not be wise, even if this DC has available stock. Considering this, our second rule incorporates the possibility of stock outs.

Figure 5. Triangular delivery cost matrix

$$\begin{bmatrix} C_{11} & C_{12} & C_{13} \\ C_{21} & C_{22} & C_{23} \\ C_{31} & C_{32} & C_{33} \end{bmatrix}=\begin{bmatrix} 0 & 3 & 1 \\ 3 & 0 & 2 \\ 1 & 2 & 0 \end{bmatrix}$$

Ratio Rule

Transshipment should be from the DC with:

$$\min_{p\in P}\left\{\frac{D_p}{S_p}C_{pk}\right\},$$

where D_p *is the expected remaining demand within the period from market p.*

With current inventory positions S_1, S_2,..., S_n, we have $D_p = \frac{\lambda_p}{\lambda}\times\sum_{i=1}^{n} S_i$ where λ_j / λ is the probability that the next unit demand comes from market *j* and $\sum_{i=1}^{n} S_i$ is the remaining system inventory. It can be simplified as Figure 6.

Hence we only need to compute $\min_{p\in P}\left\{\frac{\lambda_p}{S_p}C_{pk}\right\}$.

Using the same example described above, according to the Ratio Rule, the retailer needs to make a transshipment from DC 1 because:

$$\frac{\lambda_1}{S_1}C_{12}=\frac{1}{2}\cdot 3<\frac{3}{3}\cdot 2=\frac{\lambda_3}{S_3}C_{32}.$$

In the third heuristic rule, we take a classical approach to minimizing the total delivery cost by assuming a once-for-all transshipment based on expected future demand.

Figure 7. Linear program

$$\text{minimize } Z = \sum_{i=1}^{n}\sum_{j=1}^{n} C_{ij}Y_{ij}$$

$$\text{s.t.} \quad \sum_{j=1}^{n} Y_{ij} = X_i \qquad \forall i$$

$$\sum_{i=1}^{n} Y_{ij} = D_j = \frac{\lambda_j}{\lambda} \times \sum_{i=1}^{n} X_i \qquad \forall j$$

$$Y_{ij} \geq 0 \qquad \forall i,j$$

LP Rule

Transshipment should be from the DC with:

$$\min_{p\in P}\{C_{pk} + \min \sum_{i=1}^{n}\sum_{j=1}^{n} C_{ij}Y_{ij}\},$$

where Y_{ij} is the expected quantity of units shipped from DC i to market j.

Given current inventory positions S_1, S_2,..., S_n, first let $X_p = S_p$ -1 and $X_i = S_i$ for any $i \neq p$. We analyze the impact on the future if transshipment occurs from DC p to market k. Mathematically, this can be formulated as a linear program (Figure 7.)

After adding unit transshipment cost C_{pk} to Z_{min}, the DC with minimum sum-up value should be our choice.

Continuing to use the same example above, according to the LP Rule, suppose one unit transshipment is from DC 1, we get $Z_{min} = 3$ by solving the LP; suppose one unit transshipment is from DC 3, we get $Z_{min} = 4$. Since $C_{12} + 3 = C_{32} + 4 = 6$, the transshipment can be either from DC 1 or DC 3. As we can see, transshipping decisions from three heuristic rules are different under the described example.

To illustrate the procedure of calculating the expected total system delivery cost $T(S_1,S_2,..., S_n)$, the following numerical example is presented when using the Ratio Rule. The procedures for the Nearest Rule and the LP Rule are similar except that we need to adopt different decision polices when determining the source DC (Box 2).

NUMERICAL EVALUATIONS

In order to compare these three different rules, we set up a simulation experiment. Starting with a 3-DC system with initial inventory (3, 3, 3), different configurations can be explored by combining the demand rate and delivery cost. To determine their effects, three values of each were examined: $\lambda_j \in \{1,2,3\}$ and $C_{ij} = C_{ji} \in \{1,2,3\}$ $\forall i \neq j$. After eliminating two exact duplications, we have 22 realistic matrices and 3 nonrealistic matrices with 25 combinations of demand rates. So there are (22 + 3) · 25 = 625 different trials. Table 4 shows the simulation results of 25 trials under a triangular cost matrix. We compare the relative performance of the heuristic rules to the optimal rule.

As seen from Table 4, apparently the Ratio Rule and the LP Rule perform much better than the Nearest Rule. In addition, the relative performance of the heuristic rules seems insensitive to the variation of demand rate, although the system delivery cost does increase as the variation increases. In other words, demand variation will cause delivery costs to increase, but it will not necessarily cause poor transshipment decisions. Hence, our two new proposed heuristic rules appear robust.

Table 3 shows the average cost penalty of 550 trials based on the realistic cost matrices.

Table 5 shows the average cost penalty of 75 trials based on the nonrealistic cost matrices.

Table 3. Average penalty under realistic cost matrices

Nearest Rule	Ratio Rule	LP Rule
3%	0.51%	1.18%

Table 5. Average penalty under nonrealistic cost matrices

Nearest Rule	Ratio Rule	LP Rule
8.11%	5.59%	4.92%

Box 2. Example of cost calculation when using the Ratio Rule

3-DC system: $n = 3$

Initial Inventory: $S_1 = S_2 = S_3 = 3$

Demand Rate: $\lambda_1 = 1, \lambda_2 = 2, \lambda_3 = 3$

Delivery Cost Matrix: $\begin{bmatrix} C_{11} & C_{12} & C_{13} \\ C_{21} & C_{22} & C_{23} \\ C_{31} & C_{32} & C_{33} \end{bmatrix} = \begin{bmatrix} 0 & 1 & 1 \\ 1 & 0 & 1 \\ 1 & 1 & 0 \end{bmatrix}$

With boundary condition $T(0,0,0)=0$, we have

$$T(0,0,1) = \frac{\lambda_1}{\lambda}\cdot(C_{31} + T(0,0,0)) + \frac{\lambda_2}{\lambda}\cdot(C_{32} + T(0,0,0)) + \frac{\lambda_3}{\lambda}\cdot(C_{33} + T(0,0,0)) = \frac{1}{6}\cdot 1 + \frac{2}{6}\cdot 1 + \frac{3}{6}\cdot 0 = 0.5$$

$$T(0,1,0) = \frac{\lambda_1}{\lambda}\cdot(C_{21} + T(0,0,0)) + \frac{\lambda_2}{\lambda}\cdot(C_{22} + T(0,0,0)) + \frac{\lambda_3}{\lambda}\cdot(C_{23} + T(0,0,0)) = \frac{1}{6}\cdot 1 + \frac{2}{6}\cdot 0 + \frac{3}{6}\cdot 1 = 0.67$$

Since $\frac{\lambda_2}{S_2}C_{21} < \frac{\lambda_3}{S_3}C_{31}$, a unit transshipment should be requested from DC 2 to Market 1

$$T(0,1,1) = \frac{\lambda_1}{\lambda}\cdot(C_{21} + T(0,0,1)) + \frac{\lambda_2}{\lambda}\cdot(C_{22} + T(0,0,1)) + \frac{\lambda_3}{\lambda}\cdot(C_{33} + T(0,1,0)) = \frac{1}{6}\cdot 1.5 + \frac{2}{6}\cdot 0.5 + \frac{3}{6}\cdot 0.67 = 0.75$$

Continuing this way sequentially, we can ultimately get

$$T(3,3,3) = \frac{\lambda_1}{\lambda}\cdot(C_{11} + T(2,3,3)) + \frac{\lambda_2}{\lambda}\cdot(C_{22} + T(3,2,3)) + \frac{\lambda_3}{\lambda}\cdot(C_{33} + T(3,3,2)) = \frac{1}{6}\cdot 1.84 + \frac{2}{6}\cdot 2.21 + \frac{3}{6}\cdot 2.57 = 2.33$$

From these two summaries, we can see that the performances of heuristic rules degrade significantly when the cost matrices are nonrealistic. Although the Ratio Rule and the LP Rule are comparable to each other, we suggest using the Ratio Rule if the cost matrix is realistic; however, if the matrix is non-realistic, we suggest using the LP Rule. In general, the Nearest Rule should be avoided.

Under the same conditions, the extension to four DCs is straightforward. We keep the same setting except excluding all nonrealistic cost matrices, which we would expect to occur infrequently in practice. After adding one more DC, both time complexity and number of possible trials increase dramatically. Because we used a Microsoft Excel macro to simulate the LP Rule, it takes a much longer time for Solver to converge after the number of DCs reaches four. The estimated CPU solution time for 39,042 trials is more than 1,000 hours on a standard Pentium 4 PC. In addition, for a 3-DC system the Ratio Rule performs better than the LP Rule under realistic cost matrices; hence, we only tested the performance of the Ratio Rule and the Nearest Rule for a 4-DC system.

As seen from Table 6, the cost penalty using the Nearest Rule is more than twice as high as using the Ratio Rule. Given a very low initial inventory setting, this represents a significant improvement. Even though we only have the results of 3-DC and 4-DC systems, we expect that benefits of using the Ratio Rule will increase when the DC network continues to expand.

Table 6. Average penalty in a 4-DC system

Nearest Rule	Ratio Rule
5.29%	1.65%

Table 4. Simulation results testing the accuracy of heuristic rules

Demand Rate			Total Delivery Cost $T(3,3,3)$				Cost Penalty from Optimal Value		
λ_1	λ_2	λ_3	Optimal	Nearest	Ratio	LP	Nearest	Ratio	LP
1	1	1	1.796	1.888	1.796	1.796	5.10%	0.00%	0.00%
1	1	2	2.212	2.369	2.212	2.227	7.10%	0.00%	0.70%
1	1	3	2.795	2.956	2.795	2.811	5.80%	0.00%	0.60%
1	2	1	2.212	2.337	2.214	2.223	5.70%	0.10%	0.50%
1	2	2	2.052	2.323	2.052	2.061	13.20%	0.00%	0.40%
1	2	3	2.325	2.648	2.325	2.379	13.90%	0.00%	2.30%
1	3	1	2.795	2.935	2.795	2.819	5.00%	0.00%	0.90%
1	3	2	2.325	2.642	2.325	2.353	13.60%	0.00%	1.20%
1	3	3	2.316	2.709	2.319	2.322	17.00%	0.10%	0.30%
2	1	1	2.212	2.304	2.215	2.222	4.20%	0.10%	0.50%
2	1	2	2.052	2.205	2.06	2.056	7.50%	0.40%	0.20%
2	1	3	2.325	2.463	2.342	2.327	5.90%	0.70%	0.10%
2	2	1	2.052	2.086	2.068	2.052	1.70%	0.80%	0.00%
2	2	3	1.932	2.073	1.932	1.932	7.30%	0.00%	0.00%
2	3	1	2.325	2.362	2.343	2.341	1.60%	0.80%	0.70%
2	3	2	1.932	2.042	1.932	1.932	5.70%	0.00%	0.00%
2	3	3	1.891	2.076	1.891	1.895	9.80%	0.00%	0.20%
3	1	1	2.795	2.914	2.796	2.809	4.30%	0.00%	0.50%
3	1	2	2.325	2.541	2.327	2.351	9.30%	0.10%	1.10%
3	1	3	2.316	2.519	2.323	2.319	8.80%	0.30%	0.10%
3	2	1	2.325	2.357	2.343	2.325	1.40%	0.80%	0.00%
3	2	2	1.932	2.011	1.933	1.932	4.10%	0.10%	0.00%
3	2	3	1.891	2.013	1.893	1.895	6.50%	0.10%	0.20%
3	3	1	2.316	2.328	2.326	2.316	0.50%	0.40%	0.00%
3	3	2	1.891	1.949	1.894	1.912	3.10%	0.20%	1.10%

CONCLUSION AND DISCUSSION

In the digital age, dynamic transshipments occur frequently for online retailing. Large e-retailers can save a lot on internal fulfillment costs if they adopt correct transshipping strategies. In this chapter, we have presented a one-period model where regular transshipments are allowed. Based on minimizing the total expected delivery cost, the optimal transshipment policy can be obtained from a dynamic program. A simple but effective heuristic rule (Ratio Rule) is also provided for the practitioners to implement.

We find that the Nearest Rule, which is widely used, is not a wise approach for transshipment decision making. The LP Rule may be best for rare nonrealistic cost matrices. The Ratio Rule as we suggest is generally a much better substitute for the Nearest Rule. In addition, the performance of the Ratio Rule is robust to demand variation.

In this chapter, we assume unit-size transactions to simulate the model. Hopefully, future field research can validate our results on larger transaction sizes. A possible approach may use a stuttering Poisson demand process (Ward, 1978) for simulation. Ours is a single-period model, so there is no replenishment necessary. The extension to a system with replenishment is less than straightforward because under a continuous review inventory system with dynamic demand, the determination of optimal reorder points and batch quantities can become quite complicated.

ACKNOWLEDGMENT

Bintong Chen's research was partially supported by the National Natural Science Foundation of China No. 70640420143.

REFERENCES

Alfredsson, P., & Verrijdt, J. (1999). Modeling emergency supply flexibility in a two-echelon inventory system. *Management Science, 45*(10), 1416-1431.

Archibald, T.W., Sassen, S.A.E., & Thomas, L.C. (1997). An optimal policy for a two depot inventory problem with stock transfer. *Management Science, 43*(2), 173-183.

Axsater. S. (1990). Modeling emergency lateral transshipments in inventory systems. *Management Science, 36*(11), 1329-1338.

Axsater, S. (2003). A new decision rule for lateral transshipments in inventory systems. *Management Science, 49*(9), 1168-1179.

Das, C. (1975). Supply and redistribution rules for two-location inventory systems: One-period analysis. *Management Science, 21*(7), 765-776.

Forrester. (2005). Online retail sales will hit $210 billion in 2010. *Internet Retailer.* Retrieved November 10, 2005, from http://www.internetretailer.com

Finfacts Team. (2006). *Finfacts business news centre.* Retrieved from http://www.finfacts.com/irelandbusinessnews/publish/article_10004757.shtml

Grahovac, J., & Chakravarty, A. (2001). Sharing and lateral transshipment of inventory in a supply chain with expensive low-demand items. *Management Science, 47*(4), 579-594.

Harrington, L. (1999). Digital-age warehousing. *Industry Week, 248*(14), 52-58.

Herer, Y.T., & Tzur, M. (2001). The dynamic transshipment problem. *Naval Research Logistics, 48,* 386-408.

Herer, Y.T., & Rashit, A. (1999). Lateral stock transshipments in a two-location inventory system with fixed and joint replenishment costs. *Naval Research Logistics, 46,* 525-547.

Lee, H.L. (1987). A multi-echelon inventory model for repairable items with emergency lateral transshipments. *Management Science, 33*(10), 1302-1316.

Lin, K.Y., & Sibdari, S.Y. (2004). Dynamic price competition with discrete customer choices. *Working Paper.* Retrieved April 7, 2005, from http://www.nps.navy.mil/Faculty/Lin

Maltz, A., Rabinovich, E., & Sinha, R. (2004). Logistics: The key to e-retail success. *Supply Chain Management Review, 8*(3), 56-63.

Minner, S., Silver, E.A., & Robb, D.J. (2003). An improved heuristic for deciding on emergency transshipments. *European Journal of Operational Research, 148,* 384-400.

Robinson, E.P., & Gao, L. (1996). A dual ascent procedure for multiproduct dynamic demand coordinated replenishment with backlogging. *Management Science, 42*(11), 1556-1564.

Robinson, L.W. (1990). Optimal and approximate policies in multiperiod, multilocation inventory models with transshipments. *Operations Research, 38*(2), 278-295.

Rudi, N., Kapor, S., & Pyke, D.F. (2001). A two-location inventory model with transshipment and local decision making. *Management Science, 47*(12), 1668-1680.

Tagaras, G., & Cohen, M.A. (1992). Pooling in two-location inventory systems with non-negligible replenishment lead times. *Management Science, 38*(8), 1067-1083.

Ward, J.B. (1978). Determining reorder points when demand is lumpy. *Management Science, 24*(6), 623-632.

Chapter III
E-Com Supply Chain and SMEs

Ron Craig
Wilfrid Laurier University, Canada

ABSTRACT

This chapter considers the perspective of small and medium-sized enterprises (SMEs) in supply chains. It starts with an overview of the important role of SMEs in national and world economies. Following this is an overview of supply chains, information and communication technologies, and e-business. Both opportunities and challenges for supply chains in general and SMEs in particular are considered, and conclusions drawn. The major contribution of the chapter is in providing an extensive overview of the literature as it relates to information and communication technologies, supply chain management, and SMEs, providing researchers and practitioners with a starting point to look for further information as needed.

INTRODUCTION

This chapter presents a modest overview of the considerable literature covering supply chain management (SCM), information and communication technologies (ICTs), e-commerce, and small and medium-sized enterprises (SMEs). The reviewed papers include the perspectives of all sized firms. Since large firms have led in SCM, and continue to do so, much can be learned from their experiences and their influence over other chain members. The literature on SCM is vast, so only a few representative papers are reviewed. There is much less literature dealing with SMEs; hence this coverage is fuller. Readers are encouraged to go to the referenced articles for more information, and to future articles that cite these if the development of a particular area is of interest.

Only in the past decade has the SME perspective of SCM been seriously considered, with both theoretical and empirical research published. The SME SCM empirical literature now covers many individual countries, including Canada (Archer, Wang, & Kang, 2003; Canadian E-Business Initiative, 2004; Raymond, Bergeron, & Blili, 2005), Germany (Berlak & Weber, 2004), South Africa (Badenhorst-Weiss, Fourie, & Nel, 2004), Taiwan (Chou, Hsu, Yeh, & Ho, 2005; Wang, Chang, &

Heng, 2004), the UK (Azumah, Koh, & Maguire, 2005; Levy & Powell, 2003; Tucker & Lafferty, 2004; Wynarczyk & Watson, 2005), and the United States (Arend & Wisner, 2005; Levenburg, 2005). International comparisons have been completed by a few researchers. Beck, Wigand, and Konig (2005) compared European countries (France, Germany, Denmark) and the United States. Johnston and Wright (2004) compared Canada, Mexico, China, and Japan. There is a slight bias in the literature towards manufacturing over other sectors (such as retail/wholesale, finance, service) because manufacturing has historically controlled many supply chains. Today this control is shifting, with retailers (such as Wal-Mart) often having greater chain influence.

This chapter starts with a review of the role of SMEs in national and world economies, and then considers SCM in business today, including the major improvements facilitated by ICTs. Following this, opportunities and challenges at both the general chain and SME levels are considered. Finally, conclusions are drawn and areas for future research suggested.

SMEs in National and World Economy

The definition of what constitutes a micro, small, or medium-sized business varies from country to country, and even between government departments and programs within a country. One common segmentation approach uses number of employees—micro (or very small) businesses having less than five employees, small businesses having 100 or fewer employees, and medium-sized firms having 101-499 employees. A variation on this would have the employee limit set at 250 for small businesses. Another segmentation method uses sales volumes and is based on the type of firm (such as manufacturing, wholesale, retail, service). In all cases, only independently owned and operated firms are included (i.e., small branches and subsidiaries of large businesses are excluded).

In Canada, small firms (those with fewer than 100 employees) make up more than 97% of goods-producing employer businesses and almost 98% of all service-producing employer businesses (Industry Canada, 2005). For the U.S., small firms represent about 99.7% of all employer firms, employ half of the private workforce, have generated 75% of the net new jobs added to the U.S. economy, represent 97% of all U.S. exporters, and create more than 50% of the non-farm, private gross domestic product (U.S. Small Business Administration, 2006). At the start of 2004, within the UK, 99.9% of all enterprises were small (0 to 49 employees) or medium (50 to 249 employees), employing some 58.5% of the private sector workforce (some 12 million people), and contributing to more than 50% of the national GDP (Small Business Service, 2006). Within Europe (28 countries of the European Economic Area plus candidate countries to the European Union) in 2003 there were some 25.3 million non-primary private enterprises, of which 99.8% were craft or small and medium-sized (European Commission, 2006). In June 2004, 99 % of Australian employing businesses were SMEs (Australian Bureau of Statistics, 2004; their definition of a small business is having less than 20 employees, with a medium-sized one having fewer than 200). And in Latin America and Asia, as many as 99% of all firms are SMEs (Johnston & Wright, 2004).

With such a large number of SMEs, there are significant differences when one looks at things like profitability, industry sector, size, adoption and use of ICTs, and so forth. Many studies look at SMEs as a group (sometimes segmenting by industry sector); this can mask significant underlying differences. Similarly, looking at acceptance and use of new technology systems without considering innovators, early and late adaptors can result in 'average' results that do not reflect the full range of experiences. An exception to this approach is Levenburg (2005), who compared IT adoption for micro, small, and medium-sized firms.

Typical advantages attributed to SMEs include being able to service small markets, having a quick reaction time to changes in market conditions (both organizational and managerial flexibility), innovativeness, closeness to their customers (with a trusting relationship), and a bias for action. On the negative side, SMEs usually are 'resource poor' (in terms of finances, time, and expertise), and generally lag in integration into the new e-economy. It is important to note that a small business is not simply a scaled-down version of a large business.

We see that SMEs are very important to local and national economies, and hence to the world economy. As SMEs provide employment, create new jobs, and contribute to a country's GDP, governments are naturally concerned about their well-being and vitality. Various programs exist at national and local levels to support SMEs. There are programs with the specific goal of assisting SMEs to increase their use of e-commerce and/or supply chain initiatives; examples of these follow.

Role of SCM in Business Today

Taylor's (2004) supply chain management matrix, displayed in Figure 1, presents an illustration of several components of SCM. Rows in this matrix correspond to three different levels of management (design, planning, operations), while the columns list business processes concerned with supply, production, and demand. This matrix is for a single firm; inter-organizational networks are much more complex, as the matrix is repeated for each firm in the overall network (from tiers of upstream suppliers to the ultimate downstream customer). Even at the firm level, SCM can be very complex. Each of the component areas shown in Figure 1 has a well-established tradition with standard procedures and best practice approaches. SCM requires cooperation and coordination between these components—something that is much more common today than a few decades ago. Extending supply chain considerations externally to all the other firms in the entire network presents a much more formidable challenge.

Supply chains are on the corporate agenda today. Sheffi and Michelman (2005) point out that IBM's sale of its PC business to Lenovo and the merger of Procter & Gamble with Gillette were driven to a great extent by the supply chain success of major competitors (Dell and Wal-Mart, respectively). They state, "in an era of commoditized products, volatile markets, and expanding arenas of competition, supply chains are becoming one area where distinction is possible, powerful, and increasingly difficult to replicate."

Many SCM authors (including Harrison & van Hoek, 2005; Lee & Wang, 2001; Patterson, Grimm, & Corsi, 2003; Taylor, 2004) identify the forces contributing towards the surge in SCM interest. These forces include:

- Globalization
- Technical innovation in ICTs
- External pressure from other supply chain members, including higher expectations from customers
- Outsourcing trends
- Pressures to reduce costs and increase profits

The potential benefits of SCM and e-SCM are frequently stated (e.g., Beach, 2004; Davenport & Brooks, 2004; Serve et al., 2002; Taylor, 2004), including:

- Eliminate delays and errors associated with traditional paper-based systems
- Improve customer satisfaction (fewer stock-outs, paperwork savings)
- Reduce supply chain costs
- Improve record accuracy
- Lower data entry costs (single point of entry)
- Reduce inventory holdings (shorter lead times)
- Increase inventory turns
- Increase quality

Figure 1. Supply chain management matrix (Source: Taylor, 2004)

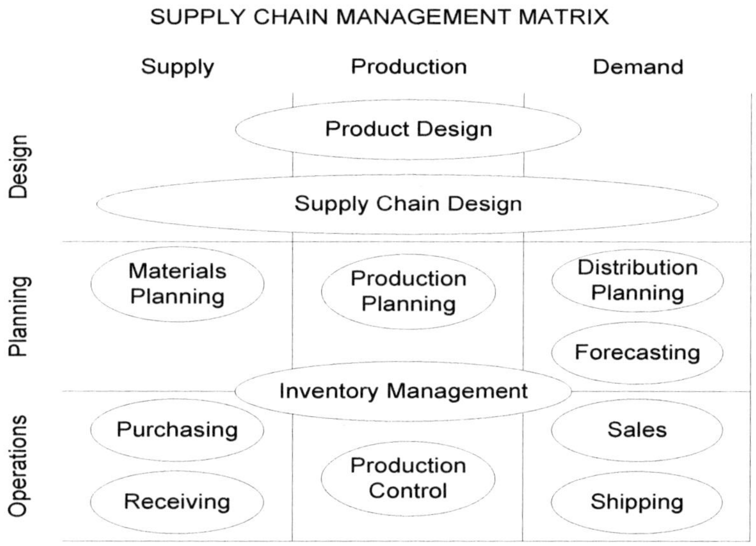

MIT has a Supply Chain 2020 project underway (Lapide, 2005)—a long-term research effort to identify and analyze the factors that are critical to the success of future supply chains. Initial research has already identified four characteristics of high-performing supply networks:

1. They support, enhance, and are an integral part of a firm's competitive business strategy (alignment).
2. They leverage a distinctive supply chain operating model to sustain competitiveness.
3. They execute well against a balanced set of operational performance objectives and metrics (measurement and feedback).
4. They focus on a few business practices that reinforce one another to support the operating model and best achieve operational excellence.

Lapide points out that strategy and operations are closely linked and particularly important. He states, "A supply chain that does not support the organization's business strategy can never be excellent. And companies have to make adjustments to supply chains when strategy changes." That SCM can be a powerful competitive weapon is demonstrated by Amazon, Dell, Wal-Mart, and other major firms.

SCM strategies and tactics continue to improve as firms develop a better understanding of how to manage the entire chain. Whereas a few years ago a fast and cost-efficient chain provided considerable competitive advantage, this is changing as more firms and chains master this. Lee (2004) points out that supply chains today need to be more than simply fast and cost effective. They need to be agile (responding quickly to sudden changes in supply or demand), adaptable (evolving over time as the environment and markets change), and aligned (with all chain member interests).

Clearly SCM is of considerable interest to large firms. However, how well does SCM fit with SMEs? Before considering this, we will first look at the role of information and communication technologies in the supply chain.

ICTs, E-Business, and Supply Chains

Information technology first took on a major role in manufacturing with the development of manufacturing resource planning (MRP) systems several decades ago. Progress continued with MRP-II, enterprise resource planning (ERP) systems (or enterprise systems—ESs), and advanced planning systems (APSs). With each advance there was increasing automation of repetitive, time-consuming tasks and improved integration of data and information used between functional areas of a department or organization, leading to first intra- and then inter-organizational data sharing.

ICTs continue to have a major impact on business in general, and supply chains in particular. Technology allows the reduction or elimination of paperwork (with its attendant delays in transmission/reception and possible data corruption if information is re-entered). Both technologies and applications continue to evolve, with the Internet now providing an efficient, effective communication link for supply chain partners. The power of the Internet comes from its open standards and widespread availability, permitting easy, universal, secure access to a wide audience at very low cost.

The term e-business has come into common use to cover the use of Internet-based ICTs within a company and between businesses, customers, and suppliers. The breadth of e-business is shown in Figure 2.

Figure 2 shows various 'application clusters' (SCM being one) that are designed to support and integrate various internal functions, and interface appropriately with external customers and/or partners and their applications. CRM (Customer Relationship Management) supports customer-centric applications covering sales, service, and marketing. ERP supports forecasting and planning, purchasing and material management, warehousing and inventory management, finished product distribution, and accounting/finance. SCM supports market demand, resource and capacity constraints, and real-time scheduling. Selling-Chain Management supports product customization, pricing and contract management, quote and proposal generation, commission management, and promotion management. Operating Resource Management supports office supplies procurement, service procurement, business travel procurement, computer equipment/software/networking, and MRO (maintenance, repair and overhaul) procurement. A key point made by Kalakota and Robinson (2000) is the integration of these various applications, both to streamline operations and compete more effectively; this requires sharing of information between internal and external applications, and internal and external people. ICTs increasingly facilitate this. Many firms now have such an e-business system in place or are well along the road to full implementation. This e-business model continues to evolve as more functionality is added to current application clusters, new applications are developed, and more members of supply chain networks become integrated. Full integration among all members of the supply chain is the ultimate goal, providing an 'e-business network'.

Let us first consider the impact of ICT and e-business on larger firms and their supply chains. After this, the research findings on SMEs will be considered. As well, government actions in support of SME e-business are reviewed.

ICT and SCM in General

Figures 1 and 2 identify the major software applications applied to SCM. The logistic, production, and distribution components of a firm's enterprise (ERP) system supports the components detailed in Figure 1. CRM systems are designed to integrate all customer-contact activities, including sales, service, and support. They have been available for several years now. Newer, are supplier relationship

Figure 2. E-business application architecture (Source: Kalakota & Robinson, 2000)

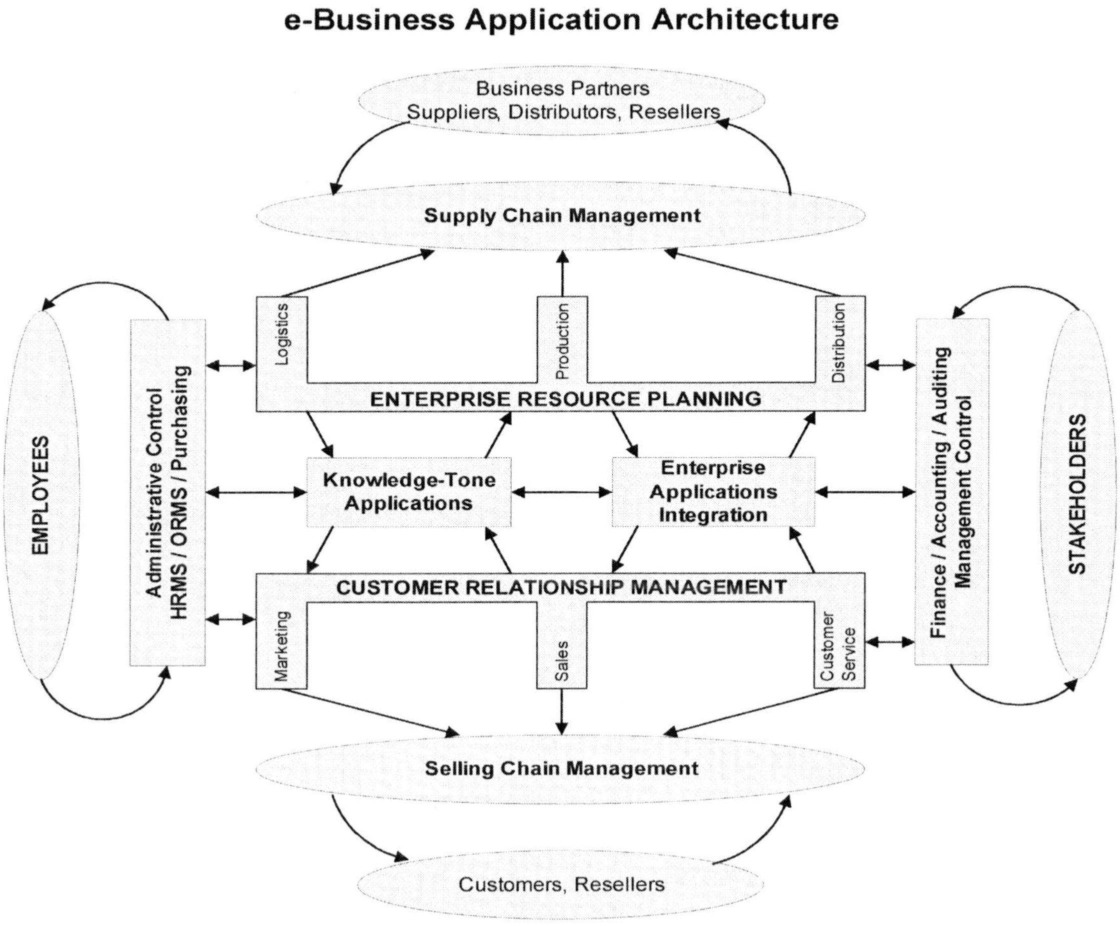

management (SRM) systems, which are a logical counterpart to CRM systems and directed to the upstream end of the supply network. Supply chain visibility and event management software is newer still and monitors supply chain activity, allowing managers to focus attention on exceptions rather than having to personally monitor the entire chain on a continuing basis.

Davenport and Brooks (2004) describe how enterprise systems in large firms have evolved to support SCM and how the Internet has brought a revolution into supply chain thinking. The low cost, ease of use, and accessibility of the Internet has facilitated growth in cross-organizational chains. However, the pace is slow because linking complex information systems and business processes is difficult. The authors encourage a view of inter-enterprise integration that spans years and even decades.

While the Internet facilitates cooperation among members of a supply chain, it has also introduced greater competition. Firms can more easily communicate with geographically distant suppliers and search for better pricing. Online auctions, for example, have brought increasing pricing pressure on many suppliers. Garcia-Dastugue and Lambert (2003) classify Internet-enabled mechanisms as either market mechanisms or coordination flows. Market mechanisms are often used for one-time transactions and include auctions, purchasing groups, electronic purchasing aids, and electronic agents. Coordination flows are implemented for ongoing relationships, so a stable business relationship is required.

Patterson et al. (2004) investigated the diffusion of supply chain intra- and inter-organizational technologies and software applications. Their study looked at 13 functional technologies (such as bar coding, electronic commerce technology, and supply chain event management systems) and two integrating technologies (ERP and supply chain planning [SCP]). Data collection was during 2001/2002, and they found a sizeable portion of firms had adopted technologies to improve functional activities but had not yet adopted integrating technologies. One would expect this to have changed in the intervening years.

Ranganathan, Dhaliwal, and Teo (2004) used a structural equation modeling (SEM) approach to empirically investigate Web technologies. They considered three organizational environment factors (managerial IT knowledge, centralization, and formalization of IT unit structure) as key drivers of internal assimilation, and three external environment factors (supplier interdependence, competitive intensity, and IT activity intensity) as the drivers of external diffusion. Their SEM approach highlighted many supply chain benefits from the deployment of Web technologies, including improved customer service, better inventory control, reduced operations costs, reduced cycle time, better relationships with suppliers, and generation of competitive advantage. Their results provide strong evidence that returns from SCM Web applications will be positive, and firms can maximize these benefits by first assimilating such technologies with their internal processes and then externally diffusing them into their supply chains.

Lee and Whang (2001) show that e-business, which they define as the use of Internet-based computing and communications to execute both front-end and back-end business processes, is a key enabler driving supply chain integration. Their paper describes the impact of e-business on four critical dimensions of supply chain integration: information integration, synchronized planning, coordinated workflow, and new business models.

ICTs and SCM in SMEs

While EDI was introduced some time ago by large firms, its cost made it difficult for even medium-sized firms. Internet technology, with its open system platform and lower cost, is proving to be of significant benefit for many SME SCM applications. Successful adoption and integration of basic e-commerce, with its extensive use of the Internet, can serve as a foundation to more sophisticated solutions, such as e-SCM. Some of the SME research has focused on the broader area of e-business, including SCM applications (but not always explicitly stating so), while other research has focused specifically on SCM applications.

Raymond et al. (2005) point out that with the advent of global competition and new organization forms based on networks of cooperating firms, the successful assimilation of e-business is bound to take added importance for many SMEs in terms of survival, growth, and competitiveness. Indeed, lacking the ability to interface electronically with supply networks could shut SMEs out of future business.

Levenburg (2005) is one of the few empirical researchers to consider size (micro, small, and medium) within the SME segment and its impact on IT adoption. She found increasing e-business technology use as firm size increased. More frequently, researchers compare SMEs as a group against larger firms, finding larger firms (on average) lead in ICT adoption and use. However, this masks the size/use relationship within the SME segment.

SCM portals have generally been successful, as those involved have significant incentives to participate. Driven by large firms, and sometimes supported by government, SMEs are important participants. Chan and Chung (2002) report on the example of Li and Fung Trading, the largest trading company in Hong Kong. With some 7,500 contract manufacturers in more than 26 countries, their average supplier has about 133 employees. The challenge for Li and Fung is to create an optimized value chain for each order, and their portal facilitates this.

Chou et al. (2005) propose a framework for evaluating industry portals and apply it to Taiwan. In 2003 the Taiwan government Ministry of Economic Affairs, Small and Medium Enterprises Administration (MOEASMEA) initiated an industry portal project. Initially 48 industry portals were to be established, followed by 10 additional portals each new year. The main goals were to: "(1) facilitate the network model for SMEs, (2) enhance associations' functions to construct SMEs' industrial databases, (3) develop the prototype SMEs' electronic marketplace, and (4) promote industry associations to become the driving centers for SMEs' e-business transformation." While this paper focuses on development and application of an assessment framework, it shows the importance of measuring portal performance from a multiple stakeholder perspective, so feedback is obtained and acted upon. Such portals could become a springboard for SMEs to form e-supply chains (as demonstrated in Germany by Berlak & Weber, 2004).

It is important to remember that as technology advances, what was once leading-edge ICT becomes cheaper, easier to install and use, and sometimes a necessity for business operation. Moore (2002) illustrates this for e-commerce (Figure 3), showing that things which were once core (providing competitive advantage) have steadily moved into the context area (where outsourcing becomes an option or even a necessity). The rise of third-party logistic providers (3PLs) illustrates this in the supply chain. Indeed, the terms 4PL and 5PL (for which there are currently various understandings) show the increasing role taken on by external specialists in supporting supply chains. Hence, possible choices for SMEs include outsourcing some supply chain responsibilities, and following a 'lag' approach to ICT, waiting for the technology and infrastructure to mature and become mainstream.

Many SME ICT and SCM empirical studies suffer from a significant time lag between data collection and journal publication (2-5 years). Given the pace of technology, these "current state" articles reflect the past, rather than the present. Another option for understanding the current state is to look at industry association and trade publications. These are usually based on smaller samples, certainly do not have the rigor of academic studies, and can misrepresent reality. Yet they are current, and hence potentially useful.

Figure 3. E-com escalator (Source: Moore, 2002)

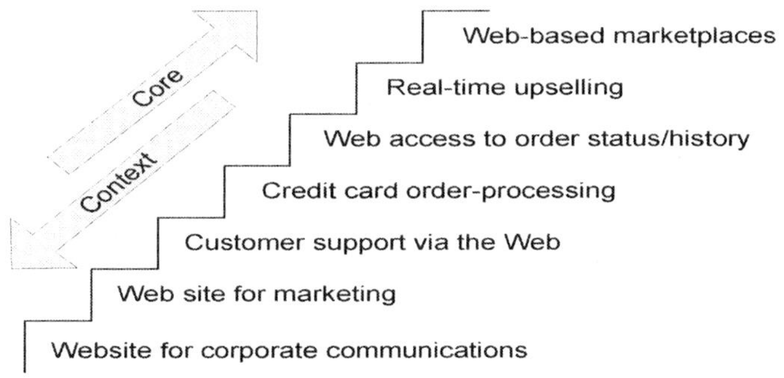

Government Involvement

With high-growth SMEs making sizeable contributions to employment and economic expansion, governments have promoted e-business as a means to sustain and increase this development. Yet, while governments are eager to support SMEs in moving to e-commerce, SMEs themselves seem rather ambivalent about government support (Beck et al, 2005). Important drivers mentioned by SMEs include such things as cost reduction, improving coordination with suppliers and customers, and market expansion (Beck et al., 2005). Government support is rated very low.

Typical of government concern, based on the slowness of SMEs to adopt Internet business solutions while larger firms move forward, is a warning from the Canadian E-Business Initiative (2004): "a lukewarm SME response to IBS adoption may weaken any national strategy to bolster Canada's international competitiveness." In Australia, the federal government's Department of Communication, Information Technology and the Arts supports ITOL (Information Technology Online), a program designed to accelerate national adoption of e-business solutions, particularly by SMEs.

An example of government support in the SCM area is the joint initiative of Industry Canada, and Supply Chain and Logistics Canada (an industry association). Their study (Industry Canada, 2003) recommended, among other things, development of fundamental guidelines for efficient supply chain technology implementation for SMEs. These guidelines were to focus on: supply chain inventory visibility, demand planning, Web-based SCM, supplier relationship management, available to promise, and supply chain event management.

OPPORTUNITIES

There are many SCM opportunities today, and firms continue to learn how to improve their supply chains. This section starts with consideration of major trends and opportunities that are particularly of interest to larger firms in the chain. Then opportunities of interest to SMEs are considered.

SCM in General

Some of the important topics in SCM today are outsourcing, agility, RFID (radio frequency identification), and pipeline design.

Outsourcing continues to grow, as firms look to focus on core functions and outsource others (context), as illustrated in Figure 3. For those firms taking on the outsourced work, this activity is their core, and their goal is to be excellent at it. Outsourcing is an option for all sizes of firms. For example, Malykhina (2004) describes how third-party logistics providers can be used by SMEs. Consultants have coined the phrases 4PL (a trademark of Accenture) to denote a higher level of SC outsourcing. Accenture defines a 4PL as "an integrator that assembles the resources, capabilities, and technology of its own organization and other organizations to design, build and run comprehensive supply chain solutions."

In some markets, it is difficult or even impossible to remove or ignore sources of turbulence and volatility. Such is the case with fashion goods, or high-tech products, where demand can be difficult to forecast and best-case/worst-case sales scenarios can differ by orders of magnitude. Agile supply chains are a partial solution (White, Daniel, & Mohdzain, 2005). Lee (2002), in an article focusing on aligning SC strategies with product supply and demand uncertainties, shows that agile chains are one of four strategy types (the others being efficient chains, risk-hedging chains, and responsive chains). Each of these SC strategies maps to a particular quadrant of supply uncertainty (low—stable process, high—evolving process) and demand uncertainty (low—functional products, high—innovative products).

Agility was first applied to flexible manufacturing systems, which stand in contrast to the traditional manufacturing approach of assembly lines, rationalization, standardization, and elimination of uncertainty. An agile system is able to sense and respond to changes in varying customer demand.

White et al. (2005) consider the trade-offs between high levels of integration between chain partners' information systems, and flexibility to frequently and rapidly make changes to trading relationships (a prerequisite to the agile paradigm). While their case study is of a very large firm (IBM), there are implications for SMEs. IBM's Integrated Supply Chain Division (ISCD) uses E2Open, a third-party electronic hub between organizations in the electronics industry that wish to achieve integration between their information systems.

Busschop, Mitchell, and Proud (2005) point out that RFID is much more than simply a technology to replace bar codes. While RFID has been in the news because of Wal-Mart's requirement that suppliers implement this new technology (an example of coercion by the major chain member), it will bring new levels of visibility, security, accountability, flexibility, and operating performance to supply chains. Davenport and Brooks (2004) identify two current impediments to full RFID deployment—the cost of tags and incompatible technology from various suppliers—and expect these to be resolved soon.

As our understanding of supply chains improves, and experience provides useful feedback, attention is turning to 'pipeline structures' and matching these to particular markets. Christopher and Towill (2002) point out that a 'one–size-fits-all' approach should not be applied to pipeline design, implementation, and control. They see matching the pipeline to the product as a key issue in the development of global supply chains. In particular, many firms are now looking at the tradeoffs between a lean chain and an agile chain.

SMEs in Particular

While the greatest benefits (by magnitude) accrue to the large players in the supply chain, there is ample evidence of opportunities for smaller members. Being a chain member does not bring automatic benefits, at least in the short term. On the other hand, not being a chain member locks a firm out of any potential benefits.

Wynarczyk and Watson (2005) studied the performance of a group of UK subcontractors to evaluate whether differences in how they managed their supply chain relationships were associated with differences in sales and employment growth rates. They concluded, "...even after allowing for sector, size, age and owner-manager motivations and supply chain opportunities and constraints, partnership firms achieved significantly higher rates of growth." However, the results of work by Arend and Wisner (2005), reported in the next section, show this growth may come at the expense of profitability.

Levy and Powell (2003) found that some SMEs see strategic potential in e-business and will invest in it. They suggest that owners' recognition of the business value of the Internet, combined with owner attitude towards business growth, are key factors determining Internet adoption strategies. One would expect these two factors to apply to e-SCM, as it is a form of e-business.

Harding (2000) looked at SME network research and suggested an incremental networking model that could be used to improve supply chain relationships. Berlak and Weber (2004) describe how to configure, establish, and operate temporary supply chains via 'competence networks'. They report on a German SME initiative, whereby a

Web portal facilitates interaction between customers and three competency networks: engineering services, rapid prototyping, and manufacturing. Participating SMEs benefit from cooperating with others in the network, as their combined competencies provide competitive advantage. Harrison and van Hoek (2005) describe a district portal initiative which assists more than 100 small companies in the Macerata shoe district of Italy with B2B relationships and order management.

Just as the ASP approach in ERP provided a viable option for medium-sized firms to move to enterprise systems, on-demand supply chain solutions are now becoming available for some SMEs (Lewis, 2005). This approach shares SCM infrastructure (hardware, software, applications) across many companies, with access via the Internet. Over time, applications aimed at a variety of SMEs should become available at reasonable cost.

CHALLENGES

SCM in General

Supply chains are complex, and managing them is not easy. Furthermore, the highest payoff supply chain projects tend to be the largest and riskiest. The trade press frequently reports on supply chain projects that have gone awry. In the following section, some of the challenges identified by researchers are reviewed. These include aligning the interests of chain members, project difficulty, taking on high rather than low payoff projects, dealing with abnormal events, and forecasting.

A Booz Allen survey, conducted in late 2002, found that overwhelmingly senior executives at large companies worldwide believed SCM had failed to live up to expectations (Heckerman et al., 2003). Technology alone was not the solution, with 45% of responding firms stating IT solutions had failed to live up to expectations. The greatest benefits were obtained by firms where SCM was part of the overall business strategy (and hence a CEO-level agenda item), and where companies were willing to reorganize the supply chain itself when appropriate, rather than simply making adjustments within the existing supply chain structure (sometimes called 'breaking the mould').

Muckstadt, Murray, Rappold, and Collins (2001) looked at the challenges of supply chain collaboration, considering both design and operation. They identified five impediments to constructing a competitive chain: (1) demand uncertainty, which is inadequately addressed; (2) long and varied response time among chain members, resulting in an inability to respond to environmental changes; (3) poor information infrastructures within firms; (4) business processes, both intra- and inter-organizational, that do not support evolving supply chain conditions; and (5) decision support systems and operating policies that cannot contend with supply chain uncertainty. In response to these challenges, they provide a set of guiding principles for the effective design and execution of supply chain systems.

As Ranganathan et al. (2004) point out, the success of e-SCM is largely contingent upon the extent to which the system is assimilated internally within each firm and diffused throughout the entire supply chain network, with every firm in the chain pulling in the same direction. End-to-end visibility, facilitated by full information sharing, can mitigate supply chain risk and build confidence among partners (Christopher & Lee, 2004). Narayanan and Raman (2004) point out that misaligned incentives can result in excess inventory, stock-outs, incorrect forecasts, inadequate sales efforts, and poor customer service. They suggest three reasons why incentive-related issues arise in supply chains: (1) when companies cannot observe other firms' actions, they find it hard to persuade those firms to do their best for the network; (2) it is difficult to align interests when one company has information or knowledge that others do not; and (3) incentive schemes are often badly designed. The authors provide a three-stage process for aligning incentives and building trust.

Major supply chain projects require great effort. Heckmann, Shorten, and Engel (2003) refer to "Herculean SCM efforts," which are commensurately rewarded—they report that companies making the biggest commitment to improving their SCM system outperform those where the effort is no more than incremental. Yet such projects bring considerable risk and are not easy to complete on time, on budget, and with the desired functionality.

Hendricks and Singhal (2005) studied the cost of SCM disruptions (project completion problems, mismatches between supply and demand, and so forth) by looking at public announcements and share prices. They found a major negative impact (average abnormal stock returns of almost -40%), with much of the underperformance observable in the year preceding and following the announcement (so the investment community recognized SCM problems before the firm acknowledged these). Further, most firms did not recover very quickly from the negative effects of the disruptions. Just as firms found ERP projects difficult, so are they finding SCM projects.

Pant, Sethi, and Bhandari (2003) present an implementation framework for e-SCM projects. They point out that "it is often overlooked that creation and implementation of integrated supply chains requires tremendous resources, a great deal of management time and energy, large organization-wide changes, huge commitment from suppliers/partners, and sophisticated technical infrastructure." They also caution that a standard software package solution cannot fit all types of supply chains. As with ERP systems, firms can go with the 'plain vanilla' version (which means changing existing internal systems to match the capabilities of the software) or customize the software to support existing in-house systems. Either approach has advantages and disadvantages.

Within the supply chain literature, the concept of 'breaking the mould' comes up more frequently now. Firms can live with their current supply chain, working to incrementally improve it. Or they can redesign the chain, which can involve relocating factories, outsourcing logistical and other responsibilities, or other fundamental changes. Experience shows the latter group obtains better results, compared to the former (Heckmann et al., 2003). Yet far greater resistance, both within the organization and from across firms within the chain, can be expected when this approach is taken.

Research attention is also being turned to abnormal events that can disrupt supply chains. Natural disasters (hurricane Katrina hitting the U.S. gulf coast in 2005), labor unrest, terrorism, health scares, (SARS, BSE, bird flu), and more mundane risks can seriously disrupt or delay the flow of material, information, and cash through an organization's supply chain. At the time this chapter was written, Danish dairy giant, Arla Foods, faced a total loss of demand within Saudi Arabia because of outrage over cartoons published in a Danish newspaper. Annual sales for Arla within Saudi Arabia were estimated at 268 million euros, and this dropped to nothing virtually overnight as consumers boycotted their products and supermarkets, and removed all Arla products from shelves. Chopra and Sodhi (2004) recommend a 'what if?' team exercise called 'stress testing' to identify potential weak links in a firm's supply chain.

Forecasting demand is proving to be difficult within many supply networks, with greater attention now being focused on this. Where possible, actual final customer demand is far better than a forecast, providing there is sufficient time for the chain to produce the necessary goods/services. Some supply chains are now providing such information to major members. In the future, it will be easier for all chain members to have access to this important information. The type of market demand experienced (volatile vs. stable, predictable vs. unpredictable) has considerable impact on the accuracy of forecasting models. Progressive firms monitor the accuracy of their forecasting models and improve them based on experience or modify them when the environment changes. However, some types of demand are not easily forecastable, and chain agility holds promise here.

SMEs in Particular

Resources (financial, people, knowledge, etc.), and specifically the lack of them, are a major challenge for most SMEs. This reflects itself in many areas, including ICT and SCM projects. Larger firms can spread the cost of ICT projects over a much greater revenue base. Also, larger firms have internal ICT development and support services, which make it easier for them to develop and maintain such systems as ERP and SCM. In addition to limited resources, there are other challenges faced by SMEs.

Some researchers have suggested the Internet levels the playing field for SME involvement in e-commerce. However, Larson, Carr, and Dhariwal (2005) did not find support for this. Their study of various sized suppliers found that larger suppliers made greater use of Internet-supported technologies than smaller ones. While the potential is there to leverage the power of the Internet, many SMEs have neither the desire nor ability to do this.

The balance of power among a supply chain's members plays a significant role in designing and operating a supply chain. SMEs, as more minor members of the chain, often have little input. So if they want to be members of the chain, they must accept what is imposed on them.

Azumah et al. (2005) examined the drivers that led SMEs to adopt Internet and communications technologies and the strategy formulation processes used to reach e-organizational goals. They found that while most SMEs (almost 80% in their sample) made considerable use of the Internet and only a minority managed their business by traditional means, no firms could yet be classified as e-organizations. Yet they see this happening soon.

Barnes, Hinton, and Mieczkowska (2004) point out that progress in many e-businesses is hampered because of an apparent mismatch between business and operations strategy. This can happen in both larger and smaller firms and within functional areas (such as marketing, finance, or human resources). Based on case studies, they suggest that:

- Operations must have technologies that are both adequate and appropriate for the required task.
- Changes to business strategy are likely to imply changes to e-operations strategy.
- Following general industry practice in the use of internet-based icts in operations may avoid the company being left behind technologically, but of itself is not likely to lead to a competitive advantage.
- Strategic use of e-operations relies on developing an operations strategy that supports business strategy.
- It is possible to use e-operations to drive business strategy.

A major Canadian survey of barriers to SME adoption of Internet solutions for procurement and supply chain interactions (Archer et al., 2003) identified three main categories: (1) perceptions, (2) economic perceptions, and (3) perceived need to adopt. Perceptions of positive benefits included reinforcing long-term relationships, reinforcing good procurement practice, developing trust with trading partners, improving customer service, and sharing useful information with supply chain partners. Negative perceptions included seeing it as more difficult to procure major needs and sell major products online, not knowing what type of e-business solution is appropriate, and employees preferring the old ways of doing business. Economic perceptions included: (1)

long-term benefits of network technology and process investment are high, (2) e-business can reduce transaction costs, and (3) e-business does not tend to reduce the price of products purchased. This study found that Canadian SMEs generally perceived a lack of need to adopt e-business. Major reasons given included: little or no competitive pressure; customers not particularly interested in online sales and supply chain interactions; most businesses in the industry apparently did not use digital networks for procurement and supply chain interactions; suppliers do not appear to promote online procurement and supply chain interactions; the company may be seen as too small to benefit; the nature of the industry does not lend itself to e-business solutions; and some companies are only interested in doing business locally, so they do not see e-business as helpful.

A similar finding was reported for the UK by Beach (2004), who states,

The [SME] manufacturing sector is failing to adopt e-commerce because firms either do not recognize its potential or perceive the risk of changing their business model to utilize the new technology to be greater than the benefits that might be derived.

He concludes:

Organizations must therefore view the adoption of Internet technology as a strategic rather than a tactical issue and develop strategies that provide the resources to facilitate the transformation of the organization's business model whilst retaining the necessary flexibility to accommodate changes in technology and market developments as they occur.

As references in the preceding section show, e-SCM projects can be massive, even for large firms. SMEs seldom have the resources or experience to take the lead on such an undertaking. Yet this does not preclude them from joining supply chains. It simply means they will work with others, often taking on a minor role, such as implementing a system that was designed by the chain master. Another option is to take the A/B/C approach used in inventory control—looking for opportunities where management of a few major supply chain areas will bring large benefits and applying efforts there.

Arend and Wisner (2005) surprisingly found that SCM was negatively associated with SME performance, after controlling for self-selection bias. They state, "It seems that although better performing SMEs may engage in SCM, SCM is not a good fit for SMEs on several performance measures." Several possible explanations for this are given by these authors. Since their data was collected in the late 1990s, a similar study today might find different results. However, with many major IT projects, firms often experience a temporary decline in productivity until bugs are worked out, users become comfortable with the system, and the foundation is laid for further improvements. Perhaps this was experienced by firms in their study. It is also possible that major chain members extracted more than their fair share of profits, leaving less for SME members.

A comparison between European and American manufacturing SMEs found both country-specific and sector-specific differences between factors driving and impeding e-commerce (Beck et al., 2005). SMEs in four countries (United States, Germany, France, and Denmark) and three sectors (manufacturing, retail/wholesale, and banking/insurance) were studied. Nine drivers and eight impediments were analyzed. The authors concluded, "Although the nature of e-commerce applications is more or less the same, each country is following its own diffusion pattern or path, based on national differences recognizable in competition, existing and emerging IT infrastructure, business concentration, governmental regulations or even national mentality."

Another international comparison (Johnston & Wright, 2004) found that Asian and Latin American

SMEs lagged North American SMEs in moving business processes to the Internet or other computer-mediated network. While firms in these countries typically have a significant cost advantage, they will need to become SCM enabled if they want to participate in global supply chains. There are certainly exceptions among firms in some of these areas, as evidenced in the papers by Chang and Chung (2002) and Chou et al. (2005).

The Internet is a technology and only one component supporting SMEs with e-SCM initiatives. Implementation challenges are faced by all firms initiating Web projects. In the cross-country commerce area, many other challenges and barriers can exist: language differences, borders and tariffs, taxation issues, government regulations, physical delivery, legal systems, payment systems, and so forth.

CONCLUSION

With the tremendous variation among SMEs in terms of size, capabilities, market reach, and profitability, the role and importance of e-SCM will vary considerably among firms. Many SMEs might have little or no need for concern, particularly among micro-businesses and those in the service industry. Others will be driven by larger firms in the supply chains they belong to, so their stance will be a reactive one. For them, the decision is whether or not the costs outweigh the benefits; in some circumstances they may be forced to accept lower margins and profits. This approach has the advantage that the network coordinating firm takes the lead in developing the complete system, ensuring both technology and applications work satisfactorily. Given the complexity of many SCM projects, only larger firms can take them on. It certainly behooves SMEs to understand their position within existing supply chains, what the opportunities are for greater involvement, and what the costs and benefits will be. From this, a decision can be made to take a proactive or reactive stance.

Portal opportunities exist, as shown by their success in Germany (Berlak & Weber, 2004) and Taiwan (Chou et al., 2005). However, these opportunities are limited and require a coordinated approach by industry associations, governments, and/or SME groups.

The literature now includes a few models of the influences on e-business and SCM adoption. These can be used for research purposes or applied to specific SME projects—identifying potential gaps and impediments.

Johnston and Wright (2004), based on their international study, propose a preliminary model of the many influences on an SME's capability to adopt supply chain-oriented networked processes (see Figure 4). Their paper explains in much greater depth the various components. One possible influence missing from this model is technology.

Other models have been proposed for e-business adoption. Raymond et al. (2005) studied e-business assimilation as a function of three contexts (environmental, organizational, and technological). In their model, e-business assimilation leads to growth and internationalization. Vidgen, Francis, Powell, and Woerndl (2004) used Venkatraman's transformation model as the basis of their Web service business transformation framework. In this framework, the three drivers of Web service-enabled information systems are business (operational efficiencies, collaborative commerce), technology (broadband Internet access, standards), and information systems (packaged software, IS outsourcing, open source, agile systems development). Wang et al. (2004) used a research model of IT adoption in the supply chain, based on external drivers (market and customer, product lifecycle, and network position of supply chain) and internal drivers (perceived benefits, firm size, and system support readiness). In their model, the level of IT adoption ranges from low (essential functions) to high (B2B integration/collaborative commerce).

Figure 4. Model of SME capability to adopt networked processes (Source: Johnson & Wright, 2004)

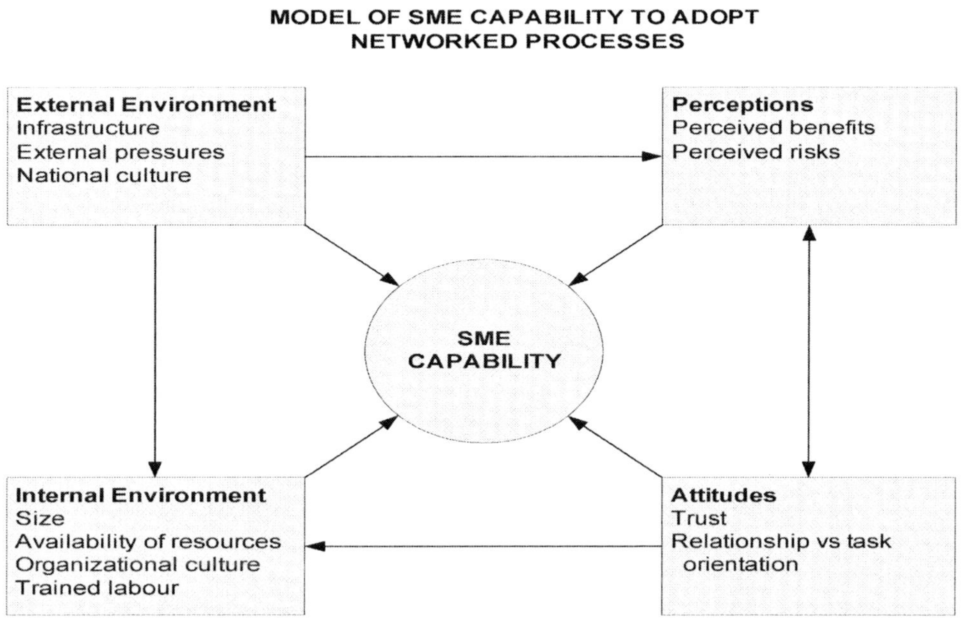

Finally, again drawing upon the reviewed papers, the following areas are suggested for future research:

- Development of an "escalator" for e-SCM (see Figure 3) by tracking empirical research results over a period of time; this will require obtaining the field work date, which is often not reported.
- Johnston and Wright (2004) see four areas concerning international issues: (1) trust, (2) cultural differences, (3) communication modes, and (4) SME structure.
- White et al. (2005), based on their study of agile supply chains and inter-organizational information system integration, suggest four areas for future research: (1) redefining the relationship between inter-organizational information system integration and flexibility, (2) coordinating mechanisms for supply chains that periodically reconfigure, (3) increased outsourcing, and (4) the application service provider (ASP) model.

REFERENCES

Archer, N., Wang, S., & Kang, C. (2003). *Barriers to Canadian SME adoption of Internet solutions for procurement and supply chain interactions.* Working Paper MeRC #5. McMaster E-Business Research Centre, Canada. Retrieved February 1, 2006, from http://cebi.ca/Public/Team1/Docs/barriers_to_canadian_sme_adoption.pdf

Arend, R.J., & Wisner, J.D. (2005). Small business and supply chain management: Is there a fit? *Journal of Business Venturing, 20*(3), 403-436.

Australian Bureau of Statistics. (2004). *8161.0.55.001—Australian Bureau of Statistics Business Register, counts of businesses—summary tables, Jun 2004.* Retrieved March 30, 2006 from http://www.abs.gov.au/AUSSTATS/abs@.nsf/productsbytitle/B34A6C8A585479F0CA25709200750356?OpenDocument

Azumah, G., Koh, S.C.L., & Maguire, S. (2005). E-organization and its future implication for SMEs. *Production Planning & Control, 16*(6), 555-562.

Barnes, D., Hinton, M., & Mieczkowska, S. (2004). The strategic management of operations in e-business. *Production Planning & Control, 15*(5), 484-494.

Badenhorst-Weiss, J.A., Fourie, I., & Nel, J.D. (2004). The application of supply chain management best practices by small business suppliers. *Proceedings of the 2004 ICSB World Conference.* Retrieved February 1, 2006, from http://www.sbaer.uca.edu/research/icsb/2004/Papers%20pdf/080.pdf

Beach, R. (2004). Adopting Internet technology in manufacturing: A strategic perspective. *Production Planning & Control, 15*(1), 80-89.

Beck, R., Wigand, R.T., & Konig, W. (2005). The diffusion and efficient use of electronic commerce among small and medium-sized enterprises: An international three-industry survey. *Electronic Markets, 15*(1), 38-52.

Berlak, J., & Weber, V. (2004). How to make e-procurement viable for SME suppliers. *Production Planning & Control, 15*(7), 671-677.

Busschop, K., Mitchell, K., & Proud, S. (2005). The role of RFID in supply chain planning. *Accenture Supply Chain Management Viewpoint.* Retrieved February 6, 2006, from http://www.accenture.com/Global/Research_and_Insights/By_Subject/Supply_Chain_Mgmt/ThePlanning.htm

Canadian E-Business Initiative. (2004). *Net impact study Canada: Strategies for increasing SME engagement in the e-economy.* Retrieved February 1, 2006, from http://www.cebi.ca/Public/Team1/Docs/net_impact_english.pdf

Chan, M.F.S, & Chung, W.W.C. (2002). A framework to develop an enterprise information portal for contract manufacturing. *International Journal of Production Economics, 75,* 113-126.

Chopra, S., & Sodhi, M.S. (2004). Managing risk to avoid supply-chain breakdown. *Sloan Management Review, 46*(1), 53-61.

Chou, T., Hsu, L., Yeh, Y., & Ho, C. (2005). Towards a framework of the performance evaluation of SMEs' industry portals. *Industrial Management & Data Systems, 105*(4), 527-544.

Christopher, M., & Lee, H. (2004). Mitigating supply chain risk through improved confidence. *International Journal of Physical Distribution and Logistics Management, 34*(5), 388-396.

Christopher, M., & Towill, D.R. (2002). Developing market specific supply chain strategies. *The International Journal of Logistics Management, 13*(1), 1-14.

Davenport, T., & Brooks, J. (2004). Enterprise systems and the supply chain. *Journal of Enterprise Information Management, 17*(1), 8-19.

European Commission. (2006). *Craft and small businesses.* Retrieved March 30, 2006, from http://ec.europa.eu/enterprise/entrepreneurship/craft/

Frohlich, M.T. (2002). E-integration in the supply chain: Barriers and performance. *Decision Sciences, 33*(4), 537-555.

Garcia-Dastugue, S.J., & Lambert, D.M. (2003). Internet-enabled coordination in the supply chain. *Industrial Marketing Management, 32*(3), 251-263.

Harding, S. (2000). *The development of a model to describe the influence of networking on an SME's ability to implement new processes.* Retrieved February 6, 2006 from http://kmc.tbs.uce.ac.uk/kmc-publications/Cardiff%20paper%20adobe.pdf

Harrison, A., & van Hoek, R. (2005). *Logistics management and strategy* (2nd ed.). Harlow, Essex: Pearson Education.

Heckmann, P., Shorten, D., & Engel, H. (2003). *Supply chain management at 21: The hard road to adulthood.* Retrieved February 6, 2006, from http://extfile.bah.com/livelink/livelink/133356/?func=doc.Fetch&nodeid=133356

Hendricks, K.B., & Singhal, V.R. (2005). An empirical analysis of the effect of supply chain disruptions on long-run stock price performance and equity risk of the firm. *Production and Operations Management, 14*(1), 35-52.

Hong, I.B. (2002). A new framework for inter-organizational systems based on the linkage of participants' roles. *Information & Management, 25*(3), 417-446.

Industry Canada. (2005). *Key small business statistics—January 2006.* Retrieved March 30, 2006, from http://strategis.ic.gc.ca/epic/internet/insbrp-rppe.nsf/en/rd01832e.html

Industry Canada. (2003). *Lean logistics technology roadmap final report.* Retrieved February 1, 2006, from http://strategis.ic.gc.ca/epic/internet/intrm-crt.nsf/en/rm00094e.html

Jeffcoate, J., Chappell, C., & Feindt, S. (2004). Assessing the impact of e-commerce on SMEs in value chains: A qualitative approach. In N.A.Y. Al-Qirim (Ed.), *Electronic commerce in small to medium-sized enterprises: Frameworks, issues and implications* (pp. 180-198). Hershey, PA: Idea Group Publishing.

Johnston, D.A., & Wright, L. (2004). The e-business capability of small and medium sized firms in international supply chains. *Information Systems and E-Business Management, 2*(2-3), 223-240.

Kalakota, R., & Robinson, M. (2000). *E-business 2.0: Roadmap for success* (2nd ed.). Boston: Addison-Wesley.

Lapide, L. (2005). The four habits of highly effective supply chains. *Supply Chain Strategy Newsletter.* Retrieved February 1, 2006, from http://ctl.mit.edu/public/four_habits_lapide.pdf

Larson, P.D., Carr, P., & Dhariwal, K.S. (2005). SCM involving small versus large suppliers: Relational exchange and electronic communication media. *Journal of Supply Chain Management, 41*(1), 18-28.

Lee, H.L. (2004). The triple-a supply chain. *Harvard Business Review, 82*(10), 102-113.

Lee, H.L. (2002). Aligning supply chain strategies with product uncertainties. *California Management Review, 44*(3), 105-119.

Lee, H.L., & Whang, S. (2001). E-business and supply chain integration. In *Stanford Global Supply Chain Management Forum, W2-2001.* Retrieved February 1, 2006, from http://www.stanford.edu/group/scforum/Welcome/White%20Papers/EB_SCI.pdf

Legris, P., John, I., & Pierre, C. (2003). Why do people use information technology? A critical review of the technology acceptance model. *Information and Management, 40*(3), 191-204.

Levenburg, N.M. (2005). Does size matter? Small firms' use of e-business tools in the supply chain. *Electronic Markets, 15*(2), 94-105.

Levy, M., & Powell, P. (2003). Exploring SME Internet adoption: Towards a contingent model. *Electronic Markets, 13*(2), 173-181.

Lewis, E. (2005). Now is SMEs' time to compete. *Industrial Distribution, 94*(9), 28.

Lim, D., & Palvia, P.C. (2001). EDI in strategic supply chain: Impact on customer service. *International Journal of Information Management, 21*(3), 193-211.

Malykhina, E. (2004, October 18). Small business' big supply chains. *Information Week*, 90.

McLaren, T., Head, M., & Yuan, Y. (2002). Supply chain collaboration alternatives: Understanding the expected costs and benefits. *Internet Research, 12*(4), 348-364.

Moore, G. (2002). *Living on the fault line, revised edition: Managing for shareholder value in any economy.* New York: HarperCollins.

Muckstadt, J.A., Murray, D.H., Rappold, J.A., & Collins, D.E. (2001). Guidelines for collaborative supply chain system design and operation. *Information Systems Frontiers, 3*(4), 427-453.

Narayanan, V.G., & Raman, A. (2004). Aligning incentives in supply chains. *Harvard Business Review, 82*(11), 94-103.

Pant, S., Sethi, R., & Bhandari, M. (2003). Making sense of the e-supply chain landscape: An implementation framework. *International Journal of Information Management, 23*(3), 201-221.

Patterson, K.A., Grimm, C.M., & Corsi, T.M. (2004). Diffusion of supply chain technologies. *Transportation Journal, 43*(3), 5-23.

Ranganathan, C., Dhaliwal, J.S., & Teo, T.S.H. (2004). Assimilation and diffusion of Web technologies in supply-chain management: An examination of key drivers and performance impacts. *International Journal of Electronic Commerce, 9*(1), 127-161.

Ratanasingam, P. (2004). Perceived barriers and risks of e-commerce supply chain management network among SMEs in Australia and New Zealand. In N.A.Y. Al-Qirim (Ed.), *Electronic commerce in small to medium-sized enterprises: Frameworks, issues and implications* (pp. 69-85). Hershey, PA: Idea Group Publishing.

Raymond, L., Bergeron, F., & Blili, S. (2005). The assimilation of e-business in manufacturing SMEs: Determinants and effects on growth and internationalization. *Electronic Markets, 15*(2), 106-118.

Sahin, F., & Robinson, E.P. (2002). Flow coordination and information sharing in supply chains: Review, implications, and directions for future research. *Decision Sciences, 33*(4), 505-536.

Serve, M., & Yen, D.C. (2002). B2B-enhancd supply chain process: Towards building virtual enterprises. *Business Process Management Journal, 8*(3), 245-253.

Sheffi, Y., & Michelman, P. (2005). The next killer app? It's your supply chain. *Supply Chain Strategy, 1*(2), 3.

Small Business Service. (2006). *SME statistics 2004.* Retrieved March 30, 2006, from http://www.sbs.gov.uk/SBS_Gov_files/researchandstats/SMEStats2004.pdf

Subramani, M. (2004). How do suppliers benefit from information technology use in supply chain relationships? *MIS Quarterly, 28*(1), 45-73.

Taylor, D.A. (2004). *Supply chains: A manager's guide.* Boston: Addison-Wesley.

U.S. Small Business Administration. (2006). *Small business statistics.* Retrieved March 30, 2006, from http://www.sba.gov/aboutsba/sbastats.html

Vakharia, A.J. (2002). E-business and supply chain management. *Decision Sciences, 33*(4), 495-504.

Vidgen, R., Francis, D., Powell, P., & Woerndl, M. (2004). Web service business transformation: Collaborative commerce opportunities in SMEs. *Journal of Enterprise Information Management, 17*(5), 372-381.

Wang, Y.C.W., Chang, C., & Heng, M.S. (2004). The levels of information technology adoption, business network, and a strategic position model for evaluating supply chain integration. *Journal of Electronic Commerce Research, 5*(2), 85-98.

White, A., Daniel, E.M., & Mohdzain, M. (2005). The role of emergent information technologies and systems in enabling supply chain agility. *International Journal of Information Management, 25*(5), 396-410.

Wynarczyk, P., & Watson, R. (2005). Firm growth and supply chain partnerships: An empirical analysis of UK SME subcontractors. *Small Business Economics, 24*(1), 39-51.

Chapter IV
Building and Managing Modern E-Services

John Hamilton
James Cook University, Australia

ABSTRACT

This chapter addresses the development cycle of recent 'services' models. It considers that all products involve services and consequently maybe be considered as service systems. First, the issue of 'services' is described; next, the enhancement of 'services' via value creation is described, along with the progression from supply and demand chains, to value chains, to service value chains, and finally to service value networks. This progression pathway has developed over time, and has enabled 'service' and 'e-service' businesses to deliver and further develop competitive business solutions. The combinations of integrated, highly competitive, e-supply chains delivering the final 'services' suite to the frontline business seller moves the e-supply chain model to a more advanced level. Today, the recent concept of utilizing service value networks offers a key to future competitive solutions. Service value networks house fully integrated e-demand and e-supply chains working in harmony to the deliver both services and e-services. They are also highly agile and offer customer-induced flexible business solutions to customer requests. This chapter highlights the progression to service value networks. In addition it also offers the manager a balanced scorecard structural mechanism via which management controls over e-services and service value networks may be developed and maintained.

DEFINITION OF SERVICES

Definitions of what constitutes a service have varied across the service sector. Clark (1940) divided all economies into three sectors: primary (agricultural), secondary (manufacturing), and tertiary (services). The service sector used three parts—domestic related services (food and lodging), business services, and others (including recreation, health care, and education)—to focus on involvement and improvement of the customer relationship. The services industry provides services, not goods (Hughes, Mitchell, & Ramson, 1993).

In 1870 the service sector employed slightly more than 20% of the U.S. workforce, while by 2002 it employed in approximately of 82% of the U.S. workforce, and 81% of the private sector GDP (U.S. Bureau of Labor Statistics, 2002/2004). Services management is a 'trans-functional' research area (Kamarkar, 2002). It covers areas including service quality (Chase, Jacobs, & Aquilano, 1996), services encounters (Cook, Goh, & Chung, 1999), and service execution (Nie & Kellog, 1999). Services operations management and services marketing provide still other perspectives to services.

Definitions of service have ranged from the narrow to the broad. In 1960 the Committee on Definitions of the American Marketing Association defined services as: "Activities, benefits, or satisfactions which are offered for sale, or are provided, in connection with the sale of goods." (p.21)

Examples of a service include: accommodation, banking, education, entertainment, finance, medical areas, real estate servicing, transportation, as well as the individual services provided by a barber shop, a piano tuner, a beautician, and assistance areas like repair, maintenance, and after-sales services, through to support services institutions like credit rating bureaus.

Judd (1964) and Rathmell (1974) believed in the service sector of the economy and emphasized the true nature of services. Murdick, Render, and Russell (1990) and Quinn, Baruch, and Paquette (1987) broadened existing services definitions to include all economic activities where output was not a physical product or construction, was usually consumed when produced, and was delivered as an intangible value-add (like travel comfort) to the customer. Thus the service definition moved again. Zeithaml et al. (1988) believed services were intangibles—like deeds, processes, and performances—but could also be tangible (e.g., health care). Czinkota, Ronkainen, and Moffett (2005) split services into tangible areas involving people (fitness centers) or possession processing (like freight transportation), and intangible areas involving mental stimulus like (education and religion) and information processing (like banking and data processing).

Often services are integrally enmeshed with manufactured goods, or to the delivery (or enabling) of goods. Thus the distinction between goods and services is imprecise, and no clear boundary between manufacturing and service firms exists (Berry & Parasuraman, 1991). Levitt (1972) suggests: "There is no such thing as a service industry. There are only industries whose service components are greater or less than those of other industries ... *Everybody is in service.*" Czinkota et al. (2005) also partially support this approach. Thus it may be suggested that all manufacturing is indeed a service, and that services may be considered from a range of viewpoints. One approach to draw such diversities of opinion together is provided by Rust and Metters (1996). They use a 'topologies' approach to group some services complexities into models. Their topologies approach, built upon other recent service industry models, may assist in the identification of key knowledge and research gaps.

As the service industry has continued to move towards globalization (Kathawala & Abdou, 2003) and incorporate more electronically based delivery systems, it has become possible to deliver a value chain, e-service operation. France, Da Rold, and Young (2002) recognized the importance of the

Figure 1. Mathematical models of service (Source: Rust & Metters, 1996)

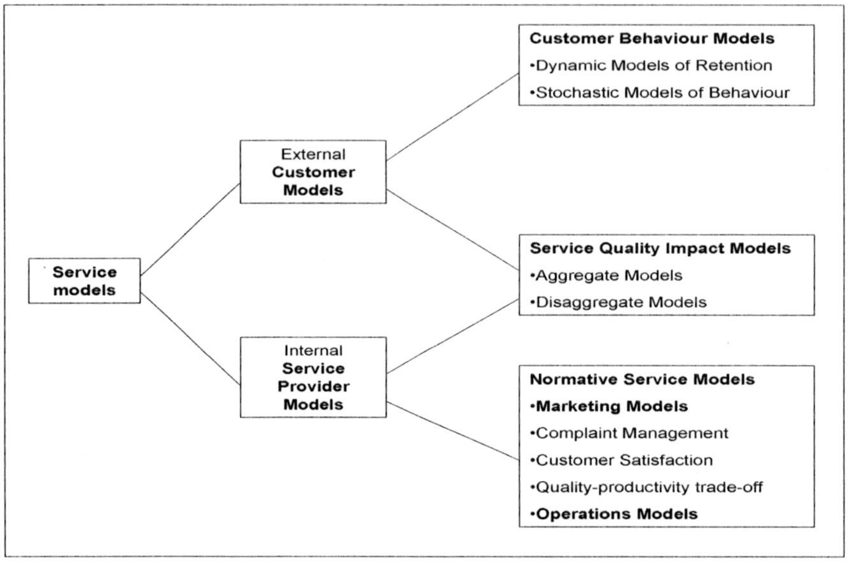

'service value chain', stating that "to satisfy client demands holistic solutions will require focused providers cooperating along services value chains." Thus 'e-service value chains' may offer a pathway to delivering enhanced customer value.

SERVICE TYPOLOGIES

From an operations and marketing perspective, topology schemes for services have generally lacked empirically tested works, but they offer a useful mechanism to draw together the constituent components applicable to the delivery of services. Empirical works (Verma & Boyer, 2000; Akkermans & Vos, 2003; Chen & Paulraj, 2004) offer some key exceptions, but overall empirical services related research is in its infancy. A topologies approach, based on recent service industry models, identifies key knowledge gaps and establishes possible empirical research areas.

SERVICE MODELS

Figure 1 presents Rust and Metters' (1996) view of services. They grouped service models as customer models (external) or service provider models (internal). Each model was then segregated, as shown in Figure 1, into two of the three models:

- **Customer behavior models**, incorporating dynamic models of customer retention (like loyalty), stochastic models of customer behavior (like satisfaction), and customer behavior models (like churn rate or a customer lost through a single service encounter).
- **Service Quality impact models**, incorporating aggregate models (like customer satisfaction effects) and disaggregated models (like financial impacts of a service component).
- **Normative service models**, housing organizationally focused marketing models (like incentive schemes and trade-offs between satisfaction and productivity) and operations models (like queuing).

Figure 2. Integrated schematic representation of services (Source: Cook et al., 1999)

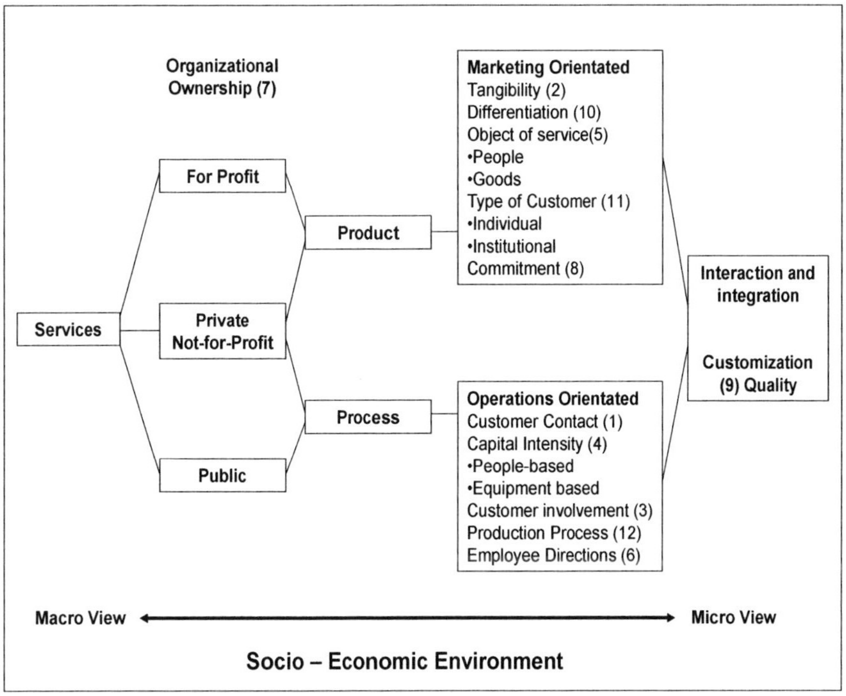

Figure 3. The service strategy triad (Source: Roth & Menor, 2003)

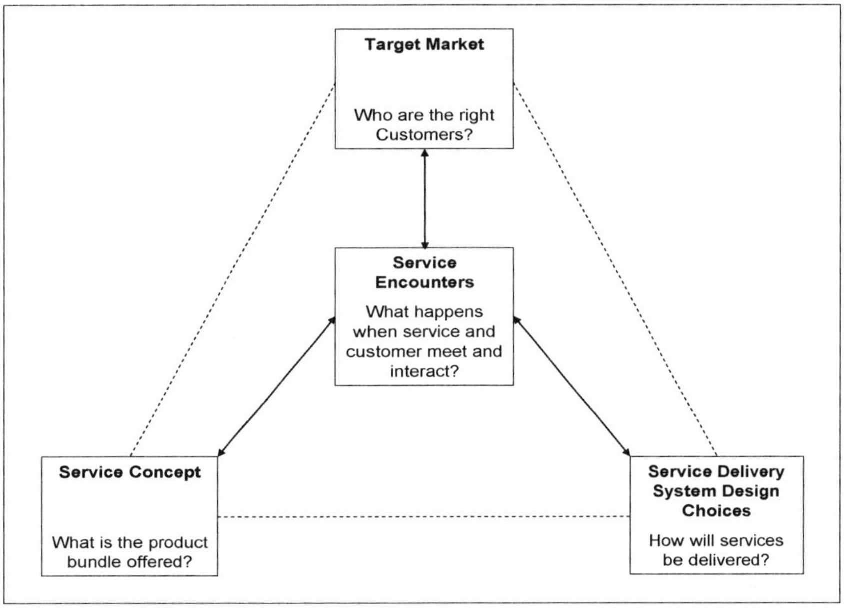

Figure 4. The service delivery systems architecture (Source: Roth & Menor, 2003)

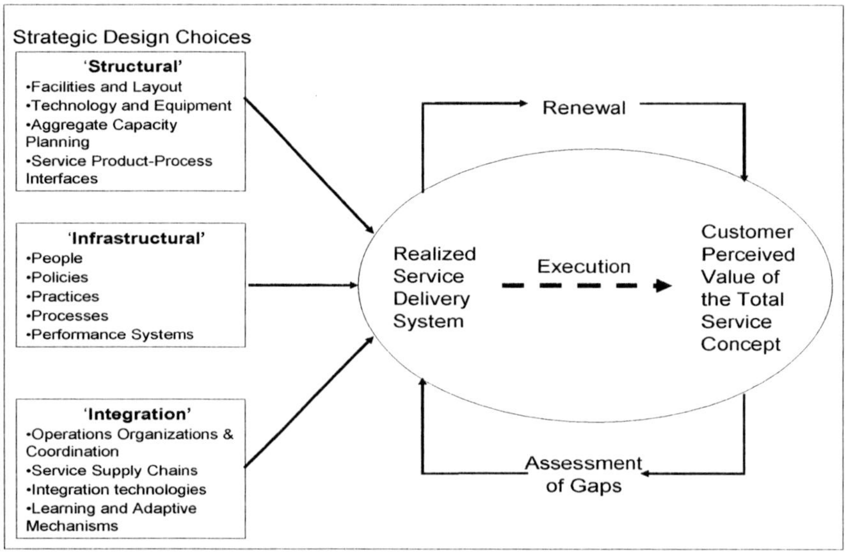

In 1999, Cook et al. developed the 'integrated schematic representation of services' matrix. Figure 2 displays this integrated services schematic.

Cook et al. (1999) recognized that services could be split into marketing (product) or operations (process) orientations. They believed that in delivering a final 'customized' solution, there remained a need to integrate and interact with both orientations. They suggested research in the 'interaction and integration' area may articulate strategies and tactics for improving services.

Roth and Menor (2003) delivered a further addition to the services topologies. Their 'service strategy triad' (displayed in Figure 3) separated the 'what', the 'how', and the 'who' of service encounters. It offered a new perspective to advance an understanding of services operations management. The 'who' defines the right customers, and not just a customer segment! These targeted customers could be defined by techniques like Forrester's 'technographics', 'psychographics', and psychographic profiling groups of customers. The interpretation of such target markets provided a means to enhance both service and performance standards, and to allow the business to competitively align its chosen degree of customer targeting with its offered service products and delivery systems.

Roth and Menor (2003) operationally defined their 'service strategy triad' into five elements:

1. **Supporting facilities** (physical and structural resources)
2. **Facilitating goods** (materials and supplies that are consumed)
3. **Facilitating information** (supporting the explicit services)
4. **Explicit services** (customer experiential and sensual benefits)
5. **Implicit services** (psychological benefits)

They realized the total service concept by the customer may differ from the service offered by the service provider. To overcome this, a feedback loop (execution, assessment of gaps, renewal) was proposed.

The 'service delivery systems architecture' model of Roth and Menor (2003), displayed in

Figure 4, allowed a framework to investigate three interrelated and dynamic components of service delivery systems:

- **Strategic service design** (portrayed as structural, infrastructural, and integration, and based on choices between time-phased content portfolios of major supply).
- **Service delivery execution system** (exemplified by programs, policies, and behavioral aspects delivering complimentary areas of customer focus), possibly using balanced scorecard approaches.
- **Customer perceived value of the total service concept** (intangibles and other effectiveness aspects of the service).

These downstream features, delivered upstream through the external integration of the service supply chain, combined with the linked internal integration of the operational functional areas and the adaptive mechanisms available to enhance the intellectual capabilities, may provide new avenues to perceived customer value.

SERVICE MODELS ANALYSIS

The above models have moved the complex concept of services delivery beyond that of the immediate services business. The models indicate that the delivery of services requires the business to adopt both an internal and an external perspective. Rust and Metters (2003) showed services to be complex in nature. They showed that a variety of approaches had been adopted, leading to the development of three key areas—customer behavior models, service quality impact models, and normative service models. Cook et al. (1999) showed services may be considered from a marketing or an operations focus. They suggested it may be possible to hold the service product constant and investigate the effects of the service process (and vice-versa). Results could then be compiled, and combined, to gain further insights into services. Roth and Menor (2003) proposed that business-customer service encounters may be considered as combinations of three functional areas—the customer, the service product, and the service delivery system. Hence, enhanced business-customer service encounters could possibly be induced when one or more of these functional areas improved. In particular, an improved business-customer service encounter may arise where the customer perceived improved customer value with the services provided or in the services package being delivered.

To deliver quality business-customer service encounters, the business's supply chain became an *integral delivery tool* for the final upstream service provider. In addition this supply chain needed to be capable of delivering customer expectations. This required sound supply chain integration and management, the integration of the above functional areas, and quality communications channels throughout the supply chain network.

SUPPLY CHAIN MANAGEMENT

Management has sought to deliver improved business-customer service encounters using a variety of approaches. The supply chain, and more specifically service supply chain management, was and is a "hot topic in business" (Chase et al., 2005). Supply chain management is defined as "the integration of business processes from end-user through to original suppliers that provide products, services and information and add value for customers" (The International Center for Competitive Excellence, 1994). It is "a technique for linking a manufacturer's operations with those of it strategic suppliers, and its key intermediaries and customers. It seeks to integrate the relationships, and operations, of both immediate, first-tier suppliers, and those several tiers back in the supply chain" and "the goal of supply chain management is to improve timing and costs in manufacturing through strong vendor relationships" (An & Fromm, 2005).

Fisher (1977) developed a management framework for product demand, and a supply chain that could best satisfy this demand. He identified specific functional products like lifecycle, percentage contribution margin, percentage product variations, average production forecast error, and make-to-order lead time. Products were categorized as primarily functional or primarily innovative. Each category required a different kind of supply chain, and mismatches between product type and supply chain could be identified.

Lee (2002) further developed Fisher's framework, and suggested that uncertainties revolving around the supply side were important drivers for correct supply chain strategies. He argued that functional products were more applicable to a more mature, and stable, supply process. Lee defined the *stable supply process*, where manufacturing process and technology were mature and 'stable', and the *evolving supply process*, where manufacturing and technology were in early stages of development and were rapidly changing. From Lee's perspective the market challenge for business was to operate a supply chain as a *responsive* or an *agile* model.

Responsive supply chains, like fashion apparel or popular music, operated in low-uncertainty, stable markets and are highly innovative. They targeted responsive, flexible, 'build-to-customer-order' strategies, and followed the changing needs of the customer. These responsive supply chains, where demand and supply communications channels intertwine, deliver business-determined, information-based, customer-targeted outcomes that may be termed *e-supply chains*.

A business engaging an agile supply chain structure—like a telecom operating in an evolving, highly uncertain market—often remains highly innovative. It employs highly responsive, agile supply chains, and remains flexible in its service offerings. It attempts to engage specific, customer needs-focused strategies, and responds rapidly to the changing, diverse, and unpredictable demands of the customer. Thus demand uncertainty and supply uncertainty remained a framework for understanding both supply chain and e-supply chain strategies.

The agile supply chain model has typically targeted the high-risk, customer-driven solutions, while minimizing the downstream risks of supply disruptions. Hence, the strategic scope of the business's supply chain now necessarily included the 'internal' integration within organizations, and also captured the 'external' expansion throughout various supply chain links.

From around 1994, when standard Internet browsers became available, the Internet has become a vital strategic management tool. Using the Internet, appropriately interconnected businesses, along with their Internet-connected supply chain partners, have the capacity to freely share information. This has allowed many competitive improvements to develop. More accurate supply and component planning, improved supplier and business performance, less stock holdings, greater efficiencies, and faster response rates have all been recognized (Reid & Sanders, 2005).

THE INTERNET

The Internet (encapsulating intranets ['internal' networks] and extranets ['external' networks]), combined with sophisticated interconnected computer networks, has delivered necessary and key enablers, to deliver responsive and agile supply chain strategies. This inter-business connectivity allows for near instantaneous, enhanced information flows (Turban, Rainer, & Potter, 2003). The Internet has driven new supply chain solutions in information storage and transmission, e-business, Web-based customer relationship management (e-CRM), and supply chain management (Lawrence, Newton, Corbitt, Braithwaite, & Parker, 2002). Dell (*www.dell.com*) and others have delivered customized e-purchasing across their Web sites, but the absolute one-on-one 'customerized' solution is still not a realistic solution for many businesses. The pressure to dynamically adjust, and adapt, the businesses supply chain strategy to the demands of the customer remains great (Frohlich & Westbrook, 2002).

DEMAND CHAIN MANAGEMENT

From the late 1990s onwards, there has been a distinct move from supply to demand chain management (Heikkila, 2002). This change in focus is driven by the desire to become both efficient and effective (Hanson, 2000), thereby delivering customer satisfaction (Kuglin, 1998), along with the right mix(es) of services (Bowen & Shoemaker, 2003). Demand chain management aims to serve customers individually with customized bundles of goods and services, thereby delivering high levels of customer satisfaction (Preis, 2003) and of customer loyalty (McAlexander, Kim, & Roberts, 2003).

The demand chain has been a near mirror image of the supply chain. It has been driven by a business competitive imperative aiming to constantly improve its supply chain efficiencies. The demand chain must balance a globally diverse mix of new customers (each with different needs and expectations), and it must also offer a degree of uniqueness to the business (Barlow-Hills & Sarin, 2003).

Beech (1998) argued for an integration of the supply and demand chains:

This challenge could only be met by developing a holistic strategic framework that leveraged the generation and understanding of demand effectiveness with supply efficiency. First, organizations needed to develop a multi-enterprise view to their supply chains. They needed to be capable of working cooperatively with other organizations

Figure 5. Demand and supply chain processes (Source: Beech, 1998)

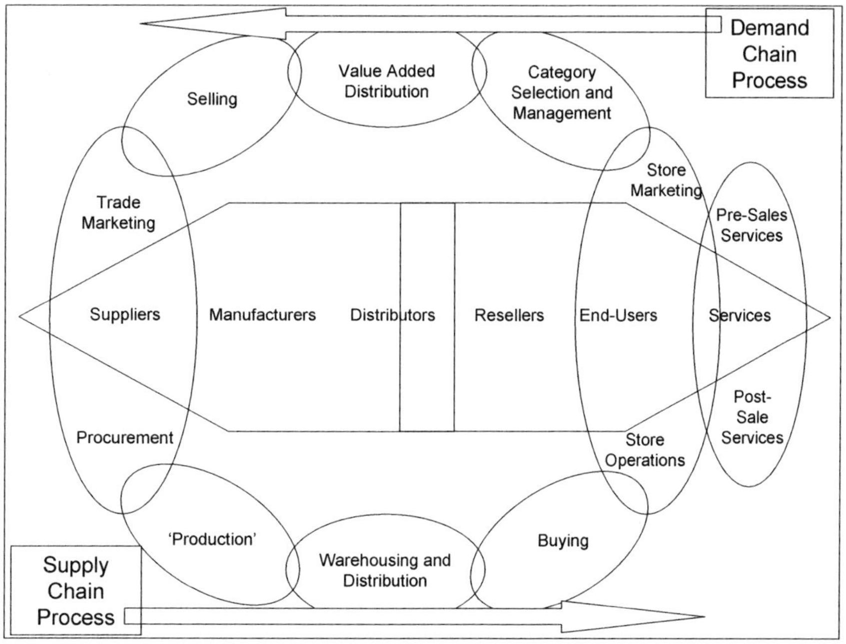

in the chain, rather than seeking to outdo them. Secondly, they needed to recognize the three key distinct supply and demand processes that must be integrated in order to gain the greatest value.

He suggested these three key elements were:

- The core processes of the supply and demand chains, as viewed from a broad cross-enterprise vantage point, rather than as discrete functions
- The integrating processes that created the links between the supply and demand chains
- The supporting infrastructure that made such integration possible

Beech's model, displayed in Figure 5, portrayed the demand chain as a sequence of backward-reaching processes, initiated by the end-customer, and enabling the business to anticipate customer demand characteristics. The supply chain structure, responsible for moving products and services upstream to the customer, remained inexorably linked to the demand chain.

However, across the virtual divide of the Internet, fundamental questions remained. Determining what the customer really wanted, and what services product variations the business could modify and/or deliver, remained as challenges. The demand chain was really about the informed customer, customers dictating what they wanted, where and why (Selen & Soliman, 2002).

Demand chain management remained strategically embedded across the whole value chain and the business's logistics infrastructure (Carothers & Adams, 1991; Shapiro, Singhal, & Wagner, 1993). It moved the 'underdeveloped' supply chain (New, 1996) into a complex Web of customer-driven supply chain systems (Choi, Dooley, & Rangtusanatham, 2001). As the supply chain strategy moved to customer driven, new demand chain capabilities emerged (Andersson & Jockel, 2002), and these became coordinated across the business supply chains (Stock, Greis, & Kasarda, 2000). They included transaction strategies, logistics, facilities, people, equipment, production, services, and intangibles like internal business processes, learning and growth, and the customer (Williamson, 1996).

From a technical viewpoint, demand chain management remained a set of applications, specifically designed, to electronically automate and 'optimize' the business processes an enterprise performed between its networks of customers and selling partners. Working independently, or in conjunction with one another, demand chain management applications were designed for easy customer use. These demand chain management applications enabled business-customer encounters, and did so at reduced servicing costs (Frohlich & Westbrook, 2002).

A raft of business-specific, integrated demand chain management frameworks emerged (Childerhouse, Aiken, & Towill, 2002). Demand chain management consultants like Comergent (*www.comergent.com*) and IBM (*www.ibm.com*) focused on the selling and ordering processes (Sarner & Desisto, 2004). Figure 6 highlights Comergent's consultancy focus areas, which focused on external 'demand chain selling' and 'ordering processes', as displayed in Figure 7.

Comergent simplified the 'external' sales processes into five key areas:

- **Analytics and metrics**, where the selling process data was collected for reporting, analysis, and business optimization
- **Product information management**, where the metrics to create, mange, and display sales-related data were housed, thereby allowing the management analysis of customers, channel partners, sales/services, and relationships
- **Pricing, configuration, and quoting**, where dynamic recommendations to customers, partners, and sales and/or services representatives were delivered in real-time

Figure 6. Demand chain selling and ordering model (Source: Comergent, 2003)

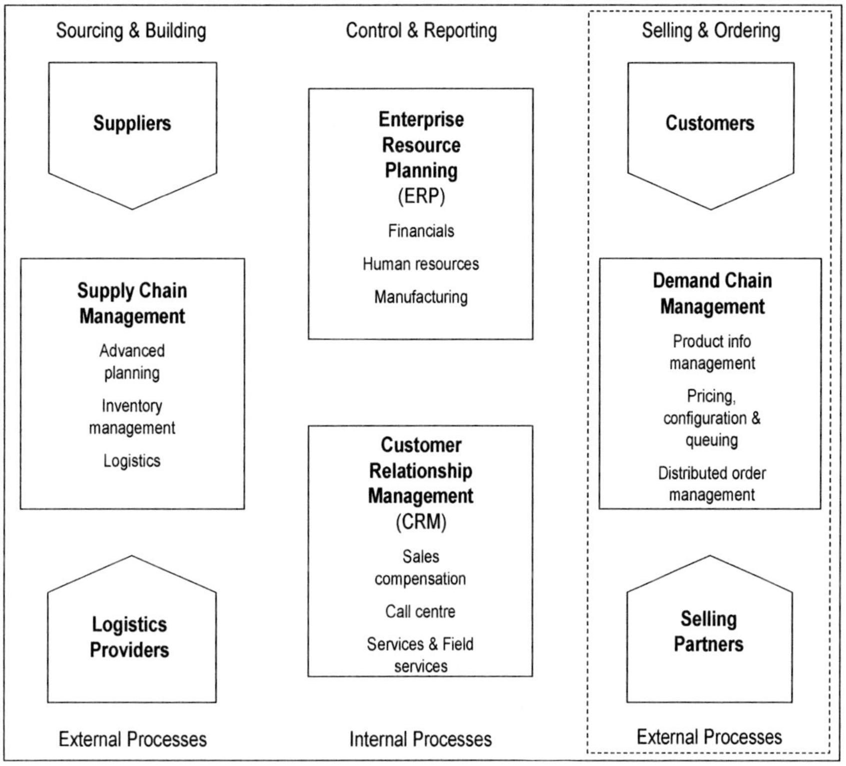

Figure 7. The external sales process (Source: Comergent, 2003)

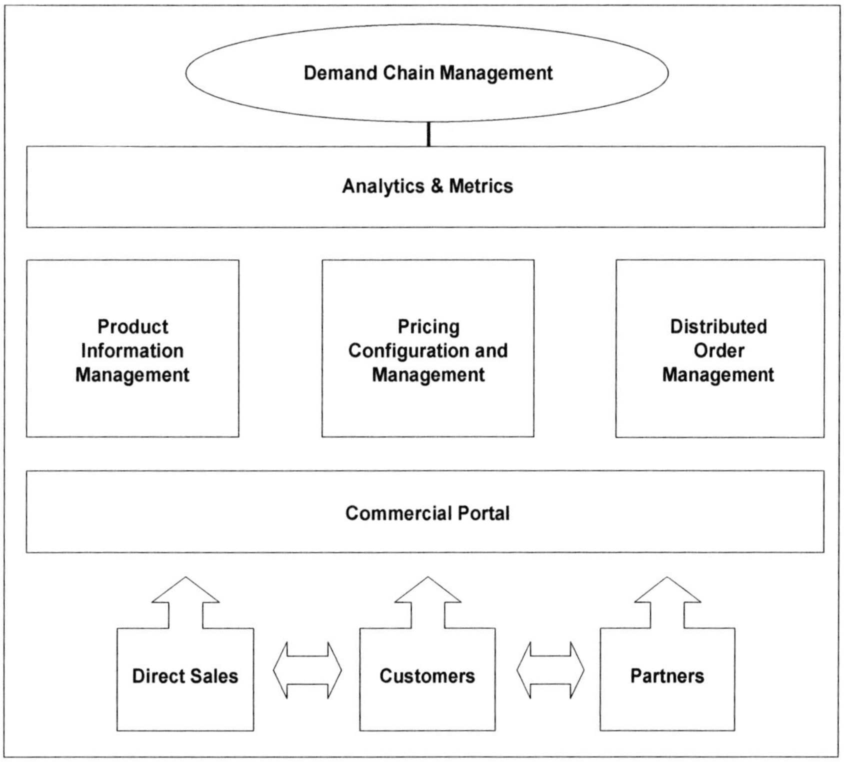

concerning the most appropriate products, solutions, prices and options, and using personalized messages and/or promotions

- **Distributed order management**, where customers were offered purchase choices across a single interface, and where their orders for processing and fulfillment were seamlessly distributed across the back-end systems or selling partners' systems.
- **Commerce portal**, where a single customer interface was offered for all applications.

Comergent then applied specific, demand chain management applications to some, or all, of the processes in these five key areas.

IBM's i2 demand chain management delivered similar collaborative solutions, aimed at maximizing profitability. It managed and shaped demand-based supply positions and delivered customers the product, price, and delivery time as coordinated services, parts, people, budgets, and facilities, and targets that maximized customer loyalty at minimal service delivery costs. IBM offered specialized business intelligence systems like: a sales configurator, a sales pricer, demand fulfillment, demand fulfillment availability, markdown optimization, distributed order management, and service parts planning.

THE VALUE CHAIN

Definitions of value have varied (Zeithaml, 1988), but common themes have indicated customer value as:

- Linked to the use of a product or service, thereby removing it from personal 'values'
- Perceived by the customers, rather than objectively determined by the seller
- Often traded between what the customer wants (including quality, benefits, worth), and what the customer gave up to acquire, and use, a product or service (such as price; sacrifices)

Value may also be loosely defined in terms of business or customer perspective equations:

- Business value = (Benefits of each delivered value chain activity minus its cost) + (Benefits of each service interface between value chain activity minus its cost).
- Customer value = (Benefits of each customer service interface interaction) + (Benefits of each added value business offering) + (Benefit perceived for the cost involved).

In 1985 Porter promoted the notion of the value chain as a key activity by which a business could manage and deliver added value to the customer. Both internal and external value chains exist. The internal value chain worked within the business itself, while the external value chain involved activities performed by, or linked through, business partners. The value chain approach sought to deliver improved efficiencies and/or greater business effectiveness. It was possible to add value to each customer by reducing cost (and/or adding value), either within each element of the value chain (for example, more efficient supplier arrangements) or at the interface between value chain components (for example, the business sales—customer interface).

Other early value creation measures arose from the supply chain (Houlihan, 1987) and the customer chain (Schonberger, 1990). These involved a series of integrated, dependent processes, whereby chosen specifications were transformed to finished deliverables. Emphasis was placed on the integration of activities, while also considering increasing customer value. Rayport and Sviokla (1996) proposed that the Internet enabled value creation by gathering, organizing, selecting, synthesizing, and distributing information. They defined two value chains: *the virtual value chain* and *the physical value chain.* The virtual value chain was information technology based, and involved the delivering of e-business-to-e-business, and e-business-to-consumer solutions. In some cases human decision making/control steps were maintained within the virtual environment, but today the approach is to use artificial intelligence software across such control points.

The value chain targeted the *real-time environment.* Online promotions by leading e-tailers could be monitored on an hourly basis to test customer response and to review the competitor's offers. This allowed the business to adjust its targeting priorities, offerings, and the like. In places where the delivery processes had become more responsive, the *deliverability of products and services* was often improved. Thus, *greater business-customer alignment* between the value chain activities and the e-customer was possible. The value chain may deliver efficiencies, and e-sales, that may be controlled from either *internal or external value chain constituents or partners.*

Kalakota and Robinson (2001) discussed disaggregation of the value chain as a means to *streamline efficiencies.* For example, logistics outsourcing, and subsequent re-aggregation of a supplier mix, may deliver new value chain components. Timmers (1999) noted that the value chain may no longer be viewed as a series of discrete steps, and that technology was offering more possibilities for *integrated solutions.* For example, Dell has used online customized ordering systems to reduce its time to market, improved customer tracking and monitoring, thereby reducing its customer response and delivery times. It deployed considerable alliance partner involvement, with its partners having instantaneous data access concerning customer purchasing and special requests. Vermijmeren (2003) suggested that *flexible, intelligent supply chain 'engines'* could drive these dynamic supply chains, delivering value in an efficient manner. Incorporating *high-level logistics* solutions offered yet another strategic solution for the online business (Docherty, 2001).

Chaffey, Mayer, Johnston, and Ellis-Chadwick (2004) and Deise, Nowikow, King, and Wright (2000) suggested the modern value chain network may involve downstream value chain partners (suppliers and buy-side intermediaries), working directly to deliver core value chain activities to the upstream value chain partners or sell-side intermediaries. They suggested both *strategic and non-strategic business partners may contribute to this value chain.*

Van Looy, Gemel, and Dierdonck (2003) considered the value chain as a "value constellation," and proposed a more "holistic view of the way in which the innovation process creates value for the final customer." This value chain constellation subsequently inspired "*innovation* managers to fully understand and articulate how the products and services are developed by the organization, in interaction with other (complementary) products and services, creating value for the customer ... leading to *integration of activities across the value chains* (rather than along the value chain) into new product and service offerings."

VALUE CHAIN MANAGEMENT

Beech's (1998) demand-supply chain model, along with Comergent's (2003) demand chain model, have each progressed towards a value chain management model (Mudimigha, Zairi, & Ahmed, 2004). Sampson (2000) demonstrated that *service supply chains were bi-directional*, and that communication between customers and suppliers, and vice versa, must occur. Thus, a partnering between participants occurred (Vokurka, 1998). Sampson also indicated bi-directional supply chains were typically *short lived,* but had *just-in-time* implications with inherent value-added expectations. To measure such information, new metrics tools have been devised. New methods to capture online measurement data (or Web metrics) have delivered new management tools. Management has increasingly incorporated such tools to interpret their Web tracking data, and to apply these findings throughout the demand-supply chain. Thus new levels of recording, understanding, and interpreting value-adding solutions have emerged (Sterne, 2002). These metrics tools helped management to:

1. Convert and distribute information, products, and services
2. Manage knowledge, quality, and connectivity
3. Work with virtual partners and customers
4. Deliver strategic information to management

The modern value chain management model has remained demand chain customer focused. Slywotzky and Morrison (1997) presented the progression of the value chain model from its traditional form into a modern form. Their model is displayed in Figure 8. This model commenced with the customer, and *linked the customer back to management core competencies.*

Many refinements that pick up the number of complex value chain relationships have since been added to value chain activities (Slywotzky & Morrison, 1997). The link between *strategy, management, investment, operations, marketing, service, and the environment* is displayed in McLarty's adaptation of Porter's value chain (Chaffey et al., 2004; Deise et al., 2000). This is displayed in Figure 9.

The link to the more complex value chain integrator (or aggregator) approach (Chaffey et al., 2004) is shown in Figure 10. Here, the downstream suppliers, the business value chain contribution blocks, and the selling operations are integrally linked, and *all contribute* to deliver an overall business package that aims to ultimately deliver customer value.

Low (2000) investigated ways of creating value and of measuring intangible assets like services. He suggested a value creation index allowing management to monitor their performance better. He further suggested that such procedures must remain flexible so they may be capable of

Figure 8. Modern value chain (Source: Slywotzky & Morrison, 1997)

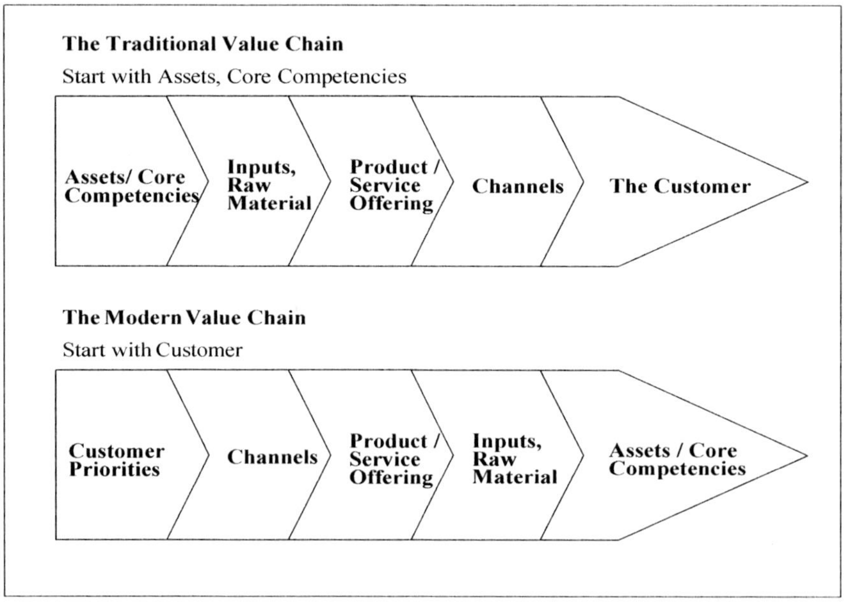

Figure 9. Revised value chain (Source: McLarty, 2003)

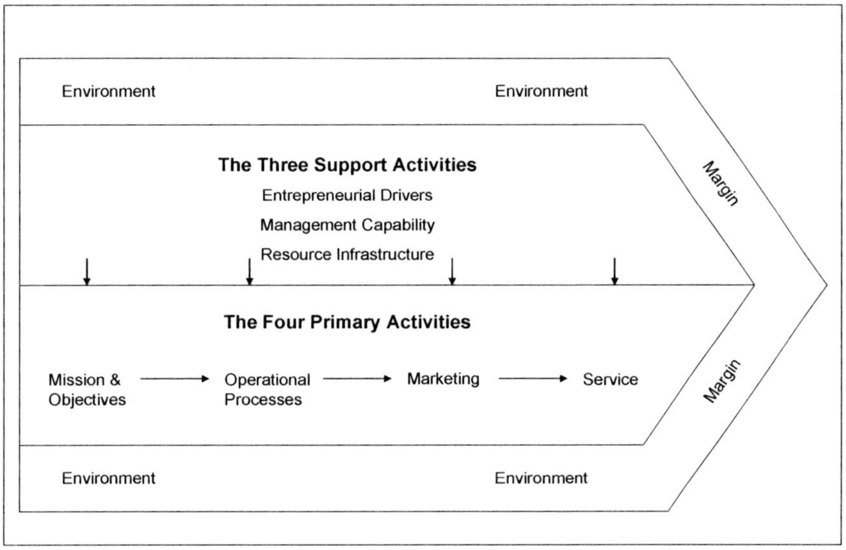

Figure 10. Value chain integrator (Source: Chaffey et al., 2004)

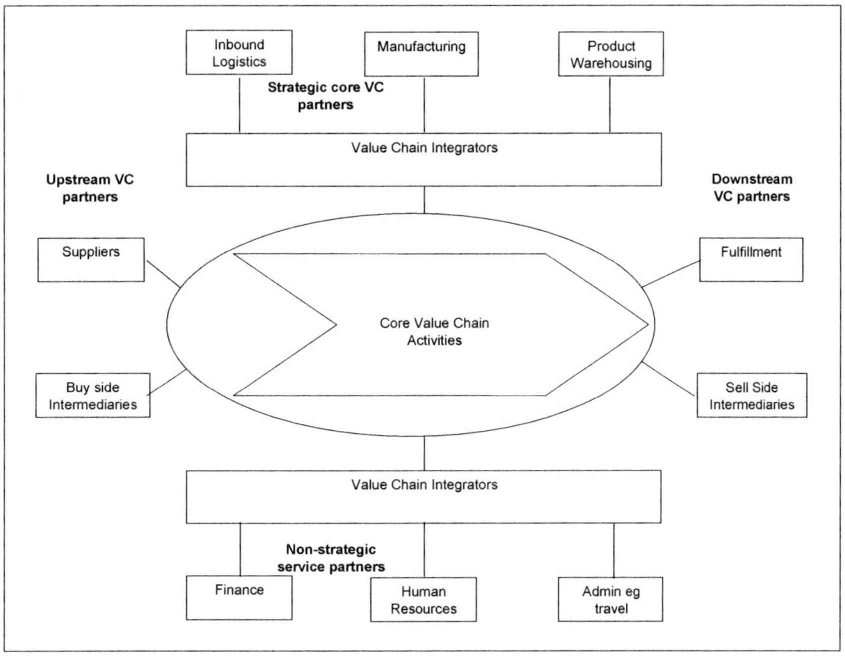

constantly adapting to the changing nature of businesses in the connected economy. Peters (1997) suggested customer segmentation issues must be continually monitored, thereby allowing for successful business-customer exchange mechanisms to be maintained. In 2001, Porter outlined how the Internet has enabled, and driven, new business solutions, forcing lower cost options and operational efficiencies across the supply side to be strategically investigated. Thus value chain management has led to a raft of networked, targeted, measurable, flexible, adaptable, supply-side innovations, and has provided a focus for customer-driven value chain strategies. Today, business services solutions have become increasingly complex, and often these can no longer be considered as simple lock-step value chains.

SERVICE VALUE CHAINS TO SERVICE VALUE NETWORKS

A more recent variant of the value chain is the services value chain. Definitions vary, but in general they refer to optimizing after-sales service situations—right across the service supply chain. The service supply chain was seen as one that, over time, delivered the fully collaborative state of low inventories, efficient planning, and high customer service levels. This may have included all planning, movement, and repair of materials activities to enable after-sales support of products (de Waart & Kemper, 2004; de Waart, 2003; Poole, 2003).

Beck (2002) suggested the 'service value chain', supported by consolidation and advances

Figure 11. Service value chain aggregator (Source: Beck, 2002)

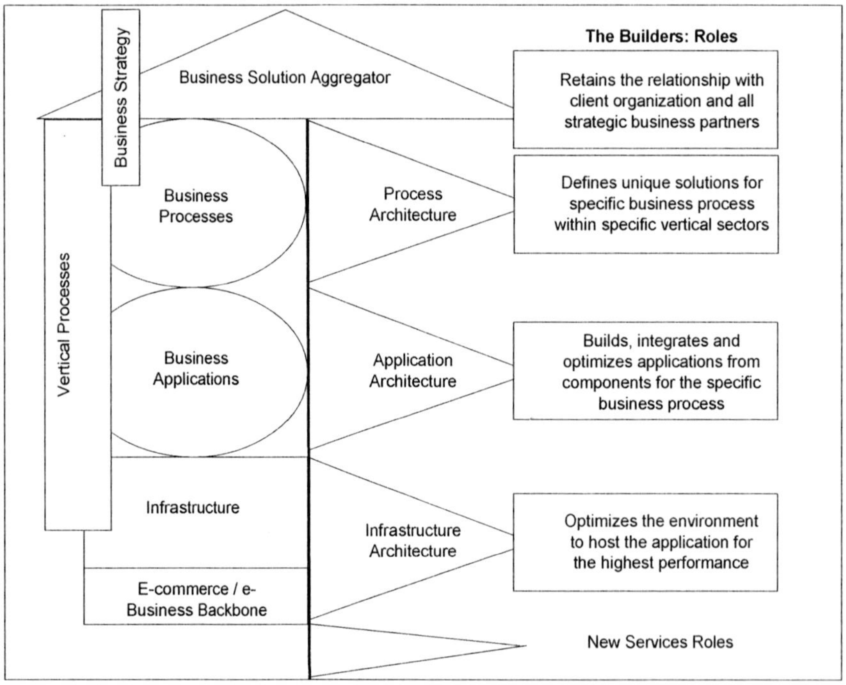

in the information technology downstream supply-side sector, would drive change during the next five years. Beck's model, displayed in Figure 11, suggested groups of equal business partners would share their specific, market-leading competencies, identify a group of similar buyers, and would deliver the required vertical solution repeatedly, reliably, and cost effectively. Beck suggested these 'consortiums of partners' could specifically target the individual customer, deliver high client satisfaction, drive new levels of profitability, and achieve competitive advantage (Bowen, & Shoemaker, 2003; Tsikriktsis & Heineke, 2004).

France et al. (2002) predicted the service value chain would be one of the most important developments for the global maturation of the services industry.

The service value chain can arise from supply chain aggregators (Zrimsek, 2002) working with other back-end providers to deliver partial, sophisticated solutions. These aggregators link the business processes (operations, supply chain, customer relationship management, service activities, finances, and others) with the business applications infrastructure backbone. These business units are also linked vertically in line with the business strategy. The necessary business architecture offers unique solutions to integrate and optimize components, their environments, movements, and hosting systems. New modes of service delivery are also delivered. Hence, the business aggregator solution delivers the 'optimized' internal systems. It 'optimizes' the relationships between the internal business and its external customer-strategic partners associates.

Businesses today are both change agents, delivering new products and services that change the lives of consumers, and change responders. For example, a firm has great difficulty in predicting when and where a useful, additional service value chain will emerge, and if it is the 'optimal' solution (one that 'best' meets the contingent trends of its service value chains; and of its buyers). In this unclear, non-linear environment of incomplete understanding, the firm and its service value chain(s) should develop *high agility* in their ability to respond to change (Kassim & Zain, 2004). Some trends have the potential to accelerate or inhibit the adoption of emerging service value chains. For example, intelligent database-driven Web sites have great advantage over Web page solutions, because they are capable of delivering specifically sourced data direct to a standard template Web page structure.

These service value chain approaches involve combinations of external supply chains, internal value integrators, and various strategic approaches. This complex aggregated structure is thus better termed a *service value network.*

A service value network may be defined as:

the flexible, dynamic delivery of a service, and/or product, by a business and its networked, coordinated value chains (supply chains and demand chains working in harmony); such that a value-adding, and target specific service and/or product solution is effectively, and efficiently, delivered to the individual customer in a timely, physical, or virtual manner. (Hamilton, 2004)

Thus a thorough and comprehensive approach to the understanding and delivery of service is defined, and integrating the downstream supplier businesses to the upstream sellers involves combinations of multiple networks—including the business's e-supply chain networked structures. *Thus, service value networks interlink the understanding and deliverability of the business's downstream business e-supply chain networks and its upstream customer service offerings.*

Measurement and strategic adjustment of the downstream e-supply chain network and the upstream service provider business remains vital to maintaining and improving competitive positioning. The balanced scorecard offers such measurement dimension.

THE BALANCED SCORECARD: BUILDING SERVICE VALUE CHAIN NETWORKS

Today, various virtual e-services and physical services models may be developed, evaluated, and monitored using a *balanced scorecard* approach. The service value network concept also fits under this measured strategic decision-making approach. Service value networks house fully integrated e-demand and e-supply chains working in harmony to the deliver both services and e-services. They are also highly agile and offer customer-induced flexible business solutions to customer requests.

This analytic balanced scorecard framework, originally developed by Kaplan and Norton (1992), is displayed in Figure 12. It delivers the enabling basis from which business industry blocks, like individual pharmacies, may be translated into powerful e-service networks of many interlinked data-sharing pharmacies. The business intelligence delivered by such an e-service network and its value adding systems is considerable.

The high-level strategies are articulated into specific, measurable performance parameters (Kaplan & Norton, 1996; Rohm, 2002). The customers must be targeted to receive their expected outcomes, the business block must develop its skills (and knowledge) and provide improved solutions. The internal processes must meet all legislative and business-specific requirements (like dispensing provisions). Finally, a set of financial outcomes (tangible and intangible) must be delivered. These financial outcomes—if correctly established, pursued, and delivered—allow the service value network to develop as a viable solution set. The business strategy subsets are broken down into objectives, measurements, targets, and initiatives, as displayed in Figure 11. Their effect on overall vision and strategy is monitored. If necessary, subset objective may also be further teased down into objective components, and even finer sets of measures may be developed.

This model delivers performance measures, allows high growth rates to be defined and targeted, differentiates competitive advantage, and delivers considerable measurable financial rewards. The

Figure 12. Balanced scorecard model

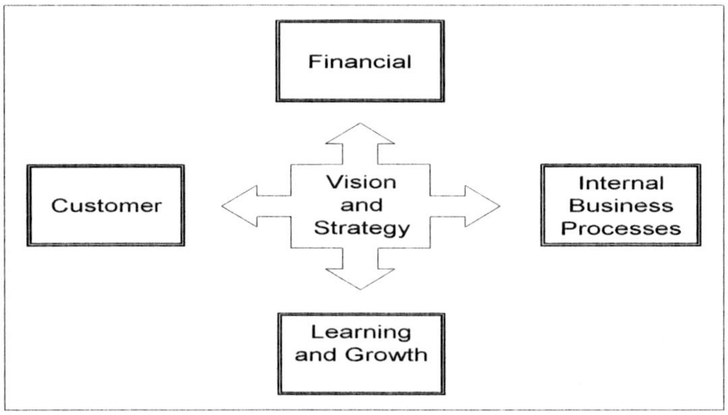

Figure 13. Balanced scorecard—nine-step strategy development cycle model (Source: Rohm, 2002)

business model has been trialed in one Australian pharmacy, is being expanded to six pharmacies, and is fully scalable and will eventually encompass an Australia-wide network of pharmacies and e-pharmacies. Revenue savings, once fully operational and Australia-wide, is projected to be over $150M per annum (physical delivery), and over $100M per annum in Internet sales (virtual delivery). This saving in real costs to the consumer translates into a net national economic benefit exceeding $900M per annum.

An e-service network may be implemented using a modified version of Rohm's (2002) nine-step balanced scorecard strategy development cycle. This model is displayed in Figure 13. It begins with the development of the visionary strategy, and delivers a global business perspective. This visionary strategy is refined and developed, via a business plan, a vision/mission top-down approach, and is combined with the evaluation of other competing or relevant business models. A set of strategic objectives (focusing on delivering customer outcomes) is developed. These strategic objectives are then mapped. Using a learning curve position/movement and knowledge approach, the strategic objectives are quantified into performance-based measures. These measures, in-turn, are tapped to deliver new initiatives, such as targeting different customer groups, offering different products and services, increasing the product and service relevance, and the like. The selected pharmacy product and services mixes (to be marketed) are automated by incorporating an e-systems approach that allowed the efficient delivery of the internal processes (in a cascading series of process requirements). This ultimately delivers efficient, productive outcomes. Such business-related outcomes provide relevant financial results including increased customer numbers and new revenue streams; greater cultural understanding and improved community involvement; upskilling of the operational staff and the business itself; enhanced local, regional, and international focus; and the like.

Figure 14. Balanced scorecard—nine-step strategic learning spiral

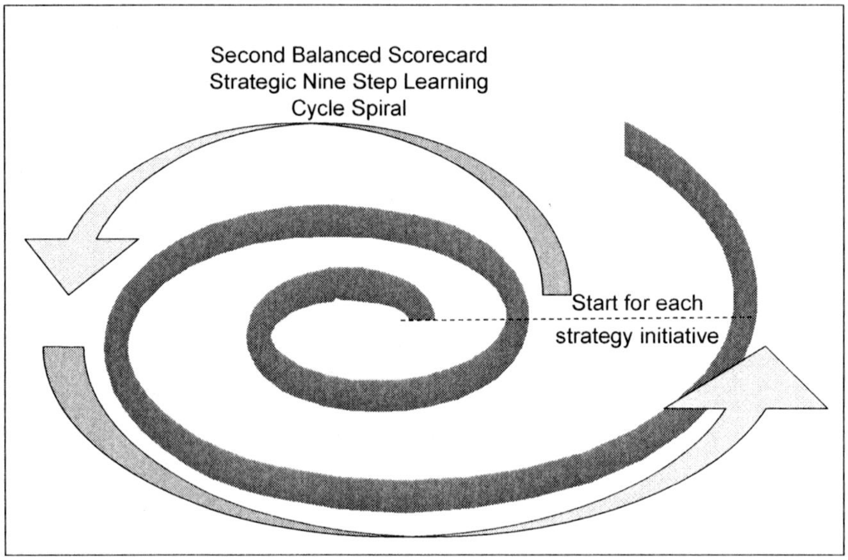

Figure 15. Balanced scorecard—strategic services components

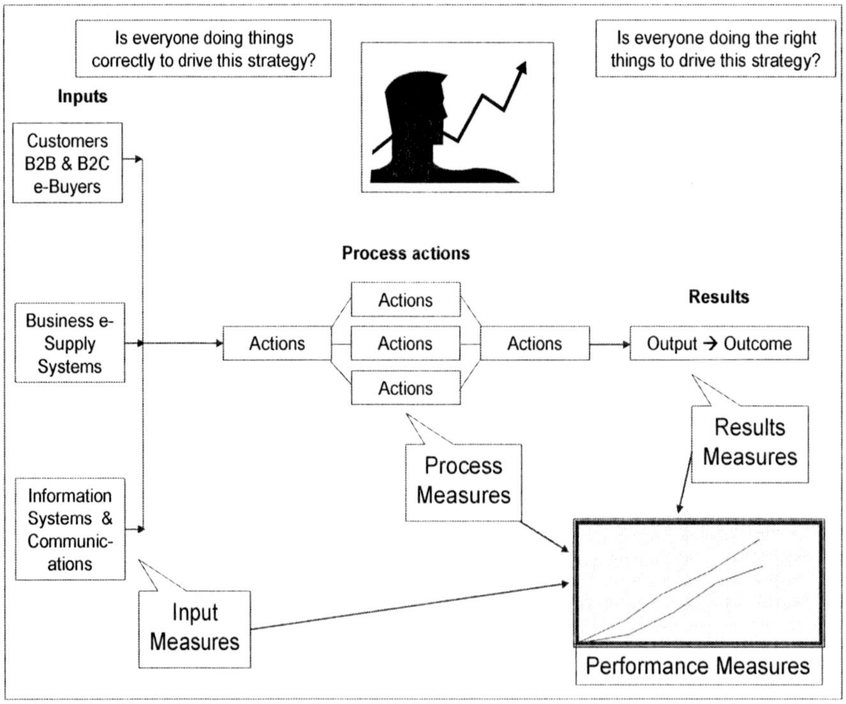

Figure 16. Pharmacy network scorecard (from Hamilton, 2004a)

	Strategy to be achieved, and how?	How success measured and traced?	Performance expectation	Key action program required to achieve objectives
	Objective	**Measure**	**Target**	**Initiatives**
Financial	Broaden the revenue mix E-Pharmacy option Local delivery	Revenue mix	65% Std Pharmacy 24% New products, services & delivery 4% Upskilled staff 6% E-services 1% Information sharing	Classifying target users Channel marketing measures Fuzzy logic/ Artificial Intelligence measures Targeted sales focus, layout, quality & learning curve effects
Customer (Local Persons)	Customer targeting Customer recognition Customer value & performance Customer satisfaction	Customer evaluations Niche growth	'05/'06 – 200% '06/'07 – 300% '07/'08 – 1000%	Intelligent integrated database interpretation and support Customer intelligence support Knowledge and learning pathways Service value network delivery Value adds and peripheral alliances 24hr customer service/ connection
Regional and Internal Business	New products New services New access & deliveries Differentiation	% revenue new products & services % uptake % approval	'05/'06 – integrated regional approach, lead pharmacies '06 – additional pharmacies added	R&D – sourcing markets Dynamic website Targeted mailing of doctors and other suppliers sourced Direct marketing
Learning and Growth	New strategic skills Learning curve	Training delivered Understanding & knowledge growth	100% to all pharmacies Well informed - all participants and leadership (100%)	Customer ed. & training Customer lifestyle support Customer expected benefits exceeded Regional and national knowledge library

When tangible (physical) and intangible (virtual) balanced scorecard measures are assessed against previous strategies, new strategic improvements are often generated. For example, joint cluster marketing, sharing of customer activities (and feedback), incremental improvements in processes, disruptive (total new pathways) improvements in target marketing and approaches used, and new funding mechanisms may be operationalized into the strategic model.

A strategic, nine-step, learning spiral and growth pattern emerges from the balanced scorecard nine-step model. The second learning cycle builds on the first learning cycle as learning occurs, and over time, faster learning along with more complex, better targeted, multifaceted approaches to business intelligence and knowledge capture arise. This growth and learning cycle is modeled in Figure 14.

The strategic components delivering the e-services balanced scorecard outcomes are displayed in Figure 15. Here specific performance measures may be identified and then tracked. For example, if the objective is to broaden the pharmacy revenue mix, all inputs related to this objective are drawn together into the required common process blocks that deliver this desired outcome. The relevant measures are then determined, delivered, and monitored.

Figure 11 considers the case of a pharmacy solution. Here, the four balanced scorecard sectors as displayed in Figure 12 are linked within the one scorecard. Using a procedure such as that outlined for Figure 13 above, and considering the relevant measures as developed via a Figure 15 approach, a series of achievable, measurable, targeted, cost related initiatives can be developed to deliver this specific part of the business strategy for the service value network.

The balanced scorecard model is a highly useful tool that can assist with the focusing, targeting, and delivery of 'optimized' growth approaches for an industry block like the pharmacy industry, the tourism industry, the financial sector, accounting services, and legal services. Figure 16 displays how this tool may be used to tease out service strategies, e-service strategies, or a combination of the two strategic blocks into a pharmacy network balanced scorecard model. This delivers strategies that may ensure necessary financial rewards and savings are deliverable to an e-service industry.

Modern business managers may use a balanced scorecard approach to monitor their business's strategy. The manager may quantify each tangible and intangible business feature into a defined and quantifiable measure. Each measure can be assessed, and specific target performance expectations can be developed, each linked to specific key outcome-related activities, and each delivering a component of the desires strategy. All activities may be costed (allocated to cost centers and with economic values), and incorporated into one of four measurable strategic areas—the customer (including business and end user); the internal business processes (like the business's e-supply chain networks); the financial area (including income and expenditure); and the innovation, learning, and growth sectors (like research and development). These four key balanced scorecard business perspectives encapsulate deliverable economic value, and each is normally directly tied into the business's common strategic vision. Thus the balanced scorecard remains a key strategic management and monitoring tool for the manager operating in the modern e-service business arena. It is also a useful strategic measurement tool in the building and maintenance of service value networks.

Thus, the progression towards highly efficient and agile e-services has been driven by businesses constantly seeking new ways to improve their performance, to deliver products and services in a more cost-effective and productive manner, and to deliver enhanced perceived customer value. This focus has driven the business beyond the e-service model and into the realm of the service value network. Industry-wide strategic management control and monitoring tools like the balanced scorecard have ready application in such business network approaches.

The service value network integrates the supply-side alliance partners and their associated peripheral partners into a highly competitive cohesive unit, striving to deliver operational and service innovation, cost savings, and value-adding solutions to its diverse customer-demanded business encounters, while the balanced scorecard delivers a set of strategic management control functions.

CONCLUSION

Today industry is seeking new pathways to competitive positioning and ways to driving business models forward. Currently, many models exist, and new additions like the e-services built around e-supply chain networks are increasingly targeting meeting customer needs. These models still lack a customerization (one-on-one business-to-individual-customer relationship) approach, and consequently need further enhancements. Service value networks offer a comprehensive pathway towards enhanced competitiveness.

To develop a service value network approach, a detailed understanding of business developments is required. Four strategic areas are required—a tactical understanding of the external business environment and its effectors on the business; a strategic, data-mined, intelligent understanding of all internal and peripheral e-supply chain networks and their information channels; an accessible business-customer interface that delivers desired information across the network and up to the targeted customer; and an alert, customer-centric solution set delivering the required service at an acceptable cost. The balanced scorecard offers a strategic measurement agenda allowing management to monitor tangible and intangible service factors across their sphere of influence.

The mechanisms underpinning these service value networks and their strategic measurement areas allow the industry and its management to cohesively move forward towards an enhanced competitive position—delivering a 'glocal' (global and local) solution.

THE FUTURE

Within the services arena, a fully operationalized e-supply chain network structure presents the participating business with an expanded array of competitive position tools. *Strategic positioning* and *extended customer value* may be utilized to develop measures and to frame new business models (Hamilton & Selen, 2003a, 2003b, 2004). Further tools like *quality functional deployment* may be used to establish e-quality dimensions (Hamilton & Selen, 2002, 2004) and the suitability of the customer directed e-service products, while *strategic e-marketing* may be used to develop strategic target market areas and measures (Gunesh & Hamilton, 2003). Additional e-supply chain-related areas including *4PL logistics* solutions (Hamilton, Hughes, & Selen, 2003; Gunesh & Hamilton, 2004a) and *learning across e-demand chain systems* (Hamilton & Selen, 2002a, 2002b) may offer additional measurement tool features. Such areas, when incorporated into e-supply chain networks, move the basic e-supply chain solutions towards comprehensive, highly agile service value networks industry-wide solutions. The early stages of industry-wide service value networks are emerging in tourism (built around local-business to national-database systems). When built into an intelligently managed (by information technology systems—incorporating fuzzy logic and artificial intelligence) e-services industry and constructed as a global, dynamic, living business network, a high degree of customer targeting and resultant customer satisfaction is deliverable. E-supply chain networks will continue to improve their capabilities in this regard, and will form an integral part of service industry business solutions into the future.

REFERENCES

Akkermans, H., & Vos, B. (2003). Amplification in service supply chains: An exploratory case study from the telecom industry. *Production and Operations Management, 12*(2), 204-223.

Al-Mudimigha, A., Zairi, M., & Ahmed, A. (2004). Extending the concept of supply chain: The effective management of value chains. *International Journal of Production Economics, 87,* 309-320.

An, C., & Fromm H. (Eds.). (2005). *Supply chain management on demand.* New York: Computer Books.

Andersson, D., & Jockel, O. (2002). Logistics competence provided and required in third-party logistics relationships. In M. Andersen & M. Marelli (Eds.), *Business Logistics and Interorganizational Electronic Networks, Proceedings of NOFOMA* (pp. 569-587). Retrieved July 31, 2003, from http://inforge.unil.ch/cimre96/papers/paper.htm

Barlow-Hills, S., & Sarin, S. (2003). From market driven to market driving: An alternative paradigm for marketing in high technology industries. *Journal of Marketing Theory and Practice, 11*(3), 13-24.

Beck, J. (2002). The services value chain provides framework for joint ventures. *Gartner Group Research Note* (AV16-2271).

Beech, J. (1998). The supply demand nexus. In I. Gattorna (Ed.), *Strategic supply chain alignment.* Aldershot, UK: Gower Press.

Berry, L., & Parasuraman, A. (1991). *Marketing services: Competing through quality.* New York: The Free Press.

Bowen, J., & Shoemaker, S. (2003). Loyalty: A strategic commitment. *Cornell Hotel and Restaurant Administration Quarterly, 44*(5/6), 31-46.

Brown, S., & Vashistha, A. (2002). Igniting the services value chain. *Services Marketing, 11*(1), 12-13.

Carothers, G., & Adams, M. (1991). Competitive advantage through customer value: The role of value based strategies. In M. Stahl & G. Bounds (Eds.), *Competing globally through customer value* (pp. 32-66). New York: Quorum Books.

Chaffey, D., Mayer, R., Johnston, K., & Ellis-Chadwick, F. (2004). *Internet marketing* (2nd ed.). Essex, UK: Pearson Education.

Chase, R. (1996). The mail is my factory: Reflections of a service junkie. *Production and Operations Management, 5*(4), 298-308.

Chase, R., Jacobs, R., & Aquilano, N. (2005). *Operations management* (10th ed.). New York: McGraw-Hill/Irwin.

Chen , I., & Paulraj, A. (2004). Towards a theory of supply chain management: The constructs and measurements. *Journal of Operations Management, 22,* 119-150.

Childerhouse, P., Aiken, J., & Towill, D. (2002). Analysis and design of focused demand chains. *Journal of Operations Management, 20,* 675-689.

Choi, T., Dooley, K., & Rangtusanatham, M. (2001). Conceptual note: Supply networks and complex adaptive systems: Control versus emergence. *Journal of Operations Management, 19,* 351-366.

Clark, C. (1940). *The conditions of economic progress.* London: Macmillan.

Comergent. (2003). *Demand chain management.* Retrieved May 20, 2004, from www.comergent.com/elibrary.cfm & http://www.comergent.com/products/architecture.cfm

Committee on Definitions, American Marketing Association. (1960). *Marketing definitions* (p. 21). Chicago: American Marketing Association.

Cook, D., Goh, C., & Chung, C. (1999). Service topologies: A state of the art survey. *Production and Operations Management, 8*(3), 318-338.

Czinkota, M., Ronkainen, I., & Moffett, M. (2005). *International business* (7th ed.). Mason, OH: Thompson/South-Western.

de Waart, D. (2003, October 6). Service supply chain management: A great untapped resource. *EBN*, 21-23. Retrieved March 20, 2004 from http://www.ebnonline.com

de Waart, D., & Kemper, S. (2004, January/February). 5 steps to service supply chain excellence. *Supply Chain Management Review*, 28-35.

Deise, M., Nowikow, C., King, P., & Wright, A. (2000). *Executive's guide to e-business. From tactics to strategy.* New York: John Wiley & Sons.

Docherty, M. (2001). Managing the supply chain: i to I. *Logistics Inc.*, (Newsletter No. 1), 1-4. Retrieved June 10, 2003, from http://www.ilogistics.com

Fisher, M. (1997). What is the right supply chain for your product? *Harvard Business Review, 75*(3), 105-116.

France, N., Da Rold, C., & Young, A. (2002). Services value chain reshapes IT services industry (pp. 1-4). *Gartner Group Research Note,* (AV-21-3090).

Frohlich, M., & Westbrook, R. (2002). Demand chain management in manufacturing and services: Web-based integration, drivers and performance. *Journal of Operations Management, 20,* 729-745.

Gunesh, K., & Hamilton, J. (2003a). Logistics—a pathway towards 'sustainable' competitive advantage for the multinational enterprise. In *Proceedings of the 3rd International Conference on Electronic Business*, Singapore (Vol. 3, no. 1, pp. 1-10, 597-599).

Gunesh, R., & Hamilton, J. (2003). Incorporating customer interface marketing design elements to leverage strategic positioning in the online real estate industry. In *Proceedings of the 3rd International Conference on Business*, Honolulu, HI (Vol. 3, no. 1, pp. 1-9).

Hamilton, J. (2004). Modeling, information flows, performance, strategy and competitiveness across the service value network. *Journal of New Business Ideas and Trends, 2*(2), 29-53.

Hamilton, J. (2004a). Service value networks: Value, performance and strategy for the services industry. *Journal of Systems Science and Systems Engineering, 13*(4), 469-489.

Hamilton, J., Hughes, K., & Selen, W. (2003). E-business enabled networks and fourth party logistics (4PL) providers: An overview. In *Proceedings of the 3rd International Conference on Electronic Business*, Singapore (Vol. 3, no. 1, pp. 1-7, 331-333).

Hamilton, J., & Selen, W. (2002). Integrating Web site design features for 'one-on-one' marketing: A QFD framework. *Proceedings of the 7th International Conference on ISO9000 and TQM,* Melbourne, Australia (vol. 7, no. 1, pp. 1-8, 93-94).

Hamilton, J., & Selen, W. (2002a). The development of the dynamic Web interface between the online e-customer and the e-business. In *Proceedings of the 6th ANZAM/IFSAM International Conference*, Gold Coast, Australia (pp. 1-12).

Hamilton, J., & Selen, W. (2002b). Learning in a demand chain management framework: Directions for business education. In *Proceedings of the 33rd Decision Sciences Institute Conference*, San Diego, CA (pp. 1-16).

Hamilton, J., & Selen, W. (2003). Development of a strategic positioning matrix for the Internet-enabled real estate industry: An Australian perspective. *The E-Business Review, 3*(1), 57-61.

Hamilton, J., & Selen, W. (2003a). Development of a regional real estate portal exhibiting an extended customer value proposition. In Spina, Vinelli, Cagliano, Kalchschmidt, Romano, & Salvador (Eds.), *One world? One view of OM?* (pp. 903-912). Italy: SGE, Pavova.

Hamilton, J., & Selen, W. (2003b). A strategic path to competitive advantage for the online, small-to-medium enterprise within the service sector. *Journal of New Business Ideas and Trends, 1*(1), 20-37.

Hamilton, J., & Selen, W. (2004). Enabling real estate service chain management through personalized Web interfacing using QFD. *International Journal of Operations and Production Management, 24*(3), 270-288.

Hanson, W. (2000). *Principles of Internet marketing.* Cincinnati, OH: Thompson Learning.

Heikkila, J. (2002). From supply to demand chain management: Efficiency and customer satisfaction. *Journal of Operations Management, 20,* 747-767.

Houlihan, J. (1987). International supply chain management. *International Journal of Physical Distribution and Materials Management, 17*(2), 51-66.

Hughes, J., Mitchell, P., & Ramson, W. (Eds.). (1993). *Australian concise Oxford dictionary.* New York: Oxford University Press.

Ismail, H., & Khatibi, A. (2004). Study of the relationship between perception of value and price and customer satisfaction: The case of Malaysian telecommunications industry. *Journal of American Academy of Business, 4*(1/2), 309-313.

Judd, R. (1964). The case for redefining services. *Journal of Marketing, 28*(1), 58-59.

Kalakota, R., & Robinson, M. (2001). *E-business 2.0: Roadmap for success.* Upper Saddle River, NJ: Addison-Wesley/Longman.

Kamarkar, U. (2002). Integrative research in marketing and operations management. *Journal of Marketing Research, 33*(2), 125-133.

Kaplan, R., &. Norton, D. (1992). The balanced scorecard—measures that drive performance. *Harvard Business Review, 70*(1), 71-79.

Kaplan, R., &. Norton, D. (1996). *The balanced scorecard: Translating strategy into action.* Boston: Harvard Business School Publishing.

Kassim, N., & Zain, M. (2004). Assessing and measurement of organizational agility. *Journal of American Academy of Business, 4*(1/2), 174-177.

Kathawala, Y., & Abdou, K. (2003). Supply chain evaluation in the services industry: A framework development compared to manufacturing. *Managerial Accounting Journal, 18*(1/2), 140-149.

Kuglin, F. (1998). *Customer-centered supply chain management.* New York: American Management Association, AMACOM.

Lawrence, E., Newton, S., Corbitt, B., Braithwaite, R., & Parker, C. (2002). *Technology of Internet business.* New York: John Wiley & Sons.

Lee, H. (2002). Aligning supply chain strategies with product uncertainties. *California Management Review, 44*(3), 105-119.

Levitt, T. (1972). Production line approach to service. *Harvard Business Review, 50*(5), 41-52.

Low, J. (2000). The value creation index. *Journal of Intellectual Capital, 1*(2), 252-262.

McAlexander, J., Kim, S., & Roberts, S. (2003). Loyalty: The influences of satisfaction and brand community integration. *Journal of Marketing Theory and Practice, 11*(4), 1-11.

McLarty, R. (2003). The attitudes of British managers in small and medium sized enterprises to the implementation of the value chain concept. *International Journal of Management, 20*(4), 430-442.

Murdick, R., Render, B., & Russell, R. (1990). *Service operations management.* Boston: Allyn and Bacon.

New, S. (1996). A framework for analyzing supply chain improvement. *International Journal of Operations and Production Management, 16*(4), 19-36.

Nie, W., & Kellogg, D. (1999). How professors of operations management view service operations. *Production and Operations Management, 8*(3), 339-355.

Peters, L. (1997). IT enabled marketing: A framework for value creation in customer relationships. *Journal of Marketing Practice, 3*(4), 213-229.

Poole, K. (2003). Seizing the potential of the service supply chain. *Supply Chain Management Review,* (July/August), 54-61.

Porter, M. (1985). *Competitive advantage: Creating and sustaining superior performance.* New York: The Free Press.

Porter, M. (2001). Strategy and the Internet. *Harvard Business Review, 79*(3), 63-78.

Preis, M. (2003). The impact of interpersonal satisfaction on repurchase decisions. *Journal of Supply Chain Management, 39*(3), 30-38.

Quinn, J., Baruch, J., & Paquette, P. (1987). Technology in services. *Scientific American, 257*(6), 50-58.

Rathmell, J. (1974). *Marketing in the service sector.* Cambridge, MA: Winthrop Publishing.

Rayport, J., & Sviokla, J. (1996). Exploiting the virtual value chain. *The McKinsey Quarterly, 1,* 20-37.

Reid, D., & Sanders, N. (2005). *Operations management* (2nd ed.). Hoboken, NJ: John Wiley & Sons.

Rohm, A., & Sultan, F. (2004 January/February). The evolution of e-business. *Marketing Management,* 32-37.

Roth, A., & Menor, L. (2003). Insights into service operations management: A research agenda. *Journal of Operations Management, 12*(2), 145-164.

Rust, R., & Metters, R. (1996). Mathematical models of service. *European Journal of Operations Research, 91*(3), 427-439.

Sampson, S. (2000). Customer-supplier duality and bidirectional supply chains in service organizations. *International Journal of Service Industry Management, 11*(2), 348-364.

Sarner, A., & Desisto, P. (2004). MarketScope: Sell-side electronic commerce, *Gartner Group Research Note,* (M21-9772), 1-4.

Schonberger, R. (1990). *Building a chain of customers.* New York: The Free Press.

Selen, W., & Soliman, F. (2002). Operations in today's demand chain management framework. *Journal of Operations Management, 20*(6), 667-673.

Tsikriktsis, N., & Heineke, J. (2004). The impact of process variation on customer dissatisfaction: Evidence from the U.S. domestic airline industry. *Decision Sciences, 35*(1), 129-142.

U.S. Bureau of Labor Statistics. (2002/2004). Retrieved May 25, 2004, from http://www.bls.gov/

Verma, R., & Boyer, K. (2000). Service classification and management challenges. *Journal of Business Strategies, 17*(1), 5-24.

Zeithaml, A. (1988). Consumer perceptions of price, quality, and value: A means-end model and synthesis of evidence. *Journal of Marketing, 52*(3), 2-22.

Chapter V
Service Value Networks:
Delivering Competitive E-Services

John Hamilton
James Cook University, Australia

ABSTRACT

This chapter addresses service value networks as a key pathway to establishing and likely retaining future strong competitive positioning within a service industry sector. A service value network may be defined as "the flexible, dynamic delivery of a service, and/or product, by a business and its networked, coordinated value chains (supply chains and demand chains working in harmony); such that a value-adding and target-specific service and/or product solution is effectively, and efficiently, delivered to the individual customer in a timely, physical, or virtual manner." The service value network offers a future pathway for a business to develop its e-supply chain systems. It captures the contacting customer, and integrates the customer's (virtual e-customer, virtual e-business customer, or physical customer) demands via its virtual or Web site interface into its integrated downstream service networks, seeks solutions, and delivers the appropriate business solutions back to the customer. Value-enhanced business encounter solutions are readily deliverable for targeted customers. The procedure to research and develop a service value network is described.

SERVICE VALUE NETWORKS

Service value networks offer a new business model and a new paradigm to service delivery mechanisms. They reconcile two conflicting, but concurrent, requirements of customers, namely to leverage economies of scale (from a diverse block of data storages), and to be able to deliver highly specific customized solutions (Brown & Vashistha, 2002). This service value network pathway is being driven by:

- Businesses—now requiring 'easy-to-implement' and 'value-proven' vertical or process-specific solutions, instead of generic 'capability-based', technical support.
- The drive towards core competency and competitive advantage.
- The requirements for holistic solutions—driving cooperation throughout the services value chains, and aiming to satisfy client demands.
- The desire for long-term (or more sustainable) competitive positioning.

The features from the previous chapter's models, when considered with other factors like customer demand-driven needs, wants, desires, and price point; supply side service feeds; the effect of the Internet, business strategic solutions; and technology options, along with their interrelated and interconnected links, can be drawn into a new topology model termed the Service Value Network Framework Model.

SERVICE VALUE NETWORK FRAMEWORK

The service value network framework offers a topology approach from which the operational, services, and customer strategies of the business are drawn together as interconnected data-sharing models delivering unique customer services encounters—ones aiming to exceed customer expectations! This business system learns from its customer encounters (by storing and analyzing customer information gathered), and improves its services database offerings by developing new, or

Figure 1. Service value network framework (Source: Hamilton, 2004a)

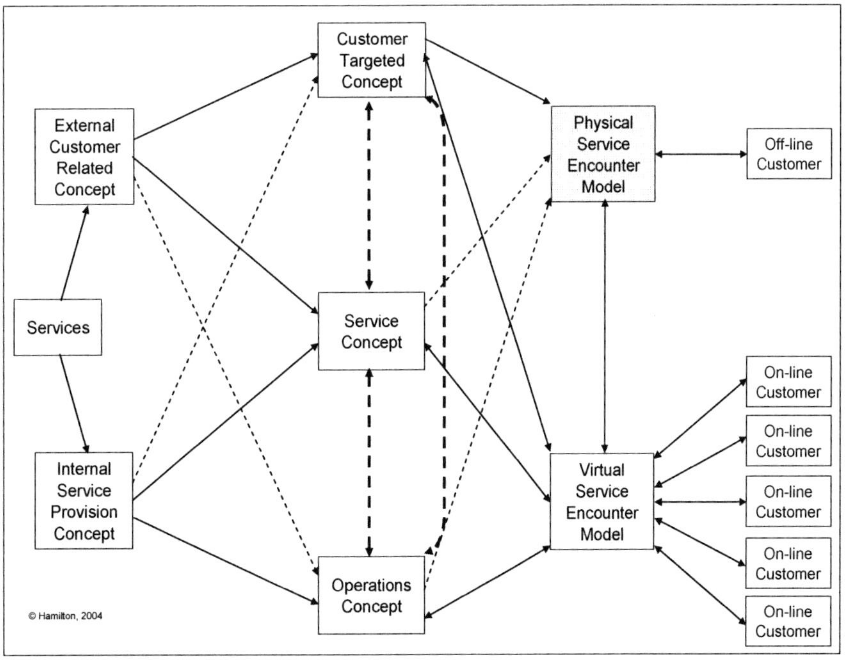

improved, upstream supply-side customer-driven solutions and housing these information sources ready for additional, or even more specific, customer encounters. This model is displayed in Figure 1.

This framework meshes with:

- Earlier works above.
- Other works (Hoffman & Novak, 2000; Chen & Wells, 1999; Biocca, Li, & Daugherty, 2002).
- Commercial services business solutions providers (Gartner, 2002; Comergent Business Strategies, 2003).
- Software developers, including SUN, Microsoft, and IBM.

The **external services** component links the environmental scanning for complementary services and added-value components, and are based on the customer-requested solution plotted.

The **internal services** component delivers the integrated demand chain/supply chain, where value chain partners work together to deliver maximum customer value in the most efficient and effective manner. Here, partners aim to deliver service quality and the service as a quality, financially accountable package.

The **customer targeted** component addresses the service being offered in terms of its efficiency, relevance, scope, and performance. In short, the customer targeted component delivers the back-end activities or the *'when' (content order), and appropriately targets these features 'to whom'.*

The **service concept** component integrates both the operations concept component and the customer targeted component. It delivers multi-dimensional information through the business and its value-adding internal and external partners, and delivers a broader customer experience. In short, the services concept model delivers the *'what'* to the service value encounter.

The **operations concept** component houses networked information systems, and extensive data storage and retrieval systems. In conjunction with developing Web measurement metrics, computer-based fuzzy logic techniques (computer-based data analysis and approximation techniques), and artificial intelligence tools (that mine the business networks databases, and provide reasoned and added-value solutions to the customer's business requests, interrogate the databases, sort and interpret available information, and deliver customized, or personalized solutions) that target perceived customer expectations. This 'renewal' and learning networked system is very different from normal Web site service offerings. It also incorporates issues related to failures and recovery. The operations concept component delivers the *'how'* to the service value encounter.

The operational, services, and customer strategies of the business are drawn together as interconnected data sharing models, delivering unique customer services encounters—ones aiming to exceed customer expectations, and house much of the business's intellectual property. They remain integrally linked downstream with their relevant partners and ad hoc additional sources, seeking to deliver dynamic service value chain network responses for their virtual customers.

The operational, services, and customer component areas are integrally connected in the modern service value chain network. Data is pooled, shared, exchanged, and cross-concept applied (between customer servicing, operations, and business strategies) to provide new learning and new customer solutions. The component areas come together at the service encounter 'touch-point'. The customer receives the business's demand-driven, appropriate, approximated, value-added set of services. This mix is intelligently sourced and retrieved from its networked combinations of databases.

The service encounter is derived via one of two components (or a combination of both):

1. The 'physical' (tangible) encounter between the customer and a business contact person or persons

2. The 'virtual' (intangible) encounter with and electronic based structure, which is often visually connected via its internal or external business Web site—in both cases information flows from customer to business, and business responds sourcing relevant, allowable (non-sensitive), correct information

Business then delivers customer-requested, value-chain sourced information (in a timely flow), across the service encounter interface and through to the customer. Chinese University of Hong Kong and National Sun Yat-Sen University research (Draaijer, 1992; Liang, 2003) indicated customers in the United States buy using multiple channels—including stores, catalogs, and online activities. The service value network operates across both physical and information pathways and networks. It is a key part of the operations management equation. Such viewpoints support the physical and virtual service value encounter model. Sterne (2002), a world authority on Web metrics, supports the notion that businesses offering both the physical and virtual encounter options tend, in the current market to be more successful, but that both models may also operate independently.

Businesses today are increasingly developing extensively networked online offerings, combined with high levels of interconnectivity between partners, alliances, and associated value-adding organizations. In addition, they are moving their supply chains into high-tech, networked, intelligent solutions—termed service value chains (Barlow-Hills & Sarin, 2003; Van Looey et al., 2003). These service value chains are networked, and thus the service value network is a better terminology.

In 2003, Australia's 'business-to-business' and 'business-to-consumer' e-commerce was valued at $11.3B (Di Gregorio & De Montis, 2003), and it was growing rapidly. It ranked fifth in the world regarding its potential to use the Internet economy! At this time, 35% of Australian businesses purchased online, and 89% of Australian businesses were online. Australian businesses (with more than 10 employees) recorded near ubiquitous Internet adoption (Di Gregorio & De Montis, 2003). The Internet has transformed many of Australia's key business and agency functions, including services delivery, customer relationship management, organizational administration, supply chain management, and knowledge (or data) management. In January 2004 over 46 million Web servers worldwide were globally connected to the Internet, with 96% connecting with the browser Internet Explorer. Thus, for many countries like Australia, the opportunity remains to deliver high-value service offerings to virtual business customers.

VIRTUAL SERVICE VALUE NETWORK FRAMEWORK

The business Web site offers a range of customer 'touch-points'. These customer encounter points have several performance and value-effector blocks. These are displayed in the virtual service value network framework, which is displayed in Figure 2.

This e-service encounter environment presents several potential virtual customer services-related weaknesses and several points of research including:

- Amplification effects
- E-services
- The web interface
- Value chain modeling
- Customer targeting
- Information communication technologies
- Bottleneck effects
- Business strategies

These factors are elaborated as follows.

Figure 2. The virtual service value network framework (Source: Hamilton, 2004a)

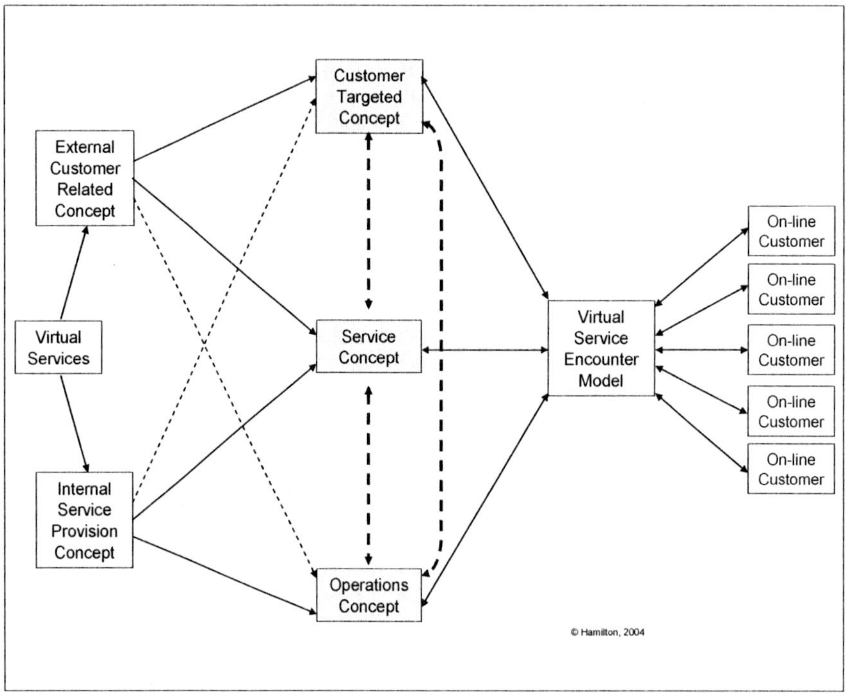

Amplification Effects

The bullwhip effect is defined as the "phenomenon where orders to the suppliers tend to have larger variances than sales to the buyer (demand distortion) and the distortion moves upstream in a amplified form (variance amplification)" (Forrester, 1961; Akkermans & Vos, 2003). Lee, Padmanabhan, and Whang (1997) consider customer ordering as a lumpy occurrence to which the supplier responds. Schmenner (1995) theorized that fast, evenflow could explain productivity gains in manufacturing settings, and that even flows were achievable when the variability in supply chain was reduced. He also noted that tight quality control reduced negative amplification effects. Finch (2003) states: "A key to eliminating the bullwhip effect and a key to any supply chain management effort is an increase in 'information' supplied by business to their suppliers." Thus the upstream amplification (or bullwhip) effects may be reduced where a Web site delivers more efficient, more direct, targeted, more uniform, information access pathways between the service value network and the customer. Improved information flows delivering manageable amounts of filtered, most relevant information to the customer may deliver one solution.

E-Service Effects

Many market forces influence the development of the service value networks. There is an ever-present economic imperative to reduce IT costs, while increasing both the business value and impact of this IT suite. Many businesses cannot afford high degrees of IT customization, and indeed this may not always be necessary—consider a mass user situation like online airline bookings. Hence size and capital remain limiting factors. Timelines to move to online service value network solutions also vary.

A true service value network integrates all aspects of its business's service supply chain—internal and external in an intelligent, coordinated manner. It then interrogates the relevant data and delivers business-specific intelligence that matches the demands of the customer, again reducing inefficiencies. This area remains one with great scope for further research and development. Various third-party logistics solutions have been developed to integrate these areas with those of other businesses, delivering new strategies, solutions, and competitive advantage.

Web Site Effects

Incorporating software programs that query the available database information for apparently 'intelligent' solutions to customer requests may be offered.

The intelligent Web site acts similarly to an intelligent, inquisitive, reasoned, language-sensitive search engine, capable of taking in customer requests by voice, e-mail, image, 'search-for ... ', and the like. Artificial intelligence, knowledge management, and fuzzy logic principles are then applied to determine efficient, appropriate business-specific solutions.

The resulting 'intelligent' Web site processes may reduce the need to revisit and reinterrogate databases, and may reduce the non-productive, time-consuming, information-seeking workload requirements on the service supply chains. Significant, tangible, and intangible cost reductions (less non-productive Web site activities) may be achievable. Less demands, per initiative, per customer, may reduce the information transmission strain across the global communications networks, and may reduce negative customer sentiment. Such solutions may require the flat Web site encounter to move to new three-dimensional approaches (Microsoft, 2004).

Value Chain Modeling Effects

Value chain modeling (Bagchi et al., 2003) has shown how changes in speed, responsiveness, and variability affect operational performance, and may enable the business to perform a solutions scenario like financial impact assessment, cost-benefit analysis, and sensitivity analysis.

Vermijmeren (2003) suggests flexible, intelligent supply chain 'engines' may drive these dynamic supply chains, delivering value, in an efficient manner. Various third-/fourth-party logistics additions offer additional new strategic solutions, scope for competitive advantage, and scope for business development. The incorporation of peripheral added-value options may further improve these offerings.

Customer Targeting Effects

When a customer encounters any aspect of a business, a 'moment of truth' arises, and positive or negative impressions can be generated (Albrecht & Zemke, 1985). In highly customer-responsive business systems, customer contact time may be lessened and sales opportunities may be enhanced. The customer may be an internal customer (working for the business, a participant in the upstream service value network, or an internal services participant in an area such as data processing, engineering, maintenance, accounting, or after-sales service (Davis, Dehning, & Stratopoulos, 2003; Swanson & Davis, 2003), or an external customer (a consumer or one who interacts with and adds value to the business service value network). To service the virtual customer, complete, responsive, flexible, adaptive service value networks often offer the most desirable options.

Finch (2003) argues that delivering quality services involves assurance and empathy. However to deliver service quality across a Web site requires a broadening of the quality dimensions to encapsulate product and service and product dimensions. Thus the customer exhibits a multidimensional impact on the business Web site. Hence, the business must maximize its virtual 'touch-point' appeal, and must develop its virtual management tools (and strategic metrics) set.

Communication and Information Technology Effects

In 2001, the five largest software providers—HP, IBM, Microsoft, Oracle, and Sun—along with a few new entrants, began promoting new standards, new Web services platforms, and new activities environments. Since 1998 the Internet Protocol version 6 (IPv6) software has been encapsulated into operating systems platforms (Comer, 2003). If adopted, IPv6 will allow marketers to segment a business's Web site customers using postcodes, geographical location, and phone numbers. Mobile devices, watches, and clothing are now capable of housing customized information solutions for business.

Third-party software operating on common platforms like Microsoft's '.Net' or IBM's WebSphere platforms may further enhance the virtual environment, delivering savings for business measured as per initiative—lower 'human' and 'capital resource requirements'. In addition, new ways to interpret, interrogate, and deliver customer requirements are unfolding, and highly intelligent, responsive Web sites are emerging. New business strategies, and the nuances of customer wants and needs, are developing and will be incorporated into solutions. Working relationships—like 'e-customer relationship management', trust, loyalty, satisfaction, addressing the dynamics of the industry structure, and cultural fit will become just as important to the customer as the provider's portfolio. Currently, latest computer application tools deliver low-level solutions (not high levels of customization) and are best utilized for standard product type applications. Hence the development (and implementation) of highly customerized and fully operational service value networks is not yet a reality.

Bottleneck Effects

Bottlenecks occur when a limiting resource affects the output level of the entire system. The business-customer Web site encounter as shown in Figure 6 is one such bottleneck! Here, multiple customers search multiple supply chain data sources, for their individual needs and business inefficiencies arise. Finch (2003) suggests bottlenecks may be considered as business constraints.

In the services industry, information is the key ingredient that moves. Some information may be physical in nature—like paperwork—whereas in the manufactured product situation, both information and products move. In both cases information bottlenecks occur.

Efficient design of the Web site (with the use of appropriate technologies) may reduce customer cycle-time (customer Web site access time to source, retrieve, and absorb desired information) (Malcinski, Dominick, & Hartrick, 2001; Cutler & Sterne, 2002), reduce bottlenecks, and possibly improve Web site effectiveness. Thus 'touch-point' information trade-rates between the customer and the business service value network remain dependent variable areas that may be improved.

Business Strategies Effects

Businesses faced with tough competition are devoting greater resources to support their e-business initiatives (Bowman, 2001). Using tools defined by IBM and others, these businesses can prioritize their financial and operational performances, and closely define their e-business and management strategies in multiple-customer environments. These strategies involve the development of semi-intelligent Web sites, and target delivery in four key areas related to the physical and virtual service encounter model. These are:

- **Technical (operations model) factors:** Including communication channels, software and hardware, artificial intelligence, fuzzy logic methodologies, natural language interpretations, Web metrics, Web site flows and information integration, presentation modes (3D screens), and telepresence.
- **Business (service operations model) factors:** Including externals (supply chain partners, peripheral partners, logistics) and internals (business, management, marketing, operations, and strategies).
- **Customer (customer targeting model) factors:** Grouped initially in technographic segments, then cyber-segmented further to eventually allow individual targeting.
- **Revenue-generator factors:** Including sales, fees, charges, advertising, partnerships, and franchises.

BUSINESS-CUSTOMER ENCOUNTER

The business-customer encounter now defined as a key to delivering individually required services to the individual customer may be further modeled by considering the information blocks contributing to actual encounter. Three main service dimensional blocks exist within the virtual service value encounter. These are: the business-related upstream strategic dimensions, the performance encounter dimensions, and the downstream customer-demanded value dimensions. Each block comes under the influence of the fourth block—the external environment. This model is displayed as Figure 3.

The close relation between the physical and virtual business-customer encounters means that service value networks have applications to the

Figure 3. Virtual service network encounter model (Source: Hamilton, 2004a)

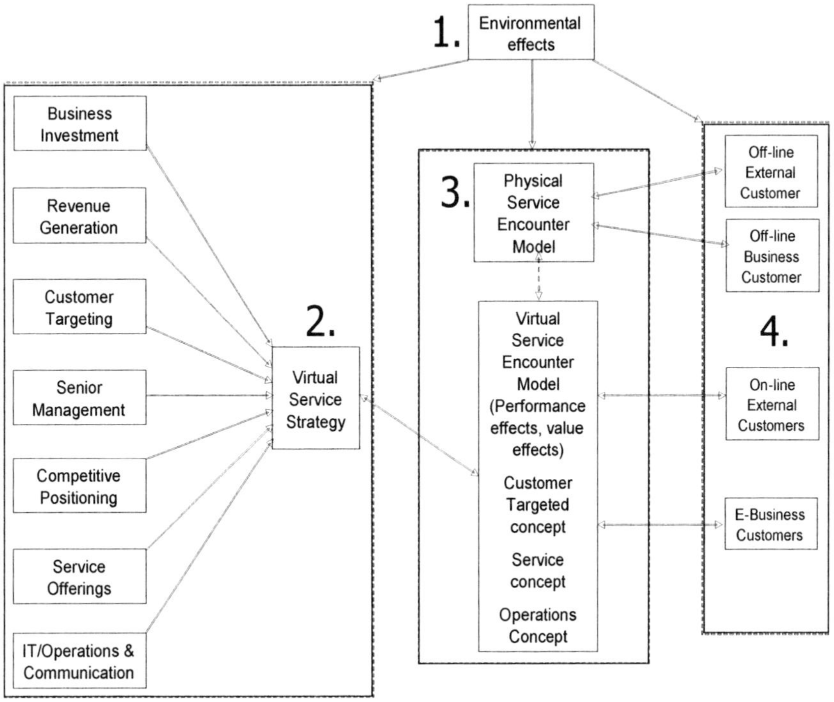

physical (tangible) 'bricks-and-mortar' service value network encounters and to the virtual (intangible) online, e- or m-business applications. In all cases (internal or external access), the business-customer encounter utilizes the same service value network IT-connected Web site structures. To ensure value is created at the virtual customer 'touch-point', the virtual service encounter (or Web interface) should be managed effectively and efficiently. Various managerial dimensions in relation to this service encounter are defined from the virtual service network encounter model.

The Strategy Dimensions

The strategy of the business has a vital connection to the virtual service encounter. If the strategy is one of low service integration, then the business will not be delivering high levels of value-added service, but rather will deliver more standard service offerings.

Investment Dimensions

The investment available may influence the degree of service offered. For example, the business may not be able to afford fully integrated services or be able to accept multiple access modes from mobile devices like phones and PDAs. The business must determine tangibles like how much it should invest; how it may optimize its financial benefits and minimize its costs; how it measures and values its information, and its customer servicing; what standard payment mechanisms it will accept; and under what standardized system. Sterne (2002) suggests other intangible finance measures must also be determined, including the delivery of customer satisfaction, importance, success, speed of sourcing, trends, and best practice. Other core business finance strategy parameters like supplier base reduction, long-term relationships, communication channels, logistics, and supplier involvement remain embedded within this dimension.

Revenue Generation Dimensions

The virtual service encounter generates its tangible financial measures from a diverse range of strategies, including sales, fees, charges, advertising, partnerships, business-customer connectivity, and the like. Intangible measures, like additional sales due to value-adds, add yet another dimension.

Customer Targeting Dimensions

Customer knowledge and data capture remains crucial to delivering appropriate services. Site personalization and high levels of recognition may enable the business to enlist its affiliates and jointly target the customer. It may also identify new markets. The service network customer encounter dimensions include the internal business-to-business customers and the external business-to-end-users (or customers). Frohlich and Westbrook (2002) have researched some internal business-to-business customer effects, but the business-to-consumer dyad has not been empirically studied (Chen & Paulraj, 2004).

Senior Management Dimensions

The business may be an innovator (like eBay.com), an early adopter (like RealEstate.com), a follower (like Zuji.com), or even a bandwagon copier (like many government departments). In today's highly competitive global environment, many models exist, but the business must maintain some points of difference, or risk being out-competed. The executive management team must understand the business environment and respond to its strategic imperatives. They set and manage framework(s), including time, flexibility, service levels, investment levels, dependability, opportunity, long-term partnerships, and control systems, to ensure the operations of the business remain competitive in the marketplace.

Figure 4. Customer performance via the service business Web site (Source: Hamilton, 2004b)

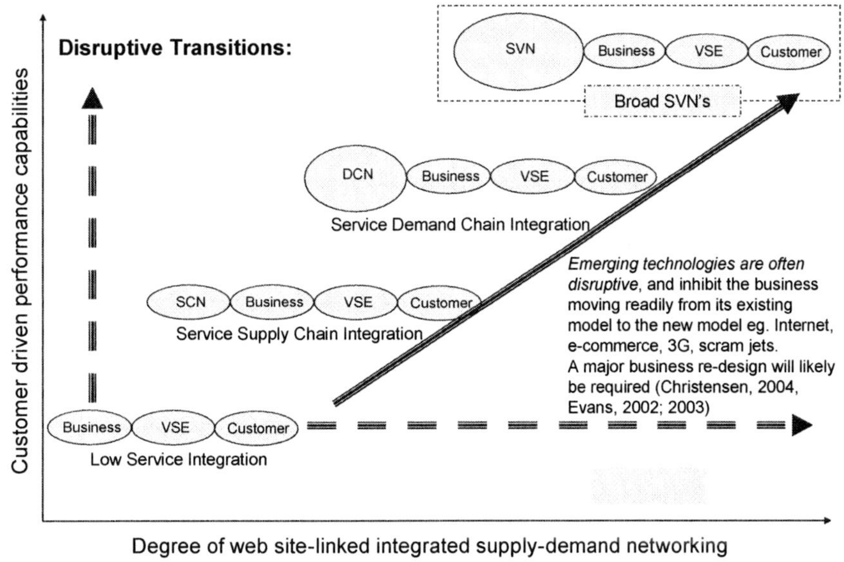

Competitive Positioning Dimensions

The business must be responsive to change (and to changes in the environment). This measure of business strategic positoning must cater for constant adjustments to the needs of its customers. The simplest strategy, shown in Figure 4, is of low service integration. Here, little or no Web-based networked integration, upon request, delivers standard service offerings from the business across the Web site interface to the customer. The second strategy (service supply chain integration) binds the virtual service business with its supply chain network, and delivers a higher level of virtual delivery—more targeted to the customer, and performance related. Here, the networked supply chain is capable of efficiently delivering its standard products, or a standard option variation, to the customer, in a timely manner.

The third strategy (service demand chain integration) further ties the virtual service business with customer-generated requests, delivering a demand chain-driven operation, where customer requests are evaluated, and where possible, a customized service solution is delivered. The fourth strategy (broad service value networks) allows the service business to operate strategically as a full service value network level, delivering agile responses to customer requests—via information sourcing across its business networks, and further complementing these services with additional value-added solutions and appropriate, externally sourced options. This requires high levels of customer-targeted performance capabilities.

Service Offerings Dimensions

The business may offer levels of service based on low service integration, service supply chain integration, service demand chain integration, or broad service networks. The levels of nctworking, agility, flexibility, customer targeting, and business supply chain focusing used vary depending on the choice of strategy. Virtual service value networks provide the most sophisticated customer service/product encounter.

IT, Operations, and Communication Dimensions

The technical areas of software, knowledge management, business intelligence, and communications must be capable of delivering the demanded customer requests, of interpreting the request and delivering sensible added value complementary features to the customer. Peer-to-peer processing may be involved.

The Virtual Service Encounter Dimensions

The strategy of the business has a vital connection to the virtual service encounter. If the strategy is one of low service integration, then the business will not be delivering high levels of value-added service, but rather will deliver more standard service offerings. The service value chain network virtual encounter dimensions house the Web site and its visible interface. This interface offers customer touch-points whereby the customer may interact, and may seek (or demand) services from the business.

Web Site Performance and Value Dimensions

Many businesses' Web site solutions deliver a virtual global presence, but do not attempt to add value (Evans, 2002), nor do they recognize customer or customer group requirements (McQueeney, 2003). The modern business services Web site is designed to offer a wide range of business options and selected corporate information. Key business-driven performance measures included volume flexibility, scheduling flexibility, on-time delivery, delivery reliability, quality, cost reductions, communication, customer complaint handling, and customer satisfaction. Other researchers add additional business performance measures including profitability, firm size, operational management experience, information delivery rate, reputation, and agility to the equation.

Web Site IT/Communications/ Operations Dimensions

Where high levels of uniform IT systems, integration, communication, performance, and sophisticated assessment and delivery exist across the entire business and its partnering networks, the business may approximate, or achieve, a service value chain network status.

The operational IT constructs permeate every aspect of the supply chain, transforming it and the way information exchange activities are delivered. Today, a lack of sophisticated computer application tools limits the implementation of highly customized solutions (approximating one-on-one customerization). In some cases highly networked business partners with specialist 'intelligent' analysis, interpretation, retrieval, and collation tools may approximate, or achieve, a service value chain network status. Such networks may include improved personalization, search, and browsing capabilities; multimodal interfaces with speech recognition, pen, and handwriting interfaces; and powerful efficient processes and wireless technologies (Fenn & Linden, 2002).

Web Site Service Dimensions

The performance of the Web site to deliver the desired levels of customer-required services may be affected by:

- **The 'bullwhip' effect**, where orders to the suppliers tend to have larger variances than sales to the business (demand distortion), and the distortion moves back downstream in an amplified form (variance amplification) (Forrester, 1961)

- **The 'bottleneck' effect**, where a limiting resource affects the output level of the entire system (Finch, 2003). For a Web site, information flows may affect overall performance, or the timeframe or capability to deliver the desired levels of customer required services.

Other measures include supplier number reduction, long-term relationships, levels of inter-business partnering, communication, and supplier involvement. Performance measures within these areas include: speed flexibility, agility (variability), management of alliances and logistics (Foss & Stone, 2001), supply chain efficiencies (including bottlenecks and bullwhip effects), lifecycle and innovation decisions, demand-driven activities, multiplicity of partners, and dynamically configured integrated networks (McCullough Johnston, 2001).

Customer Targeted Concept Dimensions

When a customer interfaces with any aspect of a business, a 'moment of truth' arises, and positive or negative impressions can be generated. In highly customer responsive business systems, customer contact time may be lessened and sales opportunities may be enhanced. The customer may be an internal customer (working for the business, a participant in the upstream service value chain network, or an internal services participant in an area such as data processing, engineering, maintenance, accounting, after-sales service) or an external customer (a consumer or one who interacts with and adds value to the business service value chain network). Parasuraman, Zeithaml, and Berry (1985) suggest that delivering quality services may involve both assurance and empathy. Sound Web site service quality should encapsulate delivery of all aspects of the service dimensions requested.

The Customer

Within this virtual Web site environment, the customer is seeking efficient, simple, effective, timely interactions with the business environment. Parasuraman et al. (1985) suggested consumers judged companies. Others are critical of this, but "reliability, responsiveness, assurance tangibles and empathy" help provide a valuable focus, while others add loyalty (and its dimensions).

Customer-perceived satisfaction levels are often influenced by the business's response(s). These may include: ease of use, degree of customization, intuitive pathways, allowable downloads, value-add offerings, recognition, price, delivery, promotion, after-sales service, and the like. The business is seeking to interpret customer requests, search its possibilities from its available sources, and deliver to the customer its best possible solution(s) in an efficient, effective, and timely manner.

The virtual service customers reside within two categories—the internal business-to-business customer category, and the end-user external business customer category (using the business service offering to add value to its operation).

E-Business Customers

The e-business customer demands its product/service requests be delivered with short lead times, on time, and every time be consistently of high quality (fault free), reliable, and supported through excellent channels and after-sales service.

External End-User Customers

The end-user external customer displays a dynamic demand for a greater variety of reliable products, delivered with short lead times (Draaijer, 1992). Customer segmented solutions are required that deliver quality, loyalty, satisfaction, individual solutions, and value adding, and do so in simple, interactive, efficient, effective, and timely ways.

The Physical Service Encounter

The business front office or salesperson deals directly with a customer—on a direct one-to-one relationship. The virtual service encounter should encapsulate Web browser technologies capable of delivering necessary information and other service-related documents to the business front office or salesperson which may then be relayed to the customer.

The Environment

The business is surrounded by and influenced by its environmental uncertainty. This uncertainty arises from a range of areas including demand uncertainty, competitor irregularities and forecasting errors, bandwagon effects ('follow the leader'), technology innovation and change, and the like. Internal business pressures arise from supply uncertainty, production uncertainty, technical uncertainty, and new product/service uncertainty.

SERVICE VALUE NETWORKS AND THE PHARMACEUTICAL INDUSTRY

The virtual service value network model discussed above may now be constructed into an operational model for the pharmacy industry. We use the Australian pharmacy industry for the discussion below.

The service value network in an e-pharmacy setting is hereby defined as a collaborative network of supply chain partners (such as pharmacists, drug companies, distributors, beauty care suppliers, health and natural product suppliers, medical practitioners); sales channels (Web site e-sales, direct over-the-counter sales, and referrals); and operational and network administration personnel, working with and serving the needs of its customers and its online e-customers.

Figure 5 displays a global perspective of the industry and the capabilities required from a service value network. Here a national data storage solution is to be developed that may be accessed by individual stores, store groups, store chains, or e-pharmacies. Development of such a service value network solution requires industry-wide information sharing, and will eventually lead

Figure 5. The service value network—global perspective (Adapted from Anwar & Hamilton, 2005a)

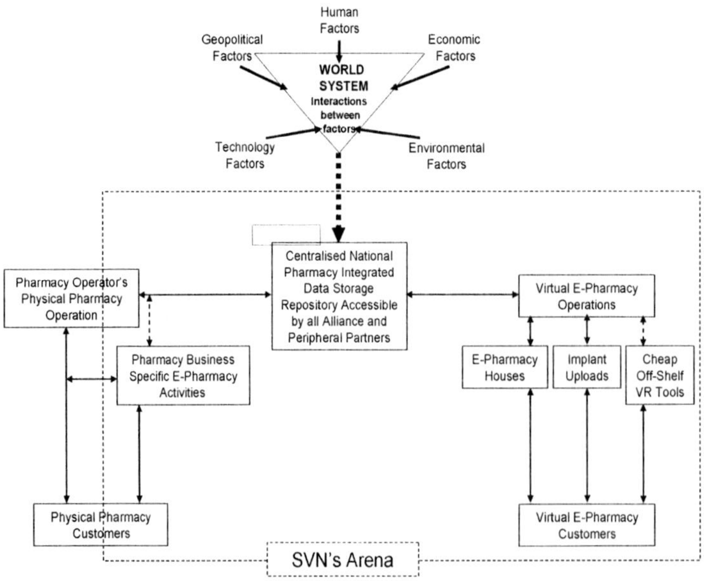

towards cost savings and enhanced value propositions (Hamilton, 2004b, 2005b).

The service value network is designed and managed by a central coordinating group, which in a pharmacy setting might be taken up by the Pharmacy Guild of Australia. Another example resides in the Australian Tourism Industry, where the Australian Tourism Export Council is currently compiling a national database in preparation for linking up its industry partners under a service value network-like framework. The generic service value network model is detailed in the following section.

BUILDING SERVICE VALUE NETWORKS INTO THE PHARMACEUTICAL INDUSTRY

The service value network for the pharmaceutical industry comprises a service-related strategy that drives the three dimensions of the virtual service encounter: the services provision, customer targeting, and the underlying operational IT infrastructures. In turn, the virtual service encounter systems may interface with the physical encounter system. For example, when a sales assistant accesses the pharmacy's databases to fill in the customer prescription details, the sales assistant may also access additional specific drug information—like the last time the customer used such a drug and if it was a successful treatment; safe drug dosages for the customer's body weight; possible complications if consumed with other drugs the customer has purchased or used; alternative, cheaper generic drug options; and the like. If appropriate, this information may then be shared with the customer. To further enhance the dialogue between the business and the customer service value network sourced, service-related value-adding options may include: consumer allowable limits, claim options, delivery options, nearest doctor, hospital, medical insurance options, tax benefits, local preferences, and so forth. The customer may directly access the service value network (via the pharmacy's industry Web site), and may source/request annual tax return data, a doctor's surgery bookings, local hospital information, health and pensioner claims, and the like.

In addition, business intelligence and knowledge/information from suppliers, research, and peripheral sources is stored on a centralized database, and this is accessible by pharmacies. Such data collation allows the customer to access a variety of pharmacy stores to obtain his or her prescriptions and medications. In addition, as stock items are consumed, or damaged, or have passed their 'use-by date', additional orders are logged with suppliers and delivery systems are informed, so that accurate planning, without bullwhip effects, is ensured. Pharmacy suppliers and logistics providers may access the service value network to facilitate production and direct shipping of products to pharmacy sales outlets—city based or regionally based. Thus supply-related efficiencies and net cost-of-delivery savings are generated. Finally, the service value network is also interconnected into other medical services—hospitals, doctors, ambulance services, police, and the like—thereby creating an efficient, better-informed, integrated medical services information network. Under agreement, peripheral partners including health and ambulance insurance funds, medical researchers, and the like may share information across some general data fields of the service value network. To build such a system requires a key stating point, and in Australia this initiator is the Pharmacy Guild of Australia. Research currently underway is seeking to align the industry with its customers at both a global and a local level, and to deliver increased performance and greater perceived customer value, and to do so in a more cost-efficient manner.

Interactions within the service value network can be viewed from an internal business perspective among supply chain partners in delivering and fulfilling customer orders, for example, a pharmacist replenishing out-of-stock items. On the other hand, the service value network responds

Figure 6. Service value network (Adapted from Hamilton, 2005a)

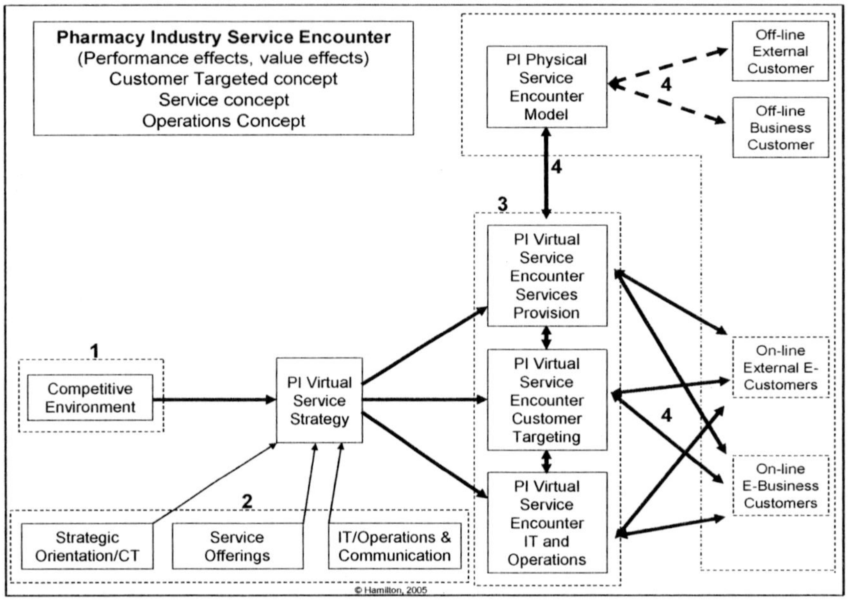

to external customers such as a local nursing home initiating bulk drugs supply directly via the service value network. Both internal and external perspectives need to be considered separately, as they need to be aligned in order to accurately respond to customer needs. The Generic Service Value Network Model is displayed in Figure 6.

SERVICE VALUE NETWORK DIMENSIONS

The various dimensions of the service value network can be grouped as follows:

- The impact of competitive environment on the industry
- The dimensions of it/communications and operations, integrated customer targeting systems, and service offerings in determining an industry strategy as set (typically by the service value network coordinating group)
- Dimensions of the service delivery system within a virtual network, and the impact of virtual network delivery on potential service performance
- The customer targeting employed by the industry

To empirically measure the necessary parameters needed to develop a cohesive service value network approach across the pharmacy industry, these four dimensions require measures. Tables 1-4 summarize the relevant measures.

Table 1 captures the competitive environment, as influenced by external forces. Strategic decisions like becoming a first mover, differentiating, focusing on specifically defined niches, being the low-cost provider, or being the dominant player interplay with this field. The industry needs to develop the agility to adapt quickly to governmental rule/regulation changes. In the pharmaceutical industry this may relate to, for example, new reporting and prescription regulations. The service value network also needs to house a capability to respond to changes in levels of competition. In Australia the introduction of pharmacies within low-cost retail chain stores/supermarket chains is

Table 1. Competitive environment

Competitive Environment	
Dimension	**Operational Characteristic**
Political	Speed to adopt governmental rule / regulation changes
Economic	Capability to respond to competition changes; Efficient cost conscious scaling of operations
Environment	Respond to competitive changes; Respond to new innovations
Cultural	Cultural monitoring of Cultural targeting
Technology	Industry wide; Networked solutions; Latest offerings; Quick accurate responses

Table 2. Inputs to industry strategy

Inputs to Industry Strategy	
Dimension	**Operational Characteristic**
Corporate	POS related Initiatives; Market positioning; Degree of service networking
Competitive	IT capability; Customer understanding; Range of service offerings
Financial	Networks; Customer knowledge; Services offerings
Customer Targeting	Customer demands met; Communicate culturally; Datamine stored information
Service	Industry wide; Networked solutions; Latest offerings; Quick accurate responses
Technology/IT	Customer delivery; Customer analysis; Customer services
Environment	Reactive to business changes; Reactive to customer changes; Updating continuous

Table 3. Virtual network and service performance

Virtual Network and Service Performance	
Dimension	**Operational Characteristic**
Cost	IT networking cost; Customer servicing cost
Quality	Internal information sorting; External customer product delivery
Dependability	Reliable business networks, Reliable customer services
Flexibility / Agility	Capability to change; Uniqueness capability
Response time	Ability to service customer
Personalization	Ability to individually target customer; Ability to individually respond to a customer
Convenience	Multiple customer access modes; Multiple customer response modes
Style fashion	Ability to deliver added value solutions
Ethics	Security and privacy of business information; Security and privacy of customer information
Technology	Strategically operationalize latest technologies

Table 4. Dimensions influencing elevated service delivery

Virtual Network and Service Performance	
Dimension	**Operational Characteristic**
Cost	22.IT and operational networking cost; 23.Customer servicing cost;
Quality	24.Internal information sorting; 25.External customer product delivery
Dependability	27.Reliable business operational networks, 28.Reliable customer services
Flexibility / Agility	29.Capability to change; 30.Uniqueness capability
Response time	31.Ability to service customer
Personalization	Ability to individually target customer; 32.Ability to individually respond to a customer
Convenience	33.Multiple customer access modes; 34.Multiple customer response modes
Style fashion	35.Ability to deliver added value solutions
Ethics	36.Security and privacy of business information; Security and privacy of customer information
Technology	37.Strategically operationalize latest technologies

imminent. In addition, the service value network requires the ability to create and work in supplier partnerships to either capture particular capabilities or to benefit from operational scale effects. As the health care market is growing rapidly because of an aging population, scale effects may become increasingly important. An example is the integration of specific health insurance coverage information with pharmaceutical prescriptions. Finally, latest technological evolutions must build alignment with each customer and with the competitive requirements, and must respond to customer demands through its various response channels.

Table 2 houses the three major classes of inputs to the service strategy: the underlying IT and operations/communications infrastructure, the customer targeting system, and the service offerings to be delivered.

Table 3 displays the dimensions of the virtual network and its service performance. The network dimension of the embedded connectivity of SC partners through varying sales channels implies that delays, incorrect information, and/or security breaches can have a leveraged negative effect on the overall service experience. Alternatively, a synchronous delivery by all partners involved may create a unique competitive edge through elevated service offerings. The quality dimension of providing relevant and targeted information, dependability of the service offering by each SC partner, flexibility to incorporate new updates from suppliers (like product information), agility to deploy new hardware/software applications, quick response time to information requests, ease of access, security with built-in privacy protection levels—these are all factors that enable or impair service delivery in a service value network framework.

Table 4 houses the resulting service offerings. These may include: contacting an online pharmacist via a video phone or videoconference or teleconference, a personal chat room, e-mail, or SMS; an evaluation of medical and cost alternatives to a prescription; a 'side-effects' report; a home-delivery service; a doctor–pharmacy direct link so that your prescription could be ready when you arrive, or be home delivered; or a database list of localities of nearby doctors and their current available appointment times. Other customer-specific attributes/knowledge bases of a pharmaceutical service value network also apply to Table 4, for example: linking of secured aspects of individual customer personal information to medical, hospital, ambulance, tax, insurance, and banking information to enable a full emergency response service related to a car accident injury that required hospital intervention.; allowing direct computer access by local doctors, thereby guaranteeing prescription communication accuracy and delivery or delivering personal prescription information (or a purchase); offering new knowledge to the customer about a purchase; and performing all levels of related interactions including drug recognition, reaction time, insurance ramifications, deals, or best price.

These measures are then teased out into two relevant questionnaire sets, each of approximately 100 questions and requiring approximately 10 to 15 minutes to complete. These survey questions are blocked to determine business-customer alignment, business performance, and customer value effects.

PHARMACY INDUSTRY: SERVICE VALUE NETWORK DEVELOPMENT

Thus, major dimensions of a generic service value network approach to an e-pharmacy-based services support strategy are identifiable (Hamilton, 2004a, 2004b, 2005a; Hamilton & Selen, 2005).

Identified service value network dimensions may be utilized to research and deliver a new approach to developing industry-wide solutions within the services industries. The pharmacy industry in Australia has been used as the test bed for this service value network theoretical approach. Here, the entire industry was analyzed from both the business and customer perspective. Answers to performance, alignment, and customer value were derived. Key investigative blocks, house resource-based, and superior-performance strategic areas enable competitive resource-based advantages to be reconstructed into efficient and/or effective market customer segment offerings (Hunt & Morgan, 1996). Where these resources were deemed valuable, hard to imitate, and not easily substituted, sustainable competitive advantage was more likely (Barney, 1991), and hence was deemed important to this industry's strategic solutions set.

Some Australian pharmacies have approached their intangible resources as a means to deliver long-term or sustainable competitive advantage. Lumpkin and Dess (1996) suggest an entrepreneurial approach may deliver competitive advantage, and suggest this entrepreneurial approach is an appropriate strategy in today's business environment. They use innovativeness, proactiveness, autonomy, competitive aggressiveness, risk taking, and employee motivation to capture such intangibles. Escrig-Tena and Bou-Liusar (2005) suggest a competency-based approach guides the development of competitive advantage, but acknowledge that the unobservables (or intangibles) affect such empirical research. Grant (1996) adopts a knowledge-based approach to deliver business uniqueness. Still others argue an evolutionary process exists where the business adapts to the environment, and changes via a stochastic process of searching for new and more beneficial routines (Winter, 1995). Jambulingam, Kathuria, and Doucette (2005) use various within-industry clusters to classify these pharmacy sectors and test the entrepreneurial orientation of these sectors. They consider the environment, organizational factors, and performance outcomes within this framework. Wright and Taylor (2003) consider inter-organizational knowledge as important and define innovative culture, information quality, accountability, strategic connection, change readiness, and clarity of response as key measures.

Chang Lee, Lee, and Kang (2005) consider knowledge utilization, accumulation, internalization, sharing, creation, understanding, and information to be important. Mayer and Davis (1999) consider trust to be another vital ingredient. Greenwald and Kahn (2005) consider all strategy must be drawn down to a local level. Swaminthan and Tayur (2003) believe decision technologies and bundling of resources can deliver competitive advantage. Chenhall (2005) believes strategic priorities must be delivered to customers offering high-quality, low-price, uniqueness, customerized, fast, and dependable service; effective availability and service; and meeting the customer's needs. He believes integrative strategic performance, strategic alignment, and organizational information and knowledge are all key business factors that must be developed. Abdinnour-Helm, Chaparro, and Farmer (2005) consider Web sites and their servicing to customers. They develop Web site customer satisfaction measures that also warrant consideration. Piccoli, Brohman, Watson, and Parasuraman (2004) also consider factors influencing business service dimensions and customer needs.

Supply chain integration also delivers market and product/services strategies that affect business performance (Narasimhan & Kim, 2005). Diversification is suggested as one means to deliver performance. Other researchers (Hamilton, 2004a, 2005a; Hamilton & Selen, 2005) have considered services, operations, IT business intelligence and knowledge provision systems, customer target marketing, and environmental considerations as vital feeds into the business-customer encounter.

Mapping Business and Customer Contact Parameters

The above factors may be drafted into a possible initial pharmacy business competitive requirements questionnaire set that encapsulated the relative level(s) of service integration offered. A customer requirements questionnaire is developed to determine the customer's needs, wants, and economic value requirements, and tested using a pre-pilot sample of pharmacies and customers. Aligned question blocks mapping business deliverables to customer perceived needs, wants, desires, and economically acceptable price tags may be used to develop suitable industry-wide questionnaires. After pilot testing in the marketplace, survey validation and reliability tests, and final survey instrument refinement, the business perspectives (business performance and customer perceived value), and business-customer dyad perspectives, may be tested across the industry according to the measures outlined in Table 5.

Business Perspectives

Existing pharmacy models may be analyzed to determine relative points of synergy and key points of difference. Existing pharmacy models include:

- An independent or owner operator pharmacy (max of 3 pharmacies)
- A member of a small pharmacy chain (3 to 10 pharmacies)
- A member of a large pharmacy chain (>10 pharmacies; typically 100-350 stores)
- A mass merchandiser pharmacy—like 'priceline' with diverse ranges of cosmetics, giftware, and food items in conjunction with a pharmacy dispensary
- A fully online pharmacy model—like e-pharmacy
- A hospital pharmaceutical outpatient dispensary
- A large 600m2 plus, price leader pharmacy warehouse
- A pharmacy prescriptions outlet attached to a medical center

Each model offers points-of-difference, ranging from independence to degrees of group purchasing and delivery, to 'bricks-and-clicks' pharmacy/online operations, through to pure online-type operations. These various models

Table 5. Aligned survey instrument questionnaire blocks

Table 5a - Business Performance – Value Perspectives	
Business Analysis Fields	**Customer Analysis Fields**
1. **Competitive positioning:** industry, innovative/entrepreneurial, positioning, risk/response	1. **Competitive positioning:** industry, management, strategy, innovation
2. **Customer targeting:** recognition, guarantees, customerization, accessibility, feel	2. **Customer targeting:** cost, quality, delivery/availability by industry
3. **Services/products offered:** brands/generics, value additions, comparisons, information/training, latest alternatives	3. **Services/products:** reliability, range/knowledge offered by industry
4. **IT deliverables:** degree of complete networking, data analysis, logistics/shipping, website, interactivity/recognition	4. **IT used:** Industry Web site /browser access, business-information /purchase option
5. **Operational delivery:** supply networks, products/services / after sales services, Web site, distributed databases access/mined information, staff, values additions/fee-for-service activities	5. **Services/products delivery:** fast, accurate, consistent, responsive, empathetic, quality assured, technically supported, trained delivers, low cost

Table 5. continued

Table 5b - Business-Customer Dyad Perspectives	
Business Analysis Fields	**Customer Analysis Fields**
1. **Customer monitoring:** visitors/purchasers, sales-per-day, prescriptions-per-day, loyalty, perceived value, revenue-per-sale	1. **Customer satisfaction:** services offered, product ranges, IT information, expectations, innovativeness, new ideas
2. **Web site usage:** ordering/purchasing, information, communications; time, reliability, accuracy and effectiveness	2. **Web site access/usage options:** accredited, save time, source contacts, product knowledge/information, order/purchase, check delivery, retrieve personal data
3. **Innovation offered:** advice sessions/customer reports (tax, expenses, drug consumption/side effects, risks, health), remote access, peripheral services, health management	3. **Innovation:** information, new fields, services/support /follow-ups, hazards, evaluations
4. **Value to customer:** needs met, wants met, customer importance level, added value feedback, additional information	4. **Customer value:** convenience, experienced efficient consultation, payments, service, information and access, relationship strength, safeguards, personalization
5. **Economic value:** market share, value-per customer, visits-per time, net earnings	5. **Economic value:** scaled quality, scaled reliability, scaled servicing skills, scaled servicing time, scaled accessibility, scaled pricing

may house synergies, including shared marketing, group innovations, and joint Australian Pharmacy Guild research activities.

Investigation of the eight active pharmacy models highlights business-customer perceived relative industry competitive positioning. This survey approach captures innovative/entrepreneurial approaches, competitive positioning strategies, and relative risk/response strategies.

Jambulingham et al. (2005) use risk taking, innovativeness, proactiveness, competitive aggressiveness, and autonomy as a key part of their pharmacy industry competitiveness scaling classification. These strategic components are captured as follows:

- The tendency to take risks
- The experimentation with new services
- The approach to challenges
- The sourcing of new opportunities in response to challenging market conditions
- The direct response to the competitive maneuvers of rivals
- The new business opportunities identified by employees

Australian pharmacies operate in a competitive world, and this affects their delivered business model and strategies. This environment should also be captured locally (Greenwald & Kahn, 2005). Immediate degree of competition, growth prospects, and competitor analysis provide such a framework. These measures are included as follows:

- The degree of local market competition between pharmacies
- The prospects for business growth in the current business environment

- The projected market growth for local competing pharmacies

The degree of responsiveness to changes in the competitive environment is tested in the pharmacy situation using correctness, completion, adaptivity, and management (Jambulingam et al., 2005). These are measured using:

- The degree of emphasis to follow formal procedures and rules
- The degree of emphasis to get things done
- The ability to adapt to changes in the business environment
- The accepted management style in handling ambiguous situations.

These measurement tools, along with the demographic measures—age group; respondent role/occupation; country where live; pharmacy access days and time; annual turnover; gender; and pharmacy postcode, locality, and population center size served—are used to analyze the respondent business surveys and its customer surveys.

The business surveys capture detailed strategic, competitive, performance, and customer alignment information (Hamilton, 2004a, 2004b, 2005a, 2005b; Hamilton & Selen, 2005). Targeting strategies deliver business points of competitiveness (Hamilton, 2005a). These competitive strategies require the business components of recognition, guarantees, customerization, accessibility, and feel to be aligned with those of the customer—cost, quality, delivery/availability by industry. Such customer targeting strategies are captured by:

- The customer response—both needs and wants
- The offer of guaranteed, high-quality brands
- The offer of cheaper generic alternatives to guaranteed, high-quality brands
- The delivery of individual attention
- The recognition of a customer's name, and the offer of personalized value-adding service(s)
- The delivery of customer service requests within timeframe(s) specified
- The lowest cost provider
- The convenience of 24-hours-a-day, 7-days-a-week, 365-days-a-year service

The services and products offered are measured using brands/generics, value additions, comparisons, information/training, and latest alternatives. These are mapped against the customer's services and product requirements of reliability, range, and explanatory information (knowledge) offered by industry. These important services and products are captured by:

- The medical and health product range offered to meet customer needs
- The general product range offered to customers—including generic (low-cost) solutions
- The specific, product-related customer information offered
- The formal annual staff training
- The supply chain networks for medical and health products

The IT deliverables and information flows are captured by the degree of complete networking, data analysis, logistics and shipping, Web site interactivity, and IT recognition IT software used (Narasimhan & Kim, 2002; Swaminthan & Tayur, 2003). These are mapped against customer industry Web site/browser access, business-information, and purchase options, and are measured by:

- The software programs used to operationalize in-store network services
- The standardized network software programs used to connect to our pharmacy group's computer networks
- The national networked pharmacy group database measures collected and shared with the group to develop better solutions and cost savings

- The degree of integrated networking with key suppliers, facilitating reduced stocking levels, automatic reordering, and shipping
- The web site delivering extended customer services and sales
- The pharmacy operating as an e-business model operation

The industry operational delivery systems of supply networks, products/services/after-sales services, partnering Web sites, distributed databases, stored and mined business information, staff, value additions, and fee-for-service activities are matched against customer-related requirements concerning services and/or product delivery. Fast, accurate, consistent, responsive, empathetic, quality-assured, technically supported, trained delivers, and low-cost options are included.

Business-Customer Dyad Perspectives

The business-customer dyad encompasses the vital delivery of services from business to customers and vice-versa (Frohlich & Westbrook, 2002; Chen & Paulraj, 2004; Jambulingam et al., 2005; Chenhall, 2005). This encounter has been rarely quantitatively investigated. This extensive study seeks to open new understandings of this vital business alignment.

The business monitors its customer encounters using visitors and their purchasers, sales-per-day, prescriptions-per-day, loyalty, perceived value, and revenue-per-sale. These features are mapped against the customer satisfaction indicators of services offered, product ranges available (Chang Lee et al., 2005), IT information accessible, customer expectations, perceived innovativeness, and new ideas. Business pharmacy monitors include:

- The pharmacy visitor numbers
- The number of sales per day
- The information requests per day or per month
- The prescriptions issued per hour, day, or month
- The loyalty measures like the number of re-visits (or sales) to a customer per unit time
- The customer perceived value in purchases
- Customer satisfaction measures
- The revenue amount per sale

Considering Web site usage, the additional dyad business measures of ordering and purchasing, information, communications, time, reliability, accuracy, and effectiveness are studied in conjunction with customer-related views of business accreditation, time savings, sourcing contacts, product knowledge/information accessibility, simple ordering and purchasing, delivery process monitoring, and personal data retrieval (Abdinnour-Helm et al., 2005). Business Web site operational areas include:

- Online business offerings to customers via an interactive 'e-pharmacist' web site
- Online customer purchases and ordering of government-allowed items
- Greater information and knowledge deliverables throughout the pharmacy group, suppliers, and in response to customer searches
- Effective and efficient retrieval of individual customer pharmacy purchase history.

The business presents various innovations including advice, sessions and customer reports (like tax, expenses, drug consumption/side effects, risks, health), remote access, peripheral services, and health management (Wright & Taylor, 2003; Narasimhan & Kim, 2002). From the customer perspective, information, new fields, services/support/follow-ups, hazards, and evaluations/feedback are measured. Innovative business options may include:

- Additional support documentation to a customer purchase
- Prescription records management

- Health information for patients
- Tax return pharmacy medical purchase history
- Asthma and/or diabetes care management
- In-pharmacy immunization
- Patient consulting and compliance programs
- Blood testing
- Talk to the doctor/pharmacist online
- Phone calls to patients to monitor pharmacotherapy and reminder scripts
- Database connections to local doctor and local health options
- Remote pharmacist advice via phone, computer, pda, or mobile connections
- Drug 'side-effects' reports
- Home delivery services
- Formal evaluation of patients' health risks
- Fees for specialist pharmacy services advice
- Prospective drug utilization reviews
- Daily drug lot packaging

The business targets delivering value to its customers by meeting their collective needs and wants; it prioritizes customers via their importance level, offers added-value feedback, and additional supporting information.

Customer-Related Perspectives

The customers' perceived value is seen as consultation advice, online or in-store payments, suitable access to their desired service(s), the strength of their relationship, safeguards regarding their personal information, and the way the service delivery is personalized and 'customerized' (or individually targeted) (Hamilton, 2004a). The business determines its customers' importance by measuring their success in:

- Meeting the needs of our customers
- Adding its database product knowledge and customer details to each customer purchase
- Ensuring its customer's desires always come first, ahead of the pharmacy's
- Anticipating and responding to our customer's evolving new wants (or new expectations)
- Giving the latest information and solutions to every customer enquiry prescription, or possible purchase

The business measures its economic value via market share, value per customer, visits per time, and net earnings (Jambulingham et al., 2005). From the customer perspective, economic value delivers quality, reliability, servicing skills, time efficiency, accessibility, and acceptable pricing. Business measures include monitoring.

- Improvements in market share
- The growth in the value of each customer's total purchase value per visit
- Employee sales per day and per month
- Improvements in earnings

Two survey data sets (business and customer) analyzed predominantly by factor analysis and structured equation modeling show relative degrees of alignment. Business performance and customer value may thus be modeled, and resultant statistical equations may be interpreted and used to build customer-targeting business solutions. Hence the industry may utilize such measurements to optimize its customer-delivered performance relative to its service offerings, operations, marketing and sales, IT/communications, positioning, and value-adding offerings.

Such solutions allow the pharmacy industry business models to reassess and map new customer-targeted pathways towards enhanced competitive positions. Data analysis to date indicates that an industry-wide service value network approach is capable of delivering the necessary connectivity, storage, and retrieval infrastructure requirements to ensure this industry remains highly competitive, and a build solution is currently being mapped, with business intelligence tools already under development.

This industry-wide analysis shows that the pharmacy industry in Australia currently operates across multiple business performance levels, typified by degrees of technological use and service encounter. The lowest level of service encounter is typified by a busy individual store with little or no computerized operations, and constitutes the oldest and least-value-adding model. The next level of customer interactivity captures those pharmacies with degrees of supply chain inter-connectivity, and some computerized operations that engage aspects of their supply chain and logistics systems. The third level of service encounter is exemplified by pharmacy groups like e-Pharmacy. This operation offers a 'bricks-and-clicks' solution (order online or off-line and have non-prescription requirements home delivered with prescriptions available at the nearest e-Pharmacy store). The e-Pharmacy solution offers a targeted customer response to a business service request. It utilizes sophisticated, well-integrated information systems. This model updates and data mines its customer databases, and delivers focused responses to individual customer demands. The fourth level of service is the industry-wide service value network. Here, fully integrated computerized solutions are intelligently delivered to the customer, via the serving staff, the pharmacist, or via direct online customer engagement. The service value network is continually mined via its business intelligence tools to deliver the most appropriate customerized (one-on-one) business-customer solutions possible from its systems. It also delivers elevated customer services incorporating additional value solutions like medicine side effects information, suggested dosage procedures, and the like. The service value network model is a complex solution, and requires substantial industry-wide knowledge sharing and reengineering. It also involves making a disruptive business transition from the simpler, less complex service models (Christensen, 2004; Evans, 2002) to a new dynamic service value network pharmacy model involving high levels of business-customer interactivity.

The service value network is a 'smart business network' solution for the pharmacy industry. It delivers a dynamic, highly competitive, agile set of solutions, which are projected to keep its business members in a strong position regarding its key potential domestic competitors like supermarkets, hospital chains, and medical services. These business sectors are all keen to enter the pharmacy marketspace, but they currently lack government approval and the market intelligence to compete directly.

Thus an industry-wide business and customer research process sets the framework and knowledge-base from which the pharmacy industry may plan its own unique forward-looking competitive pathways. It delivers industry-specific knowledge concerning competitiveness and future competitiveness, strategic alignment, higher industry performance capabilities, and their delivery; a deep understanding of value-adding solutions and their relevance, customer satisfaction measures, and customer perceived value measures; and finally, delivers the ingredients from which an aligned, high performance service value network may be constructed—one that is capable of delivering the needs, wants, desires, and value for money solutions the customer desires.

FUTURE TRENDS IN SERVICE VALUE NETWORKS

This service industry, research-based, industry-wide approach to enhancing business performance, business-customer alignment, and customer value is directly applicable to other service-based industries like the financial services sector, the real estate sector, the medical sector, the education sectors, the accountancy sector, and the like. With further refinement, this model is also predicted to also be applicable to service industries in other countries, and possibly to polycentric or geocentric service companies.

Example of an Australian Future Service Value Network

The financial services sector in Australia is closely allied with many industries, including the real estate industry. Currently, linkages between the financial services sector and real estate industry are largely informal, and beyond the control of the financial services sector industry.

The existing online real estate model is expensive and outdated. It houses all the off-line costs and numerous inefficient small-scale real estate solutions. In addition, two real estate sectors exist—the corporate and the retail sectors. It is possible to merge the corporate real estate market (focusing on its business-to-business customers) and the retail real estate market (focusing on its business-to customer markets) under a *financial services sector—real estate service value network gateway.* This model is displayed in Figure 7.

These two real estate sectors display different linkages into the financial services sector. For example, corporate real estate transaction decision making often involves detailed risk-related assessments to improve strategically aligned decision making and potential asset sales, while retail real estate transactions are more likely to pursue the best interest rate and repayment schedules, along with personalized needs-based, value-adding product solutions. Hence a dual development e-strategy (or service value networks strategy) approach may be adopted.

Once basic dual-segment, high-level, research-based deliverables have been deduced and evaluated, relationships determined, models built, and pilots tested, incorporating approaches similar to those of the pharmacy industry, then a financial services sector—real estate service value network gateway (or alliance portal) is deliverable. This relationship is outlined in Figure 8. Information aspects tracked and/or developed specifically for the corporate real estate 'one-stop-shop' model or for the retail real estate 'supermarket' model,

Figure 7. The financial services sector—real estate service value network gateway

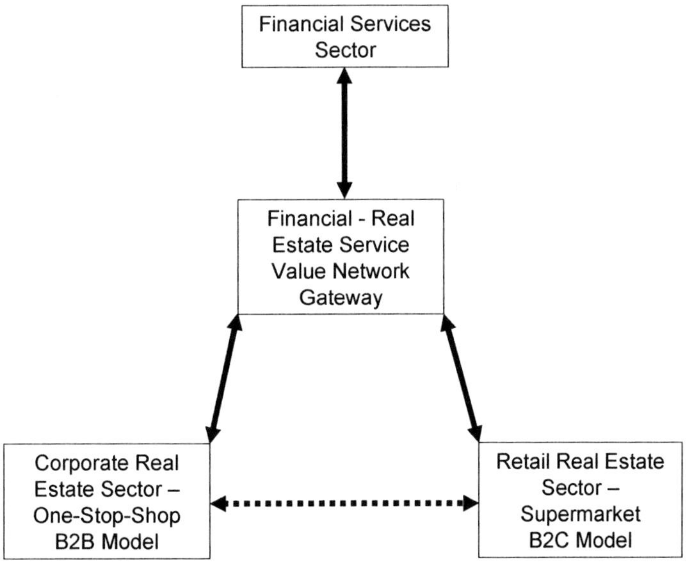

in some cases, may be of practical use (possibly incorporating deliverable variations) to the other real estate system. Such developments may then be intelligently data-mined and incorporated into the financial services sector—real estate service value network gateway.

Retail real estate is a buyer-seller service with clear intrinsic links to the financial services sector (consider mortgage, tax consulting, and risk management). Currently the retail real estate sector operates in an outdated 'corner store' business model, based on fairly fixed commission schemes and undifferentiated roles of retail real estate agents as intermediaries. The corner store model translates to retail real estate agents operating quasi-independently, each with their geographically constrained portfolio and unable to compete on cost, given the size of the market and their fixed cost structures. The online equivalent is merely all these small agents placing their offerings on a real estate portal, with sales transactions completed at a retail real estate agent's office and all existing cost structures maintained.

Corporate real estate is differentiated from retail real estate in that it encompasses all real estate assets—owned, under purchase, or leased by a business (which is not primarily engaged in real estate transactions). The corporate real estate market offers new scope for the financial services sector with its links to corporate real estate management. To date, carefully derived corporate real estate business solutions (offering research-derived, time-scoped, environmentally matched, service-analyzed, strategically planned, and financially sound solutions) are rarely available. Unleashing such information to corporations may project the corporate real estate market closer to the financial services sector, and may move significant revenue streams from real estate agents and intermediaries directly to the financial services sector. Thus corporate real estate customers would likely benefit, experiencing significant transaction savings.

The Australian financial services sector is currently in a position to enter this real estate market. Provided it operates under a new Service value network business model similar to the concept of a 'supermarket', and based on an expanded service concept and offering lower cost structures to that existing in retail real estate, greater transaction efficiencies, scalability, and increased effectiveness will likely emerge. In addition customer satisfaction is enhanced via additional and customized solutions like conveyancing, financing, and the like. Finally this service value network model also allows the financial services sector (via its gateway) to compete on cost, given the greater efficiencies and collaborate network of alliance partners. Such a 'supermarket' retail real estate model may be facilitated through the development of a 'category killer retail real estate portal platform'. By leveraging its capabilities and targeting new business/customer value propositions, the Australian financial services sector may transform its corporate real estate activities into a smart, risk-aware, networked, highly competitive, on-demand, one-stop-shop model.

Galloway and Adam (2000) believe real estate portal models in Australia deliver early productivity increases, and also may gain competitive advantage by lower operating costs. A financial services sector—real estate service value network gateway is readily capable of substantially lower transaction costs. In addition, while some portals adopt a revenue growth model, the financial services sector—real estate service value network gateway delivers gains from productivity increases and service augmentation, and not from an expanded geographic market or from a growing local market. Reduction of intermediaries, along with associated savings on property search and consultancy fees, sales commissions, and loan and insurance commissions, are also deliverable under such a service value network. In effect the financial services sector—real estate service value network gateway offers a *category killer real estate portal with* content, software, mined financial solutions, and risk analysis, along with significant cost efficiencies. This solution is distinctly different from those offered by current major retail real estate portals (like realestate.com.au) in that the underlying financial services sector business model does not feed back into a traditional retail real estate commission-based business model, but rather facilitates an end-to-end, on-demand solution with which financial service organizations may diversify their service portfolio and compete successfully with the real estate sector at large. Retail real estate portals target their value-adding activities towards effective Web presence and virtual searching facilities. A Service Value Networks Financial Services Sector Gateway offers an end-to-end and highly customized solution set to a captive primary business and end-user customer base. In addition the financial imperative to enter this arena is substantial.

In the 2002-2003 financial year, Australian Bureau of Statistics data show retail real estate transactions exceeded A$7.524 billion (ABS Data), and retail commissions generated in excess of A$188 million. The industry operated from 11,722 offices and employed around 76,599 persons. Reported corporate real estate sales in the 2002-2003 financial year were low at A$523 million. However, this figure does not accurately represent corporate real estate sales, as many are reported under different categories as partial asset sales, company asset transfers, special lease back formats, and the like. In 2006 one corporate asset sale (Woolworth's 11 distribution centers) totaled A$846 million. Thus very large revenue streams are possible when building such an industry-wide Financial Services Sector–Real Estate Service Value Networks Gateway. Real estate industries in several other countries are also in need of major updates in their approaches to corporate and retail customer deliverables, charges, and value adds. This requires e-supply chains effectively networked—as a service value network, sharing their information and being collectively mined to deliver specific 'best' business and customer-focused solutions.

CONCLUSION

The service value networks approach draws e-supply chains into a total business solution. It offers a new customer-driven perspective for business. It provides the framework from which strategic positioning of an industry or corporation may be secured. It targets delivering longer term, more sustainable, agile, and competitive solutions for the industry or corporation and its partnering businesses. A knowledge-sharing approach incorporating business intelligence tools (which sometimes incorporate approximation or fuzzy logic techniques) is used to tap into linked databases across the partnering network and supply chains. Information requested by customers is sieved, and the allowed best solutions available across the service value network are then delivered to the customer—either via online feedback or via industry-based customer service personnel delivering direct customer feedback. Customer needs, wants, desires, and economic value are generally targeted. Service value networks are under development in several places and are perceived as one pathway towards future competitiveness. This model has direct application within the services industry, and aspects of it are in development (or in operation) in the real estate, tourism, education, pharmacy, and airline industries. E-supply chains—connecting both direct and indirect (or peripheral) partners—deliver much of the back-end to service value networks, provided their connected business information systems allow for detailed sharing and mining of information back down, up, and across the fully networked e-supply chains.

To develop a service value network for any industry, a detailed knowledge base must be established. This involves business and customer research, alignment assessments, strategic partnering, and building correct, complex, and largely non-replicable networked solutions that ensure the industry has a greater chance of retaining its competitiveness in the global business arena of tomorrow. The evolution to an industry-wide service value network approach delivers improved performance and customer value, incorporating close business-customer alignment. In addition, its research-based solution set also incorporates key business-customer elevated service offerings.

REFERENCES

Abdinnour-Helm, S., Chaparro, B., & Farmer, S. (2005). Using end-user computing satisfaction (EUCS) instrument to measure satisfaction with a Web site. *Decision Sciences, 36*(2), 341-364.

Akkermans, H., & Vos, B. (2003). Amplification in service supply chains: An exploratory case study from the telecom industry. *Journal of Production and Operations Management, 12*(2), 204 -223.

Albrecht, K., & Zemke, R. (1985). *Service America! Doing business in the new economy.* Homewood, H: Dow Jones-Irwin.

Anwar, S., & Hamilton, J. (2020). Tourism into the future—towards 2020, and beyond. *Tourism Recreation Research Journal, 30*(3), 77-87.

Bagchi, S., Gallego, G., Grey, W., Katircioglu, K., Seybold, D., Shi, D., & Stefanis, S. (2003). An analytical approach for quantifying the value of e-business initiatives. *IBM Systems Journal, 42*(3), 484-497.

Barlow-Hills, S., & Sarin, S., (2003). From market driven to market driving: An alternative paradigm for marketing in high technology industries. *Journal of Marketing Theory and Practice, 11*(3), 13-24.

Barney, J. (1991). Firm resources and sustained competitive advantage. *Journal of Management, 17,* 99-120.

Biocca, F., Li, H., & Daugherty, T. (2002). Impact of 3-D advertising on product knowledge, brand attitude, and purchase intention: The mediating role of presence. *Journal of Advertising,* 1-42.

Bowman, R. (2001, October). Fast deployment—quick return help sell IT in a slow economy. *Global Logistics and Supply Chain Strategies.*

Briggs, R., & Hollis, N. (1997). Advertising on the Web: Is there a response before click-through? *Journal of Advertising Research, 37*(2), 33.

Brown, S., & Vashistha, A. (2002). Igniting the services value chain. *Journal of Marketing Management, 11*(1), 12-13.

Chang Lee, K., Lee, S., & Kang, I. (2005). KMPI: Measuring knowledge management performance. *Information and Management, 42,* 469-482.

Chen, I., & Paulraj, A. (2004). Towards a theory of supply chain management: The constructs and measurements. *Journal of Operations Management, 22,* 119-150.

Chen, Q., & Wells, W. (1999). Attitude toward the site. *Journal of Advertising Research, 39*(5), 27-38.

Chenhall, R. (2005). Integrative strategic performance measurement systems, strategic alliance of manufacturing, learning and strategic outcomes: An exploratory study. *Journal of Accounting, Organizations and Society, 30,* 395-422.

Comer, D. (1995). *Internetworking with TCP/IP volume 1: Principles, protocols, and architecture.* Englewood Cliffs, NJ: Prentice-Hall.

Comergent Business Strategies. (2003). Retrieved April 10, 2004, from http://www.comergent.com/products/valuepropositions.cfm.

Cutler, M., & Sterne, J. (2002). *E-metrics* (pp. 1-62). Cambridge, MA: NetGenesis Corp.

Davis, L., Dehning, B., & Stratopoulos, T. (2003). Does the market recognize IT enabled competitive advantage? *Journal of Information and Management, 40*(7), 705-716.

Di Gregorio, J., & De Montis, F. (2004). *NOIE information economy index 2003* (pp. 1-50). Retrieved March 12, 2004, from http://www2.dcita.gov.au/_data/assets/file/12294/NOIE_Index.pdf

Draaijer, D. (1992). Market orientedness of improvement programs in manufacturing: Results from field study research. *International Journal of Operations and Production Management, 12*(7), 24-40.

Escrig-Tena, A., & Bou-Liusar, J. (2005). A model for evaluating organizational competencies: An application in the context of a quality management initiative. *Decision Sciences, 36*(2), 221-257.

Evans, N. (2002). *Business agility: Strategies for gaining competitive advantage through mobile business solutions.* Upper Saddle River, NJ: Prentice-Hall.

Fenn, J., & Linden, A. (2002). *Key technology advances from 2003 to 2012: Disruptive advances in physical and logical connectivity, and in smart, embedded chips, will transform key business functions in the next decade*, No. AV-18-8822 (pp. 1-5). Gartner Research.

Finch, B. (2003). *OperationsNow.com.* New York: McGraw-Hill/Irwin.

Forrester, J. (1961). *Industrial dynamics.* Cambridge, MA: MIT Press.

Foss, B., & Stone, M. (2001). Business to business: Lessons on segmentation and other issues from financial services markets. *Journal of Financial Services Marketing, 9*(4), 306-313.

Frohlich, M., & Westbrook, R.(2002). Demand chain management in manufacturing and services: Web-based integration, drivers, and performance. *Journal of Operations Management, 20,* 729-745.

Galloway, J., & Adam, S. (2000). *Online property markets in Australia: Industry value transformation.* Retrieved April 25, 2006, from http://ausweb.scu.edu.au/aw2k/papers/galloway/paper.html

Gartner. (2002). *Gartner dataquest services files 2004.* Retrieved May 10, 2004, from http:// www.Gartner.com

Grant, R. (1996). Towards knowledge-based theory of the firm. *Strategic Management Journal, 17,* 109-122.

Greenwald, B., & Kahn, J. (2005). All strategy is local. *Harvard Business Review, 83*(8), 1-11.

Hamilton, J., & Selen. W. (2005, December). An e-enabled service value network for the pharmaceutical industry. In *Proceedings of the 5th International Conference on Electronic Business (ICE2005)*, Hong Kong. (pp. 1-9).

Hamilton, J. (2004a). Modeling, information flows, performance, strategy and competitiveness across the service value network. *Journal of New Business Ideas and Trends, 2*(2), 29-53.

Hamilton, J. (2004b). Service value networks: Value, performance and strategy for the services industry. *Journal of Systems Science and Systems Engineering, 13*(4), 469-489.

Hamilton, J. (2005a). Service value networks: A new approach to performance and the delivery of services. *The E-Business Review, 5*(1), 66-71.

Hamilton, J. (2005b, July). Pharmacy industry—service value networks research. *Australian Pharmacy Guild,* 1-8.

Hoffman, D., & Novak, T. (2000). How to acquiring customers on the Web. *Harvard Business Review, 78*(3), 179-188.

Hunt, S., & Morgan, R. (1996). The resource-advantage theory of competition: Dynamics, path dependencies, and evolutionary dimensions. *Journal of Marketing, 60*(3), 107-114.

Jambulingam, T., Kathuria, R., & Doucette, W. (2005). Entrepreneurial orientation as a basis for classification within a service industry: The case of retail pharmacy industry. *Journal of Operations Management, 23,* 23-42.

Lee, H., Padmanabhan, V., & Whang, S. (1997). The bullwhip effect in supply chains. *Sloan Management Review, 38*(3), 93-102.

Liang, T. (2003). The second wave of e-commerce: Successful transformation and business models. In *Proceedings of the 3rd International Conference on Electronic Business (ICEB2003)*, Singapore.

Lumpkin, T., & Dess, G. (1996). Clarifying the entrepreneurial orientation construct and linking it to performance. *Academy of Management Review, 21*(1) 135-172.

Malcinski, A., Dominick, S., & Hartrick, T. (2001). *Getting to know your audience is the key to online success—making the numbers work for you* (IBM white paper, pp. 1-11). Retrieved May 1, 2004, from http://www-106.ibm.com/developerworks/web/library/wa-mwtl/

Mayer, R., & Davis, J. (1999). The effect of the performance appraisal system on trust for management: A field quasi-experiment. *Journal of Applied Psychology, 84*(1), 123-136.

McCullough-Johnston, K. (2001). Why e-business must evolve beyond market orientation: Applying human interaction models to computer-mediated corporate communications. *Internet Research: Electronic Networking Applications and Policy, 11*(3), 213-225.

McQueeney, D. (2003). IBM's evolving strategy. *Research Technology Management, 46*(4), 20-27.

Narasimhan, R., & Kim, S. (2002). Effect of supply chain integration on the relationship between diversification and performance: Evidence from Japanese and Korean firms. *Journal of Operations Management, 20,* 303-323.

Parasuraman, A., Zeithaml, V., & Berry, L. (1985). A conceptual model of service quality and its implications for future research. *Journal of Marketing, 49,* 41-50.

Piccoli, G., Brohman, K., Watson, R., & Parasuraman, A. (2004). Net based customer service systems: Evolution and revolution in Web site functionalities. *Decision Sciences, 35*(3), 423-455.

Schmenner, R. (1995). How can services businesses survive and prosper? *Sloan Management Review, 27*(3), 21-32.

Siegel, M. (2002). *Seizing the opportunity: Exploiting Web aggregation,* White Paper No. 330 (pp. 1-14). Center for Information Systems Research, Sloan School of Management, USA.

Sterne, J. (2002). *E-metrics—business metrics for the new economy.* Cambridge, MA: NetGenesis Corp.

Swaminthan, J., & Tayur, S. (2003). Models for supply chains in e-business. *Management Science, 49*(10), 1387-1406.

Swanson, R., & Davis, J. (2003). The relationship of differential loci with perceived quality and behavioral intentions. *Journal of Services Marketing, 17*(2), 202-219.

Van Looy, B., Gemel, P., & Van Dierdonck, R. (2003). *Services management* (2nd ed.). Upper Saddle River, NJ: Pearson Education.

Vermijmeren, M. (2003). Software architecture in supply chain management. *Computers in Industry, 53,* 165-178.

Winter, S. (1995). Four R's of profitability: Rents, resources, routines, and replication. In C.A. Montgomery (Ed.), *Resource-based and evolutionary theories of the firm: Towards a synthesis* (pp. 147-178). Boston: Kluwer Academic.

Wright, G., & Taylor, A. (2003). Strategic knowledge sharing for improved public service delivery: Managing an innovative culture for effective partnerships. In E.A. Coakes. (Ed.), *Knowledge management: Current issues and challenges* (pp. 187-211). London: IRM Press.

Section II

E-Supply Chain Technologies and Infrastructure

Chapter VI
Automated Data Capture Technologies:
RFID

Vidyasagar Potdar
Curtin University of Technology, Australia

Chen Wu
Curtin University of Technology, Australia

Elizabeth Chang
Curtin University of Technology, Australia

ABSTRACT

In this chapter we provide an introduction to RFID technology. We discuss the main components of the RFID technology, which includes RFID transponders, RFID readers, RFID middleware, and RFID labels. A detailed classification and explanation for each of these components is provided, followed by the benefits and applications that can be achieved by adopting this technology. After discussing all possible applications, we describe the business benefits and how stakeholders can benefit. This is followed by a detailed outline of the adoption challenges, where we discuss issues like the security, privacy, cost, scalability, resilience, and deployment and some existing solutions. Once the issues are discussed, we divert our attention to some successful RFID deployment case studies to describe the adoption of RFID technology that has already begun and how many big organizations across the world are showing interest in this technology. Since this chapter takes into consideration a variety of audiences like researchers, business executives, business consultants, hobbyists, and general readers, we tried to cover material relevant to each target audience. For business executives and consultants interested in knowing who can offer complete RFID solutions, we allocated a dedicated section for RFID vendors where we provide a comprehensive list of RFID vendors across the globe. For researchers, we listed some open issues in the section of adoption challenges. For advanced users, in-depth technical details are provided in the section where we discuss security and privacy enhancing protocols.

INTRODUCTION

Automated data capture is an important aspect in supply chain management and logistics. In the last decade, automated identification and data capture (AIDC) has revolutionized the overall supply chain management process. AIDC includes technology to identify objects, and automatically collects data about them and updates the data into software systems without human intervention. Some examples of AIDC technologies include bar codes, RFID, smart cards, voice and facial recognition, and so forth.

An automated inventory control systems (AICS), which forms the backbone of the modern supply chain, is a software application used in a warehouse to monitor the quantity, location, and status of inventory. Modern AICS heavily relies upon *barcodes,* for automated data capture.

A barcode basically is a machine-readable visual representation of information printed on the surface of objects. There are several different kinds of barcodes, for example, barcodes which store data in the widths and spacing of printed parallel lines, and those that store data within the patterns of dots, or concentric circles, or even hidden within images. This encoded data on the barcodes is read by barcode readers, which update the backend ERP, SCM, or WMS systems. However there are some inherent issues with using a barcode, for instance, barcodes become ineffective in rain, fog, snow, dirt and grime, and so forth (Tecstra, n.d.). Since barcodes rely on optical sensors, any minor change on the barcode print can make it difficult to read. This can be commonly seen at point of sale (POS) in the supermarkets, where the POS operator scans the barcode several times because it is either wet or not aligned properly.

To overcome these issues the industry is now looking at the possibility of using new generation AIDC technology like the RFID. A radio frequency identifier (RFID) system is basically composed of an RFID transponder (tag) and an RFID interrogator (reader). The RFID transponder or the RFID tag (which is how it is often called) is a microchip connected to an antenna. This tag can be attached to an object, which needs to be uniquely identified, for example, it can be used in a warehouse to track the entry and exit of goods. This tag contains information similar to the barcode, which stores the unique properties of the object to which it is attached. An RFID reader can access this information. The RFID reader communicates with the RFID tag using radio waves. The radio waves activate the RFID tag to broadcast the information it contains. Depending on the type of tag used, the information transmitted could be merely a number or detailed profile of the object. The data fetched from the reader can then be integrated with the backend ERP or SCM or WMS systems (Tecstra, n.d.).

There are two fundamental differences between the conventional barcodes and the contemporary RFIDs. First, RFIDs do not require line of sight—that is, objects tagged with RFID can be sensed in a wide area, and there is no need to individually scan all the objects in front of an optical scanner. Second, RFIDs offer item-level tagging—that is, each item within a product range can be uniquely identified (e.g., "109839 is a bottle of orange juice manufactured by ABC Company"). However barcodes do not identify individual items; they can only identify that "this is a bottle of orange juice manufactured by ABC Company."

Some other points could also be considered. RFID has a longer read range compared to barcodes. The amount of data stored on barcodes is limited and often cannot be updated once it is printed. In comparison, RFID tags offer a considerably large amount of data storage capacity as well as reprogramming capabilities, which means the data on the tag can be updated effortlessly. These changes can be done without physically identifying the tag because the RFID reader can uniquely query the desired RFID tag and make the changes. From the security perspective RFID tags can be placed inside the objects, however barcodes have to be printed outside. Another issue with barcodes is the printing quality; substandard printing can result in reading errors (Gloeckler, n.d.; Tecstra, n.d.).

There are several inherent advantages with RFID technology; however to achieve widespread adoption of RFID, issues like security, privacy, and cost should be addressed first. In this chapter we provide a detailed insight into RFID. The rest of the chapter is organized in the following manner. The next section introduces the RFID technology. We discuss RFID tags, RFID readers, and RFID middleware. We then discuss the benefits that stakeholders can achieve by adopting RFID technology and provide an RFID Deployment Roadmap. In this section we also describe the steps that an organization should consider prior to adopting RFID to streamline its business process. The fifth section discusses the RFID adoption challenges where we outline the existing issues, which are the major obstacles in widespread adoption. These issues are security, privacy, and cost. Finally, before concluding the chapter, we discuss three case studies in the supply chain domain that have adopted RFID to enhance their business process and gain a competitive advantage.

The main objectives of this chapter are:

1. To provide *RFID novices* with an introductory illustration of the contemporary data capture technology—RFID. This is covered in the next section of this chapter.
2. To offer RFID *advanced users* a comprehensive survey of RFID technology from both technical and business perspectives. This is covered in detail in the following sub-sections where we give an in-depth explanation of the different types of RFID tags, RFID readers, and RFID middleware.
3. To illustrate the well-identified RFID adoption challenges and their corresponding deployment strategies for *business consultants*. This is covered later in the chapter, where we begin by highlighting the main challenges for RFID adoption which include cost, security, and privacy. We then provide a road map for RFID adoption where we provide a detailed deployment strategy for RFID adoption in a business environment. This can facilitate consultants, CEOs, and CIOs to make informed decisions.
4. To explain benefits of adopting RFID solutions to *business executives* using real-world proven case studies. We do this by highlighting the benefits that RFID offers to different stakeholders, and later in the chapter relating that to five successful RFID deployment case studies from supply chain domains. All these case studies provide an insight into how RFIDs can facilitate businesses across multiple domains.

TECHNOLOGY OVERVIEW

An RFID system is composed of three main elements: an *RFID tag* (inlay), which contains data that uniquely identifies an object; an *RFID reader*, which writes this unique data on the tags and, when requested, can read this unique identifier; and an *RFID middleware*, which processes the data acquired from the reader and then updates it to the backend database or ERP systems (Weis, Sarma, Rivest, & Engels, 2004).

A typical RFID system is shown in Figure 1. When the RFID tag comes in the range of the RFID reader, the reader activates the tag to transmit its unique information. This unique information is propagated to the RFID middleware, which appropriately processes the gathered information and then updates the backend database.

RFID Tags

An RFID tag is a microchip attached with an antenna to a product that needs to be tracked. The tag picks up signals from the reader and reflects back the information to the reader. The tag usu-

Figure 1. RFID architecture (Source: Potdar, Wu, & Chang, 2005)

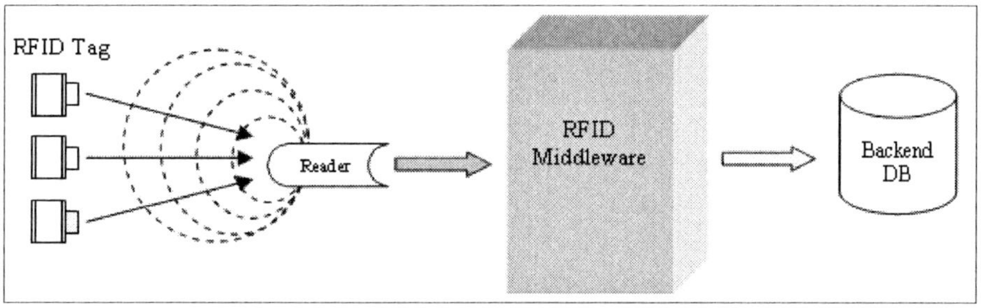

ally contains a unique serial number, which may represent information, such as a customer's name, address, and so forth (*RFID Journal*, 2006a). A detailed classification is discussed next.

Classification

RFID tags can be classified using three schemes. First, the tags can be classified based on their ability to perform radio communication—active, semi-active (semi-passive), and passive tags. Second, the tags can be classified based upon their memory—read-only, read-write or write-once, and read-many. Finally, the tags can also be classified based on the frequency in which they operate—LF, HF or UHF.

Active vs. Semi-Active (or Semi-Passive) vs. Passive RFID Tags

- **Active tags** have a battery that provides necessary energy to the microchip for transmitting a radio signal to the reader. These tags generate the RF energy and apply it to the antennae and transmit to the reader instead of reflecting back a signal from the reader (Lyngsoe, n.d.). These batteries need to be recharged or replaced once they are discharged. Some tags have to be disposed off when the batteries run out of power (Gloeckler, n.d.; Tecstra, n.d.). These tags have a read range of several 100 meters and are very expensive (more than US$20), and hence are used for tracking expensive items; for example, the U.S. military uses these tags to track supplies at ports (Lyngsoe, n.d.; *RFID Journal*, 2006a).
- **Semi-active tags** (or semi-passive or battery-assisted) also contain a battery, which is used to run the circuitry on the microchip, however it still relies on the reader's magnetic field to transmit the radio signal (i.e., information). These tags have a larger range because all the energy supplied by the reader can be reflected back to the reader (*RFID Journal*, 2006a), which means it can work at low-power signal levels as well. These tags have a read range up to 100 meters and may cost a dollar or more (Lyngsoe, n.d.; *RFID Journal*, 2006a). Some of these tags often are dormant—that is, they are activated by the presence of a reader's magnetic field. Once activated, the battery runs the circuitry and responds back to the reader. This is a mechanism to save the battery power (*RFID Journal*, 2006a).
- **Passive tags** completely rely on the energy provided by the reader's magnetic field to transmit the radio signal to and from the reader. It does not have a battery. As a result, the read range varies depending upon the reader used (Lyngsoe, n.d.). A maximum

distance of 15 meters (or 50 feet) can be achieved with a strong reader antennae and RF-friendly environment (Sweeney, 2005).

Read-Write vs. Read-Only RFID Tags

- **Read-only tags:** The reader can only read data stored on such tags. The data cannot be modified in any manner. The tag manufacturer programs the data on the tag. Such tags are comparatively very cheap (Tecstra, n.d.).
- **Write-once read-many (WORM):** The owner of the tag can program the data by writing the content on the tag. Data stored on this tag can be written only once, however it can be read many times (Sweeney, 2005; Tecstra, n.d.).
- **Read-write tags:** Data stored on such tags can be easily edited when the tag is within the range of the reader. Such tags are more expensive and are not often used for commodity tracking. These tags are reusable; hence they can be reused within an organization (Tecstra, n.d.).

LF vs. HF vs. UHF vs. Microwave Frequency RFID Tags

RFID systems are classified as radio systems because they generate and radiate electromagnetic waves. Hence the RFID systems should operate within certain frequency limits like the LF, HF, or UHF. Since some of the frequencies are already in use by police, security services, industry, medical, or scientific operations, there is a limited number of frequencies available for RFID systems to operate. Figure 2 shows the radio frequency spectrum (Beherrschen, n.d.).

RFID systems operate in four frequency bands: LF, HF, UHF, and Microwave. The RFID tags designed to operate in this frequency have special characteristics. We now discuss each of these kinds of RFID tags in detail.

Low Frequency (LF)

In LF range, RFID tags operate at 125 kHz or 134.2 kHz frequency (Lyngsoe, n.d.; *RFID Journal*, 2006a; RMOROZ, 2004). Some important characteristics of these tags are as follows:

- Tags in this range are not affected by metallic surroundings and hence are ideal for identifying metal objects like vehicles, tools, containers, and metallic equipments.
- The reading range varies from a few centimeters to a meter depending upon the size of the antennae and the reader used (*RFID Journal*, 2006a; RMOROZ, 2004).
- These tags can also penetrate through water and body tissues, and hence often used for animal identification (RMOROZ, 2004).
- These are often used at places where tagged objects are moving at a lower speed and very few objects are scanned per second (Lyngsoe, n.d.).
- Most car immobilizers rely on LF tags. The tag is embedded in the key while the reader is mounted in the ignition area (RMOROZ, 2004).
- Data transfer rate is low, for example, 70ms for read operation. This is because at low frequency the communication is slower.
- In an industrial setting, electric motors can interfere with LF RFID operation (RMOROZ, 2004).

Figure 2. Radio frequency spectrum (Adapted from http://en.wikipedia.org/wiki/Super_high_frequency)

Radio spectrum										
ELF	SLF	ULF	VLF	LF	MF	HF	VHF	UHF	**SHF**	EHF
3 Hz	30 Hz	300 Hz	3 kHz	30 kHz	300 kHz	3 MHz	30 MHz	300 MHz	**3 GHz**	30 GHz
30 Hz	300 Hz	3 kHz	30 kHz	300 kHz	3 MHz	30 MHz	300 MHz	3 GHz	**30 GHz**	300 GHz

- Most LF-based systems can only read one tag at a time—that is, they do not support reading multiple tags simultaneously (RMOROZ, 2004).
- These tags are more expensive ($2 or more) to manufacture than the HF tags because of the size of the antennae (RMOROZ, 2004).
- This frequency is used worldwide without any restrictions.

High Frequency (HF)

In the HF range, RFID tags operate at 13.56 MHz (Lyngsoe, n.d.; *RFID Journal*, 2006a; RMOROZ, 2004). Some important characteristics of these tags are as follows:

- HF tags can penetrate through most materials including water and body tissues, however they are affected by metal surroundings (Gloeckler, n.d.; RMOROZ, 2004).
- The thickness of the tag is typically less than 0.1mm and comes with variable antennae sizes. Bigger antennae offer more communication distance.
- The reading range is normally less than a meter (100cm).
- HF tags are comparatively cheaper (less than $1) than the LF tags.
- The data transfer rate is higher compared to LF tags, for example, 20ms for read operation. This is because at high frequency the communication is faster.
- In an industrial setting, electric motors do not interfere with HF RFID operation (RMOROZ, 2004).
- The reader can read multiple tags simultaneously. This is termed as anti-collision. There are many anti-collision protocols to prevent the reader from reading the same tag more than once. Depending upon the reader used, at least 50 tags can be read simultaneously (RMOROZ, 2004).
- HF tags normally work best when they are in close range with the reader (around 90cm). Secondly the orientation of the tags with respect to the reader plays a major role. For optimum communication range, the tag and the reader should be parallel. If however they are perpendicular, the communication range may reduce dramatically (RMOROZ, 2004).
- In Canada, Shell uses HF RFID for its Easy Pay customer convenience program. In Hong Kong Octopus card is used in public transit service. In the Netherlands, the Trans Link System uses contact-less smart cards to offer contact-less ticket solutions. The World Cup in Germany used tickets embedded with HF tags (RMOROZ, 2004).
- This frequency is used globally without any restrictions. However in certain countries the power of the reader is restricted.
- Global standard: ISO 15693, 14442, 18000-3.

Ultra High Frequency (UHF)

In the UHF range, RFID tags operate at 433 MHz, 860-956 MHz, and 2.45 GHz (Lyngsoe, n.d.; *RFID Journal*, 2006a; RMOROZ, 2004). Most research work is dedicated to RFID in the frequency range of 860-956 MHz. Some important characteristics of these tags are as follows:

- Multiple tags can be read simultaneously, for example, at least 200 tags (theoretically 800 possible) (RMOROZ, 2004).
- UHF tags operating at 860-956 MHz frequencies offer better read range by using short antennas.
- The reading range is normally 3-6 meters (RMOROZ, 2004).
- UHF tags are normally less expensive than HF tags because of low memory capacity and simple manufacturing process (RMOROZ, 2004).
- Such tags are commonly used on objects that are moving at a very high speed, and a large number of tags are scanned per second in the business contexts such as supply chain,

warehouse, and logistics. These devices may have a range of 7.5metres (or 25 feet) or more (Lyngsoe, n.d.; Tecstra, n.d.).

- UHF tags do not work well in liquid and in metal surroundings.
- Larger read range limits their use to banking and access control applications, because the access card may be scanned from a longer distance and some unauthorized person might gain entry in restricted premises on your behalf.
- One major hindrance for widespread adoption of UHF RFID is lack of globally accepted regulations. For example, in Australia UHF operates in the 918-926 MHz range, in North America UHF operates at 902-928 MHz, in Europe it operates at 860-868 MHz, while in Japan it operates at 950-956 MHz.
- Secondly, it operates in a highly crowded frequency range because most of the ISM (industrial, scientific, and medical) applications operate in the same range.

Components

There are four main components of a RFID tag: microchip, antennae, substrate, and in some cases an additional battery.

Microchip

An RFID tag contains a small microchip, which has some computing capabilities limited to simple logical operations and is also used for storage. The storage can be read-only, read-write, write-once read-many (WORM), or any other combination. The storage memory is used to hold a unique identification number that can identify each tag uniquely. Current generation passive tags have a memory capacity of 96 bits (characters). Passive tags have enough space to hold the identification number, however the active tags can have some additional information like the content of the container, its destination or origin, and so forth (Sweeney, 2005; Tecstra, n.d.).

Antennae

The tag antenna is the conductive element that enables the transmission of data between the tag and the reader (RFidGazzete, n.d.). Antennae play a major role in deciding the communication distance; normally a larger antenna offers more area to capture electromagnetic energy from the reader and hence provides a greater communication distance. There are several kinds of antennae, like the rectangular planar spiral antenna, fractal antennas,[1] and microstrip patch antenna (monopole, dipole). Different types of tags have different kinds of antennas, for example, low-frequency and high-frequency tags usually have a coiled antenna that couples with the coiled antenna of the reader to form a magnetic field (RFidGazzete, n.d.). UHF tag antennas look more like old radio or television antennas because UHF frequency is more electric in nature (Sweeney, 2005).

Recent advances in technology have even facilitated the deployment of printed antennas to achieve similar functionality like the traditional antennas. One possible way of printing antennas is to use silver conductive inks on plastic substrates or papers (Tecstra, n.d.). The main advantage of printed antennas is that they are cheap.

Substrate

This is a chemical (or material) that holds the antennae and the microchip together. It is something like a plastic film (Sweeney, 2005).

Battery

Unlike passive tags, active RFID tags contain a battery to power the circuitry, and generate and transmit radio signals to the reader. Onboard power supply can enable long-distance communication, as long as 1 kilometer (Sweeney, 2005).

Attributes

RFID tags can be differentiated based on several attributes. In this section we discuss seven main attributes, which should be considered when selecting RIFD tags.

Operating Frequency

This describes at what frequency the tag is designed to operate. As discussed earlier RFID tags can either operate in LF, HF, or UHF range of the radio spectrum.

Data Retention Time

This attribute describes the time for which the data can be retained on the tag, for example, RI-I16-114A-01 from Texas Instruments has a data retention time of more than 10 years.

Memory

This attribute describes the available memory on the tag. It can be classified as *factory-programmed* read-only memory and *user-programmable* memory.

Programming Cycles

This attribute defines the number of times the tag can be reprogrammed. This programming cycle is normally measured at a standard temperature (25 degrees).

Antennae Size

This attributes defines the size of the tag antennae, for example, RI-I16-114A-01 has an antennae of the following dimensions: 24.2 mm +0.1mm/-0.2mm.

Base Material

This is the material used to join the antennae with the microchip. Normally Polyethylenetherephtalate is used as a substrate.

Operating Temperature

This attribute describes the range in which the tag can operate, for example, RI-I16-114A-01 operates within -25°C to +70°C.

RFID Readers

RFID readers send radio waves to the RFID tags to enquire about their data contents. The tags then respond by sending back the requested data. The readers may have some processing and storage capabilities. The reader is linked via the RFID middleware with the backend database to do any other computationally intensive data processing. There are two different types of RFID readers (Gloeckler, n.d.).

Classification

RFID readers can be classified using two different schemes. First, the readers can be classified based on their location as handheld readers and fixed readers. Second, the tags can be classified based upon the frequency in which they operate—single frequency and multi-frequency.

Fixed Readers vs. Handheld Readers

- **Fixed RFID Readers** are fixed at one location (e.g., choke point). In a supply chain and warehouse scenario, the preferred location of a reader can be along the conveyor belt, dock door antennae or portals, depalletization stations, or any other mobile location.

- **Portable or Handheld RFID Readers** are designed for Mobile Mount Applications, for example, vehicles in a warehouse or to be carried by inventory personnel, and so forth.

Single Frequency vs. Multi-Frequency

- **Single-frequency operation readers** operate in one frequency zone, either in LF, HF, or UHF. Such readers become inconvenient if tags in a warehouse are operating in different frequencies.
- **Multi-frequency operation readers** can operate in multiple frequencies. Such readers can conveniently read tags, which operate in different frequencies (i.e., LF, HF, or UHF). Hence these are more useful from a practical perspective, however such readers come at a premium price.

Components

There are two main components in a RFID reader: antennae and the input/output (I/O) controller.

Antennae

Every RFID reader is equipped with one or more antennas. These antennas generate the required electromagnetic field to sense the RFID tags. There are many different kinds of antennas like linearly polarized, circularly polarized, or ferrite stick antennas.

I/O Controller

The data that the reader collects needs to be sent to the organization's information system like ERP or WMS. Such a communication can be achieved by using RS-232,[2] RS-485, or Ethernet. Some new generation readers also provide the Power over Ethernet (PoE) and 802.11 wireless connectivity protocol. Mostly all the readers possess a serial port for programming and data transfer. The manufacturer of RFID readers normally supplies the controllers. These controllers typically operate on 120V AC or 24V DC current.

Attributes

RFID readers can be differentiated based on several attributes. In this section we discuss 12 main attributes that should be considered when selecting RIFD readers.

Weight

Weight of the reader is an important factor if the reader is mobile or handheld because it should be handy and should not cause inconvenience for its user.

Communication Interface

Every reader has a communication interface (e.g., RS232 or Ethernet 10/100BaseT or Wireless 802.11g or infrared data connection) to transfer the data gathered from the RFID tags.

Integrated Filtering Component

The need to filter RFID tag information is vital and usually can be done using a separate server in the RFID middleware or at the place where the reader is mounted. However in order to increase efficiency, reduce cost, and decrease potential points of failure in the network, it would be desirable if the reader itself is equipped with some computing power to facilitate information filtering before propagating an excessive large amount of data to RFID middleware or backend systems (e.g., ERP). New generation readers do offer such a facility like the IF5 Intellitag Fixed Reader, which is built on Linux platform, which runs IBM's WebSphere® Everyplace® Micro Environment (WEME) (Intermec, 2006a). Some handheld readers are equipped with 700 Series Color mobile computers to do a similar job (Intermec, 2006b).

Antennae (Type and Number)

Several antennas can connect a single reader at the same time. There are different kinds of antennas that are equipped with standard readers, for example, the IP3 Intellitag Portable Reader (UHF) (Intermec, 2006b) comes with integrated circular polarized antennas. The advantage of such antennas is that it can read tags in any orientation.

Software

Most of the industry standard-compliant RFID readers are equipped with software to setup and re-configure the reader to enhance the resilience of the RFID systems.

Time for Identifying Tags

This refers to the time that is necessary to identify tags. The number of tags identified per second varies with the type of readers, for example, IP3 Intellitag Portable Reader (UHF) (Intermec, 2006b) can identity six tags per second.

Read Rate & Write Rate

This term usually describes the number of tags that can be read within a given period of time. It can also represent the maximum rate at which data can be read from a tag. The unit of measurement is in bits or bytes per second (*RFID Journal*, 2006b). Write rate usually describes the rate at which information is transferred to a tag, written into the tag's memory and verified as being correct (*RFID Journal*, 2006b). The unit of measurement is in number of bits or bytes written per second per tag.

Volatile Memory

Some readers have inbuilt volatile memory to retain a certain number of tag IDs.

Frequency Range

This term is used to describe the reader's capability to read tags in different frequencies. Some readers only operate in the UHF frequency (Intermec, 2006b), while others operate in the LF or HF range.

Operating Temperature

Depending upon the application, the operating temperature of the reader should be considered. For example, if you are going to deploy an RFID reader in the desert, it should function properly in the extreme temperature. On the other hand, if it is to be deployed in extreme freezing conditions, the same should also be considered. Many industry standard readers operate within the range of -40°C to 50°C. Apart from the operating condition the storage conditions should also be considered. Normally the storage temperate has a bit higher range.

Miscellaneous Factors

Similar to temperature, humidity is also a factor that should be considered when selecting a proper reader. Many readers can operate in 10% to 90% humidity levels (Intermec, 2006c).

Shock Resistance

In an industrial setting, shocks are almost inevitable. Hence the reader should be resistant against these conditions as well. Likewise, frequent vibrations in the industry setting give rise to vibration-resistant readers.

Legal Restrictions

Some countries have restrictions on using some frequencies because they may be allocated to ISM applications, hence before buying a reader, the country's legal restrictions should be checked.

RFID Middleware

In a general, the RFID middleware manages the readers and extracts electronic product code (EPC) data from the readers; performs tag data filtering, aggregating, and counting; and sends the data to the enterprise warehouse management systems (WMSs), backend database, and information exchange broker. Figure 1 shows the relationship between tag, reader, RFID middleware, and backend database. An RFID middleware works within the organization, moving information (i.e., EPC data) from the RFID tag to the integration point of high-level supply-chain management systems through a series of data-related services. From the architectural perspective, RFID middleware has four layers of functionality: reader API, data management, security, and integration management. The reader API provides the upper layer of the interface interacting with the reader. Meanwhile, it supports flexible interaction patterns (e.g., asynchronous subscription) and an active "context-ware" strategy to sense the reader. The data management layer mainly deals with filtering redundant data, aggregating duplicate data, and routing data to appropriate destination based on the content. The integration layer provides data connectivity to legacy data source and supporting systems at different integration levels and thus can be further divided into three sub-layers as specified in Leaver (2005): application integration, partner integration, and process integration. The application integration provides varieties of reliable connection mechanisms (e.g., messaging, adaptor, or the driver) that connect the RFID data with existing enterprise systems such as ERP or WMS. The partner integration enables the RFID middleware to share the RFID data with other RFID systems via other system communication components (e.g., the Data Exchange Broker in Figure 3). The process integration provides capability to orchestrate the RFID-enabled business process. The security layer obtains input data from the data management layer, and detects data tampering which might occur either in the tag by a wicked RFID reader during the transportation or in the backend internal database by malicious attacks. The overall architecture of RFID middleware and its related information systems in an

Figure 3. RFID middleware architecture

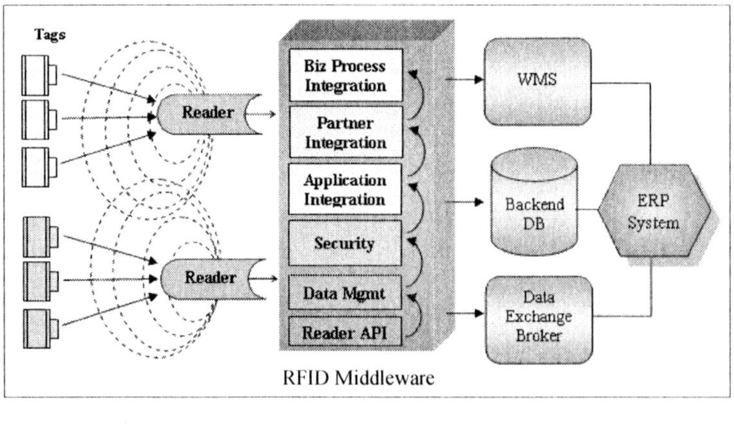

organization are depicted in Figure 3.

The backend DB component stores the complete record of RFID items. It maintains the detailed item information as well as tag data, which has to be coherent with those read from the RFID. It is worth noting that the backend database is one of the data-tampering sources where malicious attacks might occur to change the nature of RFID item data by circumventing the protection of an organization's firewall. The WMS integrates mechanical and human activities with an information system to effectively manage warehouse business processes and direct warehouse activities. The WMS automates receiving, put-away, picking, and shipping in warehouses, and prompts workers to do inventory cycle counts. The RFID middleware employs the integration layer to allow real-time data transfer towards the WMS. The data exchange broker is employed in this architecture to share, query, and update the public data structure and schema of RFID tag data by exchanging XML documents. Any update of the data structure will be reflected and propagate to all involved RFID data items stored in the backend database. From the standardization view, it enables users to exchange RFID-related data with trading partners through the Internet. From the implementation angle, it might be a virtual Web services consumer and provider running as peers in the distributed logistics network.

BENEFITS TO SUPPLY CHAIN STAKEHOLDERS

The main benefits for stakeholders of adopting RFID in their business processes are manifold. In this section, we summarize these benefits and categorize them based on different potential supply chain stakeholders (as shown in Figure 4) who would benefit from deploying the RFID technology. After reading this section, readers are able to foresee several major advantages from their own perspectives.

Benefits to Manufacturers

For manufacturers, RFID is able to support quality control by querying components and subassemblies as they enter the facility. For example, it can ensure that the correct components are included in an assembled item by automatically checking that all items from the Bill of Material are in place. Moreover, if used with appropriate modeling tools, it can help to predict the demand and supply for the products, which in turn determines the manufacturing plan, which is an essential input for the modern ERP and MRP systems.

Benefits to Distribution Centers

For distribution centers (DCs), RFID can improve its reception process—that is, a guard confirms the truck's appointment time, barcodes the trailer, and assigns a parking spot or dock. In particular, such an improvement is achieved by: (a) the RFID reader, which confirms the arrival of the truck, trailer, and all the items, eliminating the need to check the driver's Bill of Loading; (b) the RFID reader can 'query' (scan) the contents much quicker than barcoding the trailer manually; (c) the RFID system can enable the DC gate to communicate with the warehouse management system in a timely manner, thus attaining the

Figure 4. The stakeholders in the supply chain

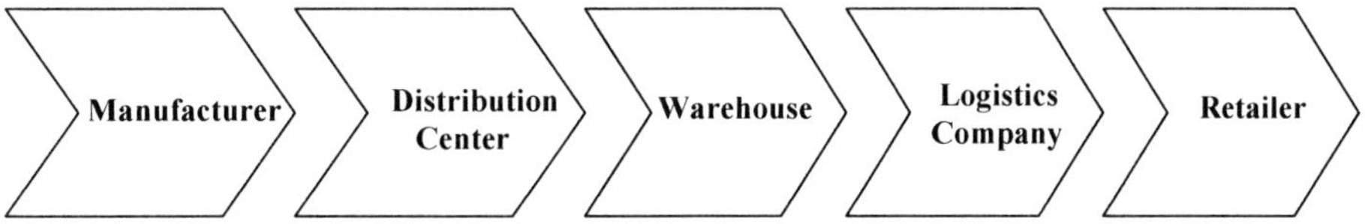

steady 'information synchrony'. In doing so, the productivity of DC is undoubtedly enhanced. The RFID solution is also seen to be beneficial when managing claims and deductions occurring at the DCs (Symbol Technologies, 2004).

Benefits to Warehouses

For warehouses, RFID can first improve the product flow by: (a) increasing the Putaway Accuracy—the measurement of the accuracy of the process that physically places inventory products into storage; and (b) removing the need for additional barcodes on the pallet. Furthermore, the RFID system can improve the temporary storage. For example, with the support of RFID, inventory items can be 'scanned' wherever they are placed, which enables a more flexible storage environment. The RFID reader can help to identify any potential inventory compatibility problems for the large warehouse and DC, which typically handle inventory for all industry sectors. For instance, an industry dealing with perishables definitely needs special inventory facilities. Last, from the cost angle, deploying RFID can reduce the cost by maintaining a reduced level of inventory, waste, manual checks, and other miscellaneous inventory handling and management costs.

Benefits to Logistics Company Administration

For company executives, RFID can improve administrative laboring. For example, RFID enables the fine-grained laboring productivity measurement by timing the uploading of the goods for particular workers. Moreover, RFID helps to avoid employee theft during the outbound shipping by identifying the nature of the items (goods or company property).

Benefits to Retailers

For retailers, RFID can help to make the price strategy. This is achieved by employing the RFID readers that capture precise information on how much product was sold from each location by placing different RFID readers in different selling place (e.g., point-of-sale machines). Next, RFID can improve customer satisfaction since it provides the right information at the right time and in the right format. For instance, DHL and FedEx each use an RFID-enabled tracking service, which helps the customer to monitor its own consignment. Customer satisfaction is further improved when the RFID allows retailers to know exactly what products are available in stock and in what capacity, which prevents the customers from being disappointed under the circumstance that their desired products are out of stock.

Benefits to the Whole Supply Chain

For SCM strategists, RFID facilitates detailed data collection and statistical analysis, from gross to very fine-grained levels. For instance, RFID readers in a retailer's store can capture data on product arrival, placement, and movement, which can present the cyclical patterns. This key capability of RFID allows the executives to link the date received with the date sold. Moreover, it can help to identify possible points of information leakage throughout the entire supply chain. As a result, RFID increases the visibility in the supply chain, which can be used to make strategic decisions to further increase competitive advantage.

ADOPTION STRATEGY

In this section, we discuss the RFID adoption strategy, which facilitates the ultimate successful RFID deployment. In general, an adoption strategy provides a roadmap to implement the technology in a way that is consistent with an organization's strategic vision and goal. It is our belief that such a road map comprises four essential fundamental principles for RFID to be thoroughly adopted in the organization. We formulate them as follows to guide the RFID adoption strategy.

Shared Understanding

In an organization, each decision maker or potential stakeholder of the RFID adoption may have a considerably different understanding from his or her own perspective towards RFID. The likelihood of successful adoption of RFID in effect hinges on the capability of the organization to enforce a broader shared understanding. This calls for a harmonious integration of each individual's opinion in a manner that benefits the organization's core competency and strategic goal, rather than that focuses on isolated areas of benefits. Hence, in the early stage, the main aim is to ensure that such a shared understanding is permeated at each level of the executive management and general administrative members of the organization.

Goal Setting

No technology deployments can be successful unless the goals of the deployment program are aligned with the business goals. Hence, at the beginning of RFID adoption, the organization has to set a very clear unambiguous goal for RFID adoption. This goal is to be aligned with the organization's existing business goal. With the goal, important stakeholders can thus be explicitly (rather than implicitly or potentially) identified. A definitive goal also helps to find the 'buy-in' among all the stakeholders of the RFID technology—a key component in achieving organization change successfully due to the fact that support from senior management is exceptionally critical.

Justification

It is well recognized that, in order to justify a new technology, a number of convincing business scenarios are of paramount importance. These scenarios must contribute to achieving the organization's business goals. They can be substantiated by collecting and investigating all the operational and technical requirements in the organization. Moreover, a cost-benefit analysis (e.g., ROI estimation) to suffice the financial concern will significantly increase the possibility of RFID being accepted by those hesitant stakeholders. Last, potential challenges and issues during and after deploying RFID have to be clearly identified at the early stage. Each challenge should be addressed by possible solutions submitted to all involved stakeholders.

Planning and Approaching

Before starting the implementation, it is very important to define a detailed deployment plan with thorough consideration to various factors like schedule, impact, and usability. This facilitates a positive and quicker realization of the technology outcomes. A good project plan includes evaluation of technology option, standard-based deployment approach, measurements and optimization techniques, and a continuous improvement roadmap. During the implementation, an incremental approach shall be taken. Thus pilot tests and milestones can be used for checking the progress of the implementation and ensuring the desired outcome is achieved through the delta part implemented in the current adoption iteration.

Based on these aforementioned principles, we then present a refined strategic step flow for the RFID adoption strategy. This is shown in Figure 5, where the elaborated steps (rectangles) of the roadmap are outlined one after another and are connected by directed edges and condition check (triangles). We explore each step one by one as follows.

Core Competency Reaffirmation

The *core competency* (*CC*) is defined as one thing that an organization can do better than its com-

Figure 5. RFID adoption roadmap

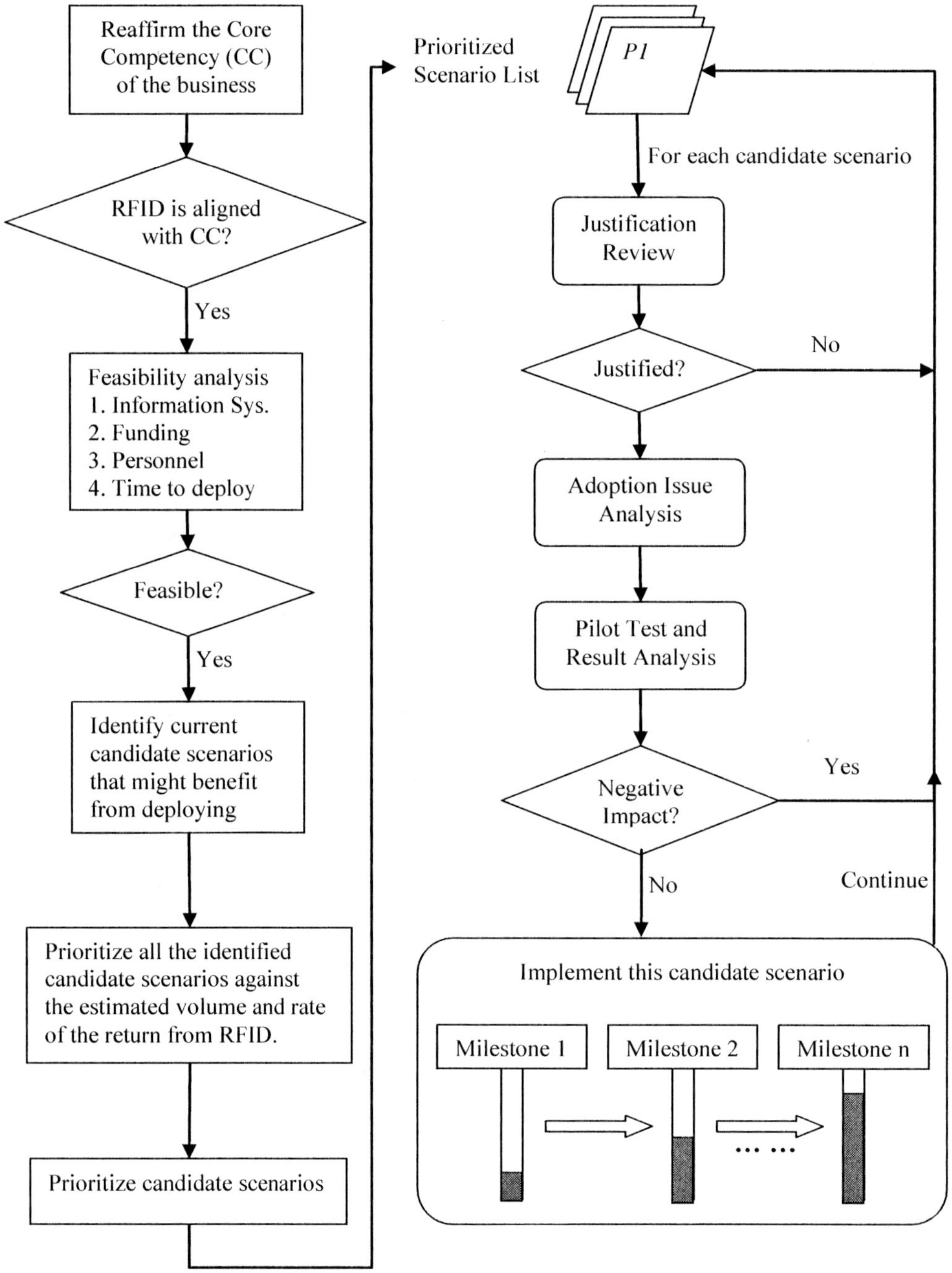

petitors, and is crucial to its success. Before the organization adopts any candidate technologies, it has to assess them against the core competency. For example, if a new technology enables the organization to maintain its CC and even gain more CC (i.e., CC-aligned), then this technology is favorable to the organization and should be given further adequate consideration. Otherwise, such a technology needs more evaluation under current business contexts even if it appears very promising from the technical perspectives or from other organizations' angles. It is highly desirable that the CC-aligned technology, once validated within the organization, receives unanimous support from senior management to the general staff. This undoubtedly paves the way for easier adoption that is less likely to be tangled with internal politics, funding difficulties, and some of the execution delays. For example, when retailer giant Wal-Mart realizes that the core competence lies in its dominant distribution channels, which can greatly benefit from RFID technology (as discussed above), it demands all of its top 100 suppliers to attach RFID tags onto their goods. On the contrary, if a company XYZ's CC is manufacturing high-quality automobile engine assemblies, it should be very cautious in adopting RFID unless its primary retailers at the downstream urge it to do so, because the distribution is not XYZ's core competencies and doing so will only distract itself from doing what they are good at. Therefore, in general, an organization should be wary of taking aggressive steps in implementing RFID solutions before the core competence has been thoroughly reaffirmed and evaluated.

Feasibility Analysis

If the RFID technology is being considered to be aligned with the CC, it is time for the organization to perform the feasibility analysis, which deals with four major aspects:

- It is very important to estimate the capability of existing information systems. Since RFID will dramatically increase the amount of the data captured from instance level tags, the information systems have to capture, process, and analyze such a huge amount of data efficiently. Any insufficiency of information systems will definitely hinder the RFID technology to realize its full potential.
- RFID solutions could be quite costly; hence continuous and dedicated RFID funding support is essential.
- Personnel preparation is another feasibility issue needing consideration. Once implemented, the RFID might change the business process as well as fundamental information systems operations, which incur substantial IT training and adaptation study. The learning capability of involved working staff also determines the success of RFID adoption.
- Lastly, the organization has to choose the appropriate time to deploy RFID. Early adoption of RFID has advantages as well as risks. The feasibility of time should study whether the company is ready for RFID at that particular time, and moreover can bear the risk associated, even if the prerequisite conditions are all met.

Candidate Scenarios

The next step is to identify candidate scenarios that would benefit from RFID and to measure the potential benefit in a self-defined scale. For example, for manufacturing units, RFID can be used to support quality control by querying components and subassemblies as they enter the facility. This is a typical candidate scenario that can be identified. It is recommended for the organization to enumerate all the potential RFID-involved candidate scenarios that can impact an organization's core competences. One efficient way to accomplish such an enumeration would be to define several business areas based on the

Table 1. A sample of candidate scenario

Scenario Name:	Shipment Status Query
Involved Stakeholders:	1. A consignee, or third-party logistics firm, or shipper 2. Consolidators, or warehousing entities, or freight forwarders, documentation personnel, carriers or custom clearing personnel
Scenario Description:	This scenario states a third-party logistics firm or shipper to query for the status of one or more shipments and a transport service provider to respond to the query.
Detail Activities:	Identifies the shipment for which status information is needed. The Shipper's and Carrier's Reference Numbers identify a particular shipment. Communicates the status of a shipment. The Shipper's and Carrier's Reference Numbers identify a particular shipment. The response references geographical location, time, and customer's entry number; it may include information about delivery exceptions. It does, if RFID technology is adopted, include order-level detail.
CC Impacts from RFID:	Increasing the shipping data accuracy: • The transport service provider's detailed shipping manifest ensures that the right number of cases is en route, thereby improving customer (e.g., consignee) service levels. • The transport service provider reduces load times by eliminating manual order auditing. • There are fewer discrepancies between shipments and invoices, because the shipping manifest can automatically generate an invoice that includes case EPCs.
Business Process:	

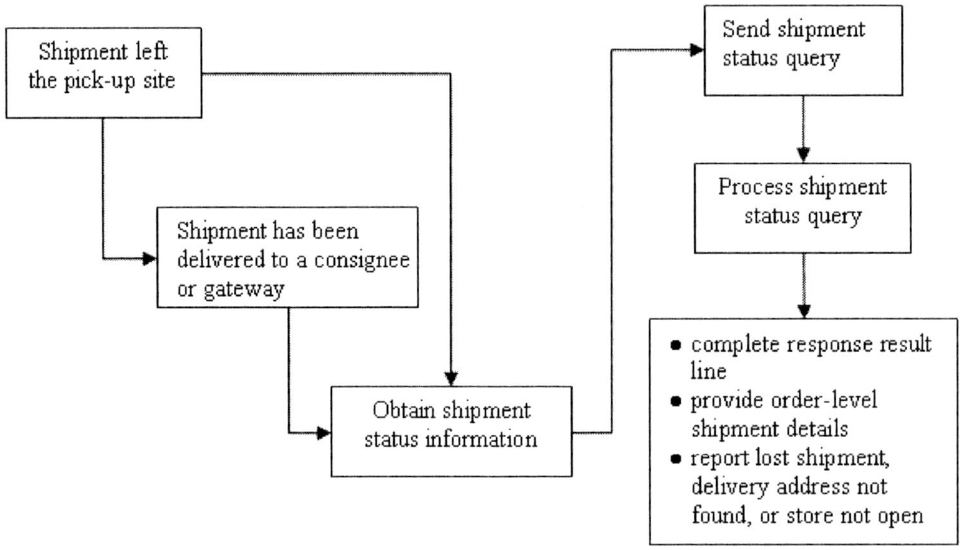

beneficiary summarized above (e.g., the manufacturing, distribution, warehouse management, etc.). For each business area, one representative candidate scenario is selected according to its relevance to the organization's CC. Also, it is a good idea to break down a large scenario into a couple of smaller scenarios, and only one of which is chosen based on the stakeholders' preferences (e.g., the one that promises the most effective impact towards the CC). In other words, as an emerging technology, RFID must be adopted in a selective and iterative manner so that the risk, cost, and organization changes can be controlled at the minimum level, whereas the positive impact to CC is pursued at the maximum level. A formal description is necessary to state the basic characteristics of each scenario. A typical tabular description of a sample candidate scenario (based on RosettaNet, 2001) is presented in Table 1.

Scenario Prioritization

The previous step produces a list of candidate scenarios, each of which represents one particular business area in this organization. (Readers shall recall that one business area comprises a set of scenarios. For each iteration, we only choose one scenario from this set in each business area). In this step, we need to prioritize this list against a set of criteria such as estimated impacts to CC, the ROI, the cost, and so forth. Such a prioritizing process also needs to consider the preference from different RFID stakeholders. This is achieved by:

1. Organizing the criteria set into a hierarchical structure
2. Performing the pair-wise comparison between any two candidate scenarios against one specific criterion
3. Providing the pair-wise comparison between any two criteria for each rfid stakeholder
4. Computing the stakeholders-aggregated preferences for each criteria
5. Calculating the overall weight for each scenario allowing for all criteria with different preferences
6. Ranking the scenario list against the weight value generated in #5, with the biggest weight value being positioned in the first rank. This step eventually generates a *prioritized scenario list* for further justification review.

Justification Review

In this step, for each candidate scenario in the *Prioritized Scenario List,* the organization conducts the justification review, a static analysis of RFID deployment only related to that particular candidate scenario. Readers are advised that several justification methods can be applied. For example, traditional ROI (return on investment) methods can be utilized to examine whether RFID technology should be deployed in this candidate scenario. However, they seem inadequate as RFID so far has a high level of uncertainty (e.g., tag prices, standards), and existing stories (eWeek.com) show that a number of possible applications are unfairly treated by existing ROI methods and tools. The appropriate justification tools are thus highly desirable and become a promising future research direction. For each candidate scenario, if the justification review produces negative results, it is removed from the prioritized scenario list, and the next scenario will be considered to perform the justification review. Otherwise, this scenario will be subsequently chosen for the following pilot test.

Adoption Issues

Before the pilot test, a clear consensus of issues and their solutions is necessary among all the stakeholders. Hence in this step, the stakeholders need to unanimously identify adoption challenges specific to this scenario. The next section of this chapter will provide a comprehensive issue list that the organization should consider. However, we believe each scenario has its own unique set of adoption issues. Even for the same issue, it has different impact on various scenarios. It is suggested that the organization itemizes all the possible problems that it might encounter during the pilot test. More importantly, the solutions that address these challenges should be proposed and planned in this step. This ensures the smooth progress of the pilot test. Moreover, the solutions can also be validated and modified during the pilot test.

Pilot Test

Once the justification review is confirmed positively, the pilot implementation can be carried out in an experimental environment. It can be an RFID prototype in a smaller scope or scale of this candidate scenario. For example, a pilot deployment in one or two locations allows evaluation of RFID vendors, equipment, and software, and provides the opportunity for different stakeholders to gain experience with RFID. Furthermore, such a pilot is to produce the impact analysis for this candidate scenario. As many impacts can be associated with the RFID deployment, some of them are beneficial to some shareholders, while some are negative to other shareholders. Hence the pilot implementation can estimate such impacts brought by RFID deployment. If most of the results tend to be negative, the likelihood that the RFID to be implemented in this scenario appears to be very low. The organization might need to consider the next candidate scenario along the *Prioritized Scenario List*. In contrast, positive pilot test results with the pilot feedback suggest the start of the RFID implementation in this candidate scenario.

Implementation

Once the pilot test is passed, the formal implementation can be carried out in an incremental manner through a set of iterations with a couple of milestones, which ensure that the implementation

Table 2. Sequential tasks within one milestone

Architecture Design	The architecture can follow some RFID reference model and must be extensible so that new architectural elements or scenarios can be added in the next milestones.
Edge Deployment	Assemble the RFID edge solution from selected vendors based on the drafted architecture rather than from one particular RFID system or product.
Verification and Validation	Measure the system performance and business impact.
Scale Deployment	Consider adding additional locations in terms of geography or business unit for next milestone.
Integration Deployment	Add the RFID data-integration middleware to enable the data sharing with other information systems, or even other partners. Consider adding business process integration infrastructure for the next milestone.
Evolve and Expand	Considering the adaptability of this milestone to ensure that it can expand and evolve to meet the changing needs of the business in the following milestones.

cost and risk can be controlled and mitigated to the minimal level. Each milestone has different focuses. Table 2 lists possible sequential tasks within one milestone. Particular attention is given for fostering the transition between milestones.

RFID ADOPTION CHALLENGES

Several key adoption issues will be discussed in this section. The main issues that we address in this section are cost associated with the deployment of RFID system, security and privacy concerns, and finally more technical issues in deployment of an RFID system.

Cost

A cost-estimation model for a full-fledged deployment of an RFID system in a supply chain environment should consider the following factors.

RFID Tags

When deploying an RFID system, one should consider the cost of buying RFID tags. It is a good idea to consider renewable tags (if possible) as a means to reduce cost. Normally the cost of active tags is more than the passive tags. The active tags are in the range of US$20 to $50 per tag (Lyngsoe, n.d.; *RFID Journal*, 2006a, 2006c) . The cost of the passive tags depends upon the frequency. Normally the LF tags are more expensive than HF or UHF because of the size of the antennae (RMOROZ, 2004). It normally costs more than $2 and goes as high as $10. The HF tags are cheaper than the LF tags and normally cost less than a dollar.

Apart from the cost of the tags, companies should also consider the *cost of testing* the passive tags. The failure rate for the UHF EPC tags ranged from 0-20% in the year 2004. This might drop down once manufacturers start using sophisticated manufacturing techniques, however there is a cost associated to ensure that the tags are functioning properly. Finally there is cost associated with *replacing* the defective tags (*RFID Journal*, 2006c).

RFID Printers

An RFID label has a similar functionality as an RFID tag. However it can be stuck on like a label. The RFID label can be printed using RFID printers. Hence if you are planning to use RFID labels, the cost of the RFID printer should be considered. In some applications RFID labels are much more preferred because of the environment and the products. For example applications like express parcel delivery, library book/video checkout, sensitive document tracking, ticketing (sports, concerts, ski lifts, etc.), and pharmaceuticals prefer RFID labels (Zebra, 2006).

RFID Readers

When deploying an RFID system, one should consider the cost of buying RFID readers. The fixed readers are normally cheaper than the portable readers. It is normally in the range of $500 to $5,000 depending on the features built into the reader (*RFID Journal*, 2006c). Dumb readers are usually cheaper, as they do not have any computing capability. On the other hand intelligent readers offer computing capability to filter data, store information, and execute commands. Agile readers can communicate with tags using a variety of protocols, while multi-frequency readers can read tags using different frequencies (*RFID Journal*, 2006c). All these features contribute to the cost of readers, and the organization should select a proper reader based on its application requirements.

RFID Antennas

Almost all the readers are equipped with one or more antennas. However in some cases the need for additional high-power antennas cannot be ruled out, and hence this additional cost should be considered before deciding to deploy an RFID system.

RFID Middleware

RFID middleware contributes a major portion of RFID investment. Many vendors supply RFID middleware, and the cost can vary depending upon the capabilities of the middleware. Usually factors that contribute to cost include complexity of the application and the number of places the middleware would be installed. Apart from the middleware, the companies should also consider the cost of edge servers, which are normally deployed in the warehouse, distribution center, or production facility. The edge servers are simple servers, which are connected to the RFID reader using a universal serial bus (USB) port.

Training Existing Staff

Introducing new technology in an organization introduces costs associated with training the concerned staff. For example an organization will need to train its employees, particularly engineering staff who will manage readers in manufacturing and warehouse facilities, and IT staff who will work on the systems that manage RFID data (*RFID Journal*, 2006c).

Hiring Technology Expertise

Most of the companies, as of now, would not have the expertise to deploy a complete RFID system. This is partly attributed to the fact that RFID is a relatively new technology. Hence an organization would need to outsource this task to a third party who knows how to install the readers, decide the appropriate location for fixing the tag on the products, ascertain that the data gathered by the reader is properly propagated to the middleware in the right format, and so on. This is quite important because RFID systems can be sometimes difficult to install, as there are several factors that can affect the optimum performance of such a system. Hence a major portion of RFID investment has to be targeted to this area.

Other Miscellaneous Costs

The miscellaneous costs might include regular maintenance of the RFID readers or replacement of damaged tags or antennas.

Cost Estimation for RFID Deployment in Supply Chain Tracking

When deploying an RFID system for inventory management and control in a supply chain, all the above-mentioned costs should be considered. According to Forrester Research, the estimated cost of middleware is around $183,000 for a $12 billion manufacturer looking to meet the RFID tagging requirements of a major retailer (*RFID Journal*, 2006c). In the same manner the estimated price of $128,000 could be spent for consulting and integration, $315,000 for the time of the internal project team, and $80,000 for tag and reader testing (*RFID Journal*, 2006c). A simple estimate is provided in Table 3.

On the lower end an estimated cost of around $3 million should be invested in an RFID project for inventory tracking and management if a total of 10 million items are tagged. The number of readers, printers, and edge servers would vary depending upon the number of distribution centers and warehouses in use. Here we assumed 100 readers and printers, and 50 edge servers. These numbers are used just as an example; it can vary depending upon each company.

Read-Rate Accuracy

Achieving 100% read-rate accuracy is a major adoption challenge with RFID deployment. Supply chains and warehouse management solutions based on RFID are highly vulnerable to read-rate

Table 3. Simple cost estimate

Investment Area	No. of Units	Cost Per Unit (USD)	Total Cost (USD)
RFID Tags	10,000,000	$ 0.15	$ 1,500,000.00
RFID Readers (*Handheld, Fixed, Forklift*)	100	$ 8,000.00	$ 800,000.00
RFID Printers	100	$ 3,000.00	$ 300,000.00
Edge Servers	50	$ 2,500.00	$ 125,000.00
RFID Middleware	N.A.		$ 200,000.00
RFID Consulting	N.A.		$ 128,000.00
RFID Training	N.A.		Variable Cost
Tag Validation	N.A.		$ 80,000.00
		Total Cost	**$ 3,133,000.00**

inaccuracy because of the number of RFID-tagged items that need to be scanned every second. Consider the scenario when a palette containing 1,000 RFID-tagged items is scanned at the warehouse exit. There is a high probability that the reader would not scan a few tags. It is difficult to list the main reasons that result in inaccurate readings because there are too many "ifs" and "buts". Accuracy is dependent on so many unrelated variables that it is difficult to list the main factors behind the cause. However we attempt to outline some basic parameters, which results in inaccurate readings. Some of the main reasons for inaccurate readings include the environment in which RFID system works, material of the item being tracked, reader configuration, reader and tag placements, tag orientation, and so forth. To successfully deploy an RFID system, some key parameters should be considered to achieve accurate readings.

Tagged Material

Maintain some consistency when tracking materials. It is not a good idea to standardize the reader configuration to track cartons, trolleys, pallets, glass materials, documents, or metal or plastic bins. This is because different materials behave differently to RF energy; some materials are RF friendly, while others are RF absorbent or RF opaque. A reader configured to read tags from RF-friendly material would definitely fail to give 100% read-rate accuracy if used to track RF-absorbent or RF-opaque items.

Preplanned Object Movement

To assure good read rates, it is advised to move the tagged objects on a predefined route (or pattern). You cannot expect good rates if the cartons are moved through a forklift, people, metals trolleys, plastic trolleys, and so forth. There should be just one or two modes of transport well tested for 100% read-rate accuracy.

Tags from Different Vendors

Read rate is also affected if tags are used from different vendors because the performance of such tags varies significantly. Another reason is the use of different standard-compliant tags (like EPC Gen1 & EPC Gen2). It is also difficult to configure the reader power level at an optimum level where it supports all different tags with 100% read rate. Ideally one should try to use a single standard and single vendor tag in one ecosystem. Nevertheless this may change as the standards improve.

Tag Orientation

Orientation is one of the big factors for providing good read rates. Even though dual dipole tags perform much better in all orientations, it is still advised to follow a policy on tag placement and tag orientation (TPTO). A standard policy on TPTO across an organization would definitely improve the read-rate accuracy.

Security

Security of RFID solutions in supply chain management is a major issue. Automated warehouse management and supply chain solutions based on RFID should leave no room for security loopholes. Security properties like confidentiality[3], integrity[4], availability[5], authentication[6], and anonymity[7] need to be considered for the successful RFID adoption. Consider the warehouse management scenario: if a malicious reader can eavesdrop (spy) on the communication between the tags and the readers, *confidentiality* and *anonymity* in such communication is lost. A malicious reader may be placed by a competing organization to study the goods movement in your warehouse. Such tactics for gathering business intelligence can be addressed if security mechanisms are in place. Secondly, information stored on the RFID tag could also be tampered with by malicious readers, which could result in wrong items being loaded from the warehouse. For example, if the malicious reader changes the information on RFID tag from *Orange* to *Apple,* then a palette containing apples might be shipped when the intention was to ship oranges. Data tampering (or *integrity*) can raise issues like quality of service and trust in logistics and supply chain, and hence needs to be addressed thoroughly. Similarly, malicious entities can employ an active jamming approach to launch denial of service attacks, which would make the RFID network unavailable. In such an attack the RFID reader cannot query the tags, and hence the warehouse management system can stop working or real-time status of the warehouse cannot be made *available* (Engberg, Harning, & Jensen, 2004; Menezes, Van Oorschot, & Vanstone, 1996).

In this section we discuss solutions from literature which can address these security issues. The details discussed in this section are explained from a security expert's perspective. Hence if the reader is a business executive or management strategist, they may skip this section. All they need to know is that there are some security mechanisms in place (as shown in Figure 7) which can be used to guarantee security in communication between the tag and the reader. These security mechanisms are based on the assumption that expensive Gen-2 RFID tags are used.

Access Control and Authentications

Several approaches to access control and authentication are proposed in the literature. We will discuss some in greater detail in this section.

Figure 6. Major security issues with RFID adoption

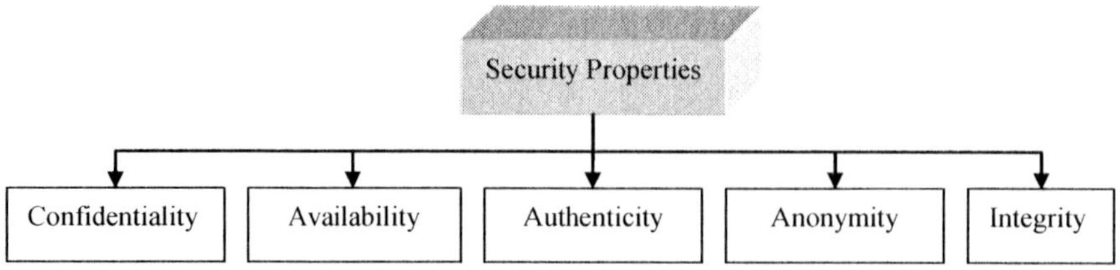

Figure 7. Security solutions to address security issues with RFID adoption

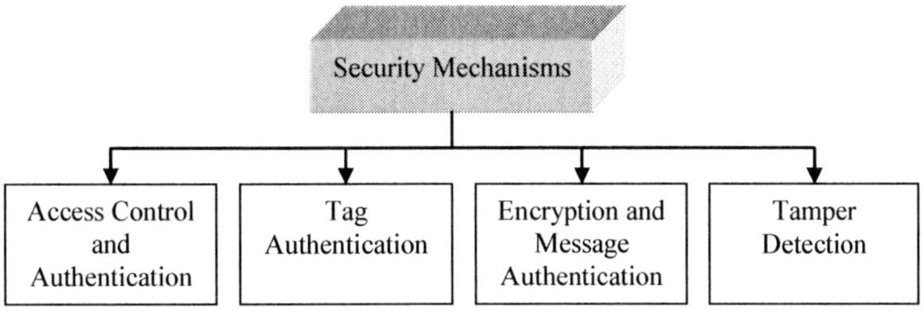

Exclusive-OR Approach for Authentication

A simple authentication scheme based on challenge-response protocol is presented in Juels, Rivest, and Szydlo (2003). It uses only simple bitwise exclusive-OR operations and no other complicated cryptographic primitives, hence it is suitable for RFIDs. However, the main issue with this approach, as pointed out by Dimitriou (2005), is that it involves the communication of four messages and frequent updates which would increase unnecessary traffic between the reader and the tag (Dimitriou, 2005; Wong & Phan, 2006). Feldhofer (2004) demonstrated that it is possible to achieve authentication without making use of computationally intensive public-key cryptography, but instead used the advanced encryption standard (AES), which is a symmetric-key technique for encryption (Stallings, 1999; Vajda & Buttyan, 2003; Wong & Phan, 2006).

Hash-based Approaches for Access Control

A hash-based access control protocol is discussed in Weis (2003). Here the tag is first in a *locked state*. When the tag moves to the *unlocked state*, the reader can access the tag's details. In order to change the state, the tag first transmits a meta ID, which is the hash value of a key. An authorized reader looks up the corresponding key in a backend system and sends it to the tag. The tag verifies the key by hashing it to return the clear text ID and remains only for a short time in an 'unlocked' state which provides time for reader authentication and offers a modest level of access security (Knospe & Pohl, 2004; Wong & Phan, 2006).

Tag Authentication

Tag authentication is another security mechanism that authenticates the tag to the reader and protects against tag counterfeiting. There are several protocols proposed for this purpose. For example, Vajda and Buttyan (2003) propose and analyze several lightweight tag authentication protocols. Similarly, Feldhofer (2004) proposes the simple authentication and security layer (SASL) protocol with AES encryption and analyzes the hardware requirements (Feldhofer, 2004; Knospe & Pohl, 2004; Wong & Phan, 2006).

Encryption and Message Authentication

Next-generation RFID systems like the ISO 14443 or MIFARE® offer encryption and authentication capability for data which is exchanged between the readers and the tags. In RFID systems the UID is the most important data, and this can be secured by encrypting the memory blocks at the application layer. The UID is usually read-only, and many RFID tags provide a permanent write lock of memory blocks. This can ensure data integrity, but of course, not message authentication (Knospe & Pohl, 2004; Wong & Phan, 2006).

Tamper Detection

RFID tags carry data that represent the unique item identifier (UID) as well as product details to which it is attached. This data is very significant and, if tampered with, can have severe conse-

Figure 8. Major privacy concerns with RFID adoption

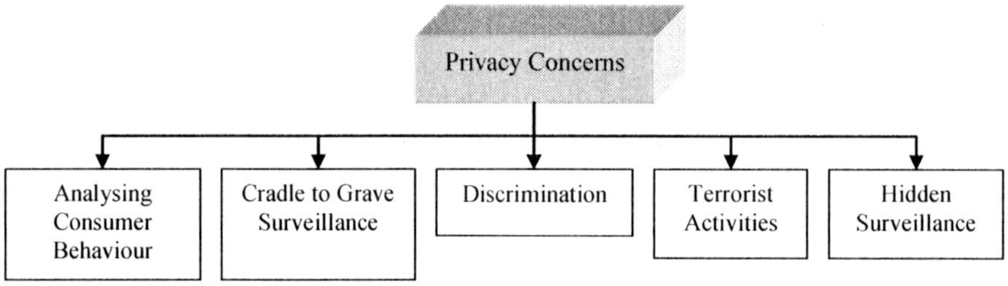

quences. For example if data representing the "nature of good" is changed, it can have severe implication—that is, instead of *Lethal Weapons*, the RFID could be modified to represent that the consignment carries *Oranges*. Such data tampering needs to be detected, as it can be a threat to national security. Potdar et al. (2005) presented a solution to address this security issue. They proposed a tamper-detection mechanism for low-cost RFID tags. The proposed algorithms for tamper detection works by embedding secret information (like a pattern) in the RFID tags. The pattern is embedded by manipulating the unique identifier in such a way that even after embedding the pattern, each RFID tag can be uniquely identified. To detect tampering, a tamper-detection component is introduced in the RFID middleware, which detects the embedded pattern. If the pattern is not present, it indicates data tampering, in which case the data from the RFID is quarantined and later processed appropriately (Potdar et al., 2005).

Privacy

The deployment of RFID in day-to-day life can raise several privacy concerns. The major concerns originate because of the inherent ability of RFID to track people who are using products that have RFID tags. Privacy experts say that marketers and retailers can gather detailed customer profiles, based on their transactions with that individual (Juels et al., 2003; Kumar, n.d.) . The privacy concern originating by the use of RFID can be categorized into five areas as shown in Figure 8.

If RFID is deployed in a full scale, it may result in many privacy concerns because RFID can be used to track *consumer behavior*, which can further be used to *analyze consumer habits*. It can even be used for *hidden surveillance*, for example, deploying secret RFIDs for tracking. With the size of RFIDs reducing day by day, it has now become possible to hide them within products without the owners' consent. For example, RFID tags have already been hidden in packaging (Hennig, Ladkin, & Siker, 2005). A scenario of hidden RFID testing was discovered in a Wal-Mart store in Broken Arrow, Oklahoma, where secret RFID readers tracked customer action (Caspian, 2003). If RFIDs are embedded in money, it could result in *discrimination*. Consider this scenario: whenever a customer enters a shop equipped with RFID readers, they would easily know the purchasing power of the customer and can automatically manipulate pricing information to the customer's credit worthiness. This results in automated prejudices (Hennig et al., 2005). Using RFIDs could even trigger anti-social activities. Criminals with RFID readers can look for people carrying valuable items and can launch selective *attacks* (Hennig et al., 2005). However most of these issues can be tackled by privacy enforcement laws, which can be incorporated into the nation's legal framework. All these privacy issues have created a lot of fear in the consumer community. In order to address these issues, several approaches are proposed in the literature. We will discuss each of these techniques and then list the pros and cons of each approach.

Kill Tag Approach

This is one of the simplest approaches to protect consumer privacy. According to this approach all the RFID tags would be killed or deactivated once they are sold to the customer—that is, when the products with the RFID tags pass through the checkout lane. Once a tag is killed, it can never be activated or used again. A password-protected 'destroy' command can also be integrated into the electronic product code (EPC) specifications, which would kill the tag permanently (Knospe & Pohl, 2004). However according to some privacy gurus, simple use of kill tag is sometimes inadequate. There are situations where the consumer would prefer the RFID tag to remain active even when the product is sold. For example, it would be wise to embed a tag in an airline ticket to allow simpler tracking of passengers within an airport. Consider embedding a tag in invoices, coupons, or return envelopes mailed to consumers; this can be used for ease of sorting upon return. Another example would be microwave ovens that read cooking instructions from food packages with embedded RFID tags (Kumar, n.d.). At the first instance, it seems that the kill tag approach would handle most of the privacy concerns, however as discussed above, in some situations it would be sensible to keep the tag active even after the product is sold. Hence this approach does not offer a satisfactory solution.

Physical Approach

There are two basic approaches to achieve privacy protection using physical techniques. They are:

- **Faraday Cage Approach:** A Faraday cage is an enclosure designed to exclude electromagnetic fields. As a result certain radio frequencies cannot penetrate through the enclosure area. It can address some privacy concerns, for example, if high-value currency notes start embedding a RFID tag, then using foil-lined wallets can guarantee privacy (Kumar, n.d.). This approach has limited application because a faraday cage cannot shield all items (mobile phones, clothing, etc).
- **Active Jamming Approach:** According to this approach the consumer can carry a radio device that would keep broadcasting radio signals in order to disrupt the normal operation of nearby RFID readers. Although this approach offers a way to protect privacy, it may be illegal in some countries. Broadcasting unnecessary radio signals can disrupt the operation of legitimate RFID readers where privacy is not concerned.

Smart Tag Approach

This approach suggests making the RFID tags smarter so that they can manage the privacy concerns in much better manner. Adding extra functionality like introducing cryptographic capabilities would enable the tags to communicate in a secure environment and can increase the smartness of the tag. Many techniques to achieve privacy protection based on cryptographic protocols are proposed in the literature; some of these were already covered earlier in this chapter.

CASE STUDIES

In this section we list a few RFID case studies from the supply chain and logistics domain.

Moraitis Fresh

Moraitis supplies fresh fruits and vegetables to major supermarkets in Australia. The shelf life of such products is one or two weeks, which means the produce must be moved from the field to the supermarket within two to five days. Moraitis was looking at ways to boost the efficiency of its supply chain. IBM Business Consulting Services proposed an RFID solution for the above problem. Moraitis realized that RFID tags could offer a cost-effective solution to streamline supply chain functions, and help reduce the time and labor required. The technology was provided by Magellan's StackTag technology, which can read and write to multiple tags moving on high-speed conveyors in any orientation—even when tags are overlapping or touching. The initial investment was around A$ 100,000. Automated inventory tracking improved the accuracy of Moraitis' inventory management decisions (IBM, n.d.).

Australia Post

Australia Post, the postal service in Australia, was looking at ways to improve its operational efficiency, focusing on a mail sorting problem. Lyngsoe Systems was approached to offer a solution. Australia Post has deployed Lyngsoe's AMQM mail-quality measurement system, which contained more than 12,500 active tags (operating at 433.92 MHz frequency) and 400 RFID readers (Lyngsoe's RD21 readers supporting 15 antennas) at several mail sorting and distribution locations. QSM software, which is an integral part of the AMQM system, is used to analyze RFID-generated mail-tracking data. The RFID readers will automatically read the tagged test envelopes as they pass through key sorting points in the network, and update the backend system (Collins, 2005).

Australian Military

The Australian Defense Force (ADF) had deployed an active RFID system for supply chain tracking to help forecast when shipments arrive at their destinations, and to ensure that material is accurately and efficiently ordered. Savi Technology deployed the RFID system, with an initial contract of US$10.1. The ADF deployed Savi's SmartChain Consignment Management Solution (CMS), which is a suite of hardware and software components that uses barcode and RFID. ADF will now be able to make its logistics network more visible by using an in-transit visibility system (ITV) (O'Connor, 2005).

CONCLUSION

Automated identification and data capture (AIDC) is a crucial technology in supply chain management as it forms the backbone of the modern supply chain. RFID, the emerging wireless AIDC technology, first appeared in tracking and access applications during the 1980s. It allowed for non-contact reading, and is very effective in manufacturing and other hostile environments where bar code labels could not survive. As a result the industry has looked into the possibility of embracing such a promising AIDC technology in a massive scale. Therefore, this chapter provided a comprehensive introduction to RFID technology and its application in supply chain management from multi-level perspectives for various readers—RFID novices, RFID advanced users, business consultants, business executives, scholars, and students. In particular, we first discussed fundamental RFID elements governed by specific RFID standards, which are further elaborated in detail. Having such basic knowledge, we identified RFID adoption challenges—mainly cost, security, and privacy—which have become the biggest concern for those early RFID adopters. Bearing these big challenges in mind, company executives and management are seeking the road-map of RFID deployment, which we offered as a dedicated section in this chapter. Before making substantial investment in RFID solutions, management would be interested in knowing existing successful case studies. We thus provided five RFID case studies to supplement this chapter for further references. All of these case studies are centered on logistics and supply chain domain, taking into consideration the overall theme of the book.

REFERENCES

Beherrschen, V. M. (n.d.). *Frequency ranges.* Retrieved February 2, 2006, from http://www.rfid-handbook.de/rfid/frequencies.html

Caspian. (2003). *Scandal: Wal-Mart, P&G involved in secret RFID testing.* Retrieved June 13, 2006 from http://www.spychips.com/press-releases/broken-arrow.html.

Collins, J. (2005). *Aussie track mail via RFID.* Retrieved January 4, 2006, from http://www.rfidjournal.com/article/articleview/2014/1/1/

Dimitriou, T. (2005). A lightweight RFID protocol to protect against traceability and cloning attacks. In *Proceedings of the Conference on Security & Privacy for Emerging Areas in Communication Networks.*

Engberg, S.J., Harning, M.B., & Jensen, C.D. (2004). Zero-knowledge device authentication: Privacy and security enhanced RFID preserving business value and consumer convenience. In *Proceedings of the Conference on Privacy, Security & Trust* (*PST'04*), Canada.

eWeek.com. (n.d.). *For many, RFID ROI still a dream.* Retrieved June 10, 2006, from http://www.eweek.com/article2/0,1895,1756872,00.asp

Feldhofer, M. (2004). A proposal for authentication protocol in a security layer for RFID smart tags. In *Proceedings of the 12th IEEE Mediterranean Electrotechnical Conference* (*MELECON*), Dubrovnik.

Gloeckler, D. (n.d.). *What is RFID?* Retrieved September 1, 2005, from http://www.controlelectric.com/RFID/What_is_RFID.html

Hennig, J.E., Ladkin, P.B., & Siker, B. (2005). *Privacy enhancing technology concepts for RFID technology scrutinized.* (Research Report # RVS-RR-04-02) Bielefield: University of Bielefield.

IBM. (n.d.). *Moraitis fresh slices supply chain costs with IBM RFID solution.* Retrieved January 8, 2006, from www.ibm.com/industries/wireless/pdfs/moratis_final.pdf

Intermec. (2006a). *IF5 IntellliTag fixed reader.* Retrieved June 14, 2006, from http://www.pointofsaleinc.com/pdf/Intermec/if5.pdf

Intermec. (2006b). *IP3 IntellliTag portable reader (UHF).* Retrieved June 14, 2006, from http://www.pointofsaleinc.com/pdf/Intermec/ip3.pdf

Intermec. (2006c). *IV7 IntelliTag vehicle mount RFID reader.* Retrieved June 14, 2006, from http://www.pointofsaleinc.com/pdf/Intermec/iv7.pdf

Juels, A., Rivest, R.L., & Szydlo, M. (2003). The blocker tag: Selective blocking of RFID tags for consumer privacy. In *Proceedings of the 10th ACM Conference on Computer and Communications Security,* Washington, DC.

Knospe, H., & Pohl, H. (2004). RFID security information security technical report. *Elsevier, 9*(4), 30-41.

Kumar, R. (n.d.). *Interaction of RFID technology and public policy.* Retrieved June 14, 2006, from http://www.wipro.com/distribution

Leaver, S. (2005). *Evaluating RFID middleware.* Retrieved August 7, 2005, from http://www.forrester.com/Research/Document/Excerpt/0,7211,34390,00.html

Lyngsoe. (n.d.) Retrieved June 14, 2006, from http://www.lyngsoesystems.com

Menezes, A., Van Oorschot, P., & Vanstone, S. (1996). *Handbook of applied cryptography.* London: CRC Press.

O'Connor, M.C. (2005). *Australia's military to track supplies.* Retrieved January 8, 2006, from http://www.rfidjournal.com/article/articleview/1838/1/1/

Potdar, V., Wu, C., & Chang, E. (2005, December 15-19). Tamper detection for ubiquitous RFID-enabled supply chain. In *Proceedings of the International Conference on Computational Intelligence and Security,* Xi'an, China.

RFidGazzete. (n.d.). *Tag shapes.* Retrieved June 14, 2006, from http://www.rfidgazette.org/2005/10/tag_shapes.html

RFID Journal. (2006a). Retrieved June 14, 2006, from http://www.rfidjournal.com/article/articleview/208#Anchor-scanners-5989

RFID Journal. (2006b). Glossary results M-S. Retrieved June 14, 2006, from http://www.rfidjournal.com/article/glossary/3

RFID Journal. (2006c). RFID system components and costs. Retrieved February 13, 2006, from http://www.rfidjournal.com/article/articleview/1336/2/129/

RMOROZ. (2004). *Understanding radio frequency identification (RFID): Passive RFID.* Retrieved June 14, 2006, from http://www.rmoroz.com/rfid.html

RosettaNet. (2001). *PIP™specification—PIP3B4: Query shipment status.* Retrieved June 14, 2006, from http://www.rosettanet.org

Stallings, W. (1999). *Cryptography and network security.* Englewood Cliffs, NJ: Prentice-Hall.

Sweeney, P.J. (2005). *RFID for dummies.* Indianapolis, IN: Wiley Publishing.

Symbol Technologies. (2004). *Business benefits from radio frequency identification (RFID).* Retrieved June 14, 2006, from http://www.symbol.com/products/rfid/rfid.html

Tecstra. (n.d.) *RFID.* Retrieved September 1, 2005, from http://glossary.ippaper.com/

Vajda, I., & Buttyan, L. (2003). Lightweight authentication protocols for low-cost RFID tags. In *Proceedings of the 2nd Workshop on Security in Ubiquitous Computing* (*Ubicomp*), Seattle, WA.

Weis, S.A. (2003). *Security and privacy in radio-frequency identification devices.* Boston: Massachusetts Institute of Technology.

Weis, S.A., Sarma, S.E., Rivest, R.L., & Engels, D.W. (2004). Security and privacy aspects of low-cost radio frequency identification systems. In *Proceedings of Security in Pervasive Computing 2003.*

Wong, D.M.-L., & Phan, R.C.-W. (2006). RFID systems: Applications versus security & privacy implications. In G. Radhamani, & G.S.V. Radha Krishna Rao (Eds.), *Web services security and e-business.* Hershey, PA: Idea Group Publishing.

Zebra. (2006). *13.56 MHz HF Zebra R-2844Z.* Retrieved February 13, 2006, from http://www.zebra.com/id/zebra/na/en/index/products/printers/rfid.html

ENDNOTES

1 http://www.rfid-handbook.de/forum/read.php?f=4&i=81&t=81

2 RS-232 is a protocol for wired communication. Readers are connected using cables (max 30m) and the data transmission rate is very low. RS-485 is an improvement to RS-232, which still used cables, but can be large sized (1200m) and the data transmission rate is higher (2.5Mb per sec).

3 Confidentiality refers to the confidentiality in communication between the tag and the reader.

4 Integrity refers to the reliability of the information on the RFID tag.

5 The RFID systems (in the UHF) work in a very congested frequency range; frequency jamming can easily attack such systems. Hence the availability of an RFID network is a security property which needs to be considered.

6 One major security issue with the RFID tag is authentication. The data on the RFID tag like the unique identifier (UID) can be easily manipulated or spoofed, as these tags are not tamper resistant (Knospe & Pohl, 2004).

7 Anonymity to undesired and anonymous scanning of items or people.

Chapter VII
Information Security Risk in the E-Supply Chain

Wade H. Baker
Virginia Tech, USA

Gregory E. Smith
Xavier University, USA

Kevin James Watson
University of New Orleans, USA

ABSTRACT

Collaboration between supply chain partners, facilitated by integration of information flows, has created more efficient and effective networks. However, the benefits of interconnectivity are not gained without risk. Though essential to support collaboration, increased use of information technology has removed internal and external protective barriers around an organization's assets and processes. Thus, supply chains are better able to satisfy the needs of customers while more vulnerable to an array of IT-specific risks. This chapter identifies the sources of IT threats in the supply chain, categorizes those threats, and validates them by means of a survey of 188 companies representing a range of supply chain functions. Analysis suggests that supply chain risk is affected by IT threats, and therefore the benefits of collaboration facilitated by IT integration must exceed the increase in risk due to IT security threats.

INTRODUCTION

Supply chain management attempts to coordinate and combine all value chain activities into a single seamless process by emphasizing collaboration and integration across functions and between organizations. Collaboration and integration are increasingly seen as necessary to improve efficiency and effectiveness across a supply chain that has grown in both scope and complexity in recent years. The strategic importance of supply chain management has changed the nature of competition, in that contemporary views of competitive rivalry increasingly see competition between supply chains rather than between firms. Facilitating supply chain management's development is information technology (IT), which has enabled integration of information flows between channel participants thereby reducing uncertainty and risk.

Supply chain management is essentially information driven; supply chains that share information for coordinated decision making achieve maximum efficiency for all channel members. However, by eliminating traditional layers of internal and external separation, which once formed protective barriers around organizational assets and processes, IT-facilitated collaboration has simultaneously improved the supply chain's ability to satisfy customer needs while making it more vulnerable to an array of IT-specific threats. This realization identifies two underappreciated aspects of current SCM. First, there is a lack of understanding as to the extent to which IT-specific threats affect the overall risk within supply chains. Second, while members within highly interconnected supply chains would appear to achieve the greatest benefits, they also appear to be especially vulnerable to IT hazards.

While supply chain risk and information technology risk have been studied in isolation, little has been done to define the impact of information security threats within highly integrated supply chains. The following addresses this issue by identifying, categorizing, and validating the sources of information security risk within the extended supply chain. To do so, several recent empirical studies, as well as a multi-company survey representing a broad range of supply chain functions, are examined and discussed. The intent is to establish a foundational conceptualization of information security risk within the overall supply chain, and to provide managers and academicians with a better understanding of the relationship between supply chain and information risk. While beyond the scope of the chapter, it is hoped that by defining IT risk in the context of the supply chain, management will be able to identify previously unrecognized or undervalued sources of threats and design improved mitigation strategies for dealing with them.

As the primary goal of this chapter is to establish a foundation from which information security can be studied within the context of supply chain management, the chapter begins with a discussion of the role of collaboration and information technology in improving supply chain performance. This is followed by a short discussion regarding how IT security events can create problems that ripple throughout the supply chain. A review of select supply chain and IT risk models is then presented, the review of IT risk factors including a categorization of IT threats. These models are then merged into a single framework capable of establishing point of origin, threat type, and type of risk to the supply chain caused by IT-specific threats. To assist in further developing the current reality and validate the proposed mode, results and analysis of a large-scale survey conducted in conjunction with a world-leading IT-security services company are presented. The remainder of the chapter contains general recommendations as to how companies may mitigate risk when establishing or operating collaborative partnerships and concluding comments.

COLLABORATION AND IT

The core tenet in developing flexible supply chains is the practice of collaboration. Supply chain collaboration is the confluence of all parties in the supply chain acting in unison towards common objectives. Collaborative partners share information, knowledge, risk, and profits (Mentzer et al., 2000) based on a foundation of trust and commitment to one another. Ultimately, as organizations move beyond mere operational-level exchanges toward collaboration, supply chains become more competitive (McLaren, Head, & Yuan, 2002). Supply chain collaboration does not happen on its own, Mentzer et al. (2000) found that certain conditions or enablers must be in place for partners to forge a collaborative union and share in the benefits of the effort. Specifically, the authors found that collaborative relationship required partners in supply chains to:

- Share the responsibility of the cooperative outcome to foster continued commitment
- Candidly discuss their operations and practices including information that might otherwise be deemed proprietary
- Trust and respect the judgments and suggestions of their fellow collaborators
- Have clear expectations of one another
- Solve problems in a unified effort which focuses on solutions, not blame
- Engage in implementing advanced information technology and commit to sustaining this practice

Engaging in these practices improves partners' ability to overcome certain obstacles that could doom supply chain collaboration. Further, Mentzer et al. (2000) identified several practices that might impede collaboration:

- Partners could resist change and discard collaborative practices by insisting on doing things the old way.
- Partners may not have a clear vision of the supply chain and maintain a silo view of the organizational structure.
- Partners may not "buy in" and fully invest in the collaboration effort.
- Partners may not sufficiently communicate with one another, leading to potentially damaging effects.
- Partners may betray one another for selfish gains rather than stay steadfast to the goal of collective gains.

Ultimately, when obstacles are overcome and enablers are in place, a supply chain can garner significant benefits. The benefits can be broadly categorized into two groups: financial and non-financial. The financial benefits arising from collaboration arise from reduction in inventory holding costs and greater efficiency of productive resources (Cachon & Fisher, 2000).

The effects of the financial benefits are reverberated throughout the supply chain and easily measurable. They receive significant attention because of their impact, but remain only one part of the benefits received. The impact of the non-financial benefits, though more subtle and often difficult to measure, are just as important, as they drive revenue growth. Non-financial gains include:

- Faster speed to market of new products
- Stronger focus on core competencies
- Enhanced public image
- Greater trust and interdependence
- Increased sharing of information, ideas, and technology
- Stronger emphasis on the supply chain as a whole
- Improved shareholder value
- Competitive advantage over other supply chains (mentzer, 2001)

The overall impact that collaboration can have on a company's bottom line can be staggering.

Based on the extent of collaboration, a company can add as much as three points to its profit margin (Wise & Fahrenwald, 2001).

Unfortunately, assessing the level of collaboration has proved a difficult measure. A number of researchers have attempted to score or assign levels of collaboration to enterprises and assess supply chain performance (Mentzer, Min & Zacharia, 2000; Barratt & Oliveira, 2001; Simatupang & Sridharan, 2005). To this end, Kolluru and Meredith (2001) developed a series of levels between partners based on the degree of collaboration. At the lowest level, partners engage in minimal arms-length relationships typified by asynchronous one-way data push communication mechanisms. Information sharing at this level is typified by the seven rudimentary information types identified by Lee, Padmanabhan, and Whang (1997) which are necessary for operation of a supply chain: inventory level, sales data, order status for tracking and tracing, sales forecasts, production and delivery schedules, performance metrics, and capacity. The highest level exists at a strategic level of collaboration across the extended enterprise facilitated by peer-to-peer client-server communication. At this level, information sharing exceeds rudimentary requirements, expanding to include product, customer, supplier, process, competitive, and marketing information (Handfield & Nichols, 1999). It appears that the degree of relationship dictates the type of information shared and the means by which it is transmitted.

Advances in IT have enabled integration and information sharing, and thus become a key driver of supply chain collaboration (Bowersox, 1990; Huang & Gangopadhyay, 2004). In fact, it has been argued that it is impossible to achieve an efficient, competitive, and collaborative supply chain without IT (Gunasekaran & Ngai, 2004). Though the supply chain literature frequently proclaims the virtues of information sharing, it is not void of warnings concerning potential drawbacks.

IT SECURITY: A SUPPLY CHAIN ISSUE

With varying levels of relationships and information sharing within supply chains, especially at the strategic level, greater importance must be placed on information security. It has been suggested (Lee & Whang, 2000; Kolluru & Meredith, 2001; Spekman & Davis, 2004) that securing information in the supply chain demands more attention than it currently receives. In fact, Lee and Whang (2000) consider identifying the amount of information that can be exchanged between supply chain partners without increasing the risk of exploitation to be one of the most challenging and frequently asked questions of the day.

The impact of IT security incidents to IT-enabled supply chains became evident as we analyzed the results of several industry surveys conducted to assess the impact of worldwide computer virus events over the past two years. The studies, done in cooperation with Cybertrust, the largest managed security services company in the world, were conducted to analyze the impact of large-scale virus events and included thousands of organizations worldwide. Although the scope of these instruments did not specifically address the source of infection, numerous respondents pointed to their partners as a source of infection in open response questions. We also noticed a number of organizations specifically commented on various impacts to their supply chain operations after partners were infected. Several examples of participant comments following four well-known viruses are included in Table 1.

Intrigued by these comments and desiring to further investigate the difficulties presented by IT security within supply chains, we cooperated with Cybertrust to conduct a large-scale industry survey to determine the scope and nature of IT risk to supply chain management. As will be shown throughout the remainder of this chapter,

Table 1. Comments from survey participants relating to the impact of recent worldwide virus events

SQL Slammer, January 2003
"The worm took down two of our data exchange partners."
"A large part of the impact for us was related to the loss of access to our external trade partners/ customers."
"Although we were not infected by Slammer, many of our partners were. This severely interfered with our work."
"We were cut off from partner sites when they went down."
Blaster, August 2003
"We were infected when a vendor hooked up his laptop to our network."
"We were infected by a 3rd party on our network."
"We got the worm through unpatched customer PCs."
"Blaster got in through a trusted partner network."
"We were infected because partners are not keeping their machines up to date with anti-virus and OS patches. This is a real problem—our IT department doesn't have control over what they do yet we suffer the consequences of their poor practices."
"Our suppliers could not confirm orders."
"We had numerous infected partners—this interfered with our work and productivity."
MyDoom, January 2004
"Our customers and suppliers sent it to us."
"It originally came in from a partner who we have a direct connection with."
"The major problems have been with our trading partners who have stopped allowing any outside e-mails to enter their system in an attempt to stop the worm's spread. In addition, some are restricting anything with an attachment. For our business, 99% of all our e-mail traffic includes attachments of one type or another and so our operations have basically been shut down."
"Several of our partners were infected causing numerous operational difficulties."
Sasser, May 2004
17% of participants infected reported a disruption of customer computing functions (order processing, sales, marketing, etc.).
16% of participants infected reported a disruption of key corporate computing functions (payroll, inventory, manufacturing, etc.).
14% of participants infected reported a disruption of partner network connectivity.

our findings imply that security incidents pose a legitimate threat to supply chain operations and call for an in-depth analysis of risk relating to the extensive usage of IT in modern supply chains.

SUPPLY CHAIN RISK

Christopher and Peck (2004) speak to the difficulty in defining risk, identifying two primary schools of thought: variance-based definitions from classical decision theory and hazard-focused definitions common to risk management. Defining the nature of and quantifying exposure to risk is often seen as the first step toward improving decision making. The Royal Society (1992) addresses this problem by defining risk in terms of an expected value measurement when they defined risk as a "combination of probability, or frequency, of occurrence of a defined hazard and the magnitude of the consequences of the occurrence." However, risk measurements are often performed qualitatively. Qualitative risk measurement evaluates descriptive variables categorically, instead of numerically, to arrive at a pragmatic solution. Categorical evaluation makes the task of quantitative risk measurement non-trivial. In either case, risk measures are fundamental to decision making and dependent on the identification of threats.

Spekman and Davis (2004) stated that risk is context specific, where different types of risk affect enterprises differently. From a business context, DeLoach (2000) identified risk as "the level of exposure to uncertainties that the enterprise must understand and effectively manage as it executes its strategies to achieve its business objectives and create value." Within this context, the definition of risk is clear yet broad, as business risk may refer to many functions of an enterprise. To hone the definition to apply to supply chain risk, it must be refined to emphasize supply and demand.

Zsidisin (2003) states that supply chain risk is "the potential occurrence of an incident associated with inbound supply from individual supplier failures or the supply market, in which its outcomes result in the inability of the purchasing organization to meet customer demand or cause threats to customer life and safety." The key elements of this definition are the identification of sources of risk and their associated threats. Christopher and Peck (2004) identify five areas that are potentially vulnerable in supply chains: processes, controls, demand, supply, and environment. These vulnerabilities fall within three risk categories: organizational, network, and environmental (Juttner, Peck, & Christopher, 2003).

Organizational risks are those found entirely within the boundaries of an organization; these risks include labor, production, and IT system uncertainties (Juttner et al., 2003). The most common types of organizational risks are process and control risks. Processes including production, sourcing, warehousing, transportation, and planning and scheduling are the activities that add value to an organization. Disruption to the execution of these processes is known as process risk. Controls are the assumptions, rules, systems, and procedures that govern how organizations exert control over processes. Misapplication or misuse of these controls is known as control risk. Cooperation between an organization's process and control mechanism is an essential supply chain strategy (Christopher, Peck, Wilding, & Chapman, 2002).

Network risks occur due to interactions between organizations linked in a supply chain. Organizations must procure materials from upstream suppliers and sell finished goods through a distribution network. However, there are risks associated with interactions between supply chain participants. Unexpected events may occur during acquisition, transportation, and employment of goods and services that negatively affect an organization's ability to serve its customers. Supply risk and demand risk, which comprise network-related risks, are defined by their role relative to the organization. Supply risk is the probability that an unexpected event occurs upstream in the supply chain, resulting in a negative consequence to the organization obtaining the goods and services. Similarly, Christopher and Peck (2004) identified demand risk as the potential for or actual disruptions of product or information flows that exist between an organization and customers. Demand risk is dependent on organizational level mechanisms (and their associated risks) of adjacent and downstream organizations.

Environmental risks, the most encompassing category, can affect the four prior sources of risk within their root categories. They are any uncertainties that occur as a result of an interaction between supply chain participants and the environment. Environmental risks could result from socio-political actions, accidents, or acts of God (Christopher & Peck 2004). These events may be far removed from an organization, but their effect could be passed to other network organizations or associated supply chains.

An appropriate line of inquiry at this juncture concerns the relationship of IT security to the supply chain risk categories above. Unfortunately, no clear and concise answer presents itself within the literature. IT system failures—which are often caused by security incidents—are considered to be an organizational risk (Juttner et al., 2003). Yet disruptions to information flows are certainly within the domain of IT security, and Christopher and Peck (2004) identified these events as a type of network-related supply chain risk. Many IT security threats, such as worms and hackers, originate outside an organization and its network of partners. These could be included among environmental risk sources in the supply chain. Based on the comments in Table 1, it is obvious that worms and viruses must be considered a network risk as well due to their tendency to propagate along the IT system interconnections among supply chain partners. Alternatively, others have classified the security of a firm's IT systems as its own dimension of supply chain risk (Spekman & Davis, 2004).

These uncertainties and conflicts exist because little has been done in the way of a unifying framework between IT security and supply chain risk. Given the growing importance of IT in SCM and the rise in IT security incidents in recent years, resolving this dilemma is critical to a resilient modern supply chain. In pursuit of such a framework, a fundamental understanding of IT security risk is essential. Therefore, an overview of IT security risk factors is supplied in the following section.

IT SECURITY RISK FACTORS

Many consider IT security to be relatively new, arising in conjunction with the increase in e-commerce since the mid-1990s. However, IT security can be traced back to the 1960s when employees of different organizations shared then scarce computer resources (Wilkes, 1991). This situation necessitated a means to control access to mutually accessible files, and the practice of computer security was born. Since that time, securing computing and IT systems within organizations and the interconnections between them has been a persistent and increasingly difficult challenge, necessitating the development of formal programs to manage IT-related risk.

Management of risk related to IT systems within a single organization has been extensively discussed in academic, professional, and governmental arenas, while the interconnections between organizations have received somewhat less attention. The National Institute of Standards and Technology (NIST) defines three basic components of an IT system interconnection: two IT systems and an interconnecting 'pipe' through which information is made available (Grance, Hash, Peck, Smith, & Korow-Diks, 2002). These components are depicted in Figure 1. Similar to the quantitative definition of risk previously discussed, most sources define IT risk as the product of the frequency of potential *threats,* the

Figure 1. Components of interconnected IT systems (Adapted from NIST, 1997)

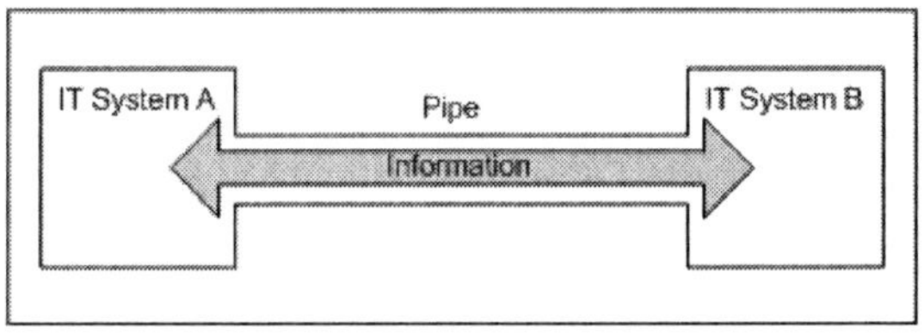

likelihood of their success, and their *impacts* to the organization (Baker & Rees, 2006).

IT Security Threats

It is beneficial to an initial investigation of IT security to define a rational categorization of threats to establish a proper foundation and facilitate understanding. Hence, numerous taxonomies have been proposed in years past to classify and systematize common IT security threats. Such efforts tend to vary greatly depending on their intended use and scope (i.e., threats identified for management attention will likely be fewer in number and less specific than those used by IT security professionals). In identifying threat categories for this study, we draw from professional experience, relevant literature, and numerous industry and government sources. As our chief purpose to discuss IT security in the context of the supply chain, we include threats identified in previous SCM literature (Warren & Hutchinson, 2000; Kolluru & Meredith, 2001; Spekman & Davis, 2004) as well as from traditional IT sources (Smith, 1989; Loch & Carr, 1992; Cheswick & Bellovin, 1994; Icove, Seger, VonStorch, & NetLibrary, 1995; Cohen, 1997; NIST, 1997; Whitman, 2003; Gordon, Loeb, Lucyshyn, & Richardson, 2004).

Categorizing IT threats from both the IT and SCM literature resulted in the selection of six general IT security threat categories. Table 2 displays these categories and provides examples from the literature as to potential threats contained within each. It is important to note that we are not claiming this list is exhaustive or descriptive, rather we consider it to be a high-level categorical representation of a large spectrum of specific threats to IT systems and interconnections. An equally important factor in our efforts was a desire to separate threats from impacts. Taxonomies often fail to make this distinction, treating causes (or threats) and effects (or impacts) interchangeably. For instance, we view various kinds of electronic theft listed by Kolluru and Meredith (2001) and Spekman and Davis (2004) as an impact associated with a successful threat—such as a network intrusion attempt or one of the many varieties of fraud and deception on the Internet. Physical theft of data or equipment is treated as a physical and environmental hazard. Separating threats and impacts in this manner becomes extremely important when attempting to measure risk.

Malicious code and programs are written to infect IT systems and then multiply, propagate, modify programs, steal information, and generally act egregiously. This category of threat is diverse and inescapable for organizations connected to the Internet. Viruses, worms, Trojans, spyware, and keyloggers are all examples of malicious code and programs. Hacking and intrusion attempts include any effort to gain unauthorized access to or alter the normal operation of IT systems. Threats of this type (denial of service, buffer overflow, and man-in-the-middle attacks) enable cyber criminals to take control of a system, allowing a range of options extending from shutting the system down to defacing Web pages to stealing information. Fraud and deception is any attempt at misrepresentation of identity to deceive and exploit. Fraud is often accomplished through non-technical means, but may take on electronic forms like phishing (a type of e-mail fraud), hoaxes, or credit card theft. Misuse and sabotage contain a diverse and particularly worrisome set of threats because persons entrusted with access to organization resources have a unique oppor-

Table 2. Categories of potential threats to IT resources

Malicious Code and Programs
Malicious Code/Programs (Amoroso, 1994; NIST, 1997; CyberProtect, 1999; NSW Guideline, 2003) *Viruses and Worm* (Loch & Carr, 1992; Landwehr et al., 1994; Icove et al., 1995; Cohen, 1997; CyberProtect, 1999; Whitman, 2003; Gordon et al., 2004) *Trojan Horse* (Landwehr et al., 1994; Icove et al., 1995; Cohen, 1997; CyberProtect, 1999) *Logic/Time Bombs* (Landwehr et al., 1994; Icove et al., 1995; CyberProtect, 1999)
Malicious Hacking & Intrusion Attempts
Hacking (Loch & Carr, 1992; NIST, 1997; CyberProtect, 1999; Spekman & Davis, 2004) *Unauthorized Access/System Penetration* (Loch & Carr, 1992; Warren & Hutchinson, 2000; NSW Guideline, 2003; Whitman, 2003; Gordon et al., 2004; Spekman & Davis, 2004) *Denial of Service Attacks* (Loch & Carr, 1992; Cheswick & Bellovin, 1994; Icove et al., 1995; NIST, 1997; CyberProtect, 1999; Warren & Hutchinson, 2000; NSW Guideline, 2003; Whitman, 2003; Spekman & Davis, 2004) *Password Sniffing/Cracking Software* (Amoroso, 1994; Icove et al., 1995; Cohen, 1997; CyberProtect, 1999; Warren & Hutchinson, 2000) *Industrial/Government Espionage* (NIST, 1997; NSW Guideline, 2003; Whitman, 2003) *Eavesdropping* (Amoroso, 1994; Icove et al., 1995; CyberProtect, 1999; NSW Guideline, 2003) *Web Site Intrusion/Defacement* (NSW Guideline, 2003; Gordon et al., 2004; Spekman & Davis, 2004) *Trap Doors* (Landwehr et al., 1994; Icove et al., 1995)
Fraud and Deception
Fraud (NIST, 1997; NSW Guideline, 2003; Gordon et al., 2004; Spekman & Davis, 2004) *Spoofing* (Icove et al., 1995; Cohen, 1997; CyberProtect, 1999; Warren & Hutchinson, 2000) *Masquerading* (Amoroso, 1994; Icove et al., 1995; Cohen, 1997; NSW Guideline, 2003) *Social Engineering* (Cheswick & Bellovin, 1994; Cohen, 1997; NSW Guideline, 2003) *Salami Attacks* (Icove et al., 1995; Cohen, 1997) *Privacy/Identity Threats* (NIST, 1997)
Misuse and Sabotage
Deliberate Acts of Sabotage or Vandalism (Loch & Carr, 1992; NIST, 1997; NSW Guideline, 2003; Whitman, 2003; Gordon et al., 2004) *Abuse/Misuse of Resources* (Amoroso, 1994; Icove et al., 1995; Cohen, 1997; Kolluru & Meredith, 2001; NSW Guideline, 2003; Gordon et al., 2004) *Abuse/Misuse of Privileges* (Amoroso, 1994; Icove et al., 1995; Cohen, 1997) *Insider Crime* (Cohen, 1997; CyberProtect, 1999) *Unauthorized Software Changes* (Cohen, 1997; NSW Guideline, 2003)

Table 2. continued

Errors and Omissions
Human Error (Cohen, 1997; NIST, 1997; NSW Guideline, 2003; Whitman, 2003)
Software/Programming Errors (Loch & Carr, 1992; Cheswick & Bellovin, 1994; Cohen, 1997; NSW Guideline, 2003; Whitman, 2003)
Accidental Entry/Destruction of Data by Employees (Loch & Carr, 1992)
Protocol/Routing/Transmission Errors (Cheswick & Bellovin, 1994; Cohen, 1997; NSW Guideline, 2003)
Physical and Environmental Hazards
Forces of Nature (fire, flood, earthquake, etc.) (Loch & Carr, 1992; NSW Guideline, 2003; Whitman, 2003)
Service Disruptions from Third-Party Provider (power, WAN, etc.) (Loch & Carr, 1992; Icove et al., 1995; Cohen, 1997; NIST, 1997; NSW Guideline, 2003; Whitman, 2003)
Weak, Ineffective, Inadequate Physical Control (Loch & Carr, 1992; Cohen, 1997)
Physical Data/Equipment Theft (Loch & Carr, 1992; Amoroso, 1994; Cohen, 1997; NIST, 1997; Kolluru & Meredith, 2001; Gordon et al., 2004; Spekman & Davis, 2004)
Dumpster Diving (Icove et al., 1995; Cohen, 1997; CyberProtect, 1999)

tunity to misuse them. An employee, partner, or contractor that abuses the access and privileges he/she has been granted within a company for malevolent purposes would fall under this category. These threats manifest themselves in the form of embezzlement, inappropriate use of an Internet connection or e-mail, sabotage, or using systems or IT resources for anything other than intended purposes. Errors and omissions are unintentional and unavoidable. They include minor nuisances like coffee on keyboards, to programming errors, to major catastrophes such as stumbling into a rack of online sales servers. Finally, physical and environmental hazards include equipment failures, power outages, natural disasters, and physical theft of property or data. Though typically rare and often outside the realm of control, an organization failing to take appropriate action will incur high downtime and equipment replacement losses due to threats in this category.

IT Security Vulnerabilities

The likelihood that any threat will be successful is largely dependent on the vulnerability of an organization's IT assets, including systems, software, information, personnel, and equipment. A vulnerability is a condition or weakness that could be accidentally or intentionally exercised by a threat (Stoneburner, Goguen, & Feringa, 2002). If no vulnerabilities are present, the likelihood of a threat's success is zero and thus IT risk is eliminated. Unfortunately, it is difficult and cost-prohibitive, if not impossible, to eliminate an organization's vulnerability to all IT threats. Therefore, the aim of IT risk management is to minimize vulnerability by implementing managerial, operational, and technical controls in an efficient and effective manner and, in the event that IT security control measures are not effective, to mitigate the negative consequences to the firm.

IT Security Impacts

The third requirement of a realistic model of IT security risk must account for potential impacts to IT assets. The practice of IT risk management has traditionally classified these impacts in terms of loss or degradation of any of the following primary security goals: confidentiality, integrity, and availability (Stoneburner et al., 2002). Confidentiality requires that information be secure from unauthorized disclosure, while integrity refers to its reliability and protection from improper modification. The goal of availability mandates that IT systems, interconnections, and information remain accessibly and uninterrupted. With these IT system impacts come numerous secondary and downstream consequences that ripple not only through the organization in which they originate but the entire supply chain.

IT SECURITY AND SUPPLY CHAIN RISK

Because modern supply chains are founded upon a series of interconnected IT systems, it is logical that they are subject to all the risks heretofore discussed as being inherent to these systems. Once an IT threat has materialized, the impact from such an incident may range from inconvenient to catastrophic and permeate all levels of the supply chain. Consequently, we now focus on the nature of the relationship between these two areas of risk and in so doing, seek a foundational model for IT security risk within the context of overall supply chain risk. In an effort to build an enveloping structure of sources by category, information flows between and within organizations, along with essential supply chain component representations, must be identified.

Figure 2. Model of supply chain information security risk

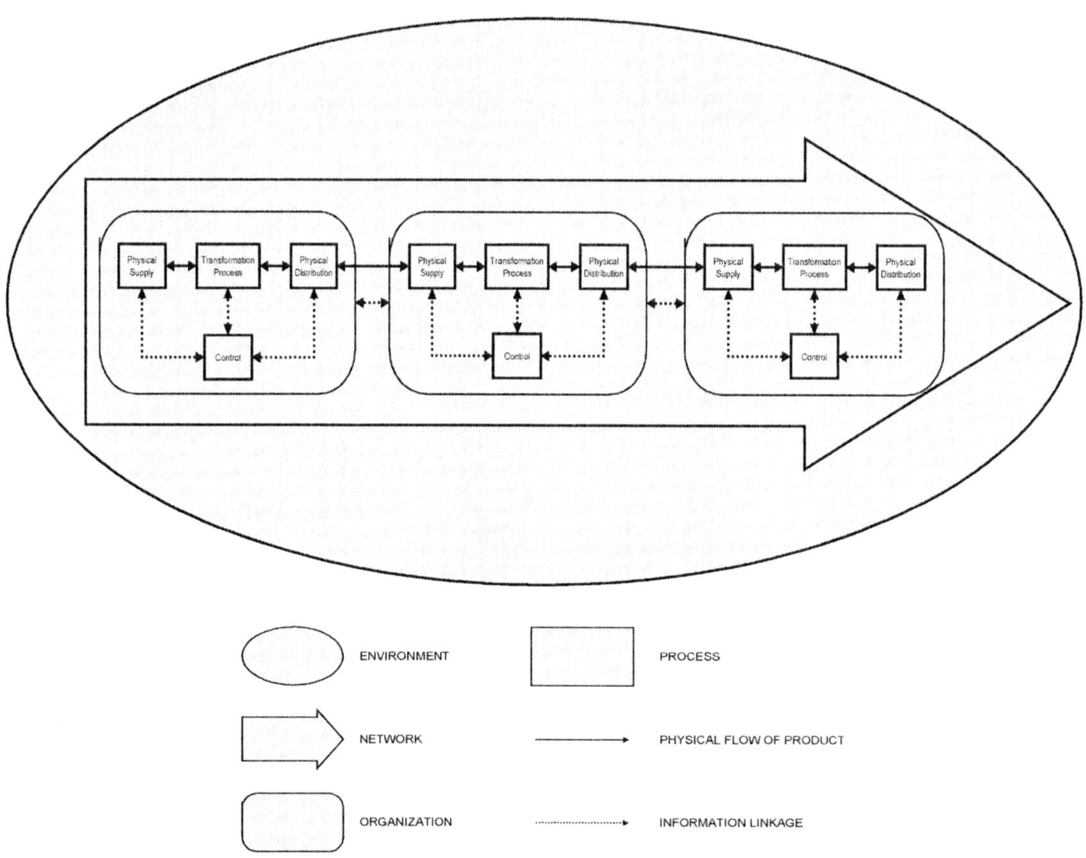

Smith, Watson, Baker, and Pokorski (2006) incorporated these informational linkages and establish a full categorical identification of supply chain risk sources (see Figure 2). In keeping with the model proposed by Juttner et al. (2003), the authors have identified the three major sources of risk originating from organizational, network, and environmental sources. Similar to the model proposed by Christopher and Peck (2004), the authors identified five areas vulnerable to information distortions within the supply chain: physical supply, the transformation process, physical distribution, control processes, and the information linkages between organizations. The information linkages and the information flowing across them are subject to compromise due to organizational, network, or environmental factors—including, of course, those related to IT security.

To understand how these information linkages are at risk, it is paramount at this point to revisit the notion of IT security risk factors—namely threats, vulnerabilities, and impacts. Though we have provided the six high-level categories of IT threats in Table 2 above for pedagogical reasons, we agree with Howard and Longstaff (1998) that categorical representations alone are insufficient to provide clarity, accuracy, and measurability of risk associated with IT security incidents. A more realistic model of how IT security incidents affect risk in the supply chain should at minimum account for: (1) threat source, (2) threat characteristics, (3) IT system vulnerabilities, (4) potential impact to IT assets, and (5) consequences to the supply chain.

As depicted in Figure 2, at a broad level, IT security and the supply chain share the same sources of risk: organizational, network, or environmental. Viruses and malicious programs, for instance, often stem from environmental risk from the far reaches of the Internet; however, because supply chain partners typically maintain high interconnectivity to support collaboration, we have found malicious code to be a substantial network risk as well. This was apparent from the respondent comments included in Table 1. Additionally, malicious code can be written and released by an organization's own employees, making this type of threat an organizational risk as well. Although we have used malicious code to show that IT security and supply chain risk share common sources, it should be understood that most IT threats span multiple sources as well.

From our previous discussion of IT security threats, it is obvious there is a myriad of vastly different methods, channels, vulnerabilities, and actors that can potentially disrupt information flows in the supply chain. For instance, intrusion attempts can be separated into virtual and physical. Obviously, the steps required to gain access to an IT system via a network are not the same as those used to gain physical access. Even when isolating virtual intrusion attempts, techniques and possibilities abound. Though seemingly elementary, characteristics such as these are critical to calculating risk and selecting proper mitigation strategies.

Figure 3 builds on our previous discussion of IT system impact, illustrating breaches to confidentiality, integrity, and availability as they specifically relate to interconnected IT systems that comprise e-supply chains.

Once the technical impacts to IT systems are clearly defined and understood, it becomes possible to draw connections to affiliated consequences within the supply chain. Previous supply chain literature is beneficial to this pursuit. Li (2002) speaks to the need to guard the confidentiality of information flows between supply chain partners from either direct or inadvertent disclosure. Findings suggest that there is a disincentive to share data due to 'information leakage' and resulting strategic actions by competitors. A recent example of how such leakage may occur and the consequence was reported in *The New York Times* (Greenhouse, 2005): a supplier lost its entire Costco account when a Wal-Mart invoice was inadvertently routed to Costco showing a lower price for items stocked

Figure 3. Impacts of IT incidents on interconnected systems

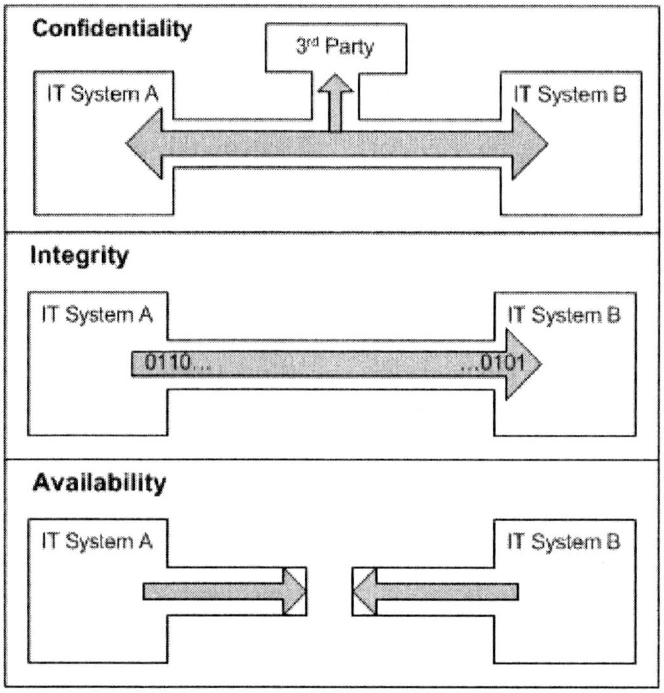

by both companies. While this disclosure was accidental, the same type of disclosure could result from the unauthorized access of company data due to any number of IT threats and could be used not only for competitive purposes, but to blackmail a company whose vulnerabilities have been exploited. To improve trust and spur increases in information sharing, three electronics trade associations proposed guidelines for the treatment of confidential information between supply chain partners (Jorgensen, 1998).

One of the most important factors for implementation of IT systems to facilitate coordination of the supply chain is data integrity. Data accuracy has been found to be a critical success factor for implementation of material requirements planning (Petroni, 2002; Ismail, 2005) and enterprise resource planning (Nelson, 2002; Xu, Nord, Brown, & Nord, 2002) systems. Data integrity is not just an issue for implementation, but extends to the operation of the supply chain. Raman, DeHoratius, and Ton (2001) point to the experience of a retailer that audited inventory on hand at a new store, finding inaccuracies in 29% of SKUs. Many of these inaccuracies can be attributed to incorrect receiving practices or incorrectly scanning products at the point of sale. A second retailer found 16% of stock outs were falsely reported to customers, reducing company profitability by an estimated 25%. Beyond these, transmission errors between channel partners or between systems may result in an incorrect product being ordered or an incorrect quantity of the correct product being delivered. For example, NIKE blamed *i2* Technologies for an estimated $80-100 million shortfall in quarterly revenues when a glitch in a new order processing system intended to match forecasts with demand created inefficiencies in its supply chain (Anonymous, 2001).

Any number of threats can create disruptions and degrade an IT system's availability. Regardless of the vulnerability, disruptions to the information infrastructure create serious consequences not only within a firm but also, by contributing to bullwhip and schedule nervousness, to those outside the originating organization. Chopra and Sodhi (2004) provide the example of the 'Love Bug' virus to illustrate consequences of information disruptions on the supply chain. In 2000, the Love Bug virus shut down many government and industry e-mail servers, including that of the Pentagon and Ford Motors, causing an estimated billion dollars in damages worldwide. Two common threats to system availability, virus and denial-of-service attacks, accounted for more than 55% of the estimated total losses in 2004 (Gordon et al., 2004). It is clear that as our reliance on IT to help manage the supply chain increases, so does the seriousness of these types of attacks on the economy.

RESULTS AND ANALYSIS

Validation of Supply Chain IT Security Risk

To validate our proposition that IT incidents affect firms in the manner discussed above, we surveyed a cross-section of production, distribution, and support functions. For obvious reasons, firms are often reluctant to divulge information about security practices and problems to outside parties. Prior research has, however, suggested that partnering with a trusted entity (i.e., government body or independent security company) when conducting information security research encourages participation and improves results (Kotulic & Clack, 2004). For this reason, the survey was again developed and conducted in cooperation with Cybertrust, the world's largest information security services company.

Due to the nature of the survey, the authors felt that the ideal target sample was individuals with knowledge or responsibility for IT, security, and operational functions within the firm. Such individuals likely have an intimate and realistic knowledge of IT in their firms, and the technological risks associated with collaboration and integration with supply chain partners. Individuals fitting this description were randomly selected from a proprietary list of firms maintained by a third-party organization and invited to participate via e-mail. Because the survey involved highly sensitive information, it was conducted anonymously to promote trust and honest responses. As an incentive, participants were offered a full report of results. Two rounds of follow-up e-mails

Figure 4. The effect of supply chain partnerships on information security risk

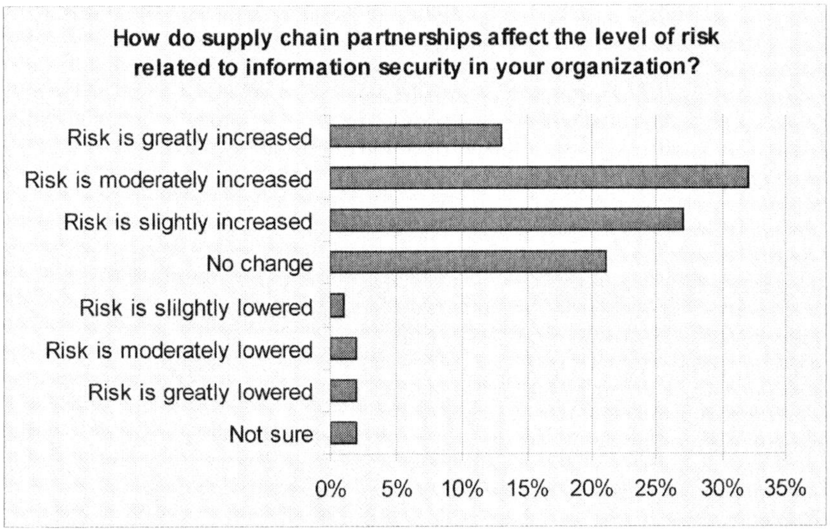

Figure 5. Preparedness of firms to mitigate IT security incidents relating to supply chain operations

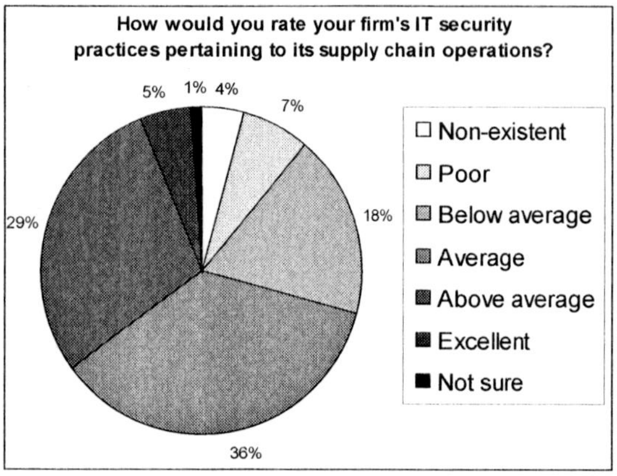

were sent to non-respondents to further encourage participation. In total, 188 companies representing a cross-section of supply chain functions and including firms ranging in size from fewer than 50 to greater than 100,000 employees provided responses to the survey instrument.

Respondents were asked about their attitudes, opinions, frustrations, and experiences of how supply chain partnerships affect the level of information risk to their firms. As seen in Figure 4, nearly three-quarters of respondents felt that their supply chain partnerships increased information risk in their organization. Research toward an understanding of this interplay is clearly a relevant and important venture. When asked about the most worrisome risks associated with their partners, participants listed unauthorized network access (67%), data theft (63%), and malicious code infections (48%) at the top of the list. Additionally, respondents did not seem overwhelmingly confident in their firm's ability to mitigate these risks. Roughly two-thirds described their security posture concerning supply chain operations as "average" or worse (see Figure 5).

Because the chief purpose of this survey was to validate the concept supply chain information security risk concept, survey respondents were presented simplified combinations from each of the six threat categories presented in Table 2, as well as impacts from Figure 3. Results showing the percent of companies reporting IT incidents for each of the six threat categories are shown in Table 3. From these results, it is evident that incidents occurred representing each of the supply chain risk sources (environmental, network, and organizational). It is also clear that a significant percentage of companies reported at least one security incident in each of the six threat categories of interest in the survey. Finally, note that several examples of confidentiality, integrity, and availability impacts are also attributed to these incidents and confirmed by the respondents.

The Effect of Collaboration on Supply Chain IT Security Risk

Toward the beginning of this chapter, we discussed different levels of collaboration that exist among supply chain partners. During this discussion, it was shown that the benefits of collaboration are tied to the number of collaborating partners, the amount and type of information exchanged, and the level of IT system integration. In light of subject matter presented in this chapter, it is appropriate for one to question whether a relationship might exist between these collaborative activities and IT security risk. Due to the nature of these activities and their dependency on IT, one could logically postulate that increased collaboration leads to increased levels of IT security risk.

To examine this hypothesis, we asked the 188 firms taking part in our study to indicate their level of various collaborative activities as being very low, low, moderate, high, or very high. Among these activities are those mentioned above—number of collaborating partners, the amount and type of information exchanged, and the level of IT system integration. Next, survey respondents were asked whether their organization had experienced an IT security incident directly traceable to supply chain partners. The percentage

Table 3. Survey respondents reporting IT security incidents

Threat Category	Type of Security Incident	%Reporting at Least One Incident
Malicious Code & Programs	Malicious code or program infection	70.9%
Malicious Hacking & Intrusion Attempts	Loss of availability of IT assets due to malicious hacking	29.1%
	Successful network intrusion from external environment	19.0%
	Successful network intrusion from within the supply network or organization	44.9%
Fraud & Deception	Reports of fraud and social engineering	24.1%
Misuse and Sabotage	Employee abuse and misuse	74.1%
Errors and Omissions	Employee errors and omissions	91.1%
Physical & Environmental Hazards	Loss of availability of IT assets due to physical and environmental hazards	75.3%
	Loss of confidentiality of IT assets due to successful physical intrusion of premises	10.1%

of respondents that reported IT security incidents of this type is depicted in Figure 6. The pattern is clear and the implications significant to supply chain management: as collaboration among partners rises, so too does IT security risk. Highly collaborative firms in our study were more than three times as likely to suffer a security incident involving their supply chain partners. Due to this finding, it is vital that IT security be included in the scope of e-supply chain management rather than relegated as a mainly "techie" problem. Most importantly, the benefits of collaboration within the e-supply chain facilitated by IT integration must be greater than the increase in risk due to IT security threats.

GENERAL RECOMMENDATIONS

Over the years, numerous volumes and documents have been written about managing IT security. The scope of these materials is vast, covering low-level technical minutia all the way to higher-level business strategies. Furthermore, a sizeable portion of IT security practices is specific to the information systems and business activities of individual organizations. It would be near impossible to extend this work with the few lines devoted to recommendations in this chapter. Because of this, the recommendations offered here are of a general nature, applicable and serviceable to most firms operating in a modern IT-enabled supply chain.

Figure 6. The effect of supply chain collaboration on IT security incidents

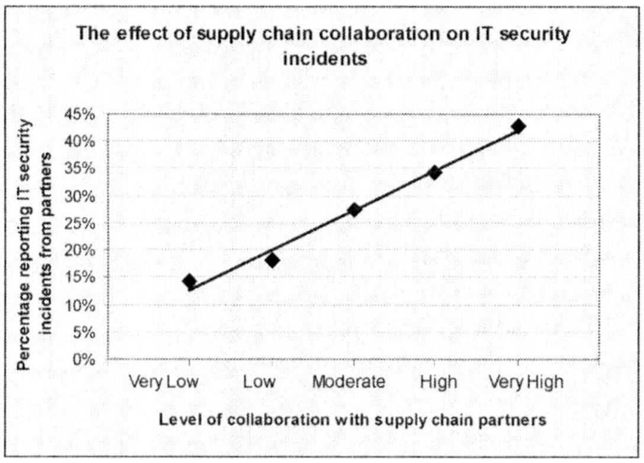

- The open and seamless lines of communication that often exist between supply chain partners tend to have a leveling effect on the IT security posture of all involved. Just because your firm takes information security seriously, it should not be assumed that partners do the same. Twelve percent of the respondents in our study reported terminating a relationship with a supply chain partner over security concerns. Treat interconnected IT systems as a "special case" of the untrusted network. Audit and protect it accordingly.
- Although there is much pressure for firms to integrate IT systems and begin collaborating, this should not be done flippantly. Plan diligently and only share the minimum assets necessary to achieve a goal. The philosophy of opening all doors and figuring out which ones can be closed while still making it work has gotten many firms into trouble.
- Audit supply chain partners before, during, and after establishing a collaborative relationship. Amazingly, many firms link themselves to partners without knowing anything about their security posture or practices. Thirty-seven percent of firms never audited their supply chain partners, and only 23% of the firms in our study audited prior, during, and after a partnership.
- Have a detailed contract (as opposed to just a policy) that clearly spells out the duties partners owe one another. These duties include personnel responsibilities and accountabilities, corrective action plans, enforceable provisions for restitution, and so forth. Only 18% of our sample reported having a formal contract relating to IT security and supply chain partners.
- Exposing assets to a trusted partner often means exposing them to your partner's partners. Trust is extremely critical within the supply chain, and it should not be a transferable property. Make ardent strides to limit the downstream exposure of sensitive assets and systems.
- Trust is a two-way street. Secure collaboration involves not only protecting your firm from supply chain partners, but also protecting those partners from your firm.
- Architectural maturity is a critical factor and classic problem when dealing with interconnected IT systems. Strive toward the use of safe(r) architectures, applications, and protocols. The IT department may resist this because it takes effort and resources, but no one ever said security was easy.
- Do not fixate solely on threats entering the organization via IT interconnections. Partners visit, attend meetings, handle and transport data, make blunders, and have access to physical resources like backup tapes and network infrastructure. Do not neglect the physical, human, and social dimensions of risk.

CONCLUSION

As IT increasingly becomes the medium of business functionality, a reliance on secure and continued operations has redefined corporate risk (Loch & Carr, 1992). In the new e-supply chain, information sharing and partner relationships are emphasized to drive down supply chain risk (Christopher & Peck, 2004). As the usage of IT becomes ubiquitous within single organizations and supply networks, its pure strategic value diminishes and the risks it creates threaten to become more important than the advantages it provides (Carr, 2003). Therefore, protecting these systems without overspending now poses the greatest difficulty.

This chapter has presented a preliminary yet thorough discussion of the relationship between supply chain and IT security risk. This relationship has received little previous investigation, yet we hope that our analysis and the results presented within this chapter will foster future research.

The findings of our study of 188 firms show that IT threats are real and that they are producing tangible impacts within the supply chain. Additional investigation is necessary to adequately quantify this risk. Most importantly, our research has established a positive correlation between collaboration and IT security incidents. To improve decision making and SCM, this relationship must be further studied and accurately modeled. Research toward this end is critical for SCM to ensure that proper consideration is given to IT security as firms seek to maximize the vast benefits of collaboration within the e-supply chain.

REFERENCES

Anonymous. (2001). JUST blame the software guys. *Business 2.0, 6*(8), 25.

Baker, W.H., & Rees, L.P. (2006). Necessary measures: Metric-driven information security risk assessment and decision-making. *Communications of the ACM,* (forthcoming).

Barratt, M., & Oliveira, A. (2001). Exploring the experiences of collaborative planning initiatives. *International Journal of Physical Distribution & Logistics Management, 31*(4), 266-289.

Bowersox, D.J. (1990). The strategic benefits of logistics alliances. *Harvard Business Review, 68*(4), 36.

Cachon, G.P., & Fisher, M. (2000). Supply chain inventory management and the value of shared information. *Management Science, 46*(8), 1032-1048.

Carr, N.G. (2003). IT doesn't matter. *Harvard Business Review, 81*(5), 41.

Cheswick, W.R., & Bellovin, S.M. (1994). *Firewalls and Internet security: Repelling the wily hacker.* Reading, MA: Addison-Wesley.

Chopra, S., & Sodhi, M.S. (2004). Managing risk to avoid supply-chain breakdown. *MIT Sloan Management Review, 46*(1), 53.

Christopher, M., & Peck, H. (2004). Building the resilient supply chain. *International Journal of Logistics Management, 15*(2), 1.

Christopher, M., Peck, H., Wilding, R., & Chapman, P. (2002). *Supply chain vulnerabilities.* Cranfield, UK: Department of Transport, Local Government and the Regions, Home Office, Department of Trade and Industry.

Cohen, F. (1997). Information system attacks: A preliminary classification scheme. *Computers & Security, 16*(1), 29.

DeLoach, J.W. (2000). *Enterprise-wide risk management: Strategies for linking risk and opportunity.* London: Financial Times/Prentice Hall.

Gordon, L.A., Loeb, M., Lucyshyn, W., & Richardson, R. (2004). *Ninth annual CSI/FBI computer crime and security survey.* San Francisco, Computer Security Institute.

Grance, T., Hash, J., Peck, S., Smith, J., & Korow-Diks, K (2002). *Security guide for interconnecting information technology systems* (p. 58). Gaithersburg, MD: National Institute of Standards and Technology.

Greenhouse, S. (2005, July 17). How Costco became the anti-Wal-Mart. *The New York Times.*

Gunasekaran, A., & Ngai, E.W.T. (2004). E.W.T. information systems in supply chain integration and management. *European Journal of Operational Research, 159*(2), 269.

Handfield, R.B., & Nichols, E.L. (1999). *Introduction to supply chain management.* Upper Saddle River, NJ: Prentice-Hall.

Howard, J.D., & Longstaff, T.A. (1998). *A common language for computer security incidents.* Albuquerque, NM: U.S. Department of Energy, Sandia National Laboratories.

Huang, Z., & Gangopadhyay, A.A. (2004). Simulation study of supply chain management to measure the impact of information sharing. *Information Resources Management Journal, 17*(3), 20.

Icove, D.J., Seger, K.A., VonStorch, W., & NetLibrary. (1995). *Computer crime: A crimefighter's handbook.* Sebastopol, CA: O'Reilly & Associates.

Ismail, S. (2005). An investigation of MRP benefit-determinant relationships: ACE model. *Problems & Perspectives in Management,* (2), 80-98.

Jorgensen, B. (1998). Confidentiality guidelines set. *Electronic Buyers' News,* (1134), 36.

Juttner, U., Peck, H., & Christopher, M. (2003). Supply chain risk management: Outlining an agenda for future research. *International Journal of Logistics: Research & Applications, 6*(4), 197.

Kolluru, R., & Meredith, P.H. (2001). Security and trust management in supply chains. *Information Management & Computer Security, 9*(5), 233-236.

Kotulic, A.G., & Clack, J.G. (2004). Why aren't there more information security research studies? *Information & Management, 41,* 597-607.

Lee, H.L., Padmanabhan, V., & Whang, W. (1997). Information distortion in a supply chain: The bullwhip effect. *Management Science, 43*(4), 546.

Lee, H.L., & Whang, S. (2000). Information sharing in a supply chain. *International Journal of Technology Management, 20*(3/4), 373.

Li, L. (2002). Information sharing in a supply chain with horizontal competition. *Management Science, 48*(9), 1196.

Loch, K.D., & Carr, H.H. (1992). Threats to information systems: Today's reality, yesterday's understanding. *MIS Quarterly, 16*(2), 173.

McLaren, T., Head, M., & Yuan, Y. (2002). Supply chain collaboration alternatives. *Internet Research: Electronic Network Applications and Policy, 12*(4), 348-364.

Mentzer, J.T. (2001). Managing supply chain collaboration. In *Supply chain management,* (pp. 83-84). Thousand Oaks, CA: Sage Publications

Mentzer, J.T., Foggin, J.H., & Golicic, S.L. (2000, September/October). Collaboration: The enablers, impediments, and benefits. *Supply Chain Management Review,* 42-46.

Mentzer, J.T., Min, S., & Zacharia, Z.G. (2000). The nature of interfirm partnering in supply chain management. *Journal of Retailing, 76*(4), 549.

Nelson, K. (2002). Bad data plagues ERP. *Bank Systems & Technology, 39*(3), 12.

NIST. (1997). *An introduction to computer security: The NIST handbook.* Gaithersburg, MD: U.S. Department of Commerce, National Institute of Standards and Technology.

Petroni, A. (2002). Critical factors of MRP implementation in small and medium-sized firms. *International Journal of Operations & Production Management, 22*(3), 329.

Raman, A., DeHoratius, N., & Ton, Z. (2001). The Achilles' heel of supply chain management. *Harvard Business Review, 79*(5), 25.

Risk Analysis. (1992). *Perception and management.* London: Royal Society.

Simatupang, T.M., & Sridharan, R. (2005). The collaboration index: A measure for supply chain collaboration. *International Journal of Physical Distribution & Logistics Management, 35*(1), 44.

Smith, G., Watson, K., Baker, W., & Pokorski, J. (forthcoming). A critical balance: Collaboration and security in the IT-enabled supply chain. *International Journal of Production Research, 45*(7).

Smith, M. (1989). Computer security—threats, vulnerabilities, and countermeasures. *Information Age, 11*(4), 205-210.

Spekman, R.E., & Davis, E.W. (2004). Risky business: Expanding the discussion on risk and the extended enterprise. *International Journal of Physical Distribution & Logistics Management, 34*(5), 414.

Stoneburner, G., Goguen, A., & Feringa, A. (2002). *Risk management guide for information technology systems* (p. 55). Gaithersburg, MD: U.S. Department of Commerce, National Institute of Standards and Technology.

Warren, M., & Hutchinson, W. (2000). Cyber attacks against supply chain management systems: A short note. *International Journal of Physical Distribution & Logistics Management, 30*(7/8), 710.

Whitman, M.E. (2003). Enemy at the gate: Threats to information security. *Communications of the ACM, 46*(8), 91.

Wilkes, M.V. (1991). Revisiting computer security in the business world. *Communications of the ACM, 34*(8), 19.

Wise, D., & Fahrenwald, B. (2001, May 6). Supply chain collaboration: Close encounters of the best kind. *Businessweek.*

Xu, H., Nord, J.H., Brown, N., & Nord, G.D. (2002). Data quality issues in implementing an ERP. *Industrial Management & Data Systems, 102*(1/2), 47.

Zsidisin, G.A. (2003). A grounded definition of supply risk. *Journal of Purchasing & Supply Management, 9*(5/6), 217.

Chapter VIII
The Use of Collaboration Tools in Supply Chain: Implications and Challenges

Ozlem Bak
University of Greenwich, UK

ABSTRACT

The supply chain environment today is a collaborative business environment in which the members of supply chains are interlinked with each other. Hence the collaboration extends in supply chains to inter- and intra-enterprise applications, the so-called collaboration tools, such as customer relationship management, supplier relationship management, e-business and employee-business integration. In order to achieve this collaboration, supply chains also realize the need to implement integrated collaboration tools, which integrate tightly their intra- and inter-supply chain processes. With new technologies like Web-enabled services, wireless applications, and software applications, the supply chain today needs frameworks that consider the requirements of collaborative supply chain scenarios. This chapter thus will introduce a framework to ensure that collaboration at all supply chain levels is considered at a very early stage of the project so that the integrated supply chain collaboration can be designed and implemented. A case study of an application of collaboration tools is presented. This framework was used successfully to design and implement a collaborative integrated-enterprise system for a manufacturing enterprise. However, collaboration in supply chain is only effective if the collaboration tools are integrated or used jointly by supply chain and their collaborative partners. Therefore, this chapter first explains the concept of collaboration tools and its importance in the supply chain, evaluates the requirements for supply chain management (SCM), and tries to ascertain the collaborative problem areas specifically within supplier and SCM relations.

INTRODUCTION

This chapter will examine issues relating to e-business technologies coordination and control between the head offices of multi-national automotive corporations' supply chains (SCM) and their suppliers. The e-business technologies facilitate the information and communication transfer in different domains without the limitation of place. E-business technologies such as business-to-business (B2B), customer relationship management (CRM), enterprise resource planning (ERP), electronic data interchange (EDI), advance planning systems (APS), and supplier relationship management (SRM) provide real-time access to demand, inventory, price, sourcing, and production data to be shared by manufacturers and their suppliers spanning the boundaries of the supply chains. The use of e-business technologies in SCM propelled companies towards collaboration and converted the way companies are conventionally organized (Bak, 2003).

In the literature the e-business technologies have been seen as a source of networking, coordination, and cooperation which are linked to collaboration, and differ in scope. The term *collaboration* encapsulates a platform that provides cooperation processes based on agreements on use of common applications, data, and information technology available to the participants (Fleisch, 2001). The scoping in this chapter is similar to Mason and Lefrere (2003), wherein networking refers mainly to exchanging information for mutual benefit, coordination in this respect includes networking and goes a step further by including the alteration of activities in order to achieve a common purpose, and cooperation steps further in that it shares the resources. Collaboration in this context can be seen as an overarching term that encapsulates and enhances the capacity of another organization and vice versa (see Figure 1).

Figure 1. Collaboration as an umbrella term[1]

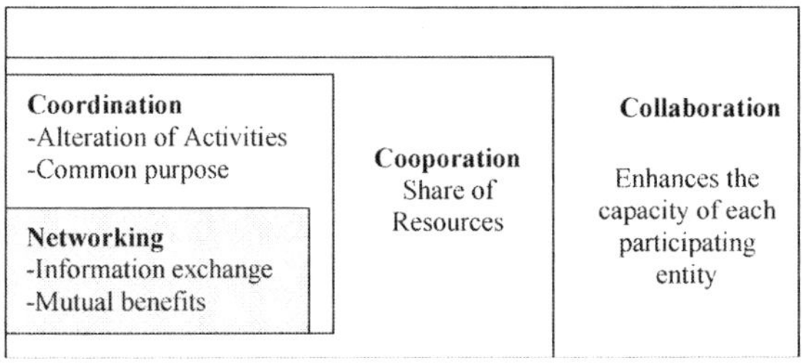

Collaboration in e-business literature enables the electronic interaction between business partners (Wigand, Picot, & Reichwald, 1997). The execution of collaboration processes requires an information infrastructure to link the partners in a supply chain. From an economic perspective two characteristics apply to the collaboration in SCM: first, SCM and its members are jointly responsible for the creation of a product or service. They have a mutual objective and a common value creation aim, which is coordinated by legal terms as well as bona-fide agreements. Second, SCM also includes legally and economically independent entities, where the economic independence is based on the reality that SCM members or entities also can belong to other SCM or on the contrary operate alone in the market. These independencies are characterized by the fact that each enterprise accepts the individual risks, where it defines its own collaboration boundaries and own goals and plans independently or jointly under collaborative benefits and risks. There are examples of possible applications for solutions such as integrated ERP system, electronic marketplaces which can consist of bilateral system links, hub and spoke architectures, and of Web service architectures.

The need for collaboration tools in SCM is of high importance as the competitive advantage remains in linking all trading partners to ensure the timely delivery of goods and services to the final consumer efficiently and effectively. To understand these issues, the research on supply chain management distinguishes between strategic, tactical, and operational level decision making in which the strategic level is concerned with supplier, formation of collaborations (Gadde & Hakansson, 1994); at the tactical level, the emphasis lies on supplier assessment, supplier selection, and resource planning; and at the operational level, it focuses on the tasks related to order fulfillment and inventory management (Kumaraswamy & Palaneeswaran, 2000). On each of these levels, several researchers have identified measures for successful collaborations based on behavioral changes; increase in long-term financial success; economic value, shareholder value, and organizational capacity; increase in performance levels; and on how well collaborations across organizations are managed and monitored. With any of these collaborative success measures, companies might differ—some may prefer to choose market share, whereas others might choose quality or innovation. Thus, collaborations can be successful on any of these levels depending on the common strategic aim of the collaboration. The aim of this chapter is not to elaborate on the success measures, but rather to ascertain the problem areas of e-business collaborations and its impact on supply chain.

When considering collaboration problem areas and their impact, it is likely that there will be a number of heterogeneous IT systems within the multiple independent/interdependent organizational units of SCM—particularly such as companies, divisions, or departments—with different databases (Garita, Afsarmanesh, & Hertzberger, 2002). These existing systems will require interfaces to various databases and file systems to access data, to store information, and to establish e-business technologies in/between the interdependent and independent organizational units of the supply chain. We may also like to bear in mind that despite the creation of such interfaces, distorted information still can be experienced unless collaboration tools are integrated or used jointly by the partners. This information distortion can occur due to knowledge sharing, resistance to change, and trust between supply chains and its entities. Therefore, collaboration tools used for IT management in SCM will need to bridge the technological and organizational gaps between its participants. This development in return would ease the IT and information transfer and its dissemination. Therefore collaboration amongst supply chain units plays a much more central role in the operation of the whole organization, and its extensive and intensive global networks of coordinated production and distribution.

THE ROLE OF E-BUSINESS TECHNOLOGIES IN COLLABORATION AMONG SCM AND ITS BUSINESS UNITS

The increasing collaboration internationally and domestically and especially within SCM business units which once were opposed profit centers have shown greater willingness to collaborate. However the difference within/between SCM is related to the nature of inter-organizational relationships. The underlying relationships can be attained from mutually defined goals and interests, again unlike traditional collaborations of supply chains which are mainly driven by market access motivations. The new forms of collaborations are a response to global competition and the strategic need of supply chains to combine resources to be competitive. Therefore we can summarize the ability to generate collaboration through the use of the following characteristics:

- **Systems and channel integration**, which leads to the empowerment of supply chain participants as they can use a common database that is available to larger constituencies. Thus, this can enable the compression of time-to-market, while enhancing the speed of response to the final customer (McIvor, Humphreys, & McCurry, 2003).
- **Openness and transparency**, which can be achieved through low-cost connectivity between the supply chain participants.

Infrastructures without expensive investments such as the use of Internet-mediated applications lead to use of collaboration tools. However, the initial investments to upgrade the systems and learning activities, and resistance to change towards the new application became main problems at the initial stage of implementation.

- **Explicit cooperation** between wealth-creating agents—The supply chain members, shareholders, employees, and external publics need to contribute resources to the successful running of the business over a longer term.
- **Learning process** and effort is needed to assimilate and/or internalize the transferred knowledge through collaborations (Lin, 2003). Learning also includes the sharing of knowledge, which is linked to embrace a collaborative relationship built on trust. This constituted a problem as "after many years of operating in a system in which trust was the last thing that they expected" (McIvor et al., 2003).
- **Knowledge transfer** needs to be considered in some cases of collaboration wherein the knowledge is not easily replicable and transferable (Kessler et al., 2000). The "stickiness" nature of the valuable knowledge demands time, effort, and cost to transfer.

Collaborations offer many value-added capabilities to the supply chain. In a perfect world, the borders of the SCM between/within its entities would blur through the use of collaboration tools. The collaboration tools were designed originally to coordinate, integrate, and restrict the information flows across several functions in the supply chain, however manufacturers began to incorporate components that extended the supply and delivery end of partner organizations' supply chains as well (Corroon, 1998), so that each supply chain had its collaboration under a network of component suppliers, distributors, and contract manufacturers that are linked through collaboration tools. The linkage and use of the collaboration tools have not been considered in the literature, hence the aim of this chapter is to create a tentative framework that can enhance the understanding in supply chain collaboration. Therefore, the author has depicted the impact of the use of collaboration tools at three levels:

- **Level 1 SCM:** At this level collaboration between and within the SCM takes place. SCM headquarters receives real-time updates on day-to-day cross-functional operations. This information can be distorted unless there is an integrated system between the participants and common strategic intent between its entities.
- **Level 2 SCM strategic business unit (SBU):** At this level the knowledge is incorporated into an organization's business unit by integrating across functional departments. The focus is on continually using technology to improve efficiency and support existing business processes. Competitive advantage is achieved through the integrated links with suppliers and customers in the logistics and purchasing functions. According to McIvor et al. (2003), this was lacking between the departments, wherein different functions and departments possessed different and often incompatible systems with incompatible objectives. The compatibility of collaboration here stems from the close relationship between the cross-functional departments.
- **Level 3 individual employee level:** At this level the individual employees or members save time through the use of collaboration tools when transferring and transmitting information and associated knowledge. As the information can be easily attained through the collaboration tools, the employees or members can react and respond to an incident quickly and independently, as the system can give the information and the

Table 1. Levels of collaboration[2]

	Level 1 Supply Chain	Level 2 Strategic Business Unit	Level 3 Individual
Scope	- Involvement, - SCM-wide inter-linkage	- Cross functional - Departmental participation	- Function orientation - Task dominated
Focus	- Enables real-time information sharing within and between SCM members	- Supports the strategic business unit strategy	- Supports empowerment of employees within the business unit
Levers	- Technological infrastructure	- Processes, workflows	- People, intellectual capital, and relationships
Enhancements	- Revenue, customer service, and existing business enhancement	- Strategic business unit coordination support	- Depending upon individual employee and tasks

employees or members do not need to wait for other individuals to complete the task at hand; unless the individual knowledge has been considered as a tool for achieving competitive advantage at an individual level, the knowledge sharing becomes bounded to a particular individual. Therefore, the issues of trust and empowerment have become the key components of collaboration. Table 1 indicates the levels and to what extent collaboration tools play a role.

CASE STUDY DESCRIPTION

This case study was embedded as part of a research setting wherein the impact of two collaboration tools/e-business applications—namely extranet and B2B—in an automotive SCM strategic business unit was examined. The sample of the SCM consisted of an independently owned local company which operated as a supplier but was restricted in its operations to the southern part of Germany. This collaboration was studied retrospectively as the collaboration took place between the SCM and its 12[3] national suppliers. This procurement collaboration stems from two main stages. The first stage involved the installation and updating of the current equipment and software for the local company to facilitate its operation. The second stage incorporated the training of the employees of the suppliers. The data was collected through a variety of methods, which included four-and-a-half months of participant observation over two projects, 10 hours of semi-structured interviews, 30 individually taken and official meeting notes, and document analysis. The formal semi-structured interviews were carried out with eight interviewees and lasted for between one and two hours. These interviews were taped and transcribed, then entered into N6 software for analysis. These interviews were conducted during and after the participant observation, in order to ascertain that the issues were covered adequately.

These various techniques of data collection are beneficial in theory generation, as they provide multiple perspectives on an issue, supply more information on emerging concepts, and allow for cross-checking and triangulation (Orlikowski, 1993; Glaser & Strauss, 1967). Therefore, similar to McPherson et al. (1993) and Sherif and Vinze

(2003), a case study research method with grounded theory approach was used. The key research question explored is the set of reasons behind the emergence of collaborations in the automotive sector, and in particular, the motivations behind the receptiveness of the supplier and original equipment manufacturer (OEM) towards investments in collaborative tools. What has persuaded the supplier to use the collaborative tools? In what respect do the new forms of partnerships reflect the concept of collaboration? What are the key benefits and limitations to collaboration?

SCM headquarters has concluded after consultation that the investment for collaboration tools was essential for its business units' future competitiveness. The initial research indicated that some of the suppliers/distributors would need to upgrade their system and thus needed funding. In particular it was estimated that an initial start-up sum would be needed annually over a period of five years to improve services in order to establish collaboration. This could not be provided by the distributors and suppliers, as they were unwilling to make additional investments on collaborative tools. In line with the IT infrastructure changes, the SCM launched the collaborative development program in order to increase the density of distributor and supplier network services in the country by subsidizing either through financial assistance, training, or technological infrastructure help in order to create a network. The main policy objectives of the program were formulated with the assistance of the SCM, consultants, and other stakeholders, with the following goals:

1. Creation of a network with distributors/suppliers with an interlinked and improved collaborative network infrastructure
2. Extension of the existing coverage of mobile services enabling overall control from suppliers to the headquarters
3. Enhancement of competitive advantage through the promotion of high-quality communication services to businesses
4. Retention of a single control-point through licensing and regulation of collaboration systems

The above-mentioned goals have had some contradictory and similar responses from the suppliers' side. The respondents, especially representatives from the suppliers, emphasized the importance of the SCM taking the coordination role, however the coordination role did not succeed as planned, as the development plans were made considering mainly the coordination aspect, rather that the capability, competencies, and resources gap. The suppliers felt that the implementation, such as sending the employees for training to the headquarters, allowing the computers to be updated to a certain level to enable the configuration, interfered with the suppliers' daily work routine. The resistance to change grew as the benefits resulting from the collaboration were more dominantly based on SCM quartile, whereas the suppliers also had to deal with other customers (from SME to SCM). The balancing act between the advantages and disadvantages came to a halt when the license agreement entailed a conflict over financial commitment of suppliers. This was rather ironic since supplier-buyer collaborations are based on the need to emphasize long-term relationship building rather than mere financial/market transactions.

DISCUSSION

From the perspective of SCM, a significant barrier to the collaborations relates to the degree of commitment and reliability of partners. In the case study of collaborations with suppliers, it appears that a change in SCM means change inter-relationships, whereas a true collaboration should be able to withstand such events. These developments are inimical to the attainment of collaboration, which in turn could motivate SCM to take a short-term perspective on relationships with the suppliers/distributors. Other collaboration problems confronting the multi-national companies relate to the limited financial strength of partners and power/trust-related issues. These problems once again support the general observation that the nature of SCM small/medium-size suppliers hinders genuine collaboration. These problems are important because of the evidence that a disproportionate contribution from one of the collaboration partners can affect the success of other collaboration partners. Thus the differences at each level can also cause distortion at collaboration levels. Similarly this conflict was found on the statements of SCM employees (see Table 2):

- "One of the limitation was the technical restructuring of our existing relationships with suppliers/distributors."
- "Suppliers who participated in this network needed also new investment."
- "The setting up of a new collaboration tool created a need for standardization of workflow, structure."
- "The change happened at supply chain level, meaning from the initial supplier to initial customer."
- "Each employee needed to acquire new skills, knowledge."

The main difference between these is that information exists without a dependency on its owner and is easily transferable, whereas on the contrary, knowledge is formed and shared in/between minds through experiences, successes, failures, learning over time, and therefore, the "stickiness" of the IT demands time, effort, and cost to transfer (Tiwana, 2001, p. 37; Kessler et al., 2000). The transferability consists of both parts: one portion that is readily transferable and the other portion which is not easily transferable. Even though the collaboration tool has been established successfully, it does not negate the success as a time-consuming learning process, and effort is needed to assimilate and/or internalize the transferred IT (Lin, 2003; Clark , 1995; Gomory, 1995).

McIvor et al. (2003) emphasized in their research the differences of electronic links with the supplier in relevance to size and level of sophistication. We can examine a similar pattern in the particular case study of the multinational corporation supply chain (SCM), where members often embed their knowledge not only in documents or repositories, but also in their organizational routines, processes, practices, and norms. Therefore, the role of collaboration systems used in SCM cannot be seen solely as a data distribution tool that is completely separated from the e-business technologies concept. The interdependency and independencies of entities call each member of the supply chain to protect their e-business technologies that exert an influence on their competitiveness. Also reflecting on practitioners' day-to-day operations in which they have to keep the information which makes them valuable to the organization (distinctive knowledge) would add value to the employees within and/or outside their organizations.

Similarly, Combs and Hull (1995) note that resting on a backbone of IT and telecommunications infrastructures, organizations should be able to shorten chains of command and thus enhance collaboration. They also suggest that external pressures, unpredictable internal conflict, and unforeseen circumstances can arise, particularly in the case of changes related to IT. The complexity is partly attributed to the Internet through its more recent business acceptance and commercial use (Hardaker & Graham, 2000). "Because businesses and supply chains operate in real-time, it only makes sense to utilize technology that does the same. In fact it can be argued that the collaboration through the use of the e-business applications were mainly based on demand

Table 2. Summary of aggravating issues on e-business applications and differences of their impact on three levels (results of the case study, authors' own presentation)

	Collaboration Issues at Level 1 Multinational Corporation (SCM)	Collaboration Issues at Level 2 Strategic Business Unit (SBU)	Collaboration Issues at Level 3 Individual
Scope What does it include?	• An integrated supply chain, meaning from initial supplier to the final customer, was introduced as the vision of the SCM • The involvement of SCM as coordinator role • Control mechanism was at SCM level	• The interdependency resulted in the bargaining power of SCM creating complications in areas of trust, commitment to change • Cross-functional department participation	• Function orientation rather than individual capabilities and learning capabilities assessment • Gaps are defined by SCM and SBU level rather than at individual level • Difference in strategic goal attainment
Focus What is the main purpose of the collaboration?	• Enables real-time information sharing within and between SCM members • Reduces the control points • Condenses the time-to-market period • E-business applications have been used as a backbone for collaborative planning	• Supports the strategic business unit strategy • Additional resources and competencies needed (i.e., the employees in some instances needed to fulfill two job descriptions for a smooth change process)	• Suppliers, employees in the process are overloaded with work, resulting in high pressure • Transferability problems: it is not possible to transfer different tasks to different employees, as this would require additional time, training, and investment
Levers What is the extent of the impact of this collaboration?	• Technological infrastructure • Organizational infrastructure • New ways of operating/introducing product/service to market	• Change of internal workflows and sub-processes • New job descriptions and tasks • Different level of impact on different departments depending on the need for sophistication of e-business applications	• People, distinctive knowledge sharing limits to a certain employee or group of employees • Confidentiality, how to create transparency without losing the competitive edge—in line with intellectual capital and relationships
Enhancements What are the benefits of this collaboration?	• Revenue, customer service, and existing business enhancement • Overall attainment of control throughout the supply chain	• Strategic business unit coordination support • SBU can also control and supervise the supplier/distributor base	• Depending upon individual employee and tasks • Employees are empowered through the visibility and attainability of the data and related information whenever needed • Enhancement at individual level depends on the individual employee and his/her capabilities and learning capacity

prediction, standardization of product/service, efficient procurement, execution and harnessing organizational expertise" (Ash & Burn, 2003).

CONCLUSION

Through the use of collaboration tools, the questions of how to create a win-win situation between suppliers, distributors, the supply chain members, and to what extent collaboration tools are used become a concern for supply chains. Littler, Leverick, & Bruce (1995) questioned the suitability of supplier collaboration; maybe his question needs to be further extended, and it should be worded as to what extent/level supply chain collaboration is considered to be beneficial?

The aim of this study has been to demonstrate factors and individual levels that are critical to the outcome of relationships where supply chain members are involved in collaboration. The case study in this collaboration enabled an in-depth insight into its characteristics, such as technological capability and competence of supplier, suppliers' level of independency or interdependency, and openness of processes in line with confidentiality. The case study also introduced a three-stage approach, wherein to achieve a smooth transition towards collaboration, the transition should include the three levels from the SCM level to SBU level to individual level and strive to create a common aim /strategic goal at each level.

FURTHER RESEARCH

The results of this research introduced supply-chain-wide views on collaboration. Supply chains are trying to come to terms with the threats and opportunities posed by these new collaborative intermediaries. The preferences for collaborative tools expressed in this study are applied at three different levels (SCM wide, SBU wide, and individual). This study also indicates that individual attitudes at level three toward collaboration may turn more positive as some of the leading supply chains start to gain advantage through their employee empowerment enabled through collaborative services. While there are no clear borders, different models might be necessary for different companies and for different types of inter-company collaborations and interactions.

REFERENCES

Ash, C.G., & Burn, J.M. (2003). A strategic framework for management of ERP enabled e-business change. *European Journal of Operational Research, 146,* 374-387.

Bak, O. (2003). A framework for transformation of supply chain management: A just in time investigation in organisations. In K.S. Pawar & M. Muffatto (Eds.), *Proceedings of the 8th International Symposium on Logistics* (pp. 59-63). Notthingham, UK: Centre for Concurrent Enterprise, University of Notthingham.

Clark, K.B. (1995). What strategy can do for technology. In K.B. Clark & S.C. Wheelwright (Eds.), *The product development challenge: Computing through speed, quality and creativity.* Boston: Harvard Business School Press.

Gadde, L., & Hakansson, H. (1994). The changing role of purchasing: Reconsidering three strategic issues. *European Journal of Purchasing and Supply Management, 1*(1), 27-35.

Gomory, R.E. (1995). From the ladder of science to the product development cycle. In K.B. Clark & S.C. Wheelwright (Eds.), *The product development challenge: Computing through speed, quality and creativity.* Boston: Harvard Business School Press.

Durlacher. (2000). *B2B e-commerce.* Durlacher Research.

Garita, C., Afsarmanesh, H., & Hertzberger, L. O. (2002). A survey of distributed information management approaches for virtual enterprise infrastructure. In U. Franke (Ed.), *Managing virtual Web organisations in the 21st century: Issues and challenges.* London.

Glaser, B.G., & Strauss, A.L. (1967). *The discovery of grounded theory.* Chicago: Aldine Press.

Graham, G., & Hardaker, G. (2000). Supply-chain management across the Internet. *International Journal of Physical Distribution and Logistics Management, 30*(3/4), 286-295.

Mason, J., & Lefrere, P. (2003). Trust, collaboration, e-learning and organisational transformation. *International Journal of Training and Development, 7*(4), 259-270.

Kumaraswamy, M., & Palaneeswaran, E. (2000). Selection matters—in construction supply chain optimisation. *International Journal of Physical Distribution & Logistics Management, 30*(7/8), 661-680.

Lin, B.-W. (2003). Technology transfer as technological learning: A source of competitive advantage for firms with limited R&D resources. *R&D Management, 33*(3), 327-341.

Littler, D., Leverick, F., & Bruce, M. (1995). Factors affecting the process of collaborative product development: A study of UK manufacturers of information and communications technology products. *Journal of Product Innovation Management, 12,* 16-32.

McIvor, R., Humphreys, P., & McCurry, L. (2003). Electronic commerce: Supporting collaboration in the supply chain? *Journal of Materials Processing Technology, 139,* 147-152.

MacPherson, S.J., Kelly. J.R., & Webb, R.S. (1993). How designs develop: Insights from case studies in building engineering services. *Construction Management and Economics, 11,* 475-485.

Orlikowski, W.J. (1993). CASE tools as organizational change: Investigating incremental and radical changes in systems development. *MIS Quarterly, 17*(3), 309-340.

Perraton, J., Goldblatt, D., Held, D., and McGrew, A. (1998). The globalization of economic activity. *New Political Economy, 2*(2), 257-277.

Sherif, K., & Vinze, A. (2003). Barriers to adoption of software reuse: A qualitative study. *Information and Management, 41,* 159-175.

Tiwana, A. (2001). *The essential guide to knowledge management.* London: Prentice-Hall.

Wigand, R.T., Picot, A., & Reichwald, R. (1997). *Information, organization and management.* Chichester, UK: John Wiley & Sons.

ENDNOTES

1. Authors' presentation of overlapping definitions
2. Authors' presentation of levels of SC
3. In order to guard the confidentiality of the supplier and SCM, the number and some details of the companies have been changed.

Chapter IX
Negotiation, Trust, and Experience Management in E-Supply Chains

Gavin Finnie
Bond University, Australia

Zhaohao Sun
Heibei Normal University, China

ABSTRACT

This chapter reviews fundamentals of e-supplhy chain management and examines the transformation from the traditional supply chains to the e-supply chains (e-SC). This chapter applies experience management (EM) and experience-based reasoning (EBR) to intellegent agents in the e-SC and explores how to use experience in extablishing trust in other agents. The role of trust and deception in supply chains for real-time enterprises is discussed, and a logical framework for fraud and deception is explained in this chapter. EBR is considered as a way to manage trust in the supply network. This chapter explores cooperation and negotiation, trust and deception in e-supply chains by providing methodologies and intelligent techniques for multiagent trust, negotiation, and deception in an e-SC. Finally, a unified model is developed for integrating cooperation and negotiation, trust and deception in e-supply chains. Although primarily theoretical, the chapter highlights new areas of research which will impact supply chain management.

INTRODUCTION

Current supply chain management (SCM) is largely based on older information retrieval methods. It generally has not taken advantage of the 'dynamic' information that is now available due to developments in information and communication technology (ICT) and knowledge management (KM). The focus of SCM has also changed from a supply-side view of optimizing production efficiency to a demand-side view of consumers driving the process. Supply chains (SCs) are developing into demand networks that adapt to consumer demand in almost real time (Silisque, Brito, Almirall, & Cortés, 2003). With moving towards real-time enterprises, there is an imperative need for rapid automated and intelligent response in the supply network. As discussed in this chapter, an e-SC can be considered as a form of agent society, with trust and negotiation between the intelligent agents as a significant issue.

Experience of suppliers and customers plays an important role in an SC. In particular, customer experience management (CEM) will become a major issue in e-SC because the latter is a customer-centered service in the Internet world (Sun & Lau, 2006). Further customer experience is a prerequisite for customer satisfaction in SC, which is highly dependent on the flexibility of the SC, such as its ability to respond to changes in demand. Because the selection and interaction space of customers in e-SC is theoretically infinite, how to manage customer experience in e-SC also becomes a significant issue for any e-SC providers.

Experience management (EM) is a new concept in information systems (IS) and information technology (IT), although KM has become well-established in business management and artificial intelligence (AI). However, experience has always played a similar rule to knowledge for organizations. Experience-based reasoning (EBR) is a reasoning paradigm using prior experiences to solve problems, and could be considered an advanced form of knowledge-based reasoning (Sun & Finnie, 2005a). This chapter will develop the concept of EM and EBR, and apply them to intelligent agents in the e-SC. In particular the use of experience in establishing trust in other agents will be explored. Any organization will have some history of dealing with problems relating to orders and perturbations in the network and the solutions applied, as well as some formal processes for dealing with these. To respond automatically, software must be capable of reacting, as one would expect a human agent to do. The information available to the agent can come from a variety of sources, including analysis of historical information/experience at the informational/planning level.

Multi-agent systems technology has been successfully applied in many fields such as e-commerce (Sun & Finnie, 2004a) and supply chain management (Finnie, Barker, & Sun, 2004). The trend for the future will be to increasingly autonomous behavior of agents. However, it is imperative that management considering relinquishing control of key aspects of the business to software systems be aware of the issues involved, in terms of how agents will need to operate and negotiate, as well as the potential for misuse of trust with adverse economic results. The increasing importance of strong IT governance and control procedures, and the possible criminal implications for failing to implement these, makes it essential that management be aware of developments in this area. The major contribution of this chapter is in establishing a basis for understanding the new field of experience management and the role it may play in the new supply chain environment. In addition the issue of trust and the role of experience in automating trust development should be appreciated. This chapter will resolve these issues by providing some methodology and intelligent techniques for multi-agent trust and negotiation in an e-SC based on EM. These include the use of EM to enable agents in an e-SC to learn from prior experience in dealing with suppliers and customers, and issues relating to trust and deception in the agent world of the e-SC.

The rest of this chapter is organized as follows: the next section examines fundamentals of e-SC management. We then review the concept of experience management, explore cooperation and negotiation in e-supply chains, and discuss trust and deception in e-supply chains. Finally this chapter proposes a unified model of integrating cooperation and negotiation, trust, and deception in e-supply chains, and the chapter ends with some concluding remarks.

FUNDAMENTALS OF E-SUPPLY CHAIN MANAGEMENT

A supply chain can be broken into three parts: an upstream part, an internal part, and a downstream part (Turban, King, Viehland, & Lee, 2006). The upstream part encompasses all the activities involved in material and service inputs from suppliers, the internal part involves the manufacturing and packaging of products, and the downstream part involves the distribution and sale of goods to distributors and customers.

There are three different viewpoints for an SC: supplier viewpoint, intermediary viewpoint, and end-customer viewpoint. From a supplier viewpoint, the SC is a tree, the root of which is the supplier. We can consider this tree as a supplier-centered supply tree of the SC, as shown in Figure 1. The output degree of the root of this tree (supply flow) should be as large as possible from a supplier viewpoint in order to obtain the most number of orders from the SC. From an end customer viewpoint, the SC is also a tree, and the root of the tree is the customer. We call this tree a customer-centered source tree with respect to the SC. The input degree of the root of the customer-centered source tree should be as large as possible, in order to obtain the most satisfactory information and source from the SC. From an intermediary viewpoint, the SC is a double tree uniquely bridged by the intermediary. On the one side, the tree is the customer-centered source tree with its root being the intermediary, because it is the customer of the upper level supplier. On the other side, the tree is a supply-centered supply tree, also with its root being the intermediary, because it is the source and information supplier of the lower level customer. These three different trees co-influence the performance of the SC. In particular, the intermediary plays a vital role in any SC, because any inefficiency of the intermediary might lead to the breakdown of the SC.

The supply network integrates the value chain and the agent chain, and extends them into a complete graph-formed value-supply network (Sun & Finnie, 2004a). With the development of the Internet/Web technology, the traditional SC is being transformed into the e-SC. The e-SC brings together widely dispersed suppliers and customers to enhance coordination and knowledge sharing,

Figure 1. A supplier-centered supply tree

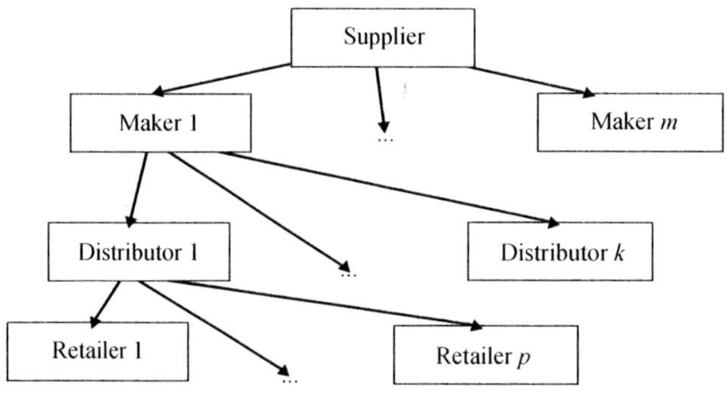

and to manage upstream and downstream value chain channels (Poirier & Mauer 2001; Ross, 2003). e-SC enables firms to improve flexibility and move toward real-time operations by sharing information and collaborating dynamically among partners. e-SC management (e-SCM) can increase revenues or decrease costs by eliminating time-consuming steps throughout the online order and delivery process. It can also improve customer satisfaction by enabling customers to view detailed information on delivery dates and order status. As an example, a mid-sized manufacturer of small loaders was reviewed. Materials management for loader assembly is extremely complex, with any shortage of required parts (e.g., pumps or engine blocks leading to significant additional costs in terms of unused labor, late delivery, possible disassembly of other components, etc.). By making the demand for specific types of loaders more visible to suppliers in an electronic form, it becomes increasingly efficient for suppliers to time the delivery of components when they are required. In addition, the manufacturer can look for alternatives if supply is impeded.

E-SCM has been a hot term for the past few years, but linking many business partners has been extremely difficult. Everyone from the raw material supplier to the ultimate seller in the chain must be able to get accurate information quickly and easily about orders, shipping, and customer responses to products and services. Business partners must decide which areas they will try to link first. Each partner then focuses on key internal groups that have the most to gain by adopting e-commerce.

Suppliers and customers in the traditional SC have been transformed into intelligent agents of suppliers or customers in the e-SC so that an e-SC can be considered as a form of agent society. Papazoglu (2001) provides a good typology of agents in such an e-business environment. Under this new situation, how to manage trust and negotiation between the intelligent agents within e-SC becomes a significant issue. This is because the trust and negotiation in the e-SC are based on interaction and communication between human suppliers and customers, between human suppliers (or customers) and their intelligent agents, and between intelligent supplier agents and intelligent buyer agents (Sun & Finnie, 2004). Experience management is also required for these activities in the e-SC.

EXPERIENCE MANAGEMENT

Experience is wealth for any individual or organization. Generally, experience can be taken as previous knowledge or skill obtained in everyday life (Sun & Finnie, 2004a, p. 13). Experience management (EM) has drawn increasing attention in IS and AI in the past few years (Bergmann, 2002; Sun & Finnie, 2005). This section will examine EM in some detail as it applies to intelligent agents in the e-SC. Although many managers are aware of the development in significance of knowledge management over the last few years, the role of experience management is still very new. Managers will be faced with a plethora of buzzwords in this area, and an intended contribution of this chapter will be to make managers aware both of experience management as a concept as well as its role in SCM. An example of experience in an organization may be in company buyers, for example, in retail who deal with a number of suppliers. Over time a buyer will learn from experience which suppliers are more reliable. This experience may be shared with other buyers, particularly inexperienced employees. In an automated environment in which suppliers and buyers are agents, the recording, management, and sharing of experience must also be automated.

Experience can be considered as a special case of knowledge. Methodologies, techniques, and tools for knowledge management (KM) can be directly reused for EM, because EM is a special kind of KM that is restricted to the management of experience. On the other hand, experience has some special features and requires special methods different from that of knowledge, just as a subclass *Y* of its superclass *X* usually possesses more special attributes and operations. Therefore, the following two issues are very important for EM:

- What features of EM are different from those of KM?
- Which special process stages does EM require?

In what follows, we will try to resolve these two issues. First of all, we define EM as a discipline that focuses on experience processing and its corresponding management (Sun, 2004), as shown in Figure 2. The experience processing mainly consists of the following process stages (Bergmann, 2002, pp. 1-14; Sun & Finnie, 2005):

- Discover experience
- Capture, gain, and collect experience
- Model experience
- Store experience
- Evaluate experience
- Adapt experience
- Reuse experience
- Transform experience into knowledge
- Use experience-based reasoning
- Maintain experience

Where management has permeated each of above-mentioned process stages.

It is significant to separate management functions from experience processing functions and then integrate them in EM (Sun, 2004).

The management of experience processing for each process stage includes analysis, planning, organization, support, collaboration (Sun & Finnie, 2005), coordination, and possible negotiation (Sun, 2004). Generally, management issues related to each or some of the experience processing stages include:

- Organization and control of experience
- Experience processing or management task assignment to specific person or teams

In the above experience processing stages, "maintain experience" includes updating the available experience regularly, while invalid or outdated experience must be identified, removed, or updated (Sun, 2004). Transforming experience into knowledge is an important process stage for EM, which is the unique feature of EM that is different from those of KM. In the history of human beings, all invaluable experience is gradually transformed into knowledge, which then is spread widely in the form of books, journals, and other means such as multimedia.

It should be noted that discovery of experience from a collection of knowledge or social practice is a significant issue for EM, just as knowledge discovery from a very large database (Sun & Finnie, 2005). Further, the processing of experience requires an experience base, where experience processing will be conducted.

EM research is providing a new way of looking at data, knowledge, experience, and its management for organizations and e-services (Sun & Finnie, 2005). This will include experience retrieval, experience similarity, and experience processing. Successful solution of these problems could provide the basis for new advances in both EM and e-SC.

As an application of EM, customer experience management (CEM) has been studied in business and commerce (Schmitt, 2003) and e-services (Sun & Lau, 2006).

Generally, CEM is the process of strategically managing a customer's entire experience with a product or a company (Schmitt, 2003, pp. 17-18). In this way, CEM changes traditional customer satisfaction from outcome oriented to process oriented. CEM also extends traditional CRM from recording transactions to building rich relations with customers and understanding the experiential world of customers, because it is imperative that organizations understand their customers' past experiences, current behaviors, preferences, and future needs (Brohman, Watson, Piccoli, & Parasuraman, 2003).

Schmitt proposes a framework to manage customer experience (Schmitt, 2003, p. 25) which targets the business managers or consultants. This framework consists of the following five steps:

1. analyzing the experiential world of the customer
2. building the experiential platform
3. designing the brand experience
4. structuring the customer interface
5. engaging in continuous innovation

The customer interface is one of the key implementation strategies for managing customer experience in e-SC, because it affects retention through the exchanges and interactions which further determine whether the customers are satisfied with the e-SC and whether they will buy the services again. Most CRM solutions merely record what can be easily tracked: the history and transactions of customer-company contracts (Schmitt, 2003, p. 141). However, this is not enough for managing customer experience in e-SC because the customer in e-SC believes that the interface of the e-SC is the agent of the e-SC, and s/he is communicating face to face with this agent. This is a new world, because the interaction between the customer and the agent of the e-SC is different from traditional face-to-face interaction or communication in traditional business or service. However, in such an interaction, the customer will still try to obtain human-like interaction with the interface agent in the e-SC.

Furthermore, humanizing and harmonizing the customer experience are important components for CEM. Humanizing the customer experience requires communicating with customers according to humanity rather than technology (Schmitt, 2003, p. 92). This is because the customer in e-SC hopes to experience a friendly human community in the virtual society such as the environment of e-SC. Harmonizing the customer experience allows the customers to increase their confidence in receiving the services or products from a company.

It should be noted that Schmidt's discussion of CEM is essentially based on his business consultation experience, in particular, in the traditional business sectors, without regards to any intelligent techniques. Sun and Lau (2006) argue that intelligent techniques can improve management of customer experience in e-services, just as had been done in other fields such as e-commerce. In the following sections we will argue that EM can facilitate cooperation, negotiation, and trust in e-SC.

COOPERATION AND NEGOTIATION IN THE E-SUPPLY CHAIN

Coordination among agents within e-SC has raised considerable interest, because cooperation across different entities is a central issue of SCM (Homburg & Schneeweiss, 2000). This is also because an agent cannot by itself just make a locally optimal decision, but must determine the effect its decisions will have on other agents and coordinate with others to choose and execute an alternative that is optimal over the entire SC (Fox, Barbuceanu, & Teigen, 2000). Therefore,

Fig. 2. EM as an integration of experience processing and management

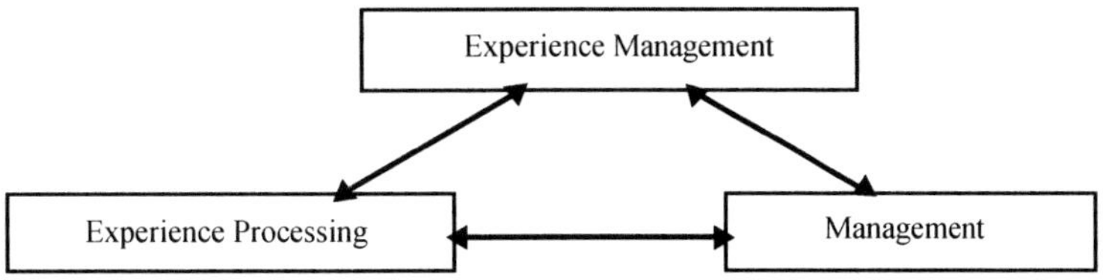

agents within an e-SC should cooperate with other agents in finding a schedule or plan or a solution to a problem. A large number of tools facilitate collaboration and communication between two parties and among members of small as well as large groups (Turban et al., 2006, p. 283).

Negotiations within the SC have also drawn increasing attention in e-SCM. For example, Homburg and Schneeweiss (2000) propose a structure for a cooperative contract negotiation between the supplier and the retailer. Barker and Finnie (2004) examine cooperation and negotiation in supply networks based on multi-agent technology. Logistics agents will negotiate over contracts with the available contractors. In this case, several rounds of offers and counteroffers should be proposed before reaching an agreement (Fox et al., 2000). As an example, factors that might be traded off would be price, delivery times, quality, delivery costs, order quantities and discounts, and so forth.

The negotiation process might be affected by uncertain events. For example, failures in agents and communication channels can occur during negotiation (Walsh & Wellman, 1999). To optimize the performance, the agents within the e-SC should work in a coordinated manner. However, the dynamics of the enterprise, the market, and agents makes this difficult (Fox et al., 2000): materials do not arrive on time, or customers change or cancel orders and negotiation between intermediaries fails. Therefore, trust and deception have become an increasing issue in e-SC. Finnie, Sun, and Barker (2005) explore trust and deception in multi-agent trading systems including supply chains. Trust among the trading partners can generate speed, agility, and lower cost (Turban et al., 2006, p. 281).

In an e-SC there is a continuous process of planning, scheduling, and management of supply and demand which requires cooperation, coordination, and negotiation by human managers. Cooperation and negotiation are thus routine activities in the e-SC. Furthermore, in recent years, cooperation and negotiation with suppliers have become increasing important in order to establish an effective and efficient supply network (Schneider & Perry, 2001). However, delegating these responsibilities to an agent requires a great deal of autonomy and intelligence.

Any organization has some history of dealing with problems relating to orders and perturbations in the supply network and the solutions applied, as well as some formal processes for dealing with these. In order to automate the response to any stochastic event, the e-SC system must be capable of reacting as one would expect a human agent to do. In many cases, a human agent responds by working from and possibly adapting solutions to previously encountered situations similar to the present problem—that is, a process of reasoning from experience using prior cases such as case-based reasoning (CBR) (Finnie & Sun, 2003) or experience-based reasoning (EBR) (Sun & Finnie, 2005).

Multi-Agent E-Supply Chain Systems

Multi-agent systems (MASs) for e-commerce probably had their origins in the pioneering work of the Autonomous Agents group of the MIT Media Lab which resulted in the Kasbah and Market Maker (Chavez & Maes, 1996). Other simple online shopping agents followed, for example, shopping bots like "Ask Jeeves." Applying multi-agent technology to e-SC has also been drawing attention since the end of the last century. Nissen and Mehra (1999) use ADE to develop a MAS for government supply chains. ADE is an integrated development environment to design, develop, debug, and deploy agents. Walsh and Wellman (1999) discuss some issues of using MAS to model supply chain formation, which is the process of bottom-up assembly of complex production and exchange relationships. However, agent interaction during SC formation might be complex, because agents do not generally have the incentive to truthfully reveal information. Papazoglu (2001) provides a good framework for intelligent agents in e-business. Singh, Salam, and Iyer (2005) describe an agent architecture for infomediary e-marketplaces which facilitates the flow of information among e-SC participants. The same group (Iyer, Singh, & Salam, 2005) further develop the concept of information exchange by agents to support collaborative business functions, using the concept of an agent-managed knowledge repository to maintain domain knowledge. This may include historical information on buyer experiences, "including the reliability and trustworthiness of the supplier." From a multi-agent viewpoint, an e-SC is composed of a set of intelligent agents, each responsible for one or more activities in the SC and each interacting with other agents in planning, bargaining, and executing their responsibilities (Fox et al., 2000). An agent is an autonomous, goal-oriented intelligent subsystem that operates asynchronously, communicating and coordinating with other agents as needed.

More and more multi-agent e-SC systems (MESC) are being developed in order to realize the transformation from conventional SC to e-SC, taking advantage of the Internet and e-commerce technology.

CBR-Based Cooperation in E-Supply Chain

Cooperation is an important characteristic of e-SC (Schneider & Perry, 2001). An agent with "perfect" knowledge and "complete" capabilities for a given task has no need to require the cooperation of other agents. However, normal agents do not have "perfect" knowledge and "complete" capabilities for a given task.

One approach to CBR-based cooperation is described by Martín, Plaza, and Arcos (1999). A cooperation mode establishes how two agents must behave to accomplish a particular task. Two cooperation modes between CBR agents are proposed in that research: Distributed CBR (DistCBR) and Collective CBR (ColCBR). The DistCBR cooperation mode is a class of cooperation protocols where a CBR agent is able to ask one or several other CBR agents to solve a problem on its behalf, and the ColCBR cooperation mode is a class of cooperation protocols where a CBR agent is able to send a specific CBR method to one or several CBR agents that are capable of using that method with their case base to solve the task at hand (Plaza, Arcos, & Martin, 1997). Therefore, the DistCBR cooperation mode enables an agent to share experiential knowledge acquired by an acquaintance by means of particular problem-solving methods, while the ColCBR cooperation mode allows a couple of CBR agents to share experiential knowledge.

CBR-Based Negotiation in E-Supply Chain

Negotiation in e-SC is a process where two parties (customers and suppliers) bargain resources for an intended gain. In order to adequately support customers, an e-SC system should possess negotiation capability. However, automated negotiation has had relatively little support to date because of the complexity of the negotiation process, which depends on the complexity of the product or service being negotiated.

The approaches to negotiation in e-SC can be classified into two classes: a cooperative approach and a competitive approach (Guttman, Moukas, & Maes, 1998). Competitive negotiation takes place if there is at least a conflict of interest between the buyer and seller/supplier. Consequently, there will be the minimum collaboration necessary between buyer and supplier to solve the negotiation problem, while cooperative negotiation tries to get as much collaboration as possible between the two parties. A competitive negotiation arises when an agent attempts to get the best deal possible, for example, to get goods at the lowest price. An example of cooperative negotiation between agents is in real-time load balancing of mobile cellular networks—all agents benefit from efficient network operation. In a supply chain environment, agents could cooperate in managing delivery across several companies to optimize utilization of trucks and so forth. However, both approaches present two extremes on a continuum of possible underlying problems. In practice, a negotiation usually lies between cooperative negotiation and competitive negotiation (Sun & Finnie, 2004a).

In the automated e-SC system, buyer agents search for a product that meets their demands. The goal of a CBR-based negotiation system is to identify these demands in cooperation with the supplier agents and to find a product that fulfils them (Sun & Finnie, 2004a, p. 186). During negotiation, the CBR-based negotiation system might suggest or even add some new demands or modify some weak demands for the purpose of finding an appropriate product. For configurable products, it is also possible for the CBR-based negotiation system to modify existing products during product adaptation to meet the customer's demands. Therefore, the task for the CBR-based negotiation system during the negotiation process is the combination of *iterative demand adaptation* and *iterative supply (product) adaptation.* The former is realized by making proposals for adjusting the demands from the buyer agent, while the latter is done by supply/product adaptation with the goal of finding an agreement point in the multidimensional demand/product space. During the negotiation, the agent or the CBR-based negotiation system is allowed to modify customer demands. If products in the product case base are configurable, it might also be possible to modify the products during negotiation.

An intelligent agent should be able to negotiate with the customer agents and to assist them during the search for an appropriate product in the e-SC. The buyer and supplier manager agents use CBR to negotiate; that is, they assess the similarity of the current negotiation to previous negotiation cases in their negotiation case base. Once a negotiation case is selected as the most relevant to the current negotiation, the agent might revise or adapt this case in order to meet any counter offer from the counterpart. Successful negotiation cases are kept in the case base for reuse in later negotiation case retrieval. These agents can use fuzzy rule-based adaptation to adapt the most similar negotiation case to the current negotiation situation (Sun & Finnie, 2004a, p. 207).

A MULTI-AGENT ARCHITECTURE FOR COOPERATION AND NEGOTIATION IN AN E-SUPPLY CHAIN

Based on the above discussion, we proposed a multi-agent architecture for cooperation and negotiation in e-SC, shown in Figure 3, in which S_i are supplier agents, SM_i are supplier manager agents, B_i are buyer agents, and BM_i is a buyer manager agent. The architecture is called MCNES (Multi-agent system for Cooperation and Negotiation in E-SC). In MCNES, CBR is used for intelligence at the buyer/supplier junctions within a specific supply network. A number of *buyer agents* control the interface between an organization and its suppliers, with each of the buyer agents using CBR to provide intelligent processing of supply needs on the basis of prior experience.

A *buyer manager (control agent)* coordinates and controls the activation and operation of the buyer agents utilizing CBR. It also uses CBR to select a suitable strategy for finding all components required for a particular product.

A *seller (supplier) agent* is at the supplier interface and is responsible for each product type. A request to purchase from an organization may itself trigger *adaptations* in the internal schedule for that organization and in turn cause its buyer agents to *negotiate* with its suppliers. To *coor-*

Figure 3. MCNES: Multi-agent cooperation and negotiation in an E-SC

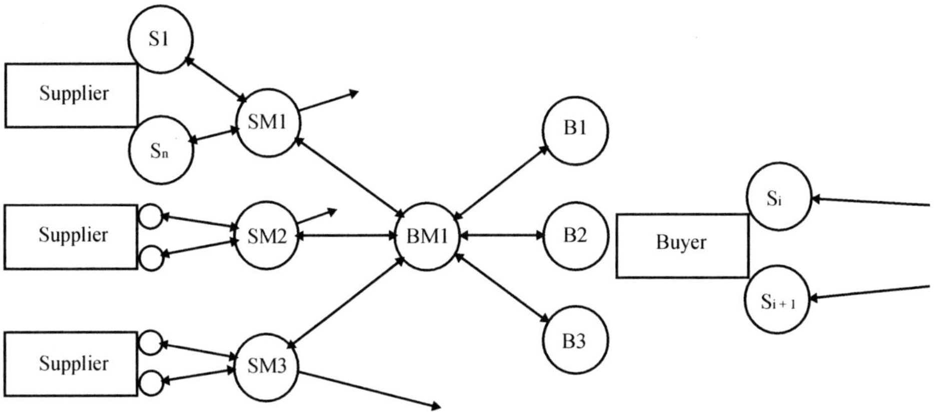

dinate the actions of supplier agents, there is a supplier manager agent for each supplier which has responsibility for checking whether the product can be supplied. Each order processed for a specific customer forms part of the *case base* for that customer and provides a historical portrait of the relationship with the customer.

Each buyer agent has a local case (experience) base. Buyer and seller manager agents need more intelligence and have their own company case base. The supplier agents will check on the impact of an order which may in turn generate a procurement need. Agents will also need to have fallback positions—that is, if there is no suitable information in the case base, there must still be a response, either by appealing for human intervention or going to other forms of reasoning (e.g., rule based).

MCNES provides two levels of agent operation: the buyer/supplier manager agents at the enterprise level and the buyer/supplier agents at the logistics level. At the enterprise level, the agents are "middle agents" (Decker, Sycara, & Williamson, 1997) who "support the flow of information in e-commerce, assisting in locating and connecting the ultimate information provider with the ultimate information requester." At the logistics level, the supplier manager agents and buyer manager agents deal with product transfer and require learning cost-effective buyer/supplier dealings for specific products.

An agent in MCNES must be capable of reasoning and learning. The CBR approach is capable of reasoning and learning dynamically; for example, as new experience is gained, it will be added to the case base for that specific product in a specific company.

Agent Interaction in MCNES

As noted above, interaction between buyers and suppliers occurs at two levels in MCNES. At the buyer agent and supplier agent level (B_i, S_i), the interaction is product based with the focus on logistics/manufacturing. Buyer agents need to keep their production optimal while supplier agents need to determine the impact of re-scheduling.

At the supplier and buyer manager agent level (BM_i, SM_i), the interaction is inter-enterprise with the focus at the trading level. Both buyer manager agents and supplier manager agents are concerned with maintaining a good trading relationship to mutual benefit. For the buyer manager agent, this may mean retaining a range of alternative suppliers. For the supplier manager agent, this is customer relationship management (CRM). The supplier agent needs to have information on the likely impact of re-scheduling which it can feed into the CRM process so that any negative effects on a customer are minimized. In essence, this is using dynamic information for real-time CRM. Obviously in many situations this will only be part of the total picture and for some time to come will probably still require human intervention if any concerns are flagged. However, the need to incorporate the capability to gather and process dynamic information is obviously an issue that will need to be part of CRM, particularly in a virtual enterprise environment. Each order that is processed for a specific customer forms part of the case base for that customer and provides a historical portrait of the relationship with the customer. A key part of the knowledge capture relates to the formation of trust between a buyer and seller. As more experience is gained of a specific supplier or buyer, the more trust (or otherwise) can be established in the relationship.

Summary

The multi-agent system approach proposed in this section provides a suitable architecture for rapid and agile response to any event. MCNES is scalable, as there is no overall controller—each organization in the chain or network will have its own agent management structure.

The MCNES system requires further development and testing both in simulated and real environments. Although initial results are encouraging for the determination of a suitable supplier (Barker & Finnie 2004), the structure of supplier agents, their relationship to CRM, the use of profiling, and the development of negotiating capability needs to be explored.

It is to be noted that in current society, negotiation between the retailer and the end-customer is not common, in particular in the supermarket. However, negotiation between business and business still exists. In the MCNES, the negotiation usually occurs between supplier agent and manufacturer agent or retailer agent. For example, Homburg and Schneeweiss (2000) discuss a model for automated negotiation between a supplier and its retailer with supply chains.

TRUST AND DECEPTION IN E-SUPPLY CHAINS

Trust and deception have been of concern to researchers since the earliest research into multi-agent e-SC (MESC). Although much of the research in MESC assumes inherent benevolence, in practice a completely open agent society must allow for the possibility of malevolent behavior. In an open trading environment, trust can be established by external mechanisms (e.g., using secret keys or digital signatures) or by internal mechanisms (e.g., learning and reasoning from experience). As noted by Ramchurn, Huynh, and Jennings (2004), many current computer applications are following a distributed model with components available through a network like the semantic Web, Web services, and grid computing. The open multi-agent system with autonomous agents has been suggested as the logical computational model for such applications (Jennings, 2001). As a result, the implications of trust and deception have broader relevance than just e-SC systems.

This section will discuss MESC systems, explore how deceptions change the reasoning required in an MESC system/environment, and will illustrate several forms of logical reasoning that involve trust and deception in an MESC. It looks at a systematic classification of reasoning techniques which can be applied between buyers and sellers. As noted earlier, it is important that management understands the issues involved in autonomous agent systems. If agents have local control and act on behalf of the organization, then the need to understand and implement controls against deception is a management imperative.

Trust and Deception in MESC

As in any other form of society, agents can exhibit malevolent behavior in the MESC environment. With the focus moving to the distributed systems paradigm and the multi-agent programming model, the study of trust and deception in agent interaction has significant implications for the operation of these systems.

Ramchurn et al. (2004) provide an extensive review of research into trust in multi-agent systems. They define trust as follows: "Trust is a belief an agent has that the other party will *do what it says it will* (being honest and reliable) or *reciprocate* (being reciprocative for the common good of both), given an *opportunity to defect* to get higher payoffs." The authors conceptualize trust as (a) individual-level trust (agent believes in honesty or reciprocation of interaction partners) and (b) system-level trust (the agents are forced to be trustworthy by the system). They further characterize individual-level trust models as learning (evolution) based, reputation based, or socio-cognitive based. Learning models are based on interactions with other agents. Reputation-based models work by asking other agents of their opinion of potential partners, often based on some form of social network (Sabater & Sierra, 2002). Rather than relying on interaction with other agents, socio-cognitive models operate on subjective perceptions of opponents. Wong and Sycara (1999) address two forms of trust: trust that agents will not misbehave and trust that agents are really delegates of whom they claim to be. Vassileva, Breban, and Horsch (2002) consider the formation of long-term coalitions of customer and vendor agents using an agent trust model. Others have done research on agent learning in an untrustworthy environment—that is, agents who will attempt to deceive each other in trading. For example, Wu, Kimbrough, and Zhong (2002) show that trust can be established if agents learn which other agents exhibit poor behavior and hence which agents not to trust.

Trust and deception are twins in MESC. Trust in MESC can be sustained only if we can understand how agents commit fraud and deception in an MESC. Furthermore, how will agents in an MESC operate autonomously in such an environment, and what precautions will they need to take to protect their "owners" from fraudulent or malevolent acts? In traditional SC systems, "caveat emptor" or "let the buyer beware" is a well-known trading rule of thumb. Humans expect the possibility of fraud and deception in trades and accordingly take whatever precautions are possible. Less well known is the Latin maxim "caveat mercator" or "let the merchant beware." The latter is particularly relevant with the increase in Internet fraud, with online merchants carrying the cost of fraudulent transactions. If this is the norm in conventional trading systems, why should it be any different in multi-agent systems?

In business and social activities, fraud depends on deception, while deception is realized through fraud. Further, the aim of both fraud and deception is to get an advantage in an environment with conflicts of interest. Therefore, in what follows, we only refer to deception, rather than fraud and deception, if necessary.

With the development of the Internet, we find ourselves in hybrid artificial societies, where real-world assumptions and the whole range of possible behaviors including deception must be taken into account (Ramchurn et al., 2004; Wooldridge & Jennings, 1994). From an e-commerce viewpoint, there are three different kinds of deception in a hybrid artificial society: deception between humans, deception between humans and intelligent agents, and deception between agents in multi-agent societies such as MESC (Sun & Finnie, 2004b). In what follows, we focus on deception in MESC.

There are many agents operating in the MESC. Some agents are generally trustworthy, for example, market coordinators, search agents, transaction agents, and payment agents. All these agents are working as a lubricant for a healthy MESC. These agents work for buyer agents, seller agents, and others such as brokers and bidders in a neutral way in order to maintain the market trading order. However, the buyer agents, seller agents, and brokers may not be trustworthy. These agents may deceive other agents in the MESC in order to obtain the maximum advantage or profit, just as buyers, sellers, and brokers may use deception in a traditional house market, where the first house buyer is usually deceived to some extent by the real estate agent on behalf of the seller.

Furthermore, Internet technology provides new opportunities and ways to deceive, because intelligent agents will also participate in deception, and agents are and will be designed, selected, or trained to deceive in MESC, and people will be also deceived by intelligent agents (Sun & Finnie, 2004b). For example, e-sellers might use all the tricks to sell something and introduce new forms of deceptive advertising. Deception in the MESC can take a variety of forms, for example, pretending to be someone else, offering goods for sale which they do not have, and so forth. This is one of the reasons why some businesses fear using an e-SC. However, we would not stop driving because we saw a fatal car accident. Similarly, we cannot stop developing e-SC or MESC, although we find some cases of deception in them. The most important issue for us is recognizing and preventing fraud and deception in MESC. To this end, it is necessary to answer the question: What is the logical foundation of fraud and deception? The essence of fraud and deception depends on its logical foundation.

Finally, to detect and defeat fraud and deception requires a theory of deceptive communication, attitudes, and behavior (Castelfranchi & Tan, 2001). In what follows, we address this issue from a logical viewpoint.

A Logical Foundation for Fraud and Deception in MESC

This subsection will examine a logical foundation for fraud and deception, and then look at how the agents commit fraud and deception in the MESC from a logical viewpoint.

Inference rules play a fundamental role in any reasoning paradigm, because any reasoning is based on an inference rule or a couple of inference rules (Sun & Finnie, 2004b). For example, *modus ponens* and *modus tollens* are central to deductive reasoning. Sun and Finnie (2004, 2005) have proposed eight basic inference rules for performing experience-based reasoning (EBR) which are summarized in Table 1. These cover all possible EBRs and constitute the fundamental for all natural reasoning paradigms at the first level. The eight inference rules are listed in the first row, and their corresponding general forms are shown in the second row respectively.

Four of them, modus ponens (MP), modus tollens (MT), abduction, and modus ponens with trick (MPT) are well known in AI and computer science, but the other four need some clarification. First of all, we illustrate modus tollens with trick with an example. We may know that:

1. If Socrates is human, then Socrates is mortal.
2. Socrates is immortal.

What we wish is to prove is "Socrates is human." In order to do so:

Let $P \to Q$: If Socrates is human, then Socrates is mortal.

- ***P*:** Socrates is human.
- ***Q*:** Socrates is mortal.

Therefore, we have P: Socrates is human, based on modus tollens with trick, and the knowledge in the knowledge base (KB) (note that $\neg Q$: Socrates is not mortal). From this example, we can see that modus tollens with trick is a kind of EBR.

Abduction with trick can be considered as a "dual" form of abduction, which is also the summary of a kind of EBR. Abduction can be used to explain that the symptoms of the patients result from specific diseases, while abduction with trick can be used to exclude some possibili-

Table 1. Experience-based reasoning: Eight inference rules

MP	MT	Abduction	MTT	AT	MPT	IMP	IMPT
P $\underline{P \to Q}$ $\therefore Q$	$\neg Q$ $\underline{P \to Q}$ $\therefore \neg P$	Q $\underline{P \to Q}$ $\therefore P$	$\neg Q$ $\underline{P \to Q}$ $\therefore P$	Q $\underline{P \to Q}$ $\therefore \neg P$	P $\underline{P \to Q}$ $\therefore \neg Q$	$\neg P$ $\underline{P \to Q}$ $\therefore \neg Q$	$\neg P$ $\underline{P \to Q}$ $\therefore Q$

ties of the diseases of the patient (Sun & Finnie, 2004b). Therefore, abduction with trick is an important complementary part for performing system diagnosis and medical diagnosis based on abduction.

It should be noted that if one does not like to use trick or deception, he can use "exception" instead. The essence is that such kinds of inferences have not yet been examined in computer science and AI, although they are necessary for EBR.

Inverse modus ponens (IMP) is also an inference rule in EBR. The "inverse" in the definition is motivated by the fact that the "inverse" is defined in logic: "if $\neg p$ then $\neg q$," provided that if p then q is given (Sun & Finnie, 2004b). Based on this definition, the inverse of $P \to Q$ is $\neg P \to \neg Q$, and then from $\neg P$, $\neg P \to \neg Q$, we have $\neg Q$ using modus ponens. Because $P \to Q$ and $\neg P \to \neg Q$ are not logically equivalent, the argument based on inverse modus ponens is not valid in mathematical logic. However, the EBR based on inverse modus ponens is a kind of common sense reasoning, because there are many cases that follow inverse modus ponens. For example, if John has enough money, then John will fly to China. Now John does not have sufficient money, then we can conclude that John will not fly to China.

The last inference rule for EBR is *inverse modus ponens with trick* (IMPT). The difference between IMPT and *inverse modus ponens* is again "with trick"; this is because the reasoning performer tries to use the trick of "make a feint to the east and attack in the west"—that is, he gets Q rather than $\neg Q$ in the *inverse modus ponens.*

These eight inference rules provide a logical foundation for any EBR paradigms at the fundamental (or atomic) level, so that they can be applied to both benevolent and deceptive agent societies. In what follows, we give several examples to illustrate this view (Finnie & Sun, 2005).

We assume that in the MESC, the seller agent S will offer goods at a specific price, while the buyer agent B will agree to purchase a specific volume at a specific price. If the MESC provides a trustworthy trading environment, we can assume that conventional reasoning applies—that is, modus ponens, modus tollens, and possible abduction are used in the agents in MESC to conduct any trading activities. For the buyer agent B, his trustworthy reasoning could be as follows:

If a seller offers goods at a price, then those goods will be available at that price. We assume that G and D are propositions: G = goods offered at known price, D = goods are available for delivery.

Modus ponens is what the buyer agent or seller agent normally uses in the trading activities: bidding, brokering, and negotiation, because they believe that If G, $G \to D$ Then D. They also use *modus tollens* in the trading activities—that is, if goods are not available, then they will not be offered for sale by an agent.

If Not D (i.e., goods are not available), Then Not G (i.e., goods will not be offered for sale).

Abduction is another common sense inference rule underpinning the marketplace: if a seller agent S has goods available for delivery D, s/he will make them available for sale. That is:

D (Goods are available and will be delivered)
$G \rightarrow D$

Therefore, we have *G* (goods will be offered at a known price).

However, the environment provided by the MESC is not always trustworthy, because some agents (e.g., buyer agents, seller agents, bankers, solicitors, and brokers) may have a conflict of interests so that they will try to deceive their trading partners. In what follows, we look at several scenarios in the simple buyer/seller context where deception or fraud could apply and consider the variations on traditional logic, which could provide a logical basis for the deceptive reasoning. A number of scenarios will be proposed where the buyer agent is misled in their dealings with the seller agent in the MESC.

1. A seller agent may offer goods at a price *G*, but those goods are not available, which case is an obvious fraud. An example could be malevolent or fraudulent behavior by a competitor of the buyer company, for example, to delay production by ensuring that materials in the SC are not delivered. This could also apply to competitors of the supplier, for example, to reduce the chances that a competitor does not achieve the deal by offering goods at a lower price. This scenario could be described as *modus ponens with trick* (MPT) (see Table 1). It takes the form:

   G (goods at known price),
   $G \rightarrow D$
   Therefore, Not D (goods are not available for delivery).

   The essence behind this fraudulent behavior is that the seller agent has used MPT to deceive the buyer agent.

2. A second form of deception could arise in the MESC, if a seller agent does not offer goods at a price but the goods are in fact available at that price. This could arise if there are limited goods available and a seller wishes to preference another buyer (agent). This is referred to as *inverse modus ponens with trick* and takes the form:

   Not *G* (not offer goods at a price)
   $G \rightarrow D$

   Therefore, *D* (goods are in fact available at that price).

3. We could also have the situation where goods are not available but are offered at a specific price. This varies slightly from case (1) above in that the starting point is that the goods are not available. This could, for example, be a negotiating tactic if goods will be available within a short time. This is called *modus tollens with trick* and takes the form:

   Not *D* (goods are not available),
   $G \rightarrow D$

   Therefore, G (goods are offered at a specific price).

4. We could have the situation where goods are available for delivery but not at that price. This could be used to fool the buyer into intending to make a purchase—again as a possible negotiating tactic or delaying tactic. This could be termed *abduction with trick* and takes the form:

   D (goods are available for delivery)
   $G \rightarrow D$

Therefore, Not *G* (goods are not offered at that price).

There are also a number of scenarios of deceiving the seller or seller agent in the MESC. As above, the seller assumes that if goods are purchased at a specific price, the seller will receive the amount in full. The most usual form of fraud and deception would be where goods are purchased, but the seller does not receive the full amount (or anything) (Finnie & Sun, 2005). This is theft or fraud and can be represented as *modus ponens with trick*. Other forms of inference rules do not apply easily to deceive the seller. *Inverse modus ponens with trick* or *abduction with trick* suggest that goods are not purchased at a specific price, but that the seller receives the full amount, which might be good for the seller but not that likely in practice.

EBR for Dealing with Trust in the E-Supply Chain

In conventional business practice, experience plays a key role in the selection of trading partners. We talk of learning from "bitter experience" when a disastrous mistake is made. Learning means that some record of past transactions together with success or failure must be made. As discussed earlier, CBR and EBR provide a practical approach to creating and manage an experience repository (Bergmann, 2002). All dealings with specific organizations would be recorded. These could then be analyzed over time to identify whether a partner is meeting the conditions of being a trustworthy collaborator.

From a buying viewpoint, buying a product in a marketplace, electronic or otherwise, can be an iterative bargaining process between an agent *S* acting on behalf of the seller and a buyer *B* initially. But it is not the only negotiation. It may also start an iterative bargaining process between *B* and bankers, delivery contractors, and so forth with the progress of the purchasing, as shown in Figure 4. First of all, *B* asks his informant (Internet agents, newspapers, acquaintances, and so forth) to search for the products for which he intends to buy. Then he will negotiate over the selling price with *S* for selling each of the products. This is also a trust and deception process between *S* and *B*, because *S* hopes to obtain the best interest by maximizing the price of the selling, while *B* also tries to obtain the best interest by minimizing the offer price to *S*. With the progress of the negotiation, the degree of deception of *S* to *B* becomes less, while the degree of trust of *B* in *S* becomes higher. If the deception degree of *S* and the trust degree of *B* can reach an equilibrium (like break-even point), as shown in Figure 5, then the price for the purchase will be fixed. Otherwise, the negotia-

Figure 4. Bargaining process in marketplace

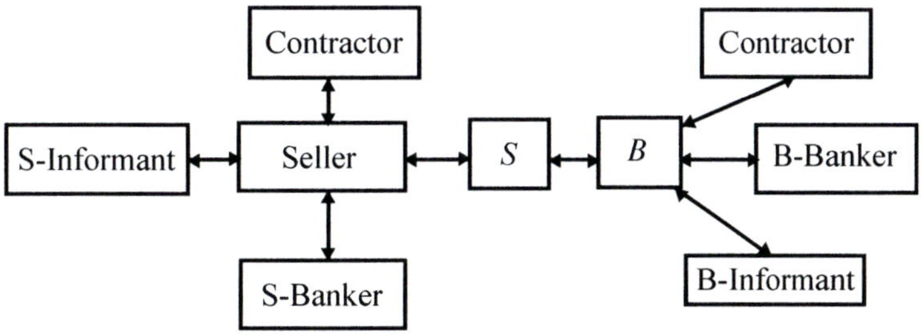

Figure 5. Trust and deception in negotiation

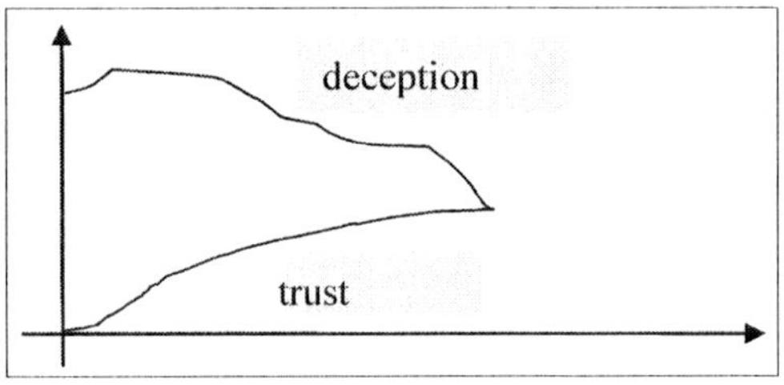

tion will be broken off and *B* will negotiate with another seller agent.

After the purchase price is fixed, *B* may ask his informant (Internet agents, newspapers, acquaintances, etc.) to search for suitable delivery contractors and then he will negotiate with each of these over the delivery price. However, *B* still uses negotiation to increase his trust in one of the contractors based on the knowledge and experience from his informant.

Although identifying partners who are not making the grade can be based on historical transactions, it would be preferable to be able to detect untrustworthy organizations fairly early in the trading relationship. One approach here relies on using data mining techniques to identify patterns of behavior which indicate possible difficulties. As one company on its own is usually unlikely to have sufficient data for effective data mining, it is possible that some form of industry-level repository could be developed (e.g., in an industry marketplace) which could be used for analysis. Although collaborative filtering techniques could possibly be used to directly identify possible problem partners, it is likely that legal issues would limit the application of these techniques. However, an industry repository based on cleaned and anonymized information might provide a good basis for learning key features for identifying trustworthy partners. Management needs to be aware of the potential role of industry marketplaces in establishing suitable trust repositories.

Summary

In the e-supply chain (e-SC), most agent models and systems assume secure and reliable communication exists between them. This ideal situation may not hold in reality. This section examined agent behaviors, in particular trustworthy behaviors, and fraud and deception behaviors of agents in the MESC. Fraud and deception are an unavoidable phenomenon for engineering MESC. Failure to understand deception will lose the "biological" balance in MESC. Benevolent agent societies assume a fundamental basis of the conventional forms of reasoning (i.e., modus ponens). In situations with malevolent or fraudulent agents, it is useful to consider other forms of reasoning to better model the processes involved. Although heuristic techniques have been applied to learn which agents could be deceptive, this section looked at the underlying models of reasoning which might apply with such agents.

Recognition of deception in e-SC remains a big issue, because wherever negotiation exists, there are issues of deception, and any bargaining in negotiation implies some justifiable concealment and deception. IT can weaken trust relationships already holding in human organizations and relations, and aggravate problems of fraud and deception (Castelfranchi & Tan, 2001). The e-medium could make matters worse by weakening the usual bonds in social control. The habit or disposition to deceive will grow stronger, because the Internet is an anonymous medium. Agents in the e-SC will deceive the users or their delegated agents, for example, we have agents that bid on our behalf from a self-interested perspective. When our agent is bidding on something in an auction, we do not want it to honestly bid our reservation price for the good, if it could possibly get that good for less money.

Many techniques have been used over time to detect and prevent fraud and deception in human communications and e-SC, for example, increasing security by security protocols, authentication, cryptography, central control, and rigid rules. All these are useful and needed, but a technical solution to protect against deception and fraud in e-SC is unrealistic. Fraud and deception was a problem 2,000 years ago, it is a problem in e-SC today, and it will be a problem in another 100 years time. It is a game of chase, catch up, run ahead, and chase all over again. Therefore, exploration of the essence of fraud and deception is at least also crucial to solve these problems.

A UNIFIED MODEL OF COOPERATION, NEGOTIATION, TRUST, AND DECEPTION IN E-SUPPLY CHAINS

So far, we have explored cooperation and negotiation, trust, and deception in e-SC respectively. These issues have drawn attention in multi-agent systems, e-commerce, and virtual society. Kraus (1997) explores cooperation and negotiation in multi-agent environments based on an intermedisciplinary approach. Sun and Finnie (2004a, 2004b) examine cooperation, negotiation, and deception in e-commerce. Weigand and van den Heuvel (2001) discuss trust, fraud, and deception in e-commerce. Castelfranchi and Tan (2001) investigate trust and deception in artificial agents and societies. However, no studies have been attempted to explore the interrelationships between communication, cooperation and negotiation, trust, and deception among the agents within the e-SC in a unified way. Without such attempts it is easy for the SC to be broken down by failures in agents, failure in communications, and intentional deception (Walsh & Wellman, 1999):

1. At least a link in an e-SC is broken or it is breakdown.
2. One part of an e-SC where many business partners involved is so weak that it is ignored.

The first case sometimes results in the bankruptcy of the lower level companies in the chain, because of delay of the materials' arrival to the company. Risk management can be used to avoid the occurrence of this case (Turban et al., 2006, p. 286).

The second case results from inefficiency of delivery of materials in the corresponding supply chain. The final results will affect the end products to end customers and negatively influence customer satisfaction.

In what follows, we will propose a unified model of cooperation, negotiation, trust, and deception in e-supply chains, as shown in Figure 6, in order to explore the above-mentioned interrelationships.

In the e-SC, an agent first communicates with its adjacent agents. However, communication between agents is normally not transitive, because indirect communication between some agents (e.g, the buyer and the seller's solicitor) is illegal or unethical. However, the communication is fundamental for any activities such as collaboration, cooperation, and coordination in the e-SC.

Agents have to coordinate their activities and cooperate based on collaboration, coordination, and cooperation protocols (3C) in order to make materials and information flow in the e-SC effectively and efficiently. For example, product design and demand forecasting can be based on 3C among the business agents. The general case of these collaborations among the business partners constitutes collaborative commerce, which implies communication, information sharing, and collaborative planning done electronically through tools such as groupware and specially designed collaboration tools (Turban et al., 2006, p. 286).

Basically, agents work trustfully in order to form coalitions, collaborate, and cooperate with other agents. This is the reason why in the majority of cases, both traditional SC and e-SC run well. Sometimes, however, the coalition, collaboration, and cooperation might terminate because one agent breaks the relevant protocols. Such a termination might lead to economic risk or

Figure 6. 3C, trust, and deception in e-supply chains

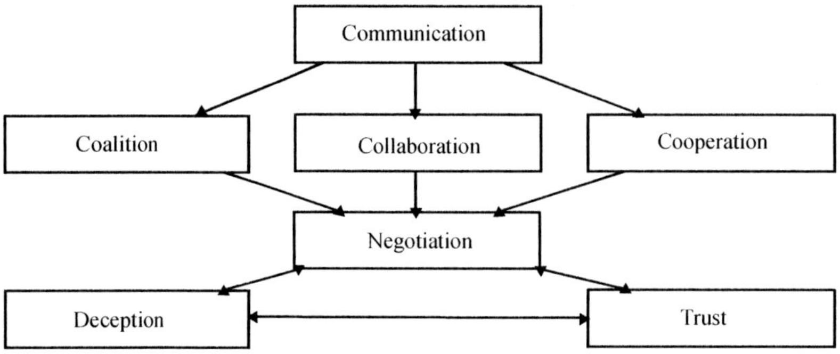

breakdown of the e-SC. In this case, a negotiation mechanism has to be activated, in order to maintain effective communication, collaboration, and cooperation with the related agents. Negotiation is a bargaining process between two or more agents over prices or service items within the e-SC. In order to obtain the maximum benefit, one party in the negotiation usually hides some truths so that there are deceptions in any negotiation. Every party makes sufficient use of their knowledge and experience to avoid any possible deception in the negotiation. Any loss of benefit in the negotiation can be considered as a result of being deceived (Sun & Finnie, 2004b). Sometimes, negotiation is also a process of improving trust among the parties. The successful negotiation can bring new coalition, collaboration, and cooperation based on new 3C protocols with improved levels of trust. In other cases, the negotiation does not improve the trust among the parties, or create new coalitions, collaboration, and cooperation among them. One of the reasons is that at least one party has not shown sufficient compromise in the negotiation so that its deception strategy has not been successful. In this case, the negotiation is broken and the e-SC has to be relinked.

Coalition, collaboration and cooperation, trust, and deception comprise a dynamic process in the e-SC. They can be considered as a subchain (i.e., deception chain, negotiation chain, or trust chain) in the e-SC. In this subchain, any change in an entity will affect the activities of other items. Negotiation plays a pivotal role in this subchain, because it can improve the trustworthiness of other entities. Deception is a unavoidable part in this subchain. It can reduce the trustworthiness, coalition, cooperation, and coordination among the agents. However, removal of deception through negotiation can improve the trustworthiness, cooperation, coalition, and coordination among the agents.

CONCLUSION

This chapter first examined the transformation from the traditional SC to the e-SC and experience management. Then it explored multi-agent cooperation and negotiation, trust, and deception in e-SCs respectively. It also proposed a unified model of cooperation, negotiation, trust, and deception in e-supply chains. The approach will facilitate research and development of negotiation, trust, and planning in e-supply chains and multi-agent systems. The trend to the future will definitely lead to increasing autonomy for agents in the electronic supply chain. With such autonomy comes an increasing requirement for management to take responsibility for the actions of agents working on their behalf. Managers must be aware of the potential for fraud and deception in the supply chain and of research in this field.

Experience management is still a new concept for e-supply chains. How to manage experience of agents within the e-supply chain in order to improve cooperation, negotiation, and trust among agents, and to control deception, remains a significant issue in e-supply chains and one that decision makers in organizations need to be aware of. Experience management is currently where knowledge management was some five to ten years ago. A contribution of this chapter is to raise awareness of this developing field. In future work, we will develop algorithms and mechanisms of integrating cooperation, negotiation, and trust, taking into account deception in e-supply chains.

REFERENCES

Barker, J., & Finnie, G. (2004, August 5-8). A model for global material management using dynamic information. In *Proceedings of the 10th Americas Conference on Information Systems,* New York.

Barker, J., & Finnie, G. (2004). Evolving platforms for process integration in supply networks. In *Proceedings of the 12th CollECTeR Workshop on eCommerce,* Adelaide, South Australia.

Bergmann, R. (2002). *Experience management: Foundations, development methodology and Internet-based applications.* Berlin: Springer (LNAI 2432).

Brohman, M.K., Watson, R.T., Piccoli, G., & Parasuraman, A.A. (2003). Data completeness: A key to effective Net-based customer service systems. *Communications of the ACM, 46*(6), 47-51.

Castelfranchi, C., & Tan, Y.H. (2001). The role of trust and deception in virtual societies. In *Proceedings of the 34th Hawaii International Conference on System Sciences.* Retrieved January 16, 2006, from http://csdl.computer.org/comp/proceedings/hicss/2001/0981/07/

Chavez, A., & Maes, P. (1996). Kasbah: An agent marketplace for buying and selling goods. In *Proceedings of the 1st International Conference on the Practical Application of Intelligent Agents and Multi-Agent Technology,* London. (pp. 75-90).

Decker, K., Sycara, K., & Williamson, M. (1997). Middle-agents for the Internet. In *Proceedings of the 15th International Joint Conference on Artificial Intelligence* (pp. 578-583).

Finnie, G., & Sun, Z. (2003, February 12-14). A knowledge-based model of multi-agent CBR systems. In *Proceedings of the International Conference on Intelligent Agents, Web Technologies, and Internet Commerce (IAWTIC'2003)*, Vienna, Austria (pp. 494-503).

Finnie, G., Barker, J., & Sun, Z. (2004). A multi-agent model for cooperation and negotiation in supply networks. In *Proceedings of the 10th Americas Conference on Information Systems* (pp. 2650-2657). New York: Association for Information Systems.

Finnie, G., & Barker, J. (2004). Adaptive agents for supply networks. In *Proceedings of the 6th International Conference on Enterprise Information Systems* (ICEIS 2004), Porto, Portugal.

Finnie, G., Sun, Z., & Barker, J. (2005). Trust and deception in multi-agent trading systems: A logical viewpoint. In N.C. Romano Jr. (Ed.), *Proceedings of the 11th Americas Information Systems (AMCIS'2005)* (pp. 1020-1026). Omaha, NE: Association for Information Systems.

Fox, M.S., Barbuceanu, M., & Teigen, R. (2000). Agent-oriented supply-chain management. *International Journal of Flexible Manufacturing Systems, 12,* 165-188.

Gates, B. (1999). *Business @ the speed of thought: Using a digital nervous system.* New York: Warner Books.

Guttman, R.H., Moukas, A.G., & Maes, P. (1998). Agent-mediated electronic commerce: A survey. *Knowledge Engineering Review, 13*(2), 147-159.

Homburg, C., & Schneeweiss, C. (2000). Negotiations within supply chains. *Computational & Mathematical Organization Theory, 6,* 47-59.

Iyer, L., Singh, R., & Salam, A.F. (2005). Intelligent agents to support information sharing in B2B e-marketplaces. *Information Systems Management, 22*(3), 37-49.

Jennings, N.R. (2001). An agent-based approach for building complex software systems. *Communications of the ACM, 44*(4), 35-41.

Kraus, S. (1997). Negotiation and cooperation in multi-agent environments. *Artificial Intelligence,* (1-2), 79-98.

Martín, F.J., Plaza, E., & Arcos, J.L. (1999). Knowledge and experience reuse through communication among competent (peer) agents. *International Journal of Software Engineering and Knowledge Engineering, 9*(3), 319-341.

Nissen, M.E., & Mehra, A. (1999). Some intelligent software supply chain agents. In *Proceedings of Autonomous Agents '99,* Seattle, WA.

Papazoglu, M.P. (2001). Agent-oriented technology in support of e-business. *Communications of the ACM, 44*(4).

Plaza, E., Arcos, J.L., & Martin, F. (1997). Cooperative case-based reasoning. In *Distributed artificial intelligence meets machine learning* (pp. 180-220). Berlin: Springer (*LNAI 1221*).

Poirier, C.C., & Bauer, M.J. (2001). *E-supply chain: Using the Internet to revolutionize your business: How market leaders focus their entire organization on driving value to customers.* San Francisco: Berrett-Koehler.

Ramchurn, S.D., Huynh, D., & Jennings, N.R. (2004). Trust in multi-agent systems. *Knowledge Engineering Review, 19*(1), 1-25.

Rea, T. (2001). Engineering trust in electronic environments: Role for a trusted third party. In C. Castelfranchi & Y.H. Tan (Eds.), *Trust and deception in virtual societies* (pp. 221-236). Dordrecht/Boston: Kluwer Academic.

Ross, D.F. (2003). *Introduction to e-supply chain management: Engaging technology to build market-winning business partnerships.* Boca Raton, FL: St. Lucie Press.

Sabater, J., & Sierra, C. (2002). Reputation and social network analysis in multi-agent systems. In *Proceedings of the 1st International Joint Conference on Autonomous Agents and Multi-Agent Systems,* Bologna, Italy.

Schillo, M., Rovatsos, M., & Funk, P. (2000). Using trust for detecting deceitful agents in artificial societies. *Applied Artificial Intelligence Journal, 14*(8), 825-848.

Schmitt, B.H. (2003). *Customer experience management: A revolutionary approach to connecting with your customers.* Hoboken, NJ: John Wiley & Sons.

Silisque, A., Brito, I., Almirall, E., & Cortés, U. (2003). From supply chains to demand networks. *Agents in Retailing. The Electrical Bazaar Artificial Intelligence Research Report,* LSI-03-41-R.

Singh, R., Salam, A.F., & Iyer, L. (2005). Agents in supply chains. *Communications of the ACM, 48*(6), 108-115.

Sun, Z., & Finnie, G. (2004a). *Intelligent techniques in e-commerce: A case-based reasoning perspective.* Heidelberg/Berlin: Springer-Verlag.

Sun, Z., & Finnie, G. (2004b, December 6-8). Experience-based reasoning for recognizing fraud and deception. In *Proceedings of the International Conference on Hybrid Intelligent Systems* (*HIS 2004*), Kitakyushu, Japan (pp. 80-85). IEEE Press.

Sun, Z., & Finnie, G. (2005a) MEBRS: A multiagent architecture for an experience-based reasoning system. In R. Khosla, R.J. Howlett, & L.C. Jain (Eds.), *Knowledge-based intelligent information and engineering system* (*LNAI 3681*) (pp. 972-978). Berlin: Springer-Verlag.

Sun, Z., & Finnie, G. (2005b). Experience management in knowledge management. In R. Khosla, R.J., Howlett, & L.C. Jain (Eds.), *Knowledge-based intelligent information and engineering systems* (pp. 979-986). Berlin: Springer-Verlag (LNAI 3681).

Sun, Z., & Lau, S.K. (2007). Customer experience management in e-services. In J. Lu, D. Run, & G. Zhang (Eds.), *E-service intelligence* (pp. 365-388). Berlin: Springer-Verlag.

Trepper, C. (2000). *E-commerce strategies.* Redmond, WA: Microsoft Press.

Turban, E., King, D., Viehland, D., & Lee, J. (2006). *Electronic commerce, a managerial perspective.* Upper Saddle River, NJ: Prentice-Hall.

Swaminathan, J., Smith, S.F., & Sadeh, N. (1998). *Modeling supply chain dynamics: A multi-agent approach.* Retrieved January 2006 from *http://interactive.wiwi.uni-frankfurt.de/ldb/articlesearch.php*

Vassileva, J., Breban, S., & Horsch, M.C. (2002). Agent reasoning mechanism for long-term coalitions based on decision making and trust. *Computational Intelligence, 18*(4), 583-595.

Walsh, W.E., & Wellman, M.P. (1999). Modeling supply chain formation in multi-agent systems. In *Proceedings of the IJCAI-99 Workshop on Agent-Mediated Electronic Commerce.*

Weigand, H., & van den Heuvel, W.-J. (2001). Trust in e-commerce: A language/action perspective. In C. Castelfranchi & Y.H. Tan (Eds.), *Trust and deception in virtual societies* (pp. 221-237). Dordrecht/Boston: Kluwer Academic.

Wheeler, R., & Aitken, S. (2000). Multiple algorithms for fraud detection. *Knowledge-Based Systems, 13*(2-3), 93-99.

Wong, H.C., & Sycara, K. (1999). Adding security and trust to multi-agent systems. In *Proceedings of the Autonomous Agents '99 Workshop on Deception, Fraud, and Trust in Agent Societies* (pp. 149-161).

Wooldridge, M., & Jennings, N.R. (1994). Agent theories, architectures, and languages: A survey. In M.J. Wooldridge & N.R. Jennings (Eds.), *Proceedings of the Intelligent Agents ECAI-94 Workshop on Agent Theories, Architectures, and Languages* (pp. 1-39). Berlin: Springer-Verlag.

Wu, D.J., Kimbrough, S., & Zhong, F. (2002). Artificial agents play the mad mex trust game: A computational approach. In R.H. Sprague (Ed.), *Proceedings of the 35th Hawaii International Conference on System Sciences* (*HICSS–35 2002*), Hawaii. IEEE Press.

Chapter X
Trading E-Coalition Modeling for Supply Chain

Pierre F. Tiako
Langston Univerisity, USA

ABSTRACT

As the Internet grew and evolved, it became more widely used by everyone. What once was utilized by the military and used for academic purposes is now employed by companies for e-business marketing strategies and alliances in the supply chain. Historically, companies have found many ways to work together, playing different roles with regard to manufacturing, supplying, selling, delivering, and buying in the supply chain. Most of the time, according to role, members of each company get together in a shared space (i.e., marketplace) to work on a particular project (i.e., delivering quality goods or services to customers). The emergence of the Internet has brought an appropriate media to expand markets and enable collaboration with partners in all stages of product manufacturing, testing, and delivering through electronic commerce. Support for these collaborations over the Internet, called e-coalition here, is what this chapter is about.

INTRODUCTION

Recently, several research works on software process technology (e.g., Tiako, Lindquist, & Gruhn, 2001) have proposed models for organizing distributed software development among autonomous and remote software enterprises. The suggested models of collaboration rely on Internet technologies, which offer a communication medium. They allow software development ventures in a dynamic manner and help automate a variety of contract types among enterprises (Tiako, 2002). The ways e-commerce companies interact to build a supply chain (Simchi-Levi, Kaminsky, & Simchi-Levi, 2000) over the Internet and deal with constraints for delivering products to customers are about the same as those used by software enterprises, as described above. Related work in e-commerce, at some level, provides framework for negotiation (Benyoucef & Keller, 2000) or mediation (Moukas, Guttman, & Maes, 1998; Guttman & Maes, 1998) in dealing with e-business relationships, but is still limited in terms of infrastructure for ad-hoc collaboration in the marketplace.

A coalition for supply chain is important in production networks where suppliers and partners work together for specific purposes. Such coalition includes several activities resulting in formal or informal arrangements. Activities define ways and constraints on what to exchange, how to exchange and when, as well as the condition. Coalition also deals with all aspects of teaming and partnering, such as partner assessment and selection, quality of product to deliver to customers, and profit and risks taken and shared. To increase individual profits in the face of globalization, participants have to work together to attain new markets and develop quality products or render services. The emergence of the Internet has brought an appropriate media to expand markets and enable collaboration with partners in all stages of product manufacturing, testing, and delivering through electronic commerce. Support for these collaborations over the Internet, called e-coalition here, is what this chapter is about.

Traditional electronic commerce models enable the online offering, ordering, payment, and delivery of goods. One common characteristic of different models is their isolation. Though they are connected to the Web, they are still isolated islands in the online universe; they cannot interact with each other without media-breaks. The isolation is enforced by the limited support for ad-hoc modeling and coordination of interactions among partners in the lifecycle for delivering quality goods or services. Support for these relationships over the Internet provides opportunities to bundle complementary needs of partners according to unpredictable requirements in the market. This chapter augments existing electronic commerce models by defining an infrastructure for collaborative electronic markets. It considers an example of a trading coalition between a travel agency and its partners. It also describes the underlying technologies for implementing the proposal.

This chapter is organized as follows: we present some basic definitions of supply chain and a brief history of electronic commerce. Then we describe an approach for e-coalition modeling and a typical scenario of usage where e-coalitions involving a travel agency and its partners for supplying flight tickets are considered. The underlying technologies used to develop this proposal are presented, followed by related work and a conclusion.

BASICS OF SUPPLY CHAIN

A production supply chain involves getting a smooth and efficient flow of goods, services, and information from raw materials through to finished goods in the hands of the ultimate customer (Ellram, 1990; Jones & Riley, 1985; Bolumole, 2000). Key supply chain activities include production planning, purchasing, materials management, distribution, customer service, and sales forecasting (Saunders, 1997; Fenstermacher & Zeng, 2000). These processes are critical to the success of any operation, whether they are manufacturers, wholesalers, or service providers.

Traditional Supply-Push Model

In the traditional supply chain model, the raw material suppliers are at one end of the supply chain. They are connected to manufacturers and distributors, which are in turn connected to a retailer and the end customer. Although the customer is the source of the profits, they are only part of the equation in this "push" model (E-Future, 2006). The order and promotion process—which involves customers, retailers, distributors, and manufacturers—occurs through time-consuming paperwork. By the time customers' needs are filtered through the agendas of all the members of the supply chain, the production cycle ends up serving suppliers every bit as much as customers.

E-Commerce Supply-Pull Model

Driven by e-commerce's capabilities to empower clients, many companies are moving from the traditional "push" business model, where manufacturers, suppliers, distributors, and marketers have most of the power, to a customer-driven "pull" model (E-Future, 2006). This new business model is less product-centric and more directly focused on the individual consumer. To succeed in the business environment, companies have recognized that there is an ongoing shift in the balance of power in the commerce model, from suppliers to customers.

The Formation of Supply Chain Relationships

A production supply chain requires the formation of partnerships and long-term relationships within and between organizations on the supply chain (Johnston & Lawrence, 1988; Balsmeier & Voisin, 1996). It has been defined more broadly as an integrative philosophy to managing the flow of products, services, and information along distribution channels from suppliers through to the ultimate consumers (Houlihan, 1985; Stevens, 1989; Bolumole, 2000b).

ELECTRONIC COMMERCE BACKGROUND

Electronic commerce and the Internet are fundamentally changing the nature of supply chains, and redefining how consumers learn about, select, purchase, and use products and services. The result has been the emergence of new business-to business supply chains that are consumer focused rather than product focused. As goods move from raw material processors through to manufacturers, distributors, and retailers, extensive coordination is required throughout the supply chain (Fenstermacher & Zeng, 2000).

Support for electronic commerce (Wrigley, Wagenaar, & Clarke, 1994; Milosevic & Bond, 1995) requires: (1) computing and communication platforms for end-to-end electronic transfer of messages; (2) electronic data interchange (EDI) structures and protocols for common understanding of messages between enterprises; and (3) enterprise models that reflect market activities, relationships among partners, as well as coalition for supply chain.

Figure 1. Electronic commerce components' hierarchy

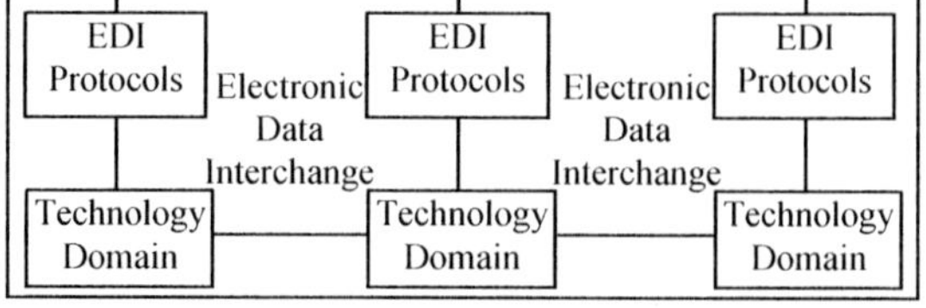

We present EC's history according to these three facets with the aim of identifying components that are still missing for fully integrated electronic commerce activities, in particular those that refer to the coordination and control of activities for manufacturing activities among partners for quality product delivery and customer satisfaction.

EDI Systems

Electronic commerce applications were first launched within transportation carriers and associated shippers, brokers, customs, freight forwarders, and bankers (Milosevic & Bond, 1995). The computing and communication framework platforms were based on the use of value-added networks. EDI is the computer-to-computer exchange of business data in standard formats. In EDI, information is organized according to a specified format set by both parties, allowing a "hands-off" computer transaction that requires no human intervention on either end. All information contained in an EDI transaction set is, for the most part, the same as on a conventionally printed document.

The motivations of the first EDI system were to extend the business scope of enterprises, as well as reduce paper flow among partners and shorten time needed for transaction execution (Wrigley et al., 1994). EDI standards come under the auspices of the United Nations with the label EDIFACT (2006). The standard was developed in the United States by the American National Standards Institute (ANSI). These two EDI standards have been used by thousands of organizations worldwide to access new business opportunities to collaborate with partners or expand their activities. EDI systems based on value-added networks have undeniably augmented business activities over the Internet. The wide penetration of the Internet enables a broader range of businesses which can utilize networking technology for their business dealings. This includes small and medium-size companies, as opposed to the scenario of the past whereby only large corporations could afford such technology. In addition to the increased types of business on the Net, EDI provides the Web with flexible ways to locate and access suitable partners to establish business relationships.

EDI Over the Internet

To support EDI for electronic commerce over the Internet was an important goal during the past decade. At that time, companies struggled with setting up EDI relationships among themselves using paper documents. Frequently, the set up was conducted in a lengthy process of agreements on EDI messages to be used. To deal with the barriers for using EDI, some initiatives have been made to improve EDI principles. Such initiatives led to the development of Open-EDI (1996) and the specification of new EDI rules. The prime thrust of this idea was to enable electronic commerce using Open-EDI to be established between trading partners without the need for upfront trading or interchange agreements. The target is to make short-term and ad hoc trading relationships practical. Jointly conducted by several organizations, new EDI rules were defined and the system labeled UNCID (UNiform rules of Conduct for Interchange of Data by teletransmission). The objective of UNCID was to complement EDIFACT (2006).

During the past decade, goals have been reached with the arrival of systems such as EDI-CORBA (Common Object Request Broker Architecture), which allows distributed components of the marketplace to communicate, as well as the emerging of EDI-XML (Extensible Markup Language) for exchanging documents over the Internet. However, new problems occurred with the need of teaming and contacting in the face of globalization, requiring organizations to work in a coalition in the supply chain. The problems are now at the level of enterprise modeling in the hierarchy of Figure 1. Current work at that level proposes how to support semantics of complex business scenarios (Milosevic & Dromey, 2002), transactions (Xiong & Ling, 2003, 2004) among partners, as well as alliances among them (Tiako, 2003). But an appropriate model of coalition to support and control supply chain formation for producing and delivering a quality product to costumers is still missing.

Below we address the problem of modeling and performing coalition to support lifecycle supply chain as well as enterprises processes. The model presented is illustrated by a detailed example.

Methodology for Modeling E-Coalition and Processes

Basically, there are two forms of e-commerce: business-to-business (B2B) and business-to-consumer (B2C). The first relates to electronic transactions that aim to automate business processes between two companies, without consideration to the final consumer. Here, companies interact with each other using Electronic Data Interchange (EDI). The second involves purchase of goods by the final consumer through the Internet, interacting with companies using electronic fund transfer. Figure 2 presents B2B and B2C in the context of a traveling agency.

An example that involves electronic data interchange transaction is the supply of flights by flying companies to travel agencies. An example of a transaction that involves electronic fund transfer is when a traveler, usually from home, sends electronic information on the checking account of a travel agency to purchase tickets. We present the different types of components, parts of chain supplies that make up the trading community, before developing the model for supporting their e-business relationships.

Components of Supply Chain

Types of components operating in the supply chain (see Figure 3) are described as follows:

- **Customer:** The end user in the trading community that buys goods or services from suppliers from home, via the Web, and using credit card for payment.
- **Supplier:** Builds shopping malls to provide products to customers. For example, it connects to banks for payment and to deliverers for delivering, besides linking with other suppliers or manufacturers for supplying.
- **Bank:** It manages the flow of money in the trading community using SET —Secure Electronic Transaction (Drew, 1999; Panurach, 1996)— for secured payments.
- **Delivery:** When needed—"*Tip:* Some itineraries may require paper tickets, and a $14.99 shipping and handling fee is charged for paper tickets." Expedia.com—it allows the physical movement of products between components.

Figure 2. Business-to-business and business-to-consumer transactions

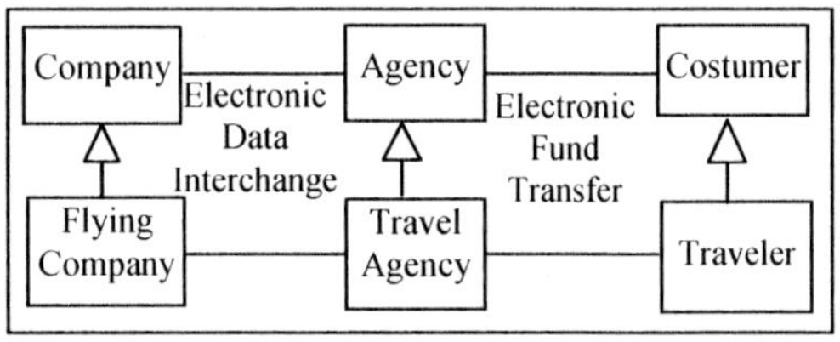

Figure 3. Components of the supply chain and their relation

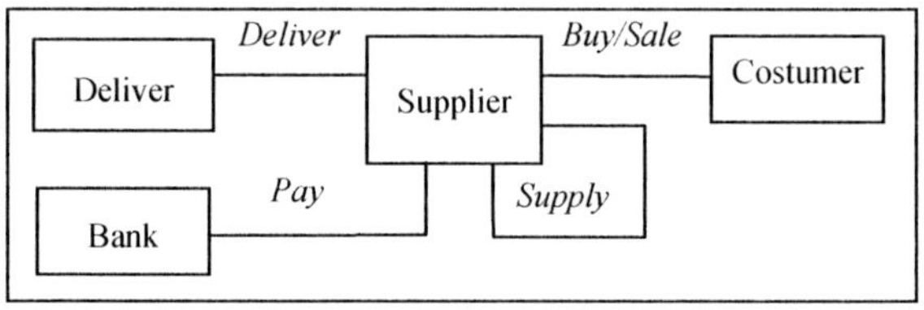

MODELING E-COALITION AND E-BUSINESS PROCESSES

Scenarios of the supply chain (see Figure 4) for travel packages in an agency are considered here. Components interacting are: (1) *customers*—families and individuals—that make reservations for packages. A package has three elements: (a) round-trip flight, (b) accommodation, and (c) car rental; (2) *travel agencies (TAs)* that interact with customers, flight companies, hotels, and car rental companies for travel arrangements; (3) *flight companies (FCs)* for traveling; (4) *car rental companies (CRCs)* for transportation at arrival; (5) *hotels* to provide accommodation; (6) *banks* for managing payments; and (7) *shipping companies (SCs)* for delivering tickets. This example is used to illustrate models of e-coalition.

E-coalition models are involved with several components, while e-business (B2B or B2C) process models are made up of single components. Both models are interdependent. E-coalitions belong to the family of organizational processes, while e-business processes are in rapport with business processes. The generic metamodel of federation introduced by Tiako (1999) and further developed by Tiako et al. (2001) can be specialized to support e-coalitions and e-business processes.

The generic metamodel supports various types of processes (software, business, and workflow) that an organization can plan to define. Each process has several activities—pieces of work that must be done. The philosophy of defining both models is the same. The definition of a model starts by creating its entities and relations from the metamodel. An activity for e-business process is composed of a name and relationships with entities' product, direction, tool, role, and sub-activities. Precisely one role is assigned to an activity. An agent will perform this role. A product can form an input to an activity, an output from an activity, or an intermediate result of an activity. An agent is a model entity that performs roles in the trading community, therefore carrying out activities. During the e-business process definition, some activities can be assigned to a role, and several agents can be identified to perform a role. A direction is a model entity that defines objectives of an activity, including constraints to be respected, and may provide advisory guidance on carrying out activities. The only requirement imposed by the model is that direction provides instructions to complete an activity.

A trading e-coalition, adopted and adapted from the organizational model (Tiako, 1999) presented in Figure 4, is composed of a name and relationships with entities events, direction, tool, competence, and eventually its sub-alliances. Competence is a model entity that defines the function a component must satisfy before involvement in a coalition. A coalition involves several competences. Several components can be identified to fulfill the same competence within an e-coalition. An *event* is a model entity that defines objects of any nature (goods, services, and information) that can be exchanged in the marketplace. *Sub-coalitions* function as e-coalitions. *Direction* and *tool* have the same semantics as defined above for e-business process. Each component can define models of an e-coalition in its own way and according to purpose of the marketplace. A model is instantiated into e-coalitions with appropriated partners. Enactment of an e-coalition allows establishing and maintaining trading collaboration. Its performance allows controlling the fulfillment of the commitment of each component during trading, including distribution of events among them.

Figure 4. High-level trading organizational modeling

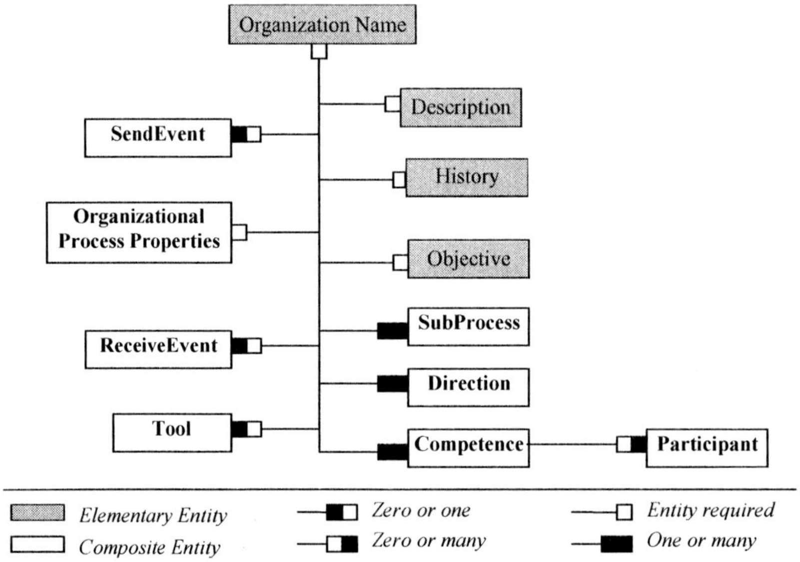

Validation of Trading E-Coalition Model

In the example, a travel agency makes a B2B inquiry for booking flights. A flight company responds by performing a process (defined in the component *Airline* in Figure 5) for supplying tickets as follows. Activity *Availability* checks flight availability before performing *Reject* for rejecting the inquiry if there is no flight. If available, *Booking* is performed to book flights and notify the travel agency. Tickets can then be delivered to the travel agency electronically or by mail. Then activity *Cash* is started to send an invoice to the travel agency with the bank account to be credited. Before closing the process, the flight company starts activity *Flight* to transport *Traveler,* for a check-in and check-out will be necessary. The trading e-coalition coordinating interactions between the travel agency and the flight company is defined as follows in Figure 5: (08) activity *Inquiry* for asking prices and flights availability; (09) *Notification* for informing the travel agency to flights availability; (10) *Ordering* to order flights for the travel agency; and (11) *Confirmation* to notify that flights are booked.

The travel agency also makes B2B inquiries to reserve rooms for accommodation at the destination. The basic process for supplying a room and its activities are defined in the component *Hotel* of Figure 5. This process is about the same as the one used by the flight company to supply tickets to the travel agency. The trading e-coalition coordinating interactions between the travel agency and hotels is defined as follows in Figure 5: (04) activity *Inquiry* for asking prices and rooms availability; (05) *Notification* to inform the travel agency to rooms' availability; (06) *Ordering* to order reservation by the travel agency; and (07) *Confirmation* to confirm rooms' reservation.

The travel agency continues by B2B inquiries for a car reservation at destination. The basic process for reservation is defined in the component *Car Rental* of Figure 5. The e-coalition for coordinating interactions between the travel agency and the car rental companies is defined as follows in Figure 5: (12) activity *Inquiry* for asking prices and cars' availability; (13) *Notification* to inform the travel

Figure 5. Model of e-coalition, including e-business processes

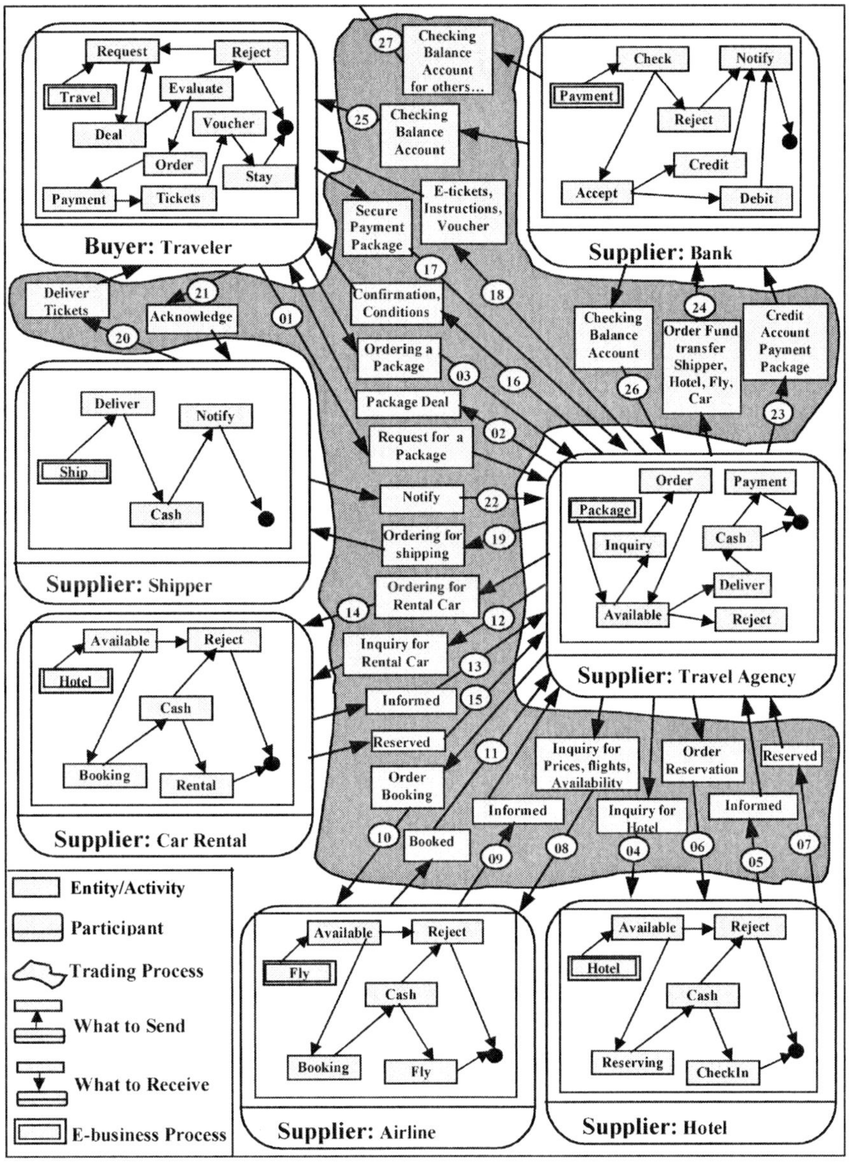

agency to availability; (14) *Ordering* by the travel agency to make reservation; and (15) *Confirmation* to confirm that cars are reserved.

At this point, the travel agency is ready to interact with the traveler for delivering packages. *Traveler*, from home's Web system, defines or uses an existing B2C procurement process for ordering tickets. The basic process *Travel* for buying packages and its activities (see the component *Traveler* of Figure 5) are defined as follows: activity *Request* is performed to inquire travel agencies for package deals. Then *Deal* is performed to receive travel agencies' proposals, before performing *Evaluate* to evaluate them.

Traveler, through the process, can receive a maximum of deals before evaluation, by just performing *Request* several times. After evaluation, *Traveler* can reject them, request other deals, or close the process. If there are good deals, the process continues by contacting the selected travel agency for ordering. *Order* will then be performed, followed by *Tickets,* for receiving tickets. If the shipping company delivers tickets, an acknowledgment is required. The performance of *Voucher* will provide information and instructions for the package. Then *Stay* starts to manage the trip. Back home, *Traveler* will close the whole processes after receiving and verifying the checking balance account from *Bank* regarding trip's expenses.

The e-coalition coordinating interactions between *Traveler, Travel Agency, Bank,* and *Shipping Company* is defined by the following activities in Figure 3: (01) *Request* that queries prices and package availability; (02) *Deals* to inform the traveler to package deals availability; (03) *Ordering* to order a package; (16) *Confirmation* to confirm package's reservation—here FCs, hotels, and car rental companies supposed already to have supplied the travel agency as presented above; (17) *Payment* uses SET to transfer account information to the travel agency for payment; (18) *E-Tickets* delivers electronic tickets to the traveler; as option, (20) *Deliver* delivers package via the shipping company and (21) *Acknowledge* for delivery's acknowledgment; (25) *Checking* allows the travel agency interacting with *Bank* to receive its checking balance account. Let us describe how the travel agency acts with its own e-business process for selling packages.

After receiving an inquiry for packages, the travel agency will start the process *Package* for selling them, as presented in the component *Travel Agency* of Figure 5. It is composed of the activities that follow: *Available* that determines the availability of stock to honor the order. If not, *Inquiry* is performed to ask additional package's elements from suppliers, before beginning *Order* to make order. If the package is still not available, the traveler's request is rejected by performing *Reject.* If available, *Deliver* is performed to deliver, electronically or by mail, the deal to the traveler. Delivery includes tickets, vouchers, and all the necessary instructions for traveling. Performance of *Cash* orders the bank to credit the travel agency's account with the traveler's payment; at the same time, the activation of *Payment* orders the bank to pay suppliers, if any. Process *Package* will close when the travel agency receives correct balance accounts from the bank regarding the package's transactions.

The e-coalition coordinating interactions between *Travel Agency, Traveler, Bank,* and *Shipping Company* is defined by the following e-coalition activities of Figure 5: (19) *Ordering* that orders the shipping company to ship the package; (22) *Notification* allows the shipping company to notify the travel agency after delivered; (23) *Credit,* orders the bank to credit the travel agency's account; (24) *Debit* debits the travel agency's account to pay suppliers involved in the package deal; and (26) *Balance* returns the travel agency's balance account from the bank. Other activities involved with the travel agency have already been defined above.

Next, the infrastructure of communication of the system is presented to validate the model suggested.

SOFTWARE INFRASTRUCTURE FOR E-COALITIONS AND PROCESSES

The Internet and proliferation of distributing technologies provide basic infrastructure for e-commerce. Unfortunately, the corresponding infrastructure for properly modeling various e-commerce activities and their evolution is still missing. The software infrastructure for supporting the supply chain has to be open enough for integrating new components. Main underlying technologies for e-commerce and other distributed Web applications are CORBA, DCOM (Distributed Component Object Model), and Java Virtual Machine (JVM), and their APIs (Jutla, Bodorik,

Hajnal, & Davis, 1999). CORBA specifies interfaces and protocols for a distributed infrastructure, working through ORBs (object request brokers). DCOM allows writing its components in several languages, including C++ and Java. Java provides a mechanism for components to discover each other's interfaces at runtime and may run on different platforms because of the JVM.

This infrastructure (see Figure 6) for supporting e-coalitions and e-business processes uses the protocol TCP/IP (Transmission Control Protocol/Internet Protocol) on which protocols HTTP (Hypertext Transfer Protocol) and IIOP (Internet Inter-ORB Protocol) are grafted. They are basic elements for distributing components in a trading community. Components functioning as customers must at least lay out a Web browser including a JVM and the plug-ins necessary for enacting and performing e-business processes, and for interacting with the community. It will interact with the different servers of the architecture through the HTTP protocol, which is the native protocol of communication between a browser and a Web server. Servers are designed using a firmware that allows querying an infrastructure's repositories of e-business products (goods, services) and e-business activities (processes, e-coalitions, artifacts, etc.).

A generic server integrated into the firmware supports e-business processes in a trading community. It allows accessing local ORB and beyond CORBA architecture, ways to reach remote ORBs, and then access other components of the community. To simplify the prototyping of the proposed architecture and the portability of the resulting platform, we have adopted the Java implementation. On each remote computer connected to the trading community resides a wrapper—a piece of software that provides a generic interface for components that cannot communicate directly with the message protocol that is the ORB. A concrete wrapper that is specific for each e-coalition component is generated from the generic wrapper at runtime using the description of the function of the component in the marketplace.

Such infrastructure allows defining, establishing, enacting, and performing various types of e-coalitions among the partners involved in

Figure 6. Infrastructure for supporting the supply chain in a trading community

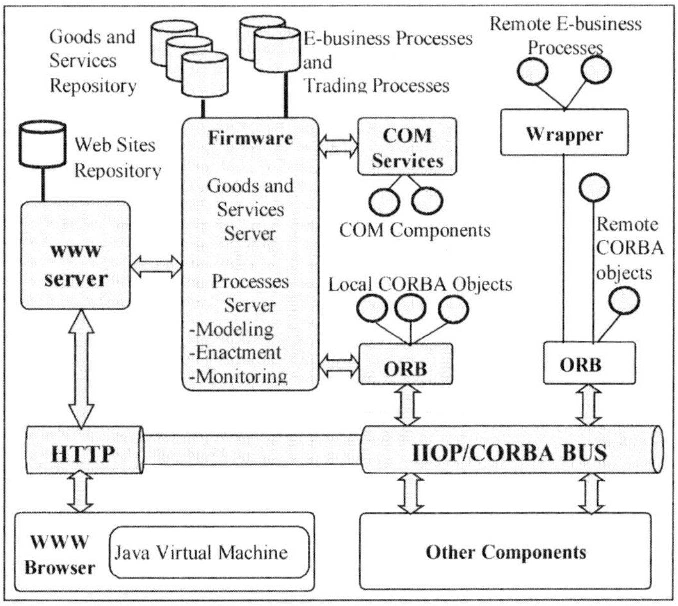

the market. E-coalition's performance allows controlling partners by requiring them to fulfill their commitments in the marketplace.

RELATED WORK AND CONCLUSION

The approach of combined negotiation (Benyoucef & Keller, 2000) is close to this work because it coordinates activities in the marketplace. It is based on a combined negotiation support system that helps users conduct negotiations. This solution does not model negotiation and its evolution for unpredictable markets. What WISE (Alonso et al., 1999; Schuldt, Scheck, & Tresch, 1998) and this chapter have in common is coordination of e-business processes. WISE provides *a priori* defined protocols for coordination, while it is explicitly modeled here by e-coalitions. Supply chain process by QPR (see www.qprsoftware.com) includes phases from customer inquiries, purchase, and production, to product delivery to the customer. Here, the customer is not considered as an equal partner or as a supplier. For instance, the customer just provides input information for processes. In this work, the customer has an equal function as other components within the supply chain and plays roles in e-coalitions. Strategic alliances (Hoffman, 1997) favor business relationship types for long-term collaboration, but the approach is different because it does not provide a support for e-business processes modeling.

Several works present possible cooperation and conditions under which the achievement of a variety of coalitions is feasible, but they are still limited because they do not model coalitions in the manner to support unpredictable aspects of the marketplace.

This work proposes an appropriated infrastructure for modeling and coordinating e-business processes using e-coalitions. The idea combines a support for modeling and coordinating relationships among e-coalition components with an architecture for their distribution. Components are not only on a different location, but also entirely autonomous. They can define, enact, and monitor all kinds of relationships they would like to establish among them.

REFERENCES

Alonso, G., Fiedler, U., Hagen C., Lazcano, A., Schuldt, H., & Weiler, N. (1999). WISE: Business to business e-commerce. In *Proceedings of the 9th International Workshop on Research Issues on Data Engineering: Information Technology for Virtual Enterprises* (*RIDE-VE'99*).

Balsmeier, P.W., & Voisin, W.J. (1996). Supply chain management: A time-based strategy. *Industrial Management, 38*(5), 24-28.

Benyoucef, M., & Keller, R. (2000). A conceptual architecture for a combined negotiation support system. In *Proceedings of the 11th International Workshop on Database and Expert Systems Application.*

Bolumole, Y. (2000). *Supply chain management: A review of relevant literature and theory.* Working Papers Series, Cranfield School of Management.

Bolumole, Y. (2000b). *Supply chain integration: A forecourt perspective.* Working Papers Series, Cranfield School of Management.

Drew, G. (1999). *Using SET for secure electronic commerce.* Englewood Cliffs, NJ: Prentice-Hall.

EDIFACT. (2006). *Electronic data interchange for administration, commerce and transport, EDIFACT syntax rules (ISO 9735) and EDIFACT data element directory (ISO 7372).* Retrieved July 4, 2006, from http://www.unece.org/trade/untdid/welcome.htm

E-Future. (2006). *Supply chain basics.* Retrieved July 4, 2006, from www.e-future.ca/alberta/pdf/efc_supply_chain_basics.pdf

Ellram, L.M. (1990). The supplier selection decision in strategic partnerships. *Journal of Purchasing and Materials Management, 26*(4), 8-14.

Fenstermacher, K.D., & Zeng, D. (2000). Know your supply chain. In *Proceedings of the AAAI'00 Workshop on Knowledge Based Electronic Markets,* Austin, TX.

Guttman, R., & Maes, P. (1998). Agent-mediated integrative negotiation for retail electronic commerce. In *Proceedings of the Workshop on Agent-Mediated Electronic Trading (AMET'98).*

Hoffman, T. (1997). *Strategic alliances for competitive advantage.* Alliance Ventures Group.

Houlihan, J. (1995). International supply chain management. *International Journal of Physical Distribution and Materials Management, 15*(1), 22-38.

Johnston, R., & Lawrence, P.R. (1988, July-August). Beyond vertical integration: The rise of value adding relationships. *Harvard Business Review*, 94-101.

Jones, T.C., & Riley, D.W. (1985). Using inventory for competitive advantage through supply chain management. *International Journal of Physical Distribution and Materials Management, 15,* 16-26.

Jutla, D., Bodorik, P., Hajnal, C., & Davis, C. (1999). *Making business sense of electronic commerce.* IEEE Computer.

Milosevic, Z., & Bond, A. (1995). Electronic commerce on the Internet: What is still missing? In *Proceedings of the Internet Society's International Networking Conference* (INET'95).

Milosevic, Z., & Dromey, R.G. (2002). On expressing and monitoring behavior in contracts. In *Proceedings of the 6th International Enterprise Distributed Object Computing Conference* (EDOC'02).

Moukas, A., Guttman, R., & Maes, P. (1998). Agent-mediated electronic commerce: An MIT media laboratory perspective. In *Proceedings of the 1st International Conference on Electronic Commerce* (ICEC'98).

Open-EDI. (1996). *The Open-EDI reference model* (working draft). Retrieved July 4, 2006, from http://www.icaris.net/icaris/newcd.doc

Panurach, P. (1996). Money in electronic commerce: Digital cash, electronic fund transfer, and e-cash. *Communications of the ACM, 39*(6).

Schuldt, H., Scheck, H.J., & Tresch, M. (1998). Coordination in CIM: Bringing database functionality to application systems. In *Proceedings of the 5th European Concurrent Engineering Conference (ECEC'98)*, Erlangen, Germany.

Simchi-Levi, D., Kaminsky, P., & Simchi-Levi, E. (2000). *Designing and managing the supply chain: Concepts, strategies, and cases.* New York: McGraw-Hill.

Stevens, G. (1989). Integrating the supply chain. *International Journal of Physical Distribution and Materials Management, 19*(8), 3-8.

Tiako, P. (1999). *Modeling the federation of process sensitive engineering environments.* PhD dissertation, Inria-Loria Lab & INPL, France.

Tiako, P. (2002). Maintenance in joint software development. In *Proceedings of the 26th IEEE International Computer Software and Applications Conference* (COMPSAC 2002), Oxford, UK.

Tiako, P.F. (2003). E-commerce approach for supporting trading alliances. *Proceedings of the International Conference in Information and Communication Technologies in Tourism.*

Tiako, P., Lindquist, T., & Gruhn, V. (2001). Report on process support for distributed team-based software development workshop. *ACM Software Engineering Notes, 26*(6).

Wrigley, C.D., Wagenaar, R.W., & Clarke, R.A. (1994). Electronic data interchange in international trade: Frameworks for the strategic analysis of ocean port communities. *Journal of Strategic Information Systems, 3*(3), 211-234.

Xiong, L., & Ling, L. (2003). A reputation-based trust model for peer-to-peer e-commerce communities. In *Proceedings of the IEEE Conference on E-Commerce* (CEC'03).

Xiong, L., & Liu, L. (2004). PeerTrust: Supporting reputation-based trust in peer-to-peer communities. To appear in *IEEE Transactions on Knowledge and Data Engineering (TKDE), Special Issue on Peer-to-Peer Based Data Management.*

APPENDIX: LIST OF ABBREVIATIONS AND TERMS

- **ANSI:** american national standards institute
- **B2B:** business-to-business
- **B2C:** business-to-consumer
- **CORBA:** common object request broker architecture
- **DCOM:** distributed component object model
- **EDI:** electronic data interchange
- **HTTP:** hypertext transfer protocol
- **IIOP:** internet inter-orb protocol
- **JVM:** java virtual machine
- **ORB:** object request broker
- **SET:** secure electronic transaction
- **TCP/IP:** transmission control protocol/internet protocol
- **XML:** extensible markup language

Section III

Best Practices and Performance Management

Chapter XI
E-Supply Chain System at Valvex and Its Integration with ERP Systems[1]

Raktim Pal
James Madison University, USA

Indranil Bose
The University of Hong Kong

Alex Ye
The University of Hong Kong

ABSTRACT

ERP and SCM systems have been used in China for some time. Although these two systems complement each other, the integration of these two systems is challenging. We present a case on a leading Chinese manufacturer of industrial valves named Valvex that successfully integrated the ERP systems from Entreplan and the SCM system from Excelvision. The project improved the operations at Valvex and resulted in many benefits. This chapter describes the implementation of the e-SCM system at Valvex and its integration with the existing ERP system. The process of implementation and integration was marked by many challenges, and some of them were unique to a Chinese manufacturing organization. Using several smart strategies the project team was able to overcome these challenges and complete the project successfully. Several lessons can be learned from the experience of Valvex which may be useful for organizations that plan to undertake similar projects.

INTRODUCTION

Chinese manufacturing industry has obtained a high growth rate in the past 25 years and is expected to maintain a speedy growth in a number of years to come. According to China's statistics bureau, the gross output of manufacturing industry is about US$709 billion and it makes up 40% of the national GDP in 2004 (China Statistical Yearbook, 2004). But a critical problem facing the Chinese manufacturing industry is its low productivity, which is only a fraction of the productivities of the United States and Japan (People's Daily, 2003).

In the last few years an increasing number of Chinese manufacturing companies have increased their investments in information technology to improve productivity. According to CCW Research, the amount of IT investments of manufacturing industry in 2005 is expected to be US$3.5 billion and it has grown by 14.8% compared to the investment figure in 2004 (CCW Report, 2005). Many large manufacturing companies in China have implemented ERP systems (Wang, Xu, Liu, & Qin, 2005; Zhang, Lee, Huang, Zhang, & Huang, 2005). These enterprise systems have not only transformed the operations of these companies and improved management efficiency, but also they have established a reasonably good information technology applications environment. For instance, most of these companies have high-end servers, multiple work terminals, and TCP/IP networks with high bandwidth. Also they have established clean data sources and have trained the employees so that the enterprise systems can be utilized well. Most of them also have established IT departments to maintain and support the hardware and software. All these efforts have created a good infrastructure base to further improve the utilization of IT in their business operations. In fact some of the companies have moved further by implementing supply chain management (SCM) systems and integrating them with ERP systems.

Logistics cost accounts for a significant part in the cost structure of manufacturing companies, especially for those with inefficient supply chain management. Poor management of supply chain causes excessive inventory, inaccurate tracking, low labor productivity, poor inventory turnover, and little or no collaboration with customers and vendors. As ERP systems are primarily not suitable to address these problems (Ball, Ma, Raschid, & Zhao, 2002; Dhingra, 2001; Tarn, Yen, & Beaumont, 2002), more and more Chinese manufacturing companies are turning to SCM systems to drive efficiency (Boston Consulting Group Report, 2005). However, implementation of ERP and SCM systems do not come easy—there are a lot of issues including system architecture design, software vendor and consulting service provider selection, disparate data sources, business process reengineering, system integration, and project management (Bakowski, 2002; Xue, Liang, Boulton, & Snyder, 2005). Apart from technical factors, appropriate organizational orientation is also critical (Wang, Ying, Jiang, & Klein, 2006). Kobayashi, Tamaki, and Komoda (2003), Kumar, Maheshwari, and Kumar (2002), and Umble, Haft, and Umble (2003) discussed the best practices in implementing enterprise systems. The benefits from enterprise systems vary a lot. Organizations across the world have seen mixed results (Hendricks, Singhal, & Stratman, 2006). Here we discuss these issues and show with the help of a case study on Valvex, a leading Chinese manufacturer of valves, how these enterprise systems can improve business operations.

ERP and SCM Systems in China

An enterprise resource planning (ERP) system is used to integrate different functions of various departments across a company into a single decision support system. ERP combines these functions into a single integrated software program that runs on a single database so that personnel from different departments can share information easily and avoid duplication. A successful ERP implementation not only needs appropriate software and hardware, but also it requires appropriate alignment of business processes with the overall goal of the organization. Many times, the ways an organization does business as well as the ways people do their jobs need to be changed. However, change does not happen overnight without pain. Transitioning to a new ERP system usually takes between one to three years on an average (Koch, 2006). As the ERP system implementations require coordination of various tasks involving multiple expertise areas including IT, business management, project management, and industry expertise, such projects usually become quite complicated.

ERP systems are designed to integrate business functions by providing information exchange capabilities among different departments in an organization. A typical ERP system consists of modules from accounting, distribution, marketing, sales, manufacturing, and human resources (Tarn et al., 2002). It helps an organization conduct key business operations using a single application package in a seamless fashion. For example, once the sales department records an order on the ERP system, it is seen by other departments in the organization. The purchasing department plans for obtaining raw materials if the inventory level is low, the manufacturing department enters the order in production plan, the transportation/logistics department plans for inbound shipment of raw materials and outbound shipment of finished goods, the customer service department prepares delivery date and quotations based on these plans, and the accounting department sends an invoice after delivery of goods. A number of companies in China have implemented an ERP system in the recent past, and many are considering an implementation in near future (Wang et al., 2005).

Although global market leaders like SAP and Oracle have significant presence in China, local vendors such as UFSoft, Kingdee, GenerSoft, HJSoft, Anyi, and Riamb play major roles in the Chinese ERP market (Xue et al., 2005). The lack of dominance by the global players in the Chinese market is due to various reasons, including incompatibilities between business requirements and the ERP package in terms of data format, issues associated with translating English instruction into pictographic Chinese language, higher cost of ownership, and disparity in business practice and corporate culture (He, 2004; Hong & Kim, 2002).

The success rate of ERP system application is quite low in China—it is lower than 20% (Enet.com Report, 2005). For instance, Valvex suffered two major setbacks in ERP system implementation before it finally selected and implemented its currently used ERP system. Besides the complexity of implementation, there are some other factors that affect ERP implementation in China. Both foreign and local ERP system providers face unique challenges. The ERP systems from foreign providers are designed based on the best business practices originating in business environments that are different from that in China. These packages are not customized well to meet the needs of Chinese companies. While the ERP packages from local providers address China-specific issues, often the packages are not mature, business concepts used in these packages are not up to date, and functionalities are not user friendly. Also from the perspective of implementation, there are many issues that hinder successful ERP projects. Due to pressure of cost-cutting initiatives, often Chinese ERP system providers are not able to provide sufficient resources during implementation. Also there is no independent party to evaluate the result of ERP system implementation and there are no agreed-on criteria to do the evaluation. Hence, it is difficult to understand where to improve and how to improve during implementation. ERP system implementation needs many consultants with diverse knowledge of IT, business processes reengineering, project management, and industry expertise. As the demand for ERP systems is growing in China, shortage of experienced consultants is turning out to be another factor in ERP implementation failures.

SCM systems are designed for supporting multi-organization-wide coordination and execution of production and distribution activities (Ball et al., 2002). The main focus of SCM systems is centered around the fact that supply chain partners should work collaboratively to drive efficiency, and an organization should look beyond its four walls to align supply chain strategies to business strategies (Lin, Huang, & Lin, 2002; Tarn et al., 2002). In an ever-changing business environment, SCM systems provide speed and agility to respond to demand uncertainty and means to influence demand to some extent with the help of well-concerted efforts from business partners.

The use of SCM systems in China has increased in recent years. SCM systems use intelligent decision rules and algorithms to help users improve the efficiency of the supply chain, including faster flow of materials and information, and reduction of inventory. With the help of SCM systems, companies can make intelligent sourcing, manufacturing, delivery, and return decisions, and different steps in business operations across multiple organizations can be automated. In China, there are many international players such as EXE, I2, and SAP, who play significant roles in the high-end SCM software market. On the other hand, local SCM providers (e.g., Boke, Dichain, Kingdee) dominate the middle and low-end SCM software markets. In 2004, revenue from the license fee of SCM software in China was about $50 million. The manufacturing industry, third-party logistics industry, and energy industry accounted for about 80% of the total SCM software market in China (CCID Consulting Report, 2005).

While ERP systems provide a means for sharing information across various departments within an organization to achieve internal efficiency, SCM systems focus on handling relationships between trading partners in the supply chain and enable collaborative workflows across organizational boundaries. Collaboration among trading partners is crucial for success in a highly competitive business environment (Hui, 2004). Modern organizations have realized that they have to move beyond internal efficiency and align business strategies with a broader view of the supply chain consisting of networks of vendors, suppliers, manufacturers, distributors, retailers, and other partners. Considering the low labor cost in China, value of SCM systems in terms of efficiency may appear to be unattractive, but its capability in offering broad visibility and channel transparency definitely helps businesses (Cecere, 2005). Some of the ERP systems rely on ad-hoc arrangements to get inventory information from different sources including warehouses, and it does not work very well. On the other hand, SCM systems are suitable for tracking inventory of different entities in the supply chain. While SCM systems are suitable for performing continuous adjustments in the decision-making process, including scenario modeling, evaluation of sourcing and logistics alternatives, and dynamic pricing and risk assessment, ERP systems are not suitable for offering these types of functionalities. They are not designed to identify problems proactively, and it takes time (a few minutes to hours) to generate reports on ERP systems. While major ERP vendors are introducing advanced planning and optimization capabilities, SCM vendors are advancing their products further with additional features (Dhingra, 2001). Nonetheless, the two types of enterprise systems have different focus, strengths, and weaknesses. While ERP captures, processes, and disseminates necessary data and business intelligence within an organization, SCM provides additional layers of decision support capabilities. It is important that organizations have access to data exchange, process integration, and analysis tools to remain competitive. Hence, it is natural that complementary capabilities of ERP and SCM are integrated to generate more benefits for businesses.

In the subsequent sections, we describe how Valvex, a leading Chinese valve manufacturing company, leverages IT to transform its supply chain and improve its business operations. We explain the issues faced by this company in managing its supply chain and how these issues are addressed with the help of an SCM system called e-SCM. We also describe how the e-SCM system is integrated with the existing ERP system. Finally, we discuss potential future improvements in supply chain management for this company.

BACKGROUND INFORMATION ON VALVEX

Valvex is a Sino-USA joint venture with more than 1,000 employees and revenue of about US$50 million in 2004. Being a leading valve manufacturer in China, Valvex has fulfilled the qualifications to manufacture a wide range of industrial valves for the most severe and demanding usage in the oil and gas, chemical, marine, power, and pipeline industry segments. Valvex's products include a wide variety of valves including ball, butterfly, check, gate, and globe valves, with sizes ranging from one-half inch to 52 inches and class ratings ranging from 150 pounds to 2,500 pounds. Using a variety of materials ranging from conventional cast or forged steel to special alloy like Monel, Inconel, Hastelloy, and Duplex steel, Valvex is able to produce valves for a working temperature range of 196°C–650°C complying with the ASTM, ANSI, API, BS, and DIN standards. Valvex's quality assurance is dedicated to the pursuit of a zero defect valve. Valvex is an ISO 9001:2000-certified firm and holds the production license of API 6D, ABS, and CE/PED. Valvex is the first valve manufacturer in China to be certified by CE/PED and TA Luft for low fugitive emission tests.

Valvex's manufacturing base is in China, and it has a distributor/agent network in North America, Europe, the Middle East, and the Far East. It sells valves to end users, engineering contractors, and stockicts. It also has two manufacturing facilities located in Suzhou, a major industrial city of Jiangsu province in China. Each of them has two raw materials warehouses, one semi-finished products warehouse, and one finished products warehouse. Approximately 3,000 models of valves are produced, and they can be classified into two main categories: one category includes ball and globe valves, and the other category includes gate, check, and butterfly valves. Each manufacturing facility produces one category of valves. There are about 20,000 types of raw materials stored in the two raw material warehouses at the two manufacturing facilities. Except for a few standard valves, Valvex primarily follows a make-to-order fulfillment policy. Around 85% of these made-to-order valves are exported.

Existing ERP System at Valvex

Valvex's existing ERP system was provided and implemented by Entreplan, a Chinese ERP system provider. The ERP system at Valvex has four major subsystems: Sales and Distribution, Manufacturing, Human Resources, and Accounting and Financial Analysis.

Sales and Distribution (S&D)

This subsystem supports customer management, order management, order fulfillment management, and distributor management. As a reporting and analytical tool for order fulfillment, the S&D subsystem gives users access to aggregated operational data from all sources, helps users complete their entire sales cycle from price quotation to invoicing and payment, and supports better decisions. By providing real-time storage information access, S&D subsystem assists users to respond faster and more efficiently to customers' demands. This subsystem includes the following features:

- Online information tracking and handling at every distributor level
- Automatic invoice generation and financial transaction
- Sophisticated customer profiling tools providing sufficient customer credit analysis and credit control
- Ability to print, edit, and manage sales reports

Manufacturing

The manufacturing subsystem supports manufacturing planning, inventory planning and control, and scheduling. This subsystem helps users manage, track, and control all phases of the product lifecycle. It enables users to communicate production information quickly and easily among production units, maintenance units, and other departments within the organization. This subsystem includes the following features:

- **Quality management:** This feature enables users to begin quality planning during the product design phase, create foundation for quality inspection processes and in-process control during production, and provide enterprise-wide instant access to the most current quality manual.
- **Asset/equipment maintenance management:** This feature manages equipment upgrades and refurbishment records, monitors equipment work-orders, keeps users informed of the conditions of assets and the status of maintenance work, automatically adjusts work schedules according to equipment availability, provides integrated procurement process, and creates acquisition for spare parts based on the inventory levels.
- **Inventory management:** This feature provides critical safety-stock information that is used for coordination of procurement, sales, and production planning.
- **Production planning management:** This feature allows manufacturers to develop optimized production schedules based on prioritization of market demand, and ensure feasibility of production schedules satisfying the material and capacity constraints.

Human Resources

This subsystem supports staff management, payroll management, time management, organizational management, performance evaluation, and career planning management. This subsystem is based on the Chinese legal welfare and tax system, and is flexible enough to support international human resource practices and salary regulations.

Accounting and Financial Analysis

This subsystem supports accounting entry, financial control, and financial analysis. It integrates all financial and business performance information during the management processes, and provides comprehensive and systematic financial reports.

Figure 1. Main subsystems of the existing ERP system at Valvex

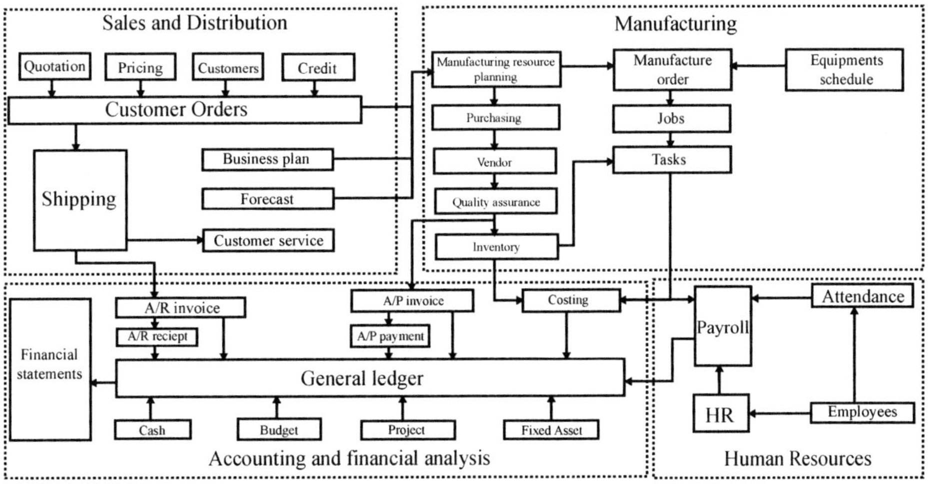

The relationship among these four subsystems is illustrated in Figure 1. As shown in Figure 1, all four subsystems are seamlessly integrated. This ERP system eliminated disorders in production planning, improved production capacity, standardized and streamlined the order-fulfillment process from purchasing to delivery, and established an open environment for corporate-wide data sharing. It has established a very good basis for Valvex to further improve its business operation with the help of information technology.

The ERP system at Valvex dealt with resource planning within the whole enterprise through fulfillment of orders. It did not track or instruct the execution of planning. During the execution activities, there was a lot of paperwork between handoff points and the business process relied upon many manual inputs from collected data. Also, the coordination with vendors and customers could not be accomplished well. Even if the company benefited from the ERP system, there was a growing need for a system to overcome the limitations of the existing ERP system and manage the execution of activities in a coordinated fashion.

Figure 2 illustrates the process flow after Valvex implemented the ERP system. It used to place purchase orders for materials largely based on anticipated demands and safety stocks. When vendors delivered materials to Valvex, they were received and put away into the warehouses. Materials were then pulled from the warehouse by the manufacturing department, and either returned to the semi-finished goods stockroom awaiting orders/instructions for assembly operations or sent to the finished goods warehouse for customer shipment. The operational processes improved substantially after the ERP system was implemented. However, a number of problems

Figure 2. Process flow with existing ERP system at Valvex

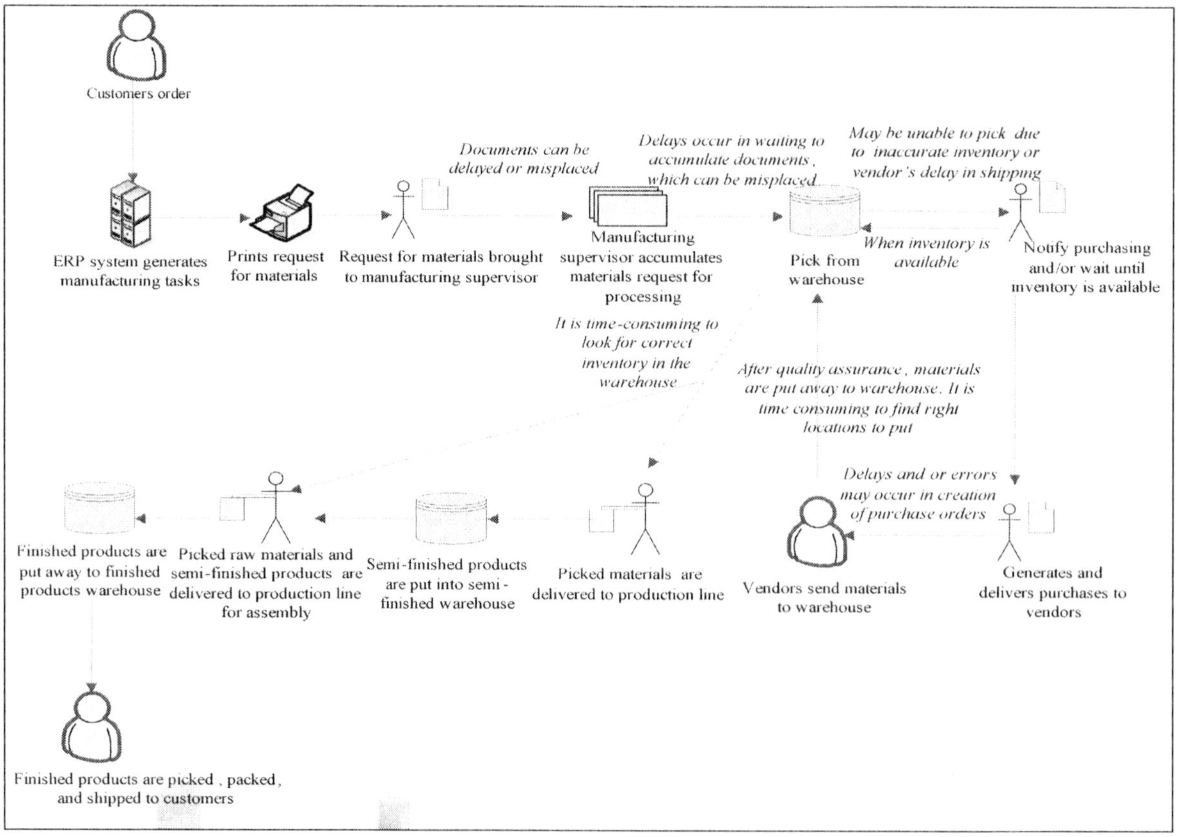

remained. Most handoff processes were through paperwork, which caused delays and human errors. Warehouse operation, one of the most critical components in the overall process, was also not managed well. In the next section we will discuss these problems.

PROBLEMS WITH EXISTING ERP SYSTEM AND BUSINESS PRACTICES

Non-Value-Added Activities

Operations at Valvex required a lot of paperwork. Printing and delivery of paper-based memos, and filing and maintaining the paperwork were non-value-added activities that consumed a lot of resources. Paperwork also caused delays in collection and recording of information in the ERP system. Lost or damaged documents as well as reading or writing errors caused incorrect recording. Hand-off delays in the operational process was another critical problem. Hand-off delays resulted in long cycle time for order fulfillment. As inventory in the warehouse was not well arranged and tracked, time was wasted in excessive travel during picking or putting away operations.

Inaccurate and Outdated Inventory in ERP System

There were various activities that would change inventory levels in the raw material warehouse, semi-finished product warehouse, or finished products warehouse. For instance, raw materials or semi-finished products were picked up and sent to the production line, semi-finished or finished products were delivered from the production line to warehouses, and finished products were picked up and shipped to customers. These activities would change the levels of raw material inventories, semi-finished product inventories, and finished goods inventories. Earlier it was taking one to two days for Valvex's employees to record the change in inventory levels on paper and input it into the ERP system. Sometimes the paperwork was misplaced or lost, and the information was not entered into ERP system. This caused inaccuracies in the inventories shown in the ERP system.

Also materials in the warehouse went missing or got damaged occasionally. However, these events were not recorded in the ERP system on time. This caused some of the manufacturing orders, which had been released and were being processed, to be sitting in an incomplete state for an indefinite period of time due to lack of raw materials. Eventually the order fill rate was low, resulting in dissatisfaction among customers.

Due to inaccurate and outdated inventory, safety stocks and purchase order quantities were set at higher levels than the levels they should be at if inventories were up to date. As a result, inventory turnover rates were low and inventory costs were higher than they should be. Sometimes inaccurate and outdated inventory created confusion, resulting in delayed supplies from vendors and unreliable forecasts as well.

Inefficient Warehouse Operation and Improper Material Tracking

Each raw material warehouse stored about 20,000 SKUs. It was very time consuming to pinpoint the right locations in the warehouse to pick up or put away materials, especially for the new employees. One type of material was usually placed at various locations within the same warehouse, which added to the difficulty of the picking job. Workers mostly relied on experience to pick up and put away materials. It used to take several weeks for new workers to get accustomed to the workplace. When the experienced workers were not on duty, it was very time consuming for relatively newer employees to do the job.

The pickers were not usually able to track materials properly as they did not have sufficient access to important information such as lot number and expiration date. Also they could not ensure proper rotation of inventory, such as first-in-first-out (FIFO) and last-in-first-out (LIFO).

After raw materials were picked up and delivered to the production line, work-in-process inventory in the production line was not recorded and tracked in the ERP system. It was not possible to track fulfillment of manufacturing orders until manufacturing was completed and associated information was entered into the ERP system.

In the finished products warehouse, workers encountered more problems. As many products were made to order, products were put into the warehouse with a label indicating which order they belonged to. Sometimes these labels got misplaced, and finished products belonging to different orders got mixed up as well.

Insufficient Productivity Measures and Low Employee Morale

As there was no accurate measurement of labor performance, supervisors were not able to provide instant feedbacks or rewards as activities were completed. As a result, employees are not motivated enough to work hard. Due to lack of visibility of operation, supervisors could not properly identify bottlenecks. Therefore, on-time corrective measures could not be undertaken.

Inefficient Interaction with Customers

In the day-to-day operation, Valvex needed to interact well with its customers. These interactions were in the form of quotations, pricing, ordering, product specification confirmation, shipping, order fulfillment inquiry, and customer service. A large number of employees were dedicated to dealing with customers. Such a system was time consuming, inefficient, and prone to human error.

Inefficient Interaction with Vendors

Valvex needed to coordinate various activities such as pricing, ordering, shipping, and product inspection with its vendors. There was much scope to improve coordination and enhance efficiency. Also, Valvex did not have effective methods to evaluate vendors and to add or drop vendors as needed from time to time.

NEW E-SCM SYSTEM AT VALVEX

In order to address the above issues and improve operational efficiency, Valvex implemented a supply chain execution information system—an e-supply chain management system (e-SCM). The system was obtained from a vendor named Excelvision. This system not only coordinates interactions with vendors and customers, but also deals with internal activities involved in warehousing and manufacturing operations. Figure 3 provides a schematic representation of the e-SCM system.

Through its interface with the ERP system, the e-SCM system obtains up-to-date planning information and generates various tasks based on this planning information. According to required durations of these tasks, the e-SCM system allocates the tasks to workers and then instructs the workers to finish assigned tasks through radio frequency handhelds which have wireless connections to the local area network. These devices measure the performance of each worker with respect to their assigned tasks. As soon as the tasks are finished, relevant feedback information on worker performance is sent to the ERP system as XML files. Using the handheld devices, the workers collect accurate inventory and other information in real time. This eliminates the need for manual paperwork that caused numerous human errors in the past. As soon as tasks are finished, relevant feedback information is sent to the ERP system as XML files through system

Figure 3. The e-SCM system at Valvex

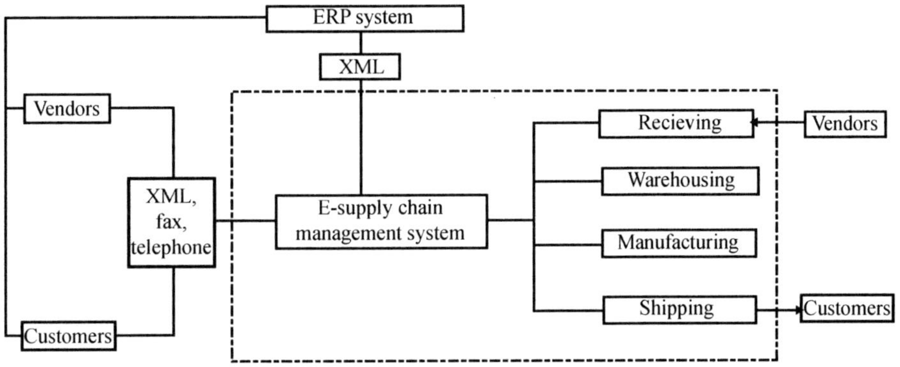

interface. The main functionalities of the e-SCM system at Valvex, namely receiving and put away, warehouse management, pickup and shipping, and order management, are discussed below.

Receiving and Put Away

Receiving and put away operations take place in all raw materials warehouses, semi-finished product warehouses, and finished product warehouses at Valvex. The ERP system sends receiving task-related information to the e-SCM system through the system interface in advance. All materials go through a quality assurance process before they are put to the warehouse. The materials that do not meet the quality standards are re-sent by the vendors. The system records these materials as well to evaluate vendors' performance. After materials are received, the system fills relevant purchase orders and prints an inspection label for each receiving activity. After materials are inspected as qualified, the system searches for the most advantageous locations and directs workers to put away. Workers scan tracking barcode labels, location-zone barcode labels, or location-address barcodes to confirm the completion of each step of the process. After finishing the put away operation in the warehouse, the system searches for shortage records. If there is any shortage of materials, the system releases and assigns picking tasks, and directs workers to pick. The e-SCM system ensures visibility of inventory as soon as materials are received and keeps track of materials in various zones. In the receiving and putting away process, materials are located in the following zones:

- **Receiving yard and receiving zone:** Vendors send materials to the receiving yard of warehouse, then receivers receive and put those materials into the receiving zone. The system prints an inspection label for each receiving task to track associated materials.
- **Quality assurance zone:** The system directs workers to pick and put the received materials into the quality assurance zone. As soon as the materials are put into the quality assurance zone, the system generates inspection tasks. Quality inspectors can inquire about the unfinished inspection tasks using personal computers. Quality inspectors inspect the materials and input inspection results through system clients installed on personal computers. Then the system auto-prints inspection result labels, and inspectors stick those labels onto associated packages of materials.
- **Return zone:** The system generates put-away-to-return-zone tasks for the materials inspected as unqualified and directs workers to put them into the return zone. Then the system notifies vendors of the inspection

results. Vendors make arrangements for taking back the unqualified materials from the return zone.

- **Put away area:** The system generates put away tasks for the materials inspected as qualified and directs workers to put them into the warehouse.

Warehouse Operation

Warehouse operation largely involves the following operations:

- **Cycle count:** Though the system can assure a high degree of inventory accuracy, there may be some missing or damaged inventories due to human error. Cycle count is done from time to time to overcome these errors. All SKUs are categorized into A, B, and C classes depending on annual dollar usage. Each class has different requirements for cycle count frequency. For instance, A class of inventory is counted every 3 months, B class of inventory is counted every 6 months, and C class of inventory is counted every 12 months. According to the ABC classification, the system generates cycle-count tasks for each SKU and assigns those tasks to workers when they are free. Hence, it is not necessary to close the warehouse during cycle counting.
- **Inventory adjustment:** Supervisors investigate the inventory discrepancies found after cycle count and figure out the root causes for it. Then supervisors take corrective measures, adjust the discrepancy, and notify the ERP system to ensure accurate inventory.
- **Inventory relocation:** There are several situations when inventories need to be relocated. For instance, if supervisors want to free up a large space, they relocate materials to other locations. Sometimes, supervisors need to combine materials from two containers into one. In these situations, the system has to track materials correctly after relocation to ensure right pick up.
- **Freeze and purge management:** Sometimes, inventory needs to be frozen for quality issues. For instance, a vendor may notify Valvex that certain lots of a component are defective. Valvex can freeze these lots of components using the lot numbers so that they cannot be picked up during the frozen period. Supervisors can freeze/unfreeze inventories by SKUs, by locations, and/or by specific receiving. Also they can purge defective inventories from the system if needed.

Pickup and Shipping

Outbound process involves picking up and shipping raw materials or semi-finished products from warehouse to production line, and picking up and shipping finished products from warehouse to customers. The system uses the following functionalities to manage the outbound process:

- **Stock allocation:** As soon as pick up orders are released, the system allocates the right amount of right materials to the orders based on appropriate material rotation rules. The stock allocation reserves the amount of stock for the outbound orders and ensures all picking tasks have enough materials to pick. Also there is provision for supervisors to free up already allocated inventory to meet higher priority outbound orders.
- **Container planning:** The system records the volume of materials when they are received. Using this information, the system calculates the number and size of containers needed for picking orders after the orders are released. Finally, the pickers are instructed to select the right containers.
- **Order consolidation:** If manufacturing and shipping schedules permit, supervisors may want to consolidate several picking tasks to

increase efficiency. The system instructs the pickers about the sequence in which orders should be picked.

Order Management

Order management has the following components:

- **Order entry:** There are two types of orders at Valvex: inbound orders and outbound orders. The system generates inbound orders based on purchase orders sent by the ERP system. It also generates outbound orders based on production orders or customer orders transmitted by the ERP system. In order to ensure order data accuracy, orders are entered electronically into the system.
- **Order maintenance:** As soon as there is change (including addition, deletion, and modification) in any purchase orders, production orders, or customer orders, the ERP system notifies the e-SCM system through system interface and the e-SCM system undertakes corrective measures.
- **Priority management:** Usually, the system processes orders in a sequence that is created internally based on required finish dates. But sometimes due to change in production schedule, these sequences need to be adjusted. In such cases, the system generates priorities for orders based on constraints imposed by supervisors as well as required finish dates.
- **Automatic order release:** Inbound orders and outbound orders are released automatically. No human intervention is required.
- **Shortage management:** The system does not release outbound orders when there is a shortage of materials to pick. However, there may be exceptions. Due to inaccurate inventory count or damaged inventory, sometimes there may not be enough inventories to pick for outbound orders that have been released. In that case, shortage is recorded and a new cycle count task is generated in the system.

BENEFITS PROVIDED BY THE E-SCM SYSTEM

Inventory Tracking

Inventory tracking is no longer a problem as before. As soon as raw materials, semi-finished products, or finished products are received, the system prints barcode labels that are stuck to the package and they help in tracking the package. A unique address is assigned to each location within the warehouse, and this appears in the barcode label. As soon as inventory is received and put away at a location, the system tracks this inventory using the barcode label of the inventory and the barcode address of the location. Then the system instructs the workers on where to pick the materials from and how much to pick at a particular location. The system even uses optimization algorithms to find out the 'best' putting away routes and picking up routes when a worker needs to put and pick multiple items in a single trip.

System-Directed Activities

The system directs all activities from incoming materials processing to manufacturing and order fulfillment, assuring that the correct materials are getting to the right place, at the right time, and in appropriate quantities to satisfy production orders or customer orders. This eliminates non-value-added activities and improves overall efficiency. Labor also has become system directed through radio frequency handheld devices. Activities are recorded on a real-time basis to ensure that inventory is accurate and current information is always available in the form of reports and for information sharing with other systems. The system also optimizes picking and putting away operations by interweaving the multiple tasks of the workers, and optimizing picking and putting routes. The system also determines the most advantageous placement of SKUs to improve the efficiency of picking.

Paperless Environment

Paperwork is no longer required at the handoff points. Data is captured at every 'hand-off' point when materials either move from one location to another or the material status changes. Data entry captures critical information including, but not limited to, SKU, time, user ID, from and to locations, lot number, serial number, and so forth. Electronic data displayed by handheld devices replaces most of the paperwork. Information can be updated almost instantaneously from the handoff points to the e-SCM system database. The paperless environment assures improved accuracy (no reading or writing errors) and elimination of lost or damaged documents. Figure 4 shows how the e-SCM has revolutionized the data capturing and data sharing activities at Valvex.

Collaboration with Suppliers and Customers

Based on information collected by the e-SCM system, Valvex also provides a Web-based application for its customers and suppliers. Now, customers can do price quotations, ordering, product inquiry, and order fulfillment inquiry on the Internet. Most of the collaboration with vendors is also achieved through the Web-based application. The customer and vendor information remains separated from each other because Valvex's customers and vendors have their own unique login and password to use this Web-based application.

IMPLEMENATION AND INTEGRATION OF E-SCM SYSTEM AT VALVEX

In this section the details of the project for implementing the e-SCM system and integrating it with the existing ERP system at Valvex are discussed.

Gathering Initial Information for Project Scoping

Before starting the project it was critical to define its scope. In order to do this job, Valvex's long-term goals were reviewed, knowledge about the existing practices was gathered, and the resource commitments from top management was estimated. As a part of the exercise, the following information was gathered:

- **Affected parties:** Valvex figured out which departments and personnel would be affected during implementation, and who would use the e-SCM system. Also it found out how they would be affected and their degree of involvement during implementation. Affected parties were various internal departments including accounting, purchasing, manufacturing, logistics, and customer service, as well as outside entities like vendors and customers. Employees in warehouse and logistics management would be primary users of the system.
- **Legacy system:** As Valvex had an existing ERP system, it became necessary to investigate the relation between the e-SCM system and the ERP system during implementation.
- **Hardware environment:** As Valvex had already implemented the ERP system, it was

Figure 4. Data capture at various handoff points at Valvex

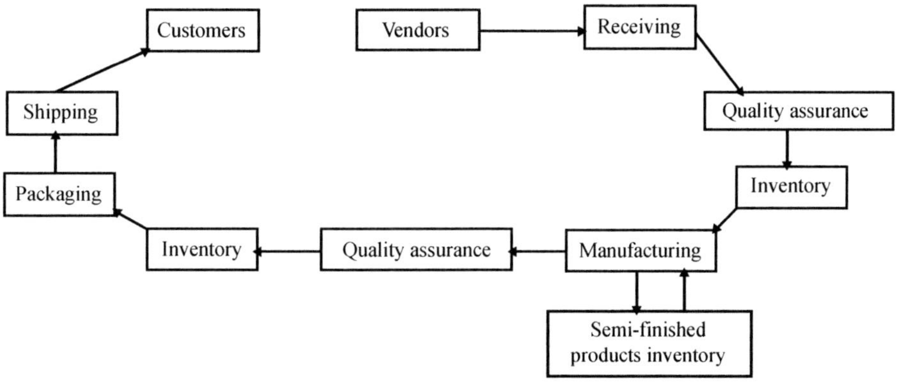

important to find out if any hardware could be shared. If purchase of new hardware was necessary, it was to be figured out as well.

- **Facilities:** It was crucial to know how materials flow through the raw material warehouse, production line, semi-finished product warehouse, and finished product warehouse. Also existing put away and pick up operations were examined as well.
- **Operational processes:** The operational processes in Valvex's supply chain including production order fulfillment, purchase order fulfillment, and internal logistics flow were investigated. A knowledge base of finished products, raw materials and components, and production environment was prepared.
- **Root cause of customers' problems:** Finding the root cause(s) of the problems faced by the customers was not always trivial. Hence, the project team worked with both customers and Valvex personnel to figure out where the real problems were and what could be done to address the issues.

Project Specifications

After outlining the broad scope of the project and coming to a consensus about it, detailed specifications were finalized. Appropriate specifications were critical for successful implementation of the project. It contained detailed information on process reengineering, software and hardware specifications, system interface, project plan, and value proposition, and was approved by the project management team. Details of some of the components are provided below:

- **Software customization:** Customer requirements were written clearly by R&D engineers to customize some functionalities of the software. Only a few people participated in this process to minimize information distortion.
- **Installation and testing of hardware environment:** As hardware configuration in the project was quite complicated, it was inspected thoroughly to ensure smooth functioning during the software testing phase. The hardware included application and database servers, TCP/IP network, wireless network, radio frequency handheld devices, barcode printers, and laser printers. The hardware testing involved inspecting individual components as well as ensuring that they function well collectively.
- **Software testing:** Software testing involved individual features testing, integrated system testing, and on-site testing. The

first two could be done internally by R&D engineers and testing engineers. After the first two tests were finished, software was installed in a real hardware environment for on-site testing that simulated the real work environment. The bugs found during on-site testing were fixed by R&D engineers, and the system was re-tested.

- **Initial data loading:** After the software was tested satisfactorily, clean and most updated data were loaded into the system. The datasets included initial inventory information, warehouse location information, purchase orders, and so forth. Extra efforts were made to ensure that accurate and high-quality data were loaded. Another set of tests was performed with these real-life datasets, and after successful completion of these, test data were reloaded and the old and new systems were run in parallel for some periods before switching to the new system.
- **Employee training:** Training with different degrees of details were conducted. For example, supply chain concept training was provided to senior managers and logistics managers, software operation training was provided to logistics managers, and training on handheld devices was provided to workers in the logistics department.
- **On-site assistance:** At the initial stage of running the system, on-site assistance from the software vendor was necessary as the users were not very comfortable with the new environment even after training. Also few bugs were not found that were not identified during the testing phase. The on-site experts addressed these issues efficiently to ensure smooth transition.
- **System backup and maintenance:** System backup is important to recover the data when data got corrupted or lost due to various unforeseen events including human error. Storage disks with the RAID mechanism were used to protect data. The system was programmed to make incremental backups every 30 minutes and a full backup at 1:00 a.m. every day automatically. The specialists from the information technology department of Valvex were trained to perform routine system maintenance.
- **Service from software vendor:** After the e-SCM system was implemented, different levels of service including 24×7 phone response, remote assistance, on-site assistance, data backup, and retrieval assistance were provided to Valvex by the software vendor based on the service contract agreement.

Organization of Implementation Team

The organization of team structure was important for successful implementation of the project. The implementation team was formed by drawing personnel from three organizations: Valvex, ERP system provider—Entreplan, and e-SCM system provider—Excelvision. The degree and length of engagement of different members varied during the implementation cycle. The designations of the different members in the team are provided below.

Valvex

- **Vice general manager:** Helped in acquiring resources as needed and ensured coordination among various departments.
- **Logistics manager:** Managed the project from the customer's side and took major decisions in the project.
- **Information technology specialist**

Entreplan

- **ERP system specialist:** Participated in the negotiation and finalization process of the system interface design, and coordinated with R&D engineer to develop interface for the ERP system.
- **R&D engineer**

Excelvision

- **Project manager**
- **Supply chain management consultant:** Played a major role in re-engineering of the business processes
- **R&D engineer**
- **System tester and trainer**

Hardware Environment

The hardware used are listed below:

Network

- **TCP/IP local area network:** Used to connect server, PCs, printers, and wireless network.
- **Wireless network:** Used to establish wireless connections needed for the operation of radio frequency handheld devices.

Servers

- **Memory:** 2 GB, two processors with 2.8 GHz.
- **Storage:** 100 GB.

Radio Frequency Handheld Devices and Scanner

Handheld devices equipped with scanners are used for instructing workers to finish tasks and collect information during their job. Each of the devices has a wireless network card to connect to the local area network.

Barcode Printer and Laser Printer

As all materials are tracked by specific barcodes, barcode printers are used quite often.

Project Management

The three major tasks of overall project management were initial project planning, progress monitoring, and transition and maintenance planning.

Initial Project Planning

This involved initial requirements gathering, IT infrastructure planning, project staffing, detailed scheduling, budgeting and financing, and transition planning. The project management team consisted of project managers from all three organizations involved: Valvex, Entreplan (ERP provider), and Excelvision (e-SCM provider). The team reported to the vice general manager of Valvex. The management team defined the scope of the project very clearly. Few key issues in inventory tracking, order management, and resource allocation were targeted to ensure rapid return on investment. Plans were made to execute necessary functional changes in the existing business processes, aligning them with the technical modifications. Some of the manually intensive activities were strategically planned to be replaced by automated processes.

Progress Monitoring and Control

All parties involved in the project conferred to come up with the project plan. Some of the tasks were carried out concurrently to keep the project duration short. Initially, one month was spent finalizing the project scope. After the kick-off, the project was finished in 15 weeks. Representatives from all groups with various job responsibilities met every other day to resolve the issues encountered during implementation. The issues were prioritized and logged, and the status of issues is updated in the next meeting. Sharing responsibilities and exchanging ideas among all team members ensured consistent progress. Most of the project went as planned except a few unexpected issues that caused changes in due dates of some tasks a few times. Progress was monitored closely by the three project managers from the three parties. At the end of the weekly update meetings, the project manager from Valvex reported the status to the vice general manager, who was the executive sponsor of the project. His intervention was necessary if a conflict/issue could not be resolved by the teams. Also he attended the status update meetings occasionally and met with project team members quite frequently on an informal basis. Active involvement of a top executive helped the team finish the project on time.

Transition and Maintenance Planning

Extensive testing initiatives were undertaken before going live. Required functionalities of both the e-SCM system and the updated ERP system were independently tested. The actual field data was loaded into the newly integrated system, and the system was tested and validated thoroughly. After finishing all functional and technical testing, the go-live was announced. Valvex personnel were trained well in advance to take over responsibilities of running the systems from Entreplan and Excelvision. Some of their early involvement in the project helped in making a smooth transition. The system was designed to make an incremental data backup once in every five minutes and a full backup for all data every night automatically. Other maintenance work was performed at night to avoid conflict with busy daytime operations. The core system maintenance team consisted of a hardware engineer from Valvex and one system engineer from Excelvision who created the system log. The IT department manager at Valvex checked the log daily and pointed out potential problems to Excelvision's system engineer for possible resolution. Valvex paid 20% of the license fee to Excelvision for maintenance support per year, which included assistance in software upgrade and resolution of day-to-day issues.

ISSUES AND CHALLENGES ENNCOUNTERED DURING IMPLEMENTATION

During the course of the implementation, the project team faced a number of issues and challenges. In the following section we discuss how these issues were discussed and resolved.

System Interface Design

Due to the complexities of the ERP and e-SCM systems, it was difficult to figure out which information should be exchanged at what stage of the business process. Also the implementation team had to decide on how the information was to be exchanged so as to ensure accuracy and security. In order to deal with the first set of issues, roles of the ERP and e-SCM systems in running the business were clearly defined and duplicate functionalities were identified. Also the information requirements of these two systems at various stages of process flow were determined. Personnel from Valvex, Entreplan, and Excelvision took part in a number of meetings to come to a consensus. Data transmission from ERP to the e-SCM system included item masters, initial inventory levels, inbound orders, and outbound orders. Data sent from the e-SCM system to ERP included receiving and put-away information, inspection result, pick-up and shipping information, and inventory adjustments.

Regarding the means of exchanging information between the ERP and e-SCM systems, the system specialist from the two system providers agreed on using XML so that data accuracy could be maintained.

Change in Business Processes

Successful use of e-SCM system required changes in some of the existing business processes. The task was quite challenging. A good amount of time was spent preparing for the transition. All the Valvex employees who were affected by the change were trained rigorously so that they could be effective in the new working environment. As the new processes were complex and involved new task-like operating handheld devices, training the workers was not easy and it required thorough planning. The training sessions were designed to cover both theoretical concepts and practical hands-on exercises in simulated environments. Also the training programs were tailored according to varying needs of system users.

Initial Data Loading

Most of the data that were loaded initially into the e-SCM system came from the databases of the ERP system. There were a few issues with these datasets. Data structures were different between the ERP and e-SCM systems, and the inventory data in the ERP system was inaccurate and outdated. Also there were many tasks that were being processed, and the corresponding data were not entered in the ERP system. Since the ERP system had to keep running during the data loading process, data often changed during this period and the data transfer was not up to date. A two-step solution was adopted to address the above issues. First, all in-process tasks were finished by a specific date. Then the data was loaded at midnight of a specific date, transformed into acceptable format, and loaded into the database of the e-SCM system. Secondly, live cycle counts for all SKUs in the warehouse were performed and accurate data were sent to the ERP system. This ensured that inventory data in both systems were in sync and accurate.

Handheld Devices and Barcode Printers

The handheld devices were to access the e-SCM system using a variety of telnet emulation terminal software. Two models of handheld devices were selected. There were some incompatibility issues with one model. Although emulation terminal software that used telnet protocol was installed in this model, it could not display Chinese characters. It was found out that incompatible character sets between the host system and the emulation terminal software was causing the problem. Compatible Chinese character set was reinstalled in the emulation terminal to resolve the problem. Also some information could not be displayed in one whole screen and some characters even disappeared. This was due to the small display screen and limited range of possible adjustment for character size. In order to address this issue, display information was simplified and the information at the host system side was adjusted according to the size of display of the handheld devices. The barcode printers also had issues with Chinese characters. Initially the printers were not able to print the Chinese characters. Compatible characters were reinstalled to eliminate the problem.

Network

There was a 2 MB bandwidth optical network connecting the two manufacturing facilities that were 10 kilometers apart. Before the e-SCM system was implemented, data transfer in the ERP system consumed almost all the network capacity. The existing optical network was not sufficient to handle the large volume of data transfer that was going to take place in a real-time system like the e-SCM system. Response time of handheld devices was quite slow due to the limited bandwidth, particularly when the ERP system was also exchanging data. In order to address the capacity issue, another optical network connection between the two manufacturing facilities was built; this took one month. The e-SCM system was not able to run well during this period. As a result, progress of the project was stalled to an extent. The lessons learned from this glitch helped the project team to be more proactive in designing IT infrastructures at later stages of the implementation.

Model Selection for Handheld Devices

A number of models of handheld devices equipped with a scanner, telnet emulation terminal, and wireless network card met the basic requirements for working with the e-SCM system. It was important to figure out which ones would be most suitable. The price of qualified handheld devices varied from US$500 to US$2,500. After long deliberation, two models were finally selected. One of them was manufactured by Symbol, the world's leading handheld provider for logistics applications; this had a price tag of US$1,625. The other model was manufactured by a Taiwanese company named Biotech with a price tag of only US$500. Since this model had not been used in the logistics industry before, there were concerns about using it in a demanding environment of a dirty and crowded warehouse. However, the price was attractive and risk was not very high as a small number of devices were to be purchased initially. Hence, the project team decided to buy a few cheaper units as well. The project was implemented in two phases. In the first phase, out of eight handheld devices needed, five were expensive units and three were cheaper units. As the cheaper model did not perform well in the first phase, all 12 units required in the second phase were procured from Symbol.

Coordination Among Team Members from Three Organizations

As project team members were drawn from three organizations, coordination among them was challenging. Especially when dealing with system interface negotiation between ERP and e-SCM system providers, it was difficult to find a final agreement. If there were multiple ways to resolve one issue, each of the system providers would choose the one(s) that minimized their workload and degree of responsibility. Often they argued for a long period of time without coming to a consensus. In order to resolve such issues, involvement of Valvex's senior management in the project was required. Every week the project manager had to evaluate the progress of implementation and take corrective actions when the status lagged behind schedule. As the project manager was from the e-SCM system provider, it was difficult for him to push the personnel from the ERP system provider to expedite their tasks. Many times senior management's interference was needed. Also the team members from the ERP system provider worked on multiple projects simultaneously. Hence, it was difficult to get full commitment from them to finish their job in the e-SCM project on time. Often negotiation and insistence from senior management was needed to complete the tasks as planned.

Unexpected Problems

Even if the project team prepared well, at the initial stage many unexpected issues surfaced which included software bugs, incorrect data, inconvenient software functionalities, human errors, and information exchange errors between ERP and e-SCM systems. Hence a problem-solving mechanism was put in place. Every two days, a meeting among representatives from all parties was arranged so that problems were recognized and necessary actions could be taken without much delay. Outstanding issues and their resolutions were discussed in the subsequent meetings. In order to make the process efficient, problems were classified into different categories according to importance and urgency, and different resolution strategies were applied for each category. Also there was a weekly status update meeting involving all team members.

Effectiveness of the E-SCM Implementation

There were many operational problems associated with the existing ERP system at Valvex which ranged from inaccurate and inefficient inventory control to poor order fulfillment. The e-SCM changed many of the basic business processes at Valvex's facilities and was able to bring in a number of benefits including real-time inventory information update, better picking activities, and establishment of effective collaboration with vendors and customers. Table 1 summarizes the benefits obtained by Valvex in terms of operational measures, one to two months after the integration of the e-SCM system with the ERP system was completed.

FUTURE IMPROVEMENTS

The traditional techniques used by Valvex for making production schedules are based on meeting forecasts or reaching preset inventory levels. Frequently, large batch orders are processed at each department based on the workflow, and materials are pushed to the next department after the jobs are finished. This type of flow usually causes excess inventories, long cycle times, and some non-value-added activities. Even after implementing the e-SCM system, these issues were not fully resolved. However, these issues can be tackled by embedding daily demand-pull subroutine in the e-SCM system, which instructs the system to react to new or changed customer orders that create the actual demand for a product. This subroutine can provide the suppliers with precise descriptions and amounts of materials to deliver to meet the demands at Valvex. The subroutine is particularly effective in reducing the capital commitments for expensive raw materials or components with short lead time when suppliers are within close proximity of Valvex's manufacturing facility. At Valvex inexpensive items and expensive items with long lead time are replenished according to a min/max inventory policy. Appropriate safety stock levels for these items are maintained, and they are ordered in economic order quantities. The demand pull subroutine can reduce the inventory levels for these items, as well result in less investment in inventory. Additional benefits include reduced space requirements in the warehouse and on the manufacturing floor.

The demand pull or Kanban system was invented and successfully implemented by the Japanese manufacturing companies. The main idea is to minimize inventory by supplying inventory only when it is needed. Work in progress is closely monitored to avoid shortage. This concept can be used for low value inventory by utilizing electronic Kanban or e-Kanban. The use of e-Kanban enables the system to pull materials efficiently as needed from the most convenient locations. When production line personnel detect a low inventory level, they can scan the SKU's barcode label to transmit the information on item description and location to the e-SCM system. Then the system displays open deliveries and open orders for that SKU. It also identifies changes in usage patterns for that SKU so that appropriate adjustments can be made to order quantities and/or delivery schedules. After the users confirm the requirements, the system determines the best course of action and assigns tasks to appropriate personnel to transfer inventory. Inventories are pulled in a predetermined sequence. One example

Table 1. Benefits of using the integrated ERP and e-SCM system at Valvex

Operational Measures	Pre-Implementation	Post-Implementation
Outbound order fulfillment		
Commitment to fulfillment percentage	80%	98%
Average lead time	45 min	30 min
On-time delivery percentage	80%	95%
Inventory		
Average safety stock period	40 days	25 days
Inventory accuracy	85%	99%
Average monthly purchase frequency	50	10

Figure 5. Workflow in the demand pull/e-Kanban subroutine

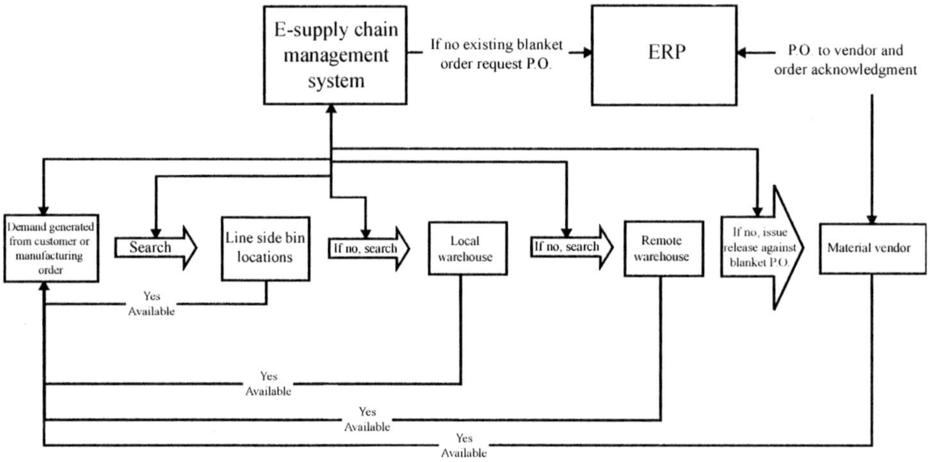

of the sequence is a search for a SKU first in the bin next to the production line followed by a search in the consignment warehouse location. After the search is over, inventory is allocated to the production line in a particular order, and personnel are directed to the specific inventory locations to perform pick, pack, and ship operations. At times, it can be found that for certain SKUs, inventory is not kept internally or inventory level is not sufficient to meet demand. In that case, the system determines first whether there is an open blanket purchase order and then issues a pull order (or e-Kanban card) to the supplier via XML, e-mail, or fax to trigger delivery activities. In the event that an open order for the SKU does not exist or an existing order is insufficient to cover the demand, the system provides alerts and notifies the purchasing department that an additional purchase order is required. Suppliers are required to provide electronic or manual acknowledgements after receiving the orders. The workflow in the demand pull subroutine that may be added in the future is provided in Figure 5.

CONCLUSION

Although the existing ERP had a number of problems, it had established a good infrastructure at Valvex to implement other information technology applications. Hardware and local area network had been established, and personnel were accustomed to working with decision support tools. Also the ERP system acted as a repository of many critical datasets that might be needed in other application software. The e-SCM system implementation at Valvex benefited from the previous ERP project. Nonetheless, there were many challenges including business processes reengineering, integration with a legacy ERP system, and new supply chain system development and installation. Eventually the challenges were handled successfully with the help of competent team selection, active executive supports, sound system architecture design, appropriate use of project management methodologies, and proper end user training.

Several lessons can be learned from the case study of Valvex. Valvex had rightly identified that it needs to look beyond the existing ERP system and implement an e-SCM system in order to maintain its competitive advantage. Also, it did not select companies like SAP or Oracle, but gave the contract to Excelvision, which had a Chinese-speaking implementation team and stressed customization. Valvex is a large manufacturing organization with a great variety of products. Hence, Valvex put emphasis on a few key manufacturing processes such as receiving and put away, picking up, and order management, which narrowed the scope of the project. This ensured rapid return on investment.

During implementation of the e-SCM system, Valvex had to deal with problems and/or issues related to design of appropriate interfaces between the two systems, data management, handling of Chinese characters in handheld devices and barcode printers, computer network capacity, and handheld device selection. Among these challenges, some were distinct for a Chinese enterprise and might not be seen in other parts of the world where standard English characters are used. The selection of XML as the standard for data exchange between the ERP and e-SCM systems proved useful because of its simplicity.

There are some interesting lessons in project management in this case. The senior management had to be responsible for moving forward the project on schedule. This was particularly important in a set up where a number of teams from different organizations worked together. Had the entire task of coordination been left with the ERP provider and e-SCM provider, the project might not have completed on time. The ERP provider had already implemented the ERP system, and there were few people from that organization who were present on-site. The active involvement of top management ensured due diligence from all sides involved. Timely meetings and well-defined follow-up procedures for various issues encountered during implementation helped smooth the progress. Staff planning with necessary skill set was also found to be one of the critical factors for success. The consultants from the ERP provider and SCM system provider comprehended the requirements of a Chinese manufacturing organization quite well. Most of the team members were Chinese and native speakers of Mandarin, which made communication among them a non-issue. The implementation started with a relatively simple workflow, and eventually more complex functionalities were added. The success of this type of approach was reported earlier in the literature (Kobayashi et al., 2003). Past implementations elsewhere have demonstrated that well-defined prior planning for undertaking the business process changes is crucial, although it often gets lost among the mess of complex technical details (Chang, 2002). The ability of the Valvex project management team to balance between the two was important for the success of the implementation.

After the implementation, Valvex benefited from increased accuracy of inventory, lower inventory tracking cost, elimination of various non-value-added activities, and improved collaboration with customers and vendors. The existing ERP system had many shortcomings that ranged from inaccurate and inefficient inventory control to poor order fulfillment. The e-SCM changed many of the basic operational processes at Valvex's manufacturing facilities and was able to bring in tangible benefits in terms of better picking activities, real-time inventory information update, and provisions of collaboration with vendors and customers. Valvex paid Excelvision US$15,000 as the license fee for the e-SCM system. The annual maintenance fee for the system was US$3,000. Valvex had to pay US$6,000 to Entreplan for modification and customization of the ERP system and US$30,000 to Excelvision as a consultation fee for installation. The initial budget required for implementation of the e-SCM system and the integration project amounted to nearly US$92,000. The project resulted in direct cost savings for Valvex. The reduction in the safety stockholding period by 15 days resulted in inventory cost reduction by approximately $1 million per year. By reducing the monthly purchase frequency from 50 to 10, the e-SCM system was able to produce a savings of US$4,800 per year. The reduction of lost sales due to unavailable inventory resulted in savings of US$20,000 per year approximately. These figures go on to show that the overall supply chain operations at Valvex have become more efficient, although there is scope for further improvement.

REFERENCES

Bakowski, M. (2002). C-commerce. Would mixing ERP, CRM, e-procurement and SCM be an efficient strategy for the future? In *Proceedings of the 10th International Systems Integration Conference*, Prague, Czech Republic (pp. 107-114).

Ball, M.O., Ma, M., Raschid, L., & Zhao, Z. (2002). Supply chain infrastructures: System integration and information sharing. *SIGMOD Record, 31*(1), 61-66.

Boston Consulting Group Report. (2005, June 1). *China is trying to cope with its logistics challenges but gaps persist.* Retrieved June 1, 2006, from http://knowledge.wharton.upenn.edu/index.cfm?fa=printArticle&ID=1167

CCID Consulting Report. (2005, October 1). *China supply chain management software market and trend.* Retrieved June 1, 2006, from http://www.ccidconsulting.com/

CCW Report. (2005). Retrieved June 1, 2006, from http://www.ccwresearch.com.cn

Cecere, L. (2005). Succeeding in China: Facing tough SCM issues in the fifth dragon economy. *AMR Research.*

Chang, H.H. (2002). A model of computerization of manufacturing systems: An international study. *Information & Management, 39*(7), 605-624.

China Statistical Yearbook. (2004). Retrieved June 1, 2006, from http://www.stats.gov.cn/english/statisticaldata/yearlydata/yb2004-e/indexeh.htm

Dhingra, V. (2001). *Enterprise resources planning systems and supply chain management.* Retrieved June 1, 2006, from http://projects.bus.lsu.edu/independent_study/vdhing1/erp/#vs

Enet.com Report. (2005, July). *How to select the ERP system.* Retrieved June 1, 2006, from http://www.enet.com.cn/cio/zhuanti/erpxx/

He, X. (2004). The ERP challenge in China: A resource-based perspective. *Information Systems Journal, 14*(2), 153-167.

Hendricks, K.B., Singhal, V.R., & Stratman, J.K. (in press). The impact of enterprise systems on corporate performance: A study of ERP, SCM, and CRM system implementations. *Journal of Operations Management.*

Hong, K.K., & Kim, Y.G.. (2002). The critical success factors for ERP implementation: An organizational fit perspective. *Information & Management, 40*(1), 25-40.

Hui, L.T. (2004). Business timeliness: The intersections of strategy and operations management. *International Journal of Operations & Production Management, 24*(6), 605-624.

Kobayashi, T., Tamaki, M., & Komoda, N. (2003). Business process integration as a solution to the implementation of supply chain management systems. *Information & Management, 40*(8), 769-780.

Koch, C. (2006). *The ABCs of ERP.* Retrieved June 1, 2006, from http://www.cio.com/research/erp/edit/erpbasics.html

Kumar, V., Maheshwari, B., & Kumar, U. (2002). ERP systems implementation: Best practices in Canadian government organizations. *Government Information Quarterly, 19,* 147-172.

Lin, F., Huang, S., & Lin, S. (2002). Effect of information sharing on supply chain performance in electronic commerce. *IEEE Transactions on Engineering Management, 49*(3), 258-268.

People's Daily. (2003, September 9). *Manufacturing industry in China still an 'Aurora Industry'.* Retrieved June 1, 2006, from http://english.people.com.cn/200309/09/eng20030909_124031.shtml

Tarn, J.M., Yen, D.C., & Beaumont, M. (2002). Exploring the rationales for ERP and SCM integration. *Industrial Management & Data Systems, 102*(1), 26-34.

Umble, E.J., Haft, R.R., & Umble, M.M. (2003). Enterprise resource planning: Implementation procedures and critical success factors. *European Journal of Operational Research, 146*(2), 241-257.

Wang, C., Xu, L., Liu, X., & Qin, X. (2005). ERP research, development and implementation in China: An overview. *International Journal of Production Research, 43*(18), 3915-3932.

Wang, E.T.G.., Ying, T.C., Jiang, J.J., & Klein, G.. (2006). Group cohesion in organizational innovation: An empirical examination of ERP implementation. *Information and Software Technology, 48,* 235-244.

Xue, Y., Liang, H., Boulton, W.R., & Snyder, C.A. (2005). ERP implementation failures in China: Case studies with implications for ERP vendors. *International Journal of Production Economics, 97*(3), 279-295.

Zhang, Z., Lee, M.K.O., Huang, P., Zhang, L., & Huang, X. (2005). A framework of ERP systems implementation success in China: An empirical study. *International Journal of Production Economics, 98*(1), 56-80.

ENDNOTE

1 Fictitious names Valvex, Entreplan, and Excelvision have been used to protect the identity of the valve manufacturer, ERP provider, and e-SCM provider respectively.

Chapter XII
Coordination of a Supply Chain with Satisficing Objectives Using Contracts

Chunming (Victor) Shi
Washington State University, USA

Bintong Chen
Washington State University, USA

ABSTRACT

Setting performance targets and managing to achieve them is fundamental to business success. As a result, it is common for managers to adopt a satisficing objective—that is, to maximize the probability of achieving some preset target profit level. This is especially true when companies are increasingly engaged in short-term relationships enabled by electronic commerce. In this chapter, our main focus is a decentralized supply chain consisting of a supplier and a retailer, both with the satisficing objective. The supply chain is examined under three types of commonly used contracts: wholesale price, buy back, and quantity flexibility contracts. Because a coordinating contract has to be Pareto optimal regardless of the bargaining powers among the agents, we first identify the Pareto-optimal contract(s) for each contractual form. Second, we identify the contractual forms that are capable of coordination of the supply chain with the satisficing objectives. In contrast to the well-known results for the supply chain with the objectives of expected profit maximization, we show that wholesale price contracts can coordinate the supply chain with the satisficing objectives, whereas buy back contracts cannot. Furthermore, quantity flexibility contracts have to degenerate into wholesale price contracts to coordinate the supply chain. This provides an important justification for the popularity of wholesale price contracts besides their simplicities and lower administration costs. Finally, we discuss possible extensions to the model by considering different types of objectives for different agents.

INTRODUCTION

The decentralized supply chain has been a major research issue in supply chain management. In particular, an important research stream has focused on the supply chain coordination with contracts. Without coordination, each agent in a decentralized supply chain tends to make decisions for his own objective instead of the interest of the whole chain. To improve the overall performance of the chain, it is necessary to have some mechanism so that each agent's interest is aligned with the interest of the whole chain. Such an alignment could be achieved through appropriately designed contracts, which provide incentives for the agents in the chain to coordinate through profit allocation and sharing.

Much of the research has assumed that each agent in a supply chain is risk-neutral and his objective is to maximize (minimize) the expected profit (cost). Under this assumption, a supply chain is said to be coordinated when the summation of individual expected profits (costs) are maximized (minimized). A number of contractual forms have been studied recently under the risk-neutral assumption. These include the three popular contracts: wholesale price (WP) contracts (Lariviere & Porteus, 2001; Corbett et al., 2004), buy back (BB) contracts (Pasternack, 1985), and quantity flexibility (QF) contracts (Tsay, 1999; Cachon, 2003).

With a WP contract, the supplier charges a constant unit wholesale price to the retailer. With a BB contract, the supplier charges a constant unit wholesale price, but offers the retailer a partial refund for all of the unsold units. With a QF contract, the supplier charges the retailer a constant unit wholesale price, but offers the retailer the flexibility of adjusting the initial order quantity without any penalty. For the one-period setting where a risk-neutral supplier sells to a risk-neutral retailer, it has been show that BB and QF contracts are capable of supply chain coordinating. However, it is well known that WP contracts are incapable of coordinating the channel due to the phenomena of double marginalization (Spengler, 1950).

With the increasingly popular use of electronic commerce, suppliers and retailers are increasingly engaged in short-term relationships. For example, in addition to their traditional long-term procurement contracts, more and more companies have gone to spot markets for procurement and/or disposal of excess inventory (Johnson & Klassen, 2005). Therefore, it is fair to say that agents in supply chains are increasingly risk-averse, instead of risk-neutral and adopting the objective of expected profit maximization, which is more appropriate for long-term relationship. To operationalize risk-aversion, an important approach is the mean-variance analysis (Markowitz, 1959). This approach works the best when the random variable under consideration is close to being symmetrically distributed, which, however, may not be the case for many inventory and supply chain management problems. Without a relatively symmetrical distribution, it is better to operationalize risk-aversion using different measures of downside risk. These measures include semi-variance and critical probability. With semi-variance, one is concerned with the volatility of the outcomes below the mean. With critical probability, one is concerned with the probability of the outcomes in some critical region. In this chapter, we choose to operationalize risk-aversion as the critical probability of achieving some predetermined target profit.

Setting performance targets and managing to achieve them is fundamental to business success. Targets provide explicit directions to an organization and motivate management to strive for even higher levels of performance. However, target setting is both an art and a science. Too high a target will provoke frustration and cynicism, whereas too low a target will engender apathy and risk the organization's survival. Different methods of target setting have been practiced by many decision makers. In the approximate order of most to least used, they include plucking it out of thin air, a percentage improvement on last period, and benchmarking (Barr, 2003). For example, Jack Welch describes the setting of stretch targets as one of General Electric's three main operating principles (McTaggart & Gillis, 1998). Lovell et al. (1997) evaluate the target-setting procedure employed by a large financial institution, whose management annually sets performance targets for each of its branch offices based on local, regional, and national economic conditions.

The satisficing objective—to maximize the probability of exceeding a target level of performance—has been commonly used in business practice. In one of the earliest studies examining the objectives of managers, Lanzillotti (1958) interviews the officials of 20 large companies (including General Electric, General Foods, and Goodyear) and verifies empirically that the most typical goal cited by the managers was a target return on investment. Simon (1959) summarizes the five most important attacks on the crucial assumption of profit maximization in the theory of the firm. One of them is due to the fact that maximizing profit is an ambiguous goal when there is imperfect competition among firms, for what action is optimal for one firm depends on the actions of the other firms. Simon then argues that most firms' goals are to attain a certain level or rate of profit, a certain share of the market, or a certain level of sales. Brown and Tang (2004) survey 250 MBA students and 6 professional buyers and find that meeting a profit target is considered as one of the most important performance metrics. In reality, missing a target often leads to serious consequences. This is clearly demonstrated by what happened to the online auction house eBay in the fourth quarter of 2004. Its profit of 33 cents a share missed the expectation of 34 cents from Wall Street analysts by just *one* cent. However, its stock price fell by 12% right after the report.

There have been a few studies investigating the newsvendor model with the objective of attaining a preset target profit. Kabak and Schiff (1978) first study the problem with zero shortage cost. Lau (1980) and Sankarasubramanian and Kumaraswamy (1983) generalize the problem to non-zero shortage cost. Lau and Lau (1988) further extend the results to a newsvendor with two products. A special case when the demand is exponentially distributed is studied by Li, Lau, and Lau (1991). More recently, Parlar and Weng (2003) study the problem of balancing two desirable but conflicting objectives: maximizing the expected profit and maximizing the probability of achieving the expected profit. Finally, Brown and Tang (2004) identify specific performance metrics, including the satisficing objective, for the newsvendor problem and analyze their impacts on the order quantity.

To the best of our knowledge, there have been few studies that deal with supply chain coordination where all agents involved adopt the satisficing objectives. This chapter attempts to fill this gap. The contractual forms we consider include WP, BB, and QF contracts. We focus these three contractual forms for three reasons. Firstly, they are popular contracts in business practice (Tayur, Ganeshan, & Magazine, 1999). Secondly, they have been extensively studied in the supply chain literature, mostly in the framework of expected profit maximization (Cachon, 2003). Thirdly, WP, BB, and QF contracts have one, two, and three contract parameters, respectively. Hence, our research will answer the question if increased degrees of freedom in contractual forms will be beneficial to coordination of supply chains with the satisficing objectives.

When the agents involved in a supply chain adopt the satisficing objectives, it is not obvious as to what the objective function of the supply chain entity should be. In our research, we adopt the general definition of supply chain coordination with contracts proposed by Gan, Sethi, and Yan (2004). A supply chain is said to be coordinated with a contract if the optimizing actions of the agents under the contract lead to Pareto optimality, that is, no agent in the chain can be better off without making any other agent worse off. The associated contract is said to be a Pareto-optimal contract. By definition, only Pareto-optimal contracts should be selected. This is due to the fact that if a contract is not Pareto optimal, it is open to counteroffers that make no one worse off and at least one of the other agents strictly better off. In another word, Pareto-optimal contracts are self-enforcing. Furthermore, a contract has to be Pareto optimal first to coordinate a supply chain. There have been limited studies on supply chain contracts utilizing Pareto optimality criterion. Cachon (2004) considers the Pareto-optimal push (same as WP), pull, and advance-purchase discount contracts in the traditional framework of expected profit maximization. However, the satisficing objective is not considered in his paper.

In this chapter, we will restrict ourselves to the feasible Pareto-optimal contracts. A contract is feasible when it satisfies the participation constraint (PC) of each agent. There are various forms of PC. For example, an agent may enter a contract only if he will get his reservation profit level. In this chapter, we operationalize PC in terms of probability of achieving a target profit: the probability must be larger than a threshold for each agent. For simplicity, the threshold probability is assumed to be zero—that is, each agent will enter a contract only if his target is attainable. Under this assumption, each agent then tries to maximize the probability of attaining that target.

In the reminder of this chapter, we first briefly review the standard newsvendor model with the satisficing objective. We then design Pareto-optimal WP, BB, and QF contracts for a supply chain where all agents adopt satisficing objectives. These Pareto-optimal contracts are then evaluated based on whether they can coordinate the supply chain or not. We then proceed to discuss possible extensions to the model by considering different objectives for different agents. Finally we summarize the results obtained in this chapter.

Newsvendor with the Satisficing Objective

In this section, we briefly review and extend the results for the newsvendor model under the satisficing objective. The purpose is to provide a basis for the subsequent analysis.

Consider a standard newsvendor with a procurement cost c and sell to his customers at a fixed unit price r. The customer demand D follows a probability density function (PDF) $f(\cdot)$ and a cumulative density function (CDF) $F(\cdot)$. The newsvendor has only one order opportunity and determines his order quantity before the actual demand is realized. If the newsvendor under-orders, he will suffer lost sales. For simplicity, we assume zero shortage cost throughout the chapter. If he over-orders, he will dispose the unsold inventory at salvage price v, which leads to a loss as well. Moreover, the newsvendor has a preset target profit of t, and his objective is to choose an order quantity q to maximize the probability of achieving the target: to maximize $P(q) = P\{\Pi(q) \geq t\}$.

The random profit of the newsvendor for a given order quantity q is given by:

$$\Pi(q) = (r-c)\,q - (r-v)\,(q-D)^+$$
$$= \begin{cases} (r-v)D-(c-v)q & \text{if } D<q \\ (r-c)q & \text{if } D<q \end{cases} \qquad (1)$$

which is shown in Figure 1.

Figure 1. The profit function of a newsvendor for a given order quantity q

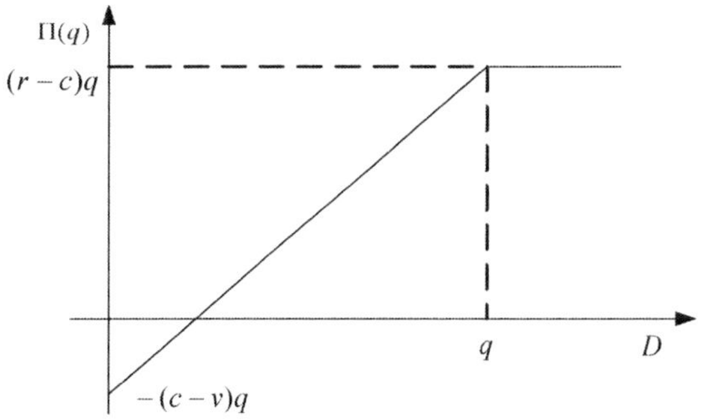

In view of Figure 1, the probability of achieving the target profit t for the newsvendor is given by:

$$P(q) = \begin{cases} 0 & \text{if } q \geq \dfrac{t}{r-c} \\ 1 - F\left(\dfrac{(c-v)q+t}{r-v}\right) & \text{if } q \geq \dfrac{t}{r-c} \end{cases} \quad (2)$$

Clearly the participation constraint (PC) for the newsvendor is $q \geq t/(r-c)$. Once the PC is satisfied, $P(q)$ decreases in q. Therefore, under the satisficing objective, the optimal order quantity and the associated maximal probability are given by $q^* = t/(r-c)$ and $P^* = 1 - F(t/(r-c))$, respectively.

Notice that the optimal order quantity takes a surprising simple form and is independent of the demand distribution. Further, with the optimal order quantity q^*, the newsvendor's maximal possible profit is the preset target profit t, which occurs only when the realized demand D is larger than the optimal order quantity.

It is interesting to compare the optimal quantity q^*above with the optimal quantity $q_e^* = F^{-1}((r-c)/(r-v))$ that maximizes the expected profit. If the newsvendor orders q^*, his expected profit is given by:

$$E\Pi(D, q^*) = t - \int_0^{q^*} F(x)dx.$$

Interestingly, although the probability of achieving t is maximized, the associated expected profit will be less than t. On the other hand, if the newsvendor sets the target profit at $t = E\Pi(D,q_e^*)$, the associated optimal order quantity to maximize the probability of achieving the target is given by:

$$q^* = q_e^* - (r-v)/(r-c)\int_0^{q_e^*} F(x)dx < q_e^*.$$

This is consistent with the finding that a risk-averse newsvendor tends to order less in comparison with a risk-neutral newsvendor.

Design of Pareto-Optimal Contracts under the Satisficing Objectives

In this section, we consider a supply chain where a supplier sells to a retailer facing a random demand from customers. The target profit levels for the supplier and the retailer are set externally at t_s and t_r, respectively. The retail price is fixed at r. The supplier procures or produces the good at a constant marginal cost c. Any unsold unit in the supply chain can be salvaged at a price v per unit. It is assumed $v < c < r$ to avoid trivial situations.

The business transaction and profit allocation between the agents are determined by a contract, which in turn is specified by its parameter set θ. The contractual forms we consider include WP, BB, and QF contracts.

Both the supplier and the retailer in the supply chain adopt satisficing objectives. The supplier wants to maximize the probability of achieving the predetermined target profit t_s, to maximize $P_s(q, \theta) = P\{\Pi_s(q, \theta) \geq t_s\}$. Similarly, the objective of the retailer is to maximize $P_s(q, \theta) = P\{\Pi_r(q, \theta) \geq t_r\}$. We assume that the target profits t_s and t_r, once endogenously determined, become common knowledge. For convenience, let $\beta = t_s / t_r$ denote the target ratio. A larger β thus indicates a higher relative target profit level of the supplier.

In the next three subsections, we design the Pareto-optimal contracts—that is, the Pareto-optimal contract parameters—for each contractual form. Moreover, we identify the associated Pareto-optimal order quantity and the maximal probabilities of achieving the target profits for the supplier and the retailer.

Design of Pareto-Optimal WP Contracts

In this subsection, we consider WP contracts. With a WP contract, the supplier charges a per unit wholesale price w to the retailer. Hence, a WP contract is characterized by its parameter set $\theta = w$.

Figure 2. The probabilities of achieving the target profits for the supplier (bold line) and the retailer under a WP contract with $w \le \hat{w}$

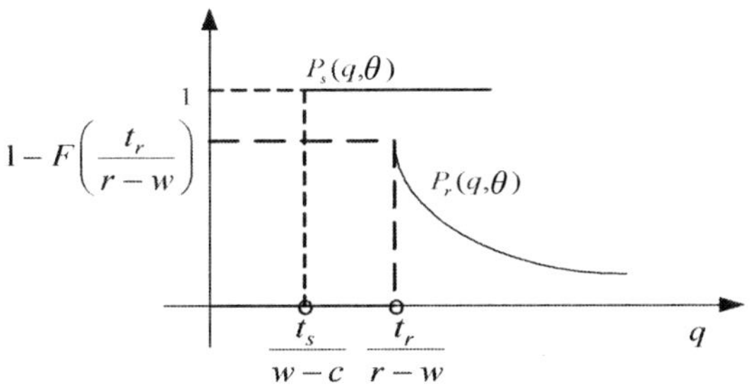

Under a WP contract with parameter set θ, the supplier's profit $\Pi_s(q,\theta)=(w-c)q$ is deterministic. Hence, the supplier's participation constraint (PC) is $q \ge t_s/(w-c)$ for a given target profit t_s. Once the PC is satisfied, the supplier's probability of achieving his target is always 1.

The retailer is a newsvendor with procurement cost w. Therefore, the PC for the retailer is $q \ge t_r/(r-w)$ and the probability of achieving her target is given by:

$$P_r(q,\theta)=\begin{cases} 0 & \text{if } q<\dfrac{t_r}{r-w} \\ 1-F\left(\dfrac{(w-v)q+t_r}{r-v}\right) & \text{iif } q\ge\dfrac{t_r}{r-w} \end{cases} \quad (3)$$

Figure 2 shows the probabilities of achieving their target profits for the supplier and the retailer when $t_r/(r-w) \ge t_s/(w-c)$, i.e., $w \le (c+\beta r)/(1+\beta) = \hat{w}$. The figure corresponding to the case of $w > \hat{w}$ is similar. Note that the wholesale price $\hat{w}$ is a linear combination of procurement cost c and selling price r, with 1 and the target ratio β as the weights, respectively.

Theorem 1

A WP contract is Pareto optimal if the wholesale price $w = \hat{w}$. The associated Pareto-optimal order quantity and maximal probabilities of achieving the targets are given by:

$$q^* = \frac{t_r + t_s}{r-c} \quad (4)$$

$$P_s^* = 1 \text{ and } P_r^* = 1 - F\left(\frac{t_r+t_s}{r-c}\right) \quad (5)$$

Proof

It can be seen from Figure 2 that, given a WP contract with parameter set $\theta = w$, the unique feasible Pareto-optimal order quantity is given by:

$$q^*(\theta) = \max\{\frac{t_s}{w-c}, \frac{t_r}{r-w}\} \quad (6)$$

The corresponding probabilities of achieving the target profits for the supplier and the retailer are, respectively:

$$P_s(q^*(\theta)) = 1 \text{ and } P_r(q^*(\theta)) = 1 - F\left(\frac{(w-v)q^*(\theta)=t_r}{r-v}\right) \quad (7)$$

Since $P_s(q^*(\theta))= 1$, for WP contracts to be Pareto optimal, it suffices to maximize $P_r(q^*(\theta))$, or equivalently, to minimize:

$$(w-v)\max\left\{\frac{t_s}{w-c}, \frac{t_r}{r-w}\right\} \quad (8)$$

Note that (8) first decreases and then increases with respect to w, and the minimum is attained when $t_s/(w-c) = t_r/(r-w)$, that is, $w = \hat{w}$. Hence, a WP contract is Pareto optimal if the wholesale price $w = \hat{w}$. Equations (4) and (5) are obtained by substituting $w = \hat{w}$ into (6) and (7).

Example

Consider a toy supply chain with a manufacturer (the supplier) and a retailer who faces a Normal demand with mean of 300 units and standard deviation of 70 units. There is only one selling season for this particular type of toy. Due to the long lead time, the retails have to commit an order quantity before the selling season so that the manufacturer can plan the manufacturing accordingly. The manufacturer produces the toys at a unit cost $c = \$18$ and the retailer sells at a unit price $r = \$25$. Any unsold toy has a unit salvage cost of $v = \$8$. The target profits for the manufacturer and the retailer are set at $t_s = \$800$ and $t_r = \$600$, respectively. If the profit allocation is implemented through a WP contract, what would be the Pareto-optimal contract parameter w and how sensitive is it?

The answer to the above example is summarized in Table 1. Under a WP contract with a wholesale price w, $q^*(w)$ and $P_r^*(w)$ denote, respectively, the associated Pareto-optimal order quantity and the retailer's maximal probability of achieving her profit target. The Pareto-optimal wholesale price is given by $\hat{w} = 22$. Note that under a feasible WP contract with a wholesale price w, the supplier's profit is deterministic and $P_s^*(w) = 1$ always holds.

It can be seen from Table 1 that the retailer's probability of achieving her profit target is quite sensitive near the Pareto-optimal wholesale price $\hat{w}$. As the wholesale price decreases from 22 to 21 (4.5%), $P_r^*(w)$ decreases from 0.92 to 0.80 (13%). As the wholesale price increases from 22 to 23 (4.5%), $P_r^*(w)$ decreases from 0.92 to 0.50 (45.7%).

The probabilities for the supplier and the retailer to achieve their respective target profits depend on not only the wholesale price but also the retailer's order quantity q. This is demonstrated by Table 2. The first and the second values in each cell, if not infeasible, represent the probabilities of achieving target profits for the supplier and the retailer, respectively. Any combination is infeasible if at least one of the PCs is not satisfied.

In Table 2, q^* is the corresponding Pareto-optimal order quantity for the satisficing objectives, and q_e^* is the optimal order quantity for the objective of expected profit maximization. Notice that the performance of the supply chain

Table 1. The associated Pareto-optimal order quantity and the retailer's maximal probability of achieving her target profit under a WP contract with wholesale price w

w	21	21.6	21.8	$\hat{w}$=22	22.2	22.4	23
$q^*(w)$	267	222	211	200	214	231	300
$P_r^*(w)$	0.81	0.89	0.91	0.92	0.89	0.84	0.50

Table 2. The probabilities of achieving the target profits for the supplier and the retailer with different combinations of wholesale price and order quantity under WP contracts

q \ w	21	21.6	21.8	$\hat{w}$ = 22	22.2	22.4	23
170	Infeasible	Infeasible	Infeasible	Infeasible	Infeasible	Infeasible	Infeasible
200 (q^*)	Infeasible	Infeasible	Infeasible	**(1,0.92)**	Infeasible	Infeasible	Infeasible
230	Infeasible	(1,0.88)	(1,0.87)	(1,0.86)	(1,0.85)	Infeasible	Infeasible
284 (q_e^*)	(1,0.75)	(1,0.70)	(1,0.69)	(1,0.67)	(1,0.65)	(1,0.63)	Infeasible

under the satisficing objectives is very sensitive to the choice of both w and q. Even though most combinations of w and q we choose are close to the optimal one ($\hat{w} = 22$, $q^* = 200$), more than half of the combinations are infeasible.

Design of Pareto-Optimal BB Contracts

With WP contracts, the supplier takes no risk from the demand uncertainty. With BB contracts, the supplier charges a unit wholesale price w, but offers the retailer a unit buy back price b for all of the unsold units. Therefore, with BB contracts, the supplier takes part of the risk from demand uncertainty. Each BB contract can be characterized by a parameter set $\theta = [w, b]$. To avoid uninteresting scenarios, we assume that $v \leq b \leq w$.

We will study the supplier first. Under a BB contract with parameter set $\theta = [w, b]$, if the retailer orders q products, the supplier's profit is given by:

$$\Pi_s(q, \theta) = (w - c)q - (b - v)(q - D)^+ \qquad (9)$$

It is worthwhile noticing that the contract parameters (w,b) need to be chosen such that $w-(c-v) \leq b \leq w$. The requirement of the second inequality is to prevent the retailer from profiting through the buy back process. Similarly, since the supplier's marginal revenue and the marginal cost are $w - b$ and $c - v$, respectively, the first inequality prevents the supplier from profiting through the buy back process.

It follows that the supplier's probability of achieving his target profit t_s is given by:

$$P_s(q,\theta) = \begin{cases} 0 & \text{if } q < \dfrac{t_s}{w-c} \\ 1 - F\left(\dfrac{(b+c-w-v)q + t}{b-v}\right) & \text{if } q \geq \dfrac{t_s}{w-c} \end{cases} \qquad (10)$$

Therefore, the PC for the supplier is $q \geq t_s/(w - c)$, which only depends on the wholesale price w.

Now we consider the retailer. The retailer is a newsvendor with a procurement cost of w and a "salvage price" of b . In view of equation (2), the retailer's probability of achieving her target t_r is given by:

$$P_r(q,\theta) = \begin{cases} 0 & \text{if } q < \dfrac{t_r}{r-w} \\ 1 - F\left(\dfrac{(w-b)q + t_r}{r-b}\right) & \text{if } q \geq \dfrac{t_r}{r-w} \end{cases} \qquad (11)$$

Hence, the PC for the retailer is $q \geq t_s/(w-c)$. The probability functions $P_s(q,\theta)$ and $P_r(q,\theta)$ when $w < \hat{w}$ are plotted in Figure 3.

Theorem 2

The three sets of BB contracts summarized in Table 3 are Pareto optimal. The second column of the table identifies the conditions for the contract parameter set $\theta = [w,b]$ to be Pareto optimal. The associated Pareto-optimal order quantity and maximal probabilities of achieving the target profits for the supplier and retailer are given by $q^*(\theta)$, $P_s(\theta)$, and $P_r(\theta)$, respectively.

Proof

We first examine the BB contracts with wholesale price $w = \hat{w}$. In this case, the PCs for both the supplier and the retailer reduce to $q \geq (t_r + t_s)/(r - c)$. Since both $P_s(q,\hat{w},b)$ and $P_r(q,\hat{w},b)$ decrease

Figure 3. The probabilities for the supplier (bold line) and the retailer to achieve their target profits under a BB contract with $w < \hat{w}$

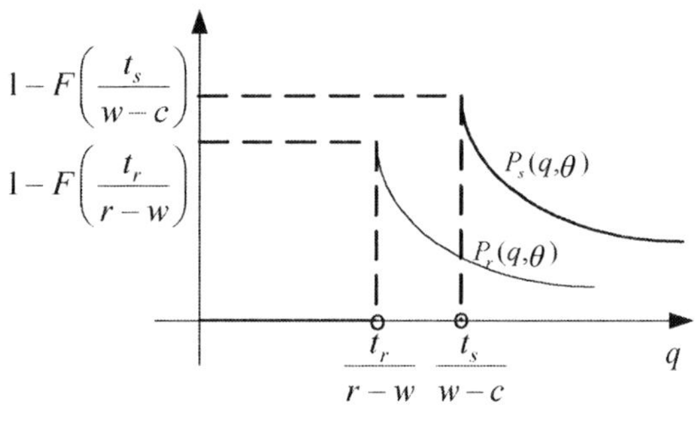

in q, the Pareto-optimal order quantity is $q^*(\hat{w}, b) = (t_r + t_s) / (r - c)$. As a result, the associated maximal probabilities for both the supplier and the retailer are given by $P_s^*(\hat{w}, b) = P_r^*(\hat{w}, b) = 1 - F((t_r + t_s)/(r - c))$. This case corresponds to Pareto-optimal set *BB1* in Table 3.

Next we consider the BB contracts with wholesale price $w < \hat{w}$. Based on Figure 3, it is clear that $q^*(\theta) = t_s/(w - c)$ is the unique feasible Pareto-optimal order quantity. The associated probability functions of achieving the supplier's and the retailer's profit targets are, respectively:

$$P_s(q^*(\theta)) = 1 - F\left(\frac{t_s}{w-c}\right) \quad (12)$$

$$P_r(q^*(\theta)) = 1 - F\left(\frac{(w-b)t_s + (w-c)t_r}{(w-c)(r-b)}\right) \quad (13)$$

Simple calculation shows that:

$$\frac{\partial P_r(q^*(\theta))}{\partial b} = -f\left(\frac{(w-b)t_s + (w-c)t_r}{(w-c)(r-b)}\right)\frac{(w-c)t_r - (r-w)t_s}{(w-c)(r-b)^2} > 0 \quad (14)$$

Hence, the Pareto-optimal buy back price satisfies $b = w$. The retailer's probability then reduces to:

$$P_r(q^*(\theta)) = 1 - F\left(\frac{t_r}{r-w}\right) \quad (15)$$

Since $P_s(q^*(\theta))$ increases in w but $P_r(q^*(\theta))$ decreases in w, any $w < \hat{w}$ is Pareto optimal. This case corresponds to the Pareto-optimal set *BB2* in Table 3.

The results for the case of $w > \hat{w}$, corresponding to set *BB3* in Table 3, can be proven similarly. Finally, one can verify that the three parameter sets identified in Table 3 are all Pareto optimal since the resulting maximal probabilities $P_s(\theta)$ and $P_r(\theta)$ do not dominate each other.

Notice that wholesale price w in a BB contract plays an important role for the contract to be Pareto optimal. When $c < w < \hat{w}$, the buy back price b needs to be at its upper bound w in order for the BB contract to be Pareto optimal. On the other hand, when $\hat{w} < w < r$, the buy back price b needs to be at its lower bound $w - (c - v)$ in order for the BB contract to be Pareto optimal. When $w = \hat{w}$, the BB contract is Pareto optimal regardless of the buy back price b, as long as the general requirement of $w - (c - v) \leq b \leq w$ holds.

Table 3. Pareto-optimal BB contracts for the supply chain with the satisficing objectives

Sets	$\theta = [w, b]$	$q^*(\theta)$	$P_s(\theta)$	$P_r(\theta)$
BB1	$w = \hat{w}$	$\frac{t_r + t_s}{r - c}$	$1 - F\left(\frac{t_r + t_s}{r - c}\right)$	$1 - F\left(\frac{t_r + t_s}{r - c}\right)$
BB2	$c < w < \hat{w},\ b = w$	$\frac{t_s}{w - c}$	$1 - F\left(\frac{t_s}{w - c}\right)$	$1 - F\left(\frac{t_r}{r - w}\right)$
BB3	$\hat{w} < w < r,\ b = w - (c - v)$	$\frac{t_r}{r - w}$		

Design of Pareto-Optimal QF Contracts

With a QF contract, the supplier charges the retailer a constant unit wholesale price w but offers the retailer the flexibility of adjusting the initial order quantity. Suppose the retailer places an initial order quantity of q. Depending on demand from customers, the retailer can adjust the initial quantity q to be anywhere within $[dq, uq]$ without extra financial charge, where $0 \le d \le 1$ and $u \ge 1$ represent the downward and upward adjustment parameters, respectively. Therefore, the retailer's actual order quantity will be dq, D, and uq if the realized demand is $D \le dq$, $dq \le D \le uq$, and $D \ge uq$, respectively. The supplier is responsible to supply up to quantity uq for the supply chain.

Each QF contract can be characterized by its parameter set $\theta = [w, u, d]$. For convenience, let $\alpha = d / u$ denote the adjustment ratio. Since the stocking level in the channel will be uq, $0 \le \alpha \le 1$ represents the fraction for which the retailer is responsible. In addition, a higher α indicates less flexibility for the retailer. A QF contract degenerates into a WP contract if $\alpha = 1$, that is, $u = d = 1$.

For notational simplicity, we define two "wholesale prices" and four order quantities:

$$w_1 = \frac{c+\alpha\beta r}{1+\alpha\beta}, w_2 = \frac{\alpha v + \alpha\beta r + c - v}{\alpha(1+\beta)} \quad (16)$$

$$q_1(\theta) = \frac{t_s}{u(w-c)}, q_2(\theta) = \frac{t_r}{u(r-w)} \quad (17)$$

$$q_3(\theta) = \frac{t_s}{d(w-v)-u(c-v)}, q_4(\theta) = \frac{t_r}{d(r-w)} \quad (18)$$

It can be easily verified that $c < w_1 \le \hat{w} \le w_2$ and $w_1 = w_2 = \hat{w}$ when $\alpha = 1$. Note that w_1 and w_2 defined in (16) are not actual wholesale prices; they are actually equation constraints for the parameter set θ. Finally, the relative magnitudes of the four order quantities depend on the parameter set θ except that inequalities $q_1(\theta) \le q_3(\theta)$ and $q_2(\theta) \le q_4(\theta)$ hold under all situations.

Under a QF contract with parameter set $\theta = [w,u,d]$, if the retailer places an initial order quantity of q, her random profit is given by:

$$\Pi_r(q,\theta) = (r-w)uq - (r-w)(uq-D)^+ - (w-v)(dq-D)^+ \quad (19)$$

It can be verified that the probability function for the retailer to achieve her target profit t_r is given by:

$$P_r(q,\theta) = \begin{cases} 0 & \text{if } q < q_2(\theta) \\ 1-F\left(\frac{t_r}{r-w}\right) & \text{if } q_4(\theta) > q > q_2(\theta) \\ 1-F\left(\frac{t_r+(w-v)dq}{r-v}\right) & \text{if } q \ge q_4(\theta) \end{cases} \quad (20)$$

Clearly, the maximal probability for the retailer to achieve her target is $1 - F(t_r/(r - w))$, which is always less than 1.

Now we consider the supplier. The profit function of the supplier, given the retailer's initial order quantity q, is given as:

$$\Pi_s(q,\theta) = (w-c)uq - (w-v)(ug-D)^+ + (w-v)(dq-D)^+ \quad (21)$$

Hence, the supplier's minimum profit is $(w-v)dq - (c-v)uq$, which occurs when $D \le dq$. It turns out that the supplier's probability of achieving his target depends on if his minimum profit is positive or not. If the contract parameter set θ is chosen such that $w \le v + (c - v)/a$, the minimum profit is non-positive. The supplier's probability of achieving his target profit t_s is given as:

$$P_r(q,\theta) = \begin{cases} 0 & \text{if } q < q_1(\theta) \\ 1-F\left(\frac{t_s+(c-v)uq}{w-v}\right) & \text{if } q \ge q_1(\theta) \end{cases} \quad (22)$$

which is always less than 1. On the other hand, if the contract parameter set θ is chosen such that $w > v + (c - v)/\alpha$, the minimum profit is positive. The supplier's probability function of achieving his target profit t_s is then given as:

$$P_r(q,\theta) = \begin{cases} 0 & \text{if } q < q_1(\theta) \\ 1 - F\left(\frac{t_s + (c-v)uq}{w-v}\right) & \text{if } q_3(\theta) > q \geq q_1(\theta) \\ 1 & \text{if } q \geq q_3(\theta) \end{cases} \quad (23)$$

Therefore, if $w > v + (c-v)/a$, the supplier's probability of achieving his target can be as high as 1.

Now we proceed to design Pareto-optimal QF contracts for the supply chain under the satisficing objectives. For the clarity of exposition, we first summarize our results on Pareto-optimal QF contracts in Table 4 (see the Appendix for a derivation). The second column of the table identifies the conditions for the contract parameter set θ to be Pareto optimal. The associated Pareto-optimal order quantity and maximal probabilities of achieving their target profits are given by $q^*(\theta)$, $P_s(\theta)$ and $P_r(\theta)$, respectively.

So far we have derived the Pareto-optimal QF contracts, for which we have the following observations. First, for a QF contract to be Pareto optimal, its contract parameters must satisfy $w_1 \leq w \leq \hat{w}$. When $w = \hat{w}$, the adjustment ratio α has to be 1. This means a QF contract will be Pareto optimal if it degenerates into a WP contract with wholesale price $w = \hat{w}$. Second, the Pareto-optimal QF contracts depend on the downward and upward adjustment parameters only through the adjustment ratio α. However, the associated Pareto order quantity may depend on the upward adjustment parameter only, which is the case for the Pareto set *QF1*. Finally, the Pareto-optimal QF contracts depend on the supplier's and the retailer's target profits only through the target ratio β.

Example

Consider a supply chain with a supplier and a retailer who faces a Gamma demand with mean 400 and coefficient of variation 0.5. The supplier procures the good at a unit cost $c = 15$ and the retailer sells at a unit price $r = 20$. Any unsold unit has a salvage cost $v = 8$. The terms of trade between the supplier and the retailer are specified by a QF contract. Both the supplier and the retailer adopt the satisficing objective. The target profits for the supplier and the retailer are set at $t_s = 1200$ and $t_r = 800$, respectively.

What are the pareto-optimal QF contracts?

Figure 4 illustrates the Pareto optimality. The region bounded by the solid line and the dotted line represents the Pareto-optimal QF contracts under the satisficing objectives. We use the dotted line to emphasize the fact that the dotted line is excluded from the region.

Table 4. Pareto-optimal QF contracts for the supply chain with the satisficing objectives

Sets	θ = [w, u, d] or [w, α]	$q^*(\theta)$	$P_s(\theta)$	$P_r(\theta)$
*QF*1	$\frac{c+\alpha\beta r}{1+\alpha\beta} \leq w < \frac{c+\beta r}{1+\beta}$	$\frac{t_s}{u(w-c)}$	$1-F\left(\frac{t_s}{w-c}\right)$	$1-F\left(\frac{t_r}{r-w}\right)$
*QF*2	$w = \frac{c+\beta r}{1+\beta}, \alpha = 1$	$\frac{t_r+t_s}{r-c}$	1	$1-F\left(\frac{t_r+t_s}{r-c}\right)$

Figure 4. The Pareto-optimal QF contracts for the supply chain with the satisficing objectives (the region bounded by the dotted line and the solid line)

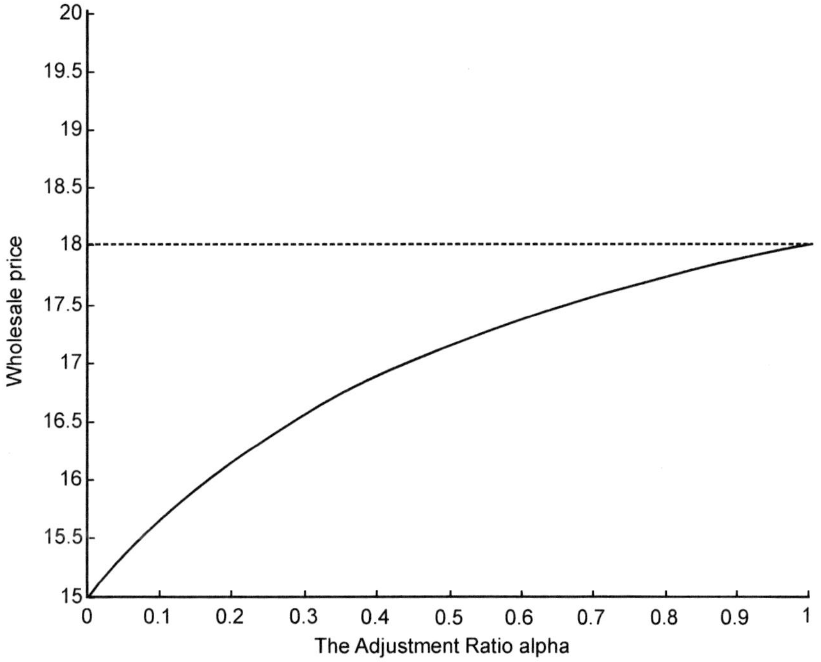

Coordination of the Supply Chain with the Satisficing Objectives

So far we have designed the Pareto-optimal contracts for the three contractual forms under the satisficing objectives. In this section, our goal is to identify the contractual forms that are capable of coordination of the supply chain with satisficing objectives.

To this end, we adopt the general definition of supply chain coordination with contracts proposed by Gan et al. (2004). A supply chain is said to be coordinated with a contract if the optimizing actions of the agents under the contract lead to Pareto optimality, that is, no agent in the chain can be better off without making any other agent worse off. We have the following theorem (see the Appendix for proof) on supply chain coordination with contracts under the satisficing objectives.

Theorem 3

Let t_s and t_r be the profit targets for the supplier and the retailer, respectively. If both of them adopt the satisficing objective, the supply chain is coordinated if and only if:

(1) The retailer chooses the optimal order quantity $q^*=(tr + ts)/(r - c)$, which is the solution to the chain optimization problem: $\max P\{\Pi(q)\geq t_s + t_r\}$, *where $\Pi(q)=\Pi_s(q,\theta) + \Pi_r(q,\theta)$ is the total profit of the supply chain.*

(2) The supplier and the retailer follow the optimal profit allocation rule $\Psi^*=[\Pi^*_s, \Pi^*_r]$, where Π^*_s and Π^*_r *are profits allocated to the supplier and the retailer, respectively: For any demand realization $\Pi(q^*)$, set $\Pi^*_s\geq t_s$ and $\Pi_r \geq t_r$ if $\Pi(q^*) \geq t_s + t_r$; Otherwise, set either $\Pi^*_s= t_s$ and $\Pi^*_r = \Pi(q^*) - t_s$, or $\Pi^*_r= t_r$ and $\Pi^*_s= \Pi (q^*) - t_r$.*

Based on Theorem 3, the coordinating contract for the supply chain with the satisficing objectives has a very simple structure. First, the retailer's order quantity needs to be chosen so that the probability for the whole chain to achieve the chain profit target $t_s + t_r$ is maximized. Second, the supply chain's profit should be allocated such that at least one of the agents (either the supplier or the retailer), and both agents whenever possible, achieve their profit targets. The resulting probability pair for the supplier and the retailer is either $[1, 1-F((t_r + t_s)/(r - c))]$ or $[1-F((tr + ts)/(r - c)), 1]$.

Obviously the Pareto-optimal WP contract (see Theorem 1) can coordinate the supply chain with satisficing objectives, which results in the probability pair $[1, 1-F((t_r + t_s)/(r - c))]$. However, the Pareto-optimal BB contracts (see Table 3) cannot coordinate the supply chain with satisficing objectives. This is because all three resulted probability pairs are dominated by either $[1, 1-F((t_r + t_s)/(r-c))]$ or $[1-F((t_r + t_s)/(r - c)), 1]$. As for Pareto-optimal QF contracts (see Table 4), the probability pair from set *QF1* is dominated by $[1-F((t_r + t_s)/(r-c)), 1]$. Therefore, the Pareto-optimal QF contracts in set *QF1* cannot coordinate such a supply chain. However, the Pareto-optimal QF contract in set *QF2*, which is a WP contract with wholesale price $\hat{w}$, coordinates the supply chain. Hence, for a QF contract to coordinate the supply chain under the satisficing objective, it has to degenerate into a WP contract.

The results above provide an important additional justification for the popularity of WP contracts besides their simplicities and lower administration costs. Recall that WP, BB, and QF contracts have one, two, and three contractual parameters, respectively. Intuitively, more contractual parameters mean more design freedom, which is indeed the case for the supply chain with the objective of expected profit maximization (Cachon, 2003). However, we show that WP contracts are better BB contracts when it comes to coordination of the supply chain with the satisficing objectives. For a QF contract to coordinate such a supply chain, it has to degenerate into a WP contract.

It is also worthwhile noticing the interesting wholesale price $\hat{w}$, for which we have the following observations. First, it is a linear combination of procurement cost c and selling price r, with 1 and the target ratio β as the weights, respectively. Second, for a WP contract to coordinate the supply chain, its wholesale price has to be $\hat{w}$. Third, by setting the wholesale price to $\hat{w}$, a BB contract will be Pareto optimal regardless of the buy back price b. Finally, for a QF to coordinate the supply chain, it has to degenerate into a WP contract with wholesale price $\hat{w}$.

However, the resulting probability pair of the coordinating WP and QF contracts is $[1, 1-F((t_r + t_s)/(r - c))]$. This is equivalent to saying that the supplier gets his target profit and the retailer gets the rest. There is another type of Pareto-optimal profit allocation where the retailer gets her target profit of t_r and the supplier gets the rest—that is, the resulting probability pair will be $[1-F((t_r + t_s)/(r - c)), 1]$. This can be implemented through simple slotting fee contracts (Lariviere & Padmanabhan, 1997), in which the retailer receives a fixed slotting fee and the supplier gets the rest of the profit (or loss). By setting the slotting fee equal to the retailer's profit target t_r, the slotting fee contract is Pareto optimal and coordinates the supply chain with the satisficing objectives.

Coordination of the Supply Chain with Different Objectives

Our work so far assumes that both the supplier and the retailer in the supply chain adopt the satisficing objectives. However, there are other types of objectives for managers and/or companies in business practice. These objectives include expected profit maximization (EPM), expected utility maximization, and expected profit maximization subject to downside-risk constraint (Gan et al., 2005). If this is the case, how could we design Pareto-optimal and/or coordinating contracts for such a supply chain?

For the purpose of illustration, we consider the same decentralized supply chain as the one in the previous sections. The terms of trade between the two agents are specified by a simple WP contract. For simplicity, we assume the demand follows a uniform distribution on $[0, z]$. If the supply chain is centralized and both agents adopt the EPM objective, it can be verified that the Pareto-optimal order quantity is given by $q_e^* = F^{-1}((r-c)/(r-v)) = (r-c)z/(r-v)$ and the maximal expected profit is given by:

$$\prod{}^{o} = \frac{z(r-c)^2}{2(r-v)} \tag{24}$$

Now we consider the supply chain where the retailer adopts the EPM objective while the supplier still adopts the satisficing objective. How does one design the Pareto-optimal WP contract for such a supply chain?

Given a WP contract with wholesale price w, the retailer will order $q_r = F^{-1}((r-w)/(r-v))$ to maximize her expected profit. For the supplier, his PC is $q_s \geq t_s/(w-c) = q_s$ given his target profit level t_s. Once the PC is satisfied, the probability to achieve his target profit will always be 1, and thus is maximized. Here we also assume $\Pi^o/2 \leq t_s \leq 2\,\Pi^o$. Note that setting his target profit to at least half of Π^o indicates the supplier has relatively larger bargaining power. In addition, it is reasonable to set his target profit no more than twice Π^o.

Therefore, the Pareto-optimal order quantity for the supply chain is $q^* = \max(q_r, q_s)$. The associated probability for the supplier to achieve his target is 1, and the associated expected profit of the retailer is given as:

$$E\prod{}_r(q^*) = (r-w)q^* - (r-v)\int_0^{q^*} F(x)dx \tag{25}$$

Under the assumption of $\Pi^o/2 \leq t_s \leq 2\,\Pi^o$, it can be verified that $q^* = t_s / (w-c)$ and:

$$\frac{\partial E\Pi_r}{\partial w} = \frac{t_s}{z}\frac{(r-v)t_s - z(r-c)(w-c)}{(w-c)^3} \tag{26}$$

which increases first and then decreases with regard to w. By setting (26) equal to 0, we obtain the Pareto-optimal wholesale price:

$$w^* = c + \frac{t_s(r-v)}{z(r-c)} \tag{27}$$

which maximizes $E\Pi_r(q^*)$. It can be verified that w^* lies in the interval of $[c + (r-c)/4, r]$, and hence is economically sensible. Furthermore, the Pareto-optimal order quantity becomes $q^* = (r-c)z/(r-v)$, which is independent of t_s. It is also interesting to note that $q^* = q_e^*$, which is Pareto optimal for the supply chain where both agents adopt the EPM objective.

Of course, the results we obtained above are unlikely to hold for more general cases. It would be interesting to design Pareto-optimal and/or coordinating contracts for the supply chain where different agents adopt other different objectives, and/or some agent adopts multiple objectives.

CONCLUSION

Setting performance targets and managing to achieve them is fundamental to business success. As a result, it is common for managers to adopt a satisficing objective, that is, to maximize the probability of achieving some preset target profit level. This is especially true when companies are increasingly engaged in short-term relationships enabled by electronic commerce. However, there has been little research in supply chain literature with such a satisficing objective. We attempt to fill the gap in this chapter. The supply chain consists of a supplier and a retailer, selling a short lifecycle goods/service to the customer. Furthermore, the profit allocation between the two agents could be implemented by one of the three contractual forms, namely, WP, BB, and QF contracts.

For each contractual form, we first design the Pareto-optimal contracts. By definition, only Pareto-optimal contracts should be selected in practice, no matter what the negotiation process and negotiation powers among the agents. This is due to the fact that if a contract is not Pareto optimal, it is open to a counteroffer that makes no one worse off and at least one of the other agents strictly better off. Furthermore, a contract has to be Pareto optimal first to coordinate a supply chain.

Next, we identify the contractual forms that are capable of supply chain coordination. It is shown that WP contracts can coordinate the supply chain with the satisficing objective, whereas BB contracts cannot. Furthermore, QF contracts have to degenerate into WP contracts to coordinate a supply chain with satisficing objectives.

We then proceed to discuss the possible extension to the model by considering different objectives for different agents, and/or some agent may adopt multiple objectives simultaneously. For the purpose of illustration, we design the Pareto-optimal WP contract for the supply chain where the supplier adopts the satisficing objective and the retailer adopts the objective of expected profit maximization.

It is worthwhile noticing that the results we obtained in this chapter are contrary to those obtained for supply chain coordination with the objective of expected profit (cost) maximization (minimization). Under such an objective, BB and QF contracts can coordinate the supply chain, whereas WP contracts cannot. As a result, advanced contracts, such as the BB and QF contracts, have been advocated to improve the performance of the supply chain (Tayur et al., 1999). However, our results indicate that for the supply chain with the satisficing objectives, the simple WP contracts, instead of BB contracts, can coordinate the supply chain and should be adopted. Furthermore, a QF contract has to degenerate into a WP contract to coordinate such a supply chain. Since the satisficing objective is quite realistic and popular in business practice, we provide another important justification of the wide use of WP contracts besides the simplicities and lower administration costs.

ACKNOWLEDGMENT

Bintong Chen's research was partially supported by the National Natural Science Foundation of China, Grant No. 70640420143.

REFERENCES

Brown, A., & Tang, C.S. (2004). *The impact of alternative performance measures on single-period inventory policy.* working paper, UCLA, USA.

Barr, S. (2003). Target setting: Art or science? ... Or both? *Mezhermnt, 4,* 1-5.

Cachon, G. (2003). Supply chain coordination with contracts. In A.G. de Kok & S.C. Graves (Eds.), *Supply chain management: Design, coordination and operation.* Elsevier.

Cachon, G. (2004). The allocation of inventory risk in a supply chain: Push, pull, and advance-purchase discount contracts. *Management Science, 50,* 222-238.

Gan, X., Sethi, S., & Yan, H. (2004). Coordination of a supply chain with risk-averse agents. *Production and Operations Management, 13,* 135-149.

Gan, X., Sethi, S., & Yan, H. (2005). Channel coordination with a risk-neutral supplier and a downside-risk-averse retailer. *Production and Operations Management, 14,* 80-89.

Kabak, I.W., & Schiff, A.I. (1978). Inventory models and management objectives. *Sloan Management Review, 19,* 53-59.

Johnson, P.F., & Klassen, R.D. (2005). E-procurement. *Sloan Management Review, 46,* 6-10.

Lanzillotti, R.F. (1958). Pricing objectives in large companies. *American Economics Review, 48,* 921-940.

Lariviere, M., & Padmanabhan, V. (1997). Slotting allowances and new product introductions. *Marketing Science, 16,* 112-128.

Lariviere, M., & Porteus, E. (2001). Selling to the newsvendor: An analysis of price-only contracts. *Manufacturing and Service Operations Management, 3,* 293-305.

Lau, H. (1980). The newsboy problem under alternative optimization objectives. *Journal of the Operational Research Society, 31,* 393-403.

Lau, A., & Lau, H. (1988). Maximizing the probability of achieving a target profit level in a two-product newsboy problem. *Decision Sciences, 19,* 392-408.

Li, J., Lau, H., & Lau, A. (1991). A two-product newsboy problem with satisficing objective and independent exponential demands. *IIE Transaction, 23,* 29-39.

Lovell, C.A.K., & Pastor, J.T. (1997). Target setting: An application to a bank branch network. *European Journal of Operational Research, 98,* 290-299.

McTaggart, J., & Gillis, S. (1998). Setting targets to maximize shareholder value. *Strategy Leadership, 26,* 18-21.

Pasternack, B. (1985). Optimal pricing and returns policies for perishable commodities. *Marketing Science, 4,* 166-176.

Sankarasubramanian, E., & Kumaraswamy, S. (1983). Optimal order quantity for pre-determined level of profit. *Management Science, 29,* 512-514.

Simon, H.A. (1959). Theories of decision-making in economics and behavioral science. *American Economics Review, 49,* 253-283.

Spengler, J. (1950). Vertical integration and antitrust policy. *Journal of Political Economics, 58,* 347-352.

Tsay, A.A. (1999). The quantity flexibility contract and supplier-customer incentives. *Management Science, 45,* 1339-1358.

Tayur, S., Ganeshan, R., & Magazine, M. (Eds.). (1999). *Quantitative models for supply chain management.* Boston: Kluwer.

Van Neumann, J., & Morgenstern, O. (1944). *Theory of games and economic behavior.* Princeton, NJ: Princeton University Press.

APPENDIX

Derivation of Pareto-Optimal QF Contracts

To design Pareto-optimal QF contracts, it is worthwhile noticing that the supplier's probability function takes different forms depending on if the parameter set θ satisfies inequality $w > v + (c - v)/\alpha$ or not. Hence, we design Pareto-optimal QF contracts for Case 1 of $w > v + (c - v)/\alpha$ and Case 2 of $w \le v + (c - v)/\alpha$, respectively.

Case 1: $w > v + (c - v)/\alpha$

Under Case 1, the probability function of the supplier to achieve his target profit is given by (23). Furthermore, it can be seen below that Pareto optimality depends on the relative magnitudes of $q_1(\theta)$, $q_2(\theta)$, $q_3(\theta)$, and $q_4(\theta)$. Therefore, we consider the following three subcases.

Case 1.1: $w \ge w_2$
Under Case 1.1, we have $q_1(\theta) \le q_3(\theta) \le q_4(\theta)$. The probability functions $P_s(q,\theta)$ and $P_r(q,\theta)$ for the supplier and the retailer are plotted in Figure A1. Note that it is also possible that $q_3(\theta) \le q_2(\theta)$ under Case 1.1.

It can be seen from Figure A1 that the Pareto-optimal order quantity set is given by:

$$q^*(\theta) \in [\max(q_2(\theta), q_3(\theta), q_4(\theta)] \quad \text{(A1)}$$

The associated probabilities for the supplier and the retailer are:

$$P_s(q^*(\theta),\theta) = 1 \text{ and } P_r(q^*(\theta),\theta) = 1 - F\left(\frac{t_r}{r - w}\right) \quad \text{(A2)}$$

Obviously $P_r(q^*(\theta),\theta)$ decreases with respect to w. Hence we choose $w^*(u,d)=w_2$. The associated retailer's probability is:

$$P_r(q^*(w_2,u,d)\theta) = 1 - F\left(\frac{\alpha(t_r + t_s)}{\alpha(r - v) - (c - v)}\right) \quad \text{(A3)}$$

which is maximized at $\alpha=1$. Note that $w_2=\hat{w}$ when $\alpha=1$. Moreover, substituting $\alpha=1$ into (A1) an (A3), we have the Pareto-optimal set $QF2$ in Table 4.

Figure A1. The probability functions of achieving their target profits for the supplier (bold line) and the retailer under Case 1.1

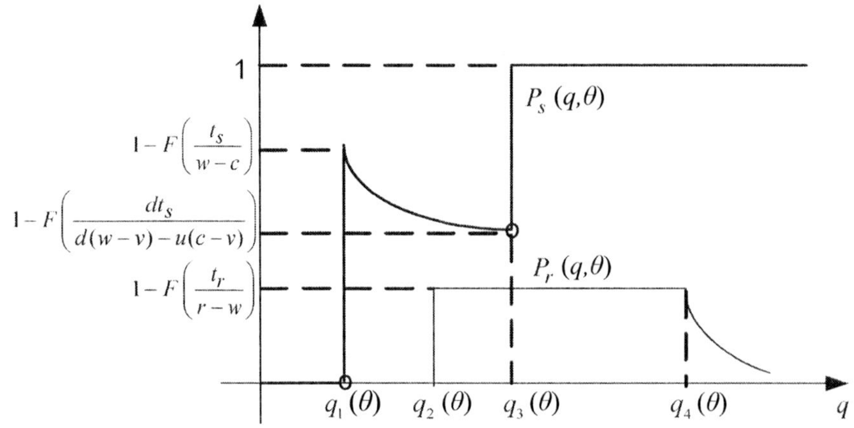

Case 1.2: $w \leq w_1$

Under Case 1.2, we have $q_2(\theta) \leq q_4(\theta) \leq q_1(\theta) \leq q_3(\theta)$. The probability functions of the supplier and the retailer are shown in Figure A2.

Therefore, both $q_3(\theta)$ and $q_1(\theta)$ are Pareto-optimal order quantities. It can be verified that the order quantity $q_3(\theta)$ will eventually lead to the Pareto-optimal set *QF2* in Table 4. On the other hand, if the retailer orders $q_1(\theta)$, the probabilities for the supplier and the retailer are given by:

$$P_s(q_1(\theta),\theta) = 1 - F\left(\frac{t_s}{w-c}\right) \text{ and } P_r(q_1(\theta),\theta) = 1 - F\left(\frac{1}{r-v}\left(t_r + \frac{w-v}{w-c}\alpha\, t_s\right)\right) \quad \text{(A4)}$$

Since both $P_r(q_1(\theta),\theta)$ and $P_s(q_1(\theta),\theta)$ increase with respect to w, we choose $w^*(u,d) = w_1$. The associated Pareto-optimal order quantity $q_1(\theta)$ then becomes:

$$q^*(w_1,u,d) = \frac{dt_s + ut_r}{ud(r-c)} \quad \text{(A5)}$$

The associated probabilities for the supplier and the retailer are:

$$P_s(q^*(w_1,u,d),\theta) = 1 - F\left(\frac{t_r + \alpha t_s}{\alpha(r-c)}\right) \quad \text{(A6)}$$

$$P_r(q^*(w_1,u,d),\theta) = 1 - F\left(\frac{t_r + \alpha t_s}{r-c}\right) \quad \text{(A7)}$$

Because the two probabilities vary in different directions as α changes, any α is Pareto optimal. In summary, the resulting Pareto-optimal set is a special case of the Pareto-optimal set *QF1* in Table 4 when $w = w_1$.

Case 1.3: $w_1 \leq w < w_2$

Under Case 1.3, we have $q_1(\theta) \leq q_4(\theta) \leq q_3(\theta)$. Once again, it can be verified that both $q_3(\theta)$ and $q_1(\theta)$ are Pareto optimal, and $q_3(\theta)$ will eventually lead to the Pareto-optimal set *QF2* in Table 4. If the retailer orders $q_1(\theta)$, the supplier's probability of achieving his target profit $P_s(q^*(\theta),\theta)$ is less than 1, and the retailer's probability is

Figure A2. The probabilities of achieving their target profits for the supplier (bold line) and the retailer under Case 1.2

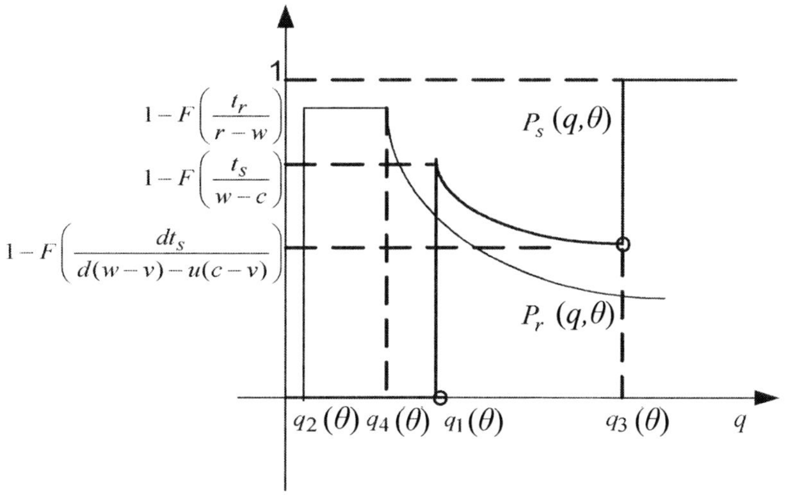

Figure A3. The probabilities of achieving their target profits for the supplier (bold line) and the retailer under Case 1.3

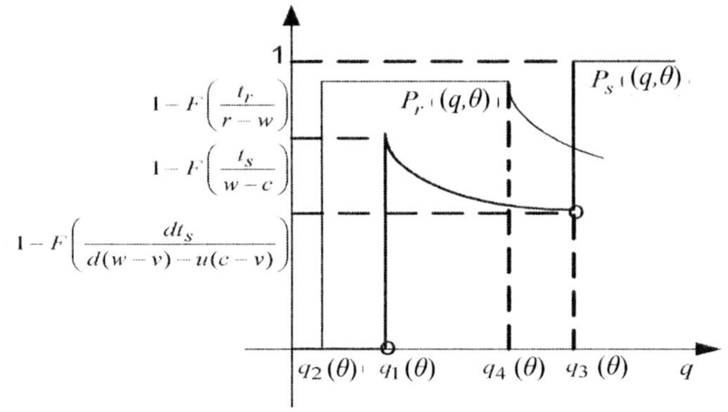

$P_r(q_r^*(\theta),\theta)=1-F(t_r/(r-w))$. To make sure that the resulting Pareto-optimal set will not be dominated by set *QF2*, we need to have:

$$P_r(q_1(\theta),\theta) > 1-F\left(\frac{t_s+t_r}{r-c}\right) \quad \text{(A8)}$$

which is equivalent to $w < \hat{w}$. Therefore, we only need to consider the case when $w_1 \leq w < \hat{w}$, for which $q_2(\theta) \leq q_1(\theta)$. The probability functions of the supplier and the retailer are plotted in Figure A3.

It can be seen from Figure A3 that the probabilities of the supplier and the retailer associated with order quantity $q_1(\theta)$ are:

$$P_r(q_1(\theta),\theta) = 1-F\left(\frac{t_s}{w-c}\right) \text{and } P_r(q_1(\theta),\theta) = 1-F\left(\frac{t_r}{r-w}\right) \quad \text{(A9)}$$

Because the two probabilities vary in different directions as w changes, any w is Pareto optimal. In summary, this Pareto-optimal set is given as *QF1* in Table 4.

Case 2: w ≤ v + (c – v) / α

Under Case 2, the probability of the supplier to achieve his target profit is given by (22), which is always less than 1. Furthermore, the retailer's probability will be no larger than $1-F(t_r/(r-w))$. Therefore, to guarantee the resulting Pareto-optimal set is not dominated by set *QF2* in Table 4, we need to have:

$$1-F\left(\frac{t_r}{r-w}\right) > 1-F\left(\frac{t_s+t_r}{r-c}\right) \quad \text{(A10)}$$

which is equivalent to $w < \hat{w}$ or $q_2(\theta) \leq q_1(\theta)$. Now we consider the two subcases as follows.

Case 2.1: $w_1 \leq w < \hat{w}$

Under Case 2.1, we have $q_2(\theta) \leq q_1(\theta) \leq q_4(\theta)$. It can be verified that the order quantity $q_1(\theta)$ is Pareto optimal, with the supplier's and the retailer's probabilities given by:

$$P_s(q_1(\theta),\theta) = 1-F\left(\frac{t_s}{w-c}\right) \text{and } P_r(q_1(\theta),\theta) = 1-F\left(\frac{t_r}{r-w}\right) \quad \text{(A11)}$$

Therefore, any w in Case 2.1 is Pareto optimal, which gives the Pareto-optimal set *QF1* in Table 4.

Case 2.2: $w \le w_1$
Under Case 2.2, we have $q_2(\theta) \le q_4(\theta) \le q_1(\theta)$. It can be verified that the order quantity $q_1(\theta)$ is Pareto optimal, with the supplier's and the retailer's probabilities given by:

$$P_s(q_1(\theta),\theta) = 1 - F\left(\frac{t_s}{w-c}\right) \text{and } P_r(q_1(\theta),\theta) = 1 - F\left(\frac{1}{r-v}\left(t_r + \frac{w-v}{w-c}\alpha\, t_s\right)\right) \quad \text{(A12)}$$

Because both probabilities increase with respect to w, we have $w^*(u,d)= w_1$. Substituting $w^*(u,d)= w_1$ into $q_1(\theta)$ and (A12), we end up with a special case of the Pareto-optimal set *QF1* in Table 4 when $w = w_1$.

Proof of Theorem 3

ONLY IF: We show that the optimal profit allocation rule Ψ^* is necessary by contradiction. First note with the optimal allocation rule Ψ^*, we have $P\{\Pi^*_s \ge t_s\}$=1 and $P\{\Pi^*_r \ge t_r\}$=1 if $\Pi(q^*) \ge t_s + t_r$. Otherwise, we have $P\{\Pi^*_s \ge t_s\}$=1 or $P\{\Pi^*_r \ge t_r\}$=1. Now consider ANY other allocation rule $\Psi = [\Pi'_s, \Pi'_r]$. If the chain profit $\Pi(q^*) \ge t_s + t_r$, rule Ψ implies either $\Pi'_s < t_s$ or $\Pi'_r < t_r$, and hence, $P\{\Pi'_s \ge t\}_s$=0 or $P\{\Pi'_r \ge t_r\}$=0. If $\Pi(q^*) < t_s + t_r$, rule Ψ implies $\Pi'_s < t_s$ and $\Pi'_r < t_r$, and hence, $P\{\Pi'_s \ge t_s\}$= 0 and $P\{\Pi'_r \ge t_r\}$= 0. In either case, the probability pair $[P\{\Pi'_s \ge t_s\}, P\{\Pi'_r \ge t_r\}]$ is dominated by $[P\{\Pi^*_s \ge t_s\}, P\{\Pi^*_r \ge t_r\}]$. Therefore the profit allocation rule Ψ^* is Pareto optimal.

Next we show that order quantity q^* is necessary. Consider ANY other order quantity $q' \neq q^*$. If $q' < q^*$, the maximum chain profit is $\Pi(q') = (r-c)q' < t_s + t_r$. This implies that it is impossible for both the supplier and the retailer to achieve their profit targets simultaneously, no matter what the demand realization. Therefore, $q' < q^*$ cannot be Pareto optimal. Now we consider the case of $q' > q^*$. We have the following based on Figure 1:

$$\begin{cases} \Pi(q') > \Pi(q^*) = t_r + t_s & \text{if } D > \overline{q} \\ \Pi(q') < \Pi(q^*) = t_r + t_s & \text{if } \overline{q} > D > q^* \\ \Pi(q') < \Pi(q^*) < t_r + t_s & \text{if } D < \overline{q} \end{cases} \quad \text{(A13)}$$

where:

$$q^* < \overline{q} = \frac{t_r + t_s + (c-v)q'}{r-v} < q' \quad \text{(A14)}$$

If $D > \overline{q}$ or $D < q^*$, the order quantities q^* and q' lead to the same probability pair with the allocation rule Ψ^*. If $\overline{q} > D > q^*$, the order quantity q^* leads to the probability pair [1,1] for the supplier and retailer. Hence, q^* Pareto dominates q' under the case of $\overline{q} > D > q^*$. In summary, the order quantity q^* is Pareto optimal.

IF: Let $\lambda = P\{\Pi(q^*) < t_r + t_s, \Pi^*_s = t_s\}$, based on the profit allocation rule Ψ^*, we have:

$$P\{\Pi^*_s \ge t_s\} = P\{\Pi(q^*) \ge t_r + t_s\} + (1 - P\{\Pi(q^*) \ge t_r + t_s\})\lambda \quad \text{(A15)}$$

Similarly, we also have:

$$P\{\Pi^*_r \ge t_r\} = P\{\Pi(q^*) \ge t_r + t_s\} + (1 - P\{\Pi(q^*) \ge t_r + t_s\})(1-\lambda) \quad \text{(A16)}$$

Since both $P\{\Pi^*_s \ge t_s\}$ and $P\{\Pi^*_r \ge t_r\}$ increase in $P\{\Pi(q^*) \ge t_r + t_s\}$ and $P\{\Pi(q^*) \ge t_r + t_s\}$ is maximized at q^*, $[P\{\Pi^*_s \ge t_s\}, P\{\Pi^*_r \ge t_r\}]$ is Pareto optimal.

Chapter XIII
Information Feedback Approach for Maintaining Service Quality in Supply Chain Management

R. Manjunath
Bangalore University, India

ABSTRACT

Maintaining the service quality in a supply chain has become a challenging task with increased complexity and number of players down the line. Often several supply chains cross over the common resources, calling for the sharing of resources and prioritization. This leads to the definition of pre-specified service quality as seen by the end user of the supply chain. In this chapter, a feedback mechanism that conveys the status of the supply line starting from the tail end is discussed. The advantages of using a predicted and shifted slippage or loss rate as the feedback signal are highlighted. Based on the feedback, the source is expected to change the rate of transfer of the commodity over the supply chain. With this, the resources would get utilized effectively, reducing the stranded time of the commodity down the line. The service quality in terms of delay and loss rate gets improved.

INTRODUCTION

The enormous business size in recent days call for distributed supply units to be located across the globe and connected through a sophisticated network. Throughout this work, these isolated business structures are referred to as mobile business units. They resemble the distributed computing environment in the sense that a time-bound, constraint-based command, signal, and information get exchanged among them.

In this work the concept of differential feedback is explored for the effective utilization of the information for the communication among the members of the supply chain. The model that translates individual behavior to the collective behavior of the chain is given. The resource contention for communication along the chain is addressed and the solution is modeled.

Maintaining a constant agreed ratio of defects or losses—quality of service (QoS)—in a supply chain is often tricky. The problem gets further complicated when the supply chain contains multiple source streams. In this work, a differential feedback-based model has been developed to predict the defects or losses. A shifted version of the same will be used as a feedback signal. Simulation results show that the number of defects observed at any point in the supply chain gets reduces with the shifted feedback signal. With the defects getting reduced, for a given demand at any point down the supply chain, the quantum of input may be reduced with differential feedback to achieve the same performance. The defense supply and deployment into the battlefield, the fair mixing of reactants in a chemical reaction chamber, and so forth stand as good examples.

The shifted feedback information from the end user or any other intermediate player in the line may be used to achieve some additional quality of service deadlines such as the absolute delay guarantee, fraction of the service loss, and so forth. The same would be agreed up on with the different units down the line, well in advance. Simulation results prove that the usage of shifted signals can stabilize the QoS and improve the service quality in terms of overall successful operations in a given time. This reduces the stranded time of the information or loss along the supply chain.

Analysis shows that a system exhibits self-similarity to maximize the entropy (Manjunath & Gurumurthy, 2005a). It is proved that, to maximize entropy, the system makes use of differential feedback of different degrees. They form various levels of abstraction and by and large carry redundant information (Manjunath & Gurumurthy, 2005a). The self-similar property has been exploited here to maintain the quality of service constraints

Because of abstraction and redundancy, even if a portion of the information is lost or if it is required to predict the future uncertainties with minimum available information, it can be repaired or re-synthesized using the available information.

The self-similar property of the component induces interesting properties into the system. This property may be used as lead-lag components in controlling the information transfer over the network. Closed-loop feedback is utilized to control the signals transferred over the network. Intermediate self-similar structures or switches may modulate feedback signals and control the system behavior.

In order to meet the real-time transfer of the signal, stringent service quality parameters are defined over the data transfers down the supply chain. This chapter provides techniques to meet these requirements with minimal resources. In-time flow of the commodities to the end user is the basic requirement in a supply chain. The tools and techniques used to meet this goal are different in different supply chains. The example of real-time transfer of information for the end user is considered throughout this chapter. The supply chain involves various routers, switches, and media in between. The goal is to get the real-time performance in the chain with minimal retransmissions. The concepts may be easily extended to any other form of supply chain.

A supply chain has four areas of decision: location, production, inventory, and transportation or distribution. It is known that the rate of production bears a direct relation with the rate of consumption. However, the other factors during the transportation, such as the influence of adjacent supply chains and the stranded time of commodities within the chain, need to be considered. In this chapter, these factors are explained in depth.

Simulation plays an important role in the modeling of a supply chain before it becomes operational. It provides a closer look at the issues that may crop up in a supply chain and handle them appropriately during the implementation.

Supply chains have to make two categories of decisions—he long-term strategic and short-term operational decisions. A lot of data is required for making decisions. A model-based approach is extremely helpful to reduce the sample size. The model consists of an auto regressive (AR) and a moving average (MA) part. The ARMA followed by a non-linear limiter can enhance the predictability in the data set. The model described here is called differentially fed artificial neural network (DANN) (Manjunath & Gurumurthy, 2002) and is a variant of ANN.

BACKGROUND

A supply chain is basically a network from production to the consumption, involving the producer, the end consumer, and the intermediate distribution agents or brokers. The underlying philosophy of a supply chain exists in diverse fields such as manufacturing industries, the troops deployed in the battlefield, and so forth.

In an industrial supply chain, the material undergoes changes metamorphically along the chain. The models that describe the supply chain are very specific in nature. In this work a more generic approach has been taken.

The literature in supply chain management dates back to the work of Geoffrion and Graves (1974). Their work describes an optimal flow of multi-commodity logistics from the plants to the end users. This model is further explored in Geoffrion and Powers (1995) as a review of the evolution of the distribution strategies.

In the supply chain the intervening agents can have distinct characteristics.

Cohen and Lee (1985) gave a framework for manufacturing strategy analysis, with several stochastic sub-models describing the supply chain. Finally these sub-models got integrated heuristically, which they presented in Cohen and Lee (1988). The other successful implementation of the supply chain model is at General Motors by Breitman and Lucas (1987). The optimal resource utilization in a supply chain has been considered by the work of Cohen and Lee (1989). Another cost and time optimization model has been considered in Arntzen, Brown, Harrison, and Trafton (1995).

Differential feedback of the status of the commodity that flows along the supply chain improves the performance of the supply chain. Here the differential feedback model is introduced (Manjunath, 2004).

The different components of an organization, such as marketing, distribution, planning, and production in the supply chain, operate quite independently with their own agendas and priorities. The marketing department targets maximum profit while the production division calls for more investment. The scientific way of bringing together these conflicting goals is the theme of supply chain management.

The real-time supply chain solution has to provide up-to-the-minute information for the end user. Hence the quality of the information is very important. The system cannot afford to undo the implications of usage of information of bad quality or transmit the data again. Stringent service quality parameters are imposed over the supply chain. Especially when multiple chains pass through the common resources in between, priority would come into the picture for the logical sharing of the resources.

INFORMATION FEEDBACK FOR SUPPLY CHAIN

When feedback information—that is, the information to the source about the status at the tail end of the supply chain—is provided, the system starts exhibiting interesting behavior (Manjunath & Gurumurthy, 2002). As a result of feedback that uses a set of previous values, the feedback signal exhibits multi-resolution property. That is, the output signal can be expressed as a weighted sum of a set of orthogonal signals, each of which is a replica of the other but for a scale (Manjunath & Gurumurthy, 2003). These replicas are called hyperplanes, as they form a linear transformation in the hyperspace. Any of these hyperplanes may be obtained from the other plane by convolving with a Gaussian pulse of appropriate scale factor.

The architecture is based on feedforward and feedback paths. The feedforward path consists of the actual information or data or commodity flow departing from the source depending up on the simulation application. It is data packets in a communication network, a commodity in a product supply chain, and investment in a finance supply chain. The feedback signal comprises the position and status of the commodity or information as observed at the destination. The differentially fed neural network sits as a controller in the loop comprising the source, the forward path, the destination, and the feedback path.

The presence of such a controller imparts all of its properties to the system. That is, the supply chain on either direction behaves as a system with differential feedback provided.

In general, when a controller is used as an estimator, it starts throwing the output depending up on the underlying algorithm and decision rules. An ideal estimator gives the weighted sum of the outputs from the different estimators. When the differentially fed controller is used as an estimator, there will be different output for each order of the differential feedback. The ideal controller is the one that corresponds to infinite ordered feedback. As the order of differential feedback is increased, it starts moving closer to the ideal estimator. Also, any of the estimators may be expressed as the weighted sum of other estimators.

The feedback information in a supply chain results in the reduction or increase of the source operation rate. It in turn helps in proper supply line scheduling. Based on the congestion status, different congestion control algorithms are used. Each one of them may be thought of as an estimator. A DANN works as an ideal estimator to replace all of them.

Since the differentially fed artificial neural network is a part of the loop, its presence has profound effect on the traffic in the loop. Traffic here refers to the movement of the commodity or the like. The DANNs make use of a large number of previous samples for decision making. Decisions thrown out by such a system contribute to long-range dependency in the movement of the commodity or the traffic. The abstract levels of hyperplanes of DANN contribute to self-similarity of the traffic when observed over different time scales.

In essence, insertion of DANN in the traffic loop makes the entire network behave as a differentially fed neural network, manifesting all its properties. The network here refers to the forward and feedback paths. Hence DANNs play a role more than replacing the conventional ANNs in traffic shaping. The traffic shaping involves maintaining the schedules, reduction in the delays, and reduction in stranded times or reschedules, while keeping up the agreed service parameters.

A multi-bit closed-loop feedback mechanism is assumed here, with the bits representing the drop or failure probability and express congestion status of the network. The notification signal or feedback signal is time shifted to get better performance. This algorithm is called random early prediction (REP) (Manjunath, 2004). Generally, feedback-based control is used in systems that need precise adaptive control. Any mismatch in the feedback would drive the system into an unstable region.

Models of the traffic are critical in providing a high quality of service. The complexity of traffic in a network is a natural consequence of integrating diverse ranges of members from different sources that significantly differ in their traffic patterns as well as their performance requirements over the same path.

Shifted Feedback in Data Network Supply Chain

The similarities between supply chain model and the data propagation over a network are exploited in this section. Basically the data network is a particular form of the supply chain. The concept developed with the networks is applicable for all variants of the chain. This perception throws all the associated problems of the network on to the supply chain. Consider two different classes of the data flow. It may be generalized for multiple classes. The relative service parameters come into the picture when the different classes of the flow contend for the common resources such as the operating path, buffering space, or docking space that tend to get choked and require the maintenance of a fixed ratio of the flow members.

The resource status in a network may be simulated with the DANN included. The application of a DANN component in network traffic shaping may be studied with this setup, and the parameters of the DANN may be fine tuned until the desired response is achieved. The simulations are basically used to analyze and tune the quality of service metrics and allow exploring different implementation options by conducting experiments.

The simulation setup and the underlying methodology is valid for other supply chains as well.

In the proposed scheme the predicted version of the probability of cell loss is given as feedback to the source. The DANN gets the training data from the background RED algorithm. For some time, the DANN will be in a learning phase. It then predicts the data and arbitrary k steps in advance. This is provided as the feedback signal to the source. The source then re-computes the transmission rate. It may be seen that the cell loss ratio has been reduced with feedback.

In a simulation, 42 data points computed with RED are used for training. The input consists of 20 sources supporting background traffic that exist over the entire simulation time. The maximum buffer size is 8,000 and the cell size is 512. The total cell loss ratio of an ordinary RED scheme is found to be 1.6. With a neural network prediction, it has been reduced to 0.05, and in a first-order differentially fed neural network, it is reduced further to 0.04.

It is desirable to keep the variance of the resource occupancy less. The variance can be brought down with the increase of the differential feedback order. The use of a differentially fed artificial neural network in Web traffic shaping has been explained at length in Manjunath (2006). As the order of differential feedback increases, the error reduces.

The proposed input rate prediction process captures the actual input traffic rate reasonably well. In the steady state, the average queue size changes more slowly compared to the instantaneous queue size. This means that the proposed active queue management method is successful in controlling the average size at the router in response to a dynamically changing load, and there is no global synchronization among the sources. There will be some large variation of mean queue length during the initialization phase. This is because it is assumed that the queue is initially empty and it takes some time for the proposed scheme to operate correctly.

Because the proposed scheme randomly drops incoming packets according to the severity of the incipient congestion, there is no global synchronization. The large variation of the transient queue size is due to the bursty input traffic.

With the number of traffic sources that exist from the start to end of the simulation increasing from 20 to 80, the total probability of cell loss or area under the error signal remains the same. However, the variance of the queue length is considerably reduced with the proposed scheme. The reduction in the variance is more pronounced with large traffic.

The variance will be reduced with increase in the prediction. This happens for some time. Again the variance shows upward trend. This is because the autocorrelation function of a long-range dependent series exhibits oscillations. As the number of sources increases, LRD is more pronounced, with peaks of correlation separated far apart.

RED detects incipient congestion by calculating the average queue size at each packet arrival. In other words, in RED, congestion detection and the packet drop are performed in a small time scale. On the contrary, in the case of the proposed scheme, the congestion detection and the packet drop are performed at different time scales. When network congestion occurs, it takes some time for a traffic source to detect the congestion and reduce sending rate to resolve the congestion situation. The shift for which further increase of shift shows a reverse trend in the variance increases with the increase in the load.

The proposed scheme can reduce the time for a traffic source to detect congestion, because the congestion detection is determined in a large time scale. In case an incipient congestion is detected at a large time scale and a packet is lost within a sequence of packets, the successfully delivered packets following the lost packets will cause the receiver to generate a duplicate acknowledgement ACK. The reception of these duplicate ACKs is a signal of packet loss at the sender. So, the traffic sources can detect incipient congestion before it really occurs.

By using the proposed scheme, the source can respond to the incipient congestion signal faster than in the case of using RED gateway. Therefore, both the average queue length and the variation of the average queue length are smaller when the gateway uses the active queue management scheme proposed in this chapter rather than when the gateway uses RED. Because the proposed active queue management scheme can control the average queue size and the variation of the average queue size while accommodating transient bursty input traffic, it is well suited to provide high throughput, low average delay, and low average jitter in high-speed networks.

The variance of queue is found to vary linearly with the shift given to the feedback signal for different traffic loads. This confirms the existence of a constant term in the variance modulated by a variable term. The slope is independent of the load, while the constant depends on it.

Since the variance can be written as variance $= k_1 + k_2/\text{shift}$, k_1 and k_2 being constants, the plot of variance against the reciprocal of shift is a straight line. The constant variance term represents the bias. The second term happens to be the multi-resolution decomposition of variance and is the sum of n terms, n being the order of differential. By the weighted averaging of hyperplanes, the two parts in the second term can be replaced by a single term of highest degree or shift. The plot of variance against load also behaves similar to variance against the shift. In both cases, the variance initially gets reduced and later increases.

The growth of buffer size is a reflection of the efficiency of the algorithm followed in routing the cells. When differential feedback concept is applied, the maximum buffer occupancy is reduced, resulting in reduced cell loss. Depending on the network condition and the kind of traffic, an appropriate algorithm or rule may be applied for packet scheduling and discard. A set of ANNs, each learning a different scheduling algorithm, may be used. Any of them may be triggered based on the cost function, once again decided by another ANN. Each scheduling algorithm is an estimator. A single differentially fed ANN may be used since an ideal estimator can replace all the Bayesian estimators. A differentially fed neural network can merge and learn the multiple rules in one shot. It results in reduced hardware as well as improved switching efficiency in routing of the cells. It may be observed that the differentially fed ANN-based estimator outperforms the multiple scheduling schemes.

The past history associated with the differential feedback imparts a kind of long-range dependency in the output. With this, the switch performance is found to be better in terms of maximum buffer size and the total time to flush the cells. The proposed algorithm is independent of the underlying scheduling algorithm. Green is another standard scheduling algorithm like RED. The proposed algorithm of random early prediction works well with Green. For small shift, variance is reduced with not much change in the cell loss. It is the reverse for large shifts.

The peak instantaneous value falls as the sources go off. When more sources come on, with shift, it builds slowly and thus reduces rapid fluctuations of Q size. When Q changes rapidly, queuing models do not work well.

When the optimization problem does not yield a solution, meaning that it is impossible to satisfy all service guarantees simultaneously, some of the QoS guarantees are selectively ignored, based on a precedence order specified in advance. Due to the form of the constraints, the optimization problem is non-linear and can be solved only numerically.

The computational cost of solving a non-linear optimization upon each arrival to the link under consideration may be prohibitive to consider the implementation of an optimization-based algorithm at high speeds. The REP algorithm is effective in providing proportional and absolute per-class QoS guarantees for delay and cancellation or reschedule. The closed-loop algorithm reacts immediately when the routes are going from underload to overload and reacts swiftly when the routes go from overload to underload. This indicates that the delay feedback loops used in the closed-loop algorithm are stable.

Proportional delay differentiation does not match the target proportional factors when the route is underloaded, due to the fact that the algorithms are work conserving and therefore cannot artificially generate delays when the load is small.

Results for ratios of delays indicate that proportional loss differentiation (i.e., schedule cancellation) is achieved when the outbound route is overloaded and traffic is dropped. However, it is not met in any of the algorithms when the queue falls to 0. This implies that the algorithms basically manipulate the queue of the flow members and scheduling of the members to meet the relative delay and loss guarantees. With this the REP feedback loops used in the closed-loop algorithm appear to be robust to variations in the offered load, and the results of the REP closed-loop algorithm are found to be better than the one without any shift.

The delays and losses experienced by classes are monitored. It allows the algorithm to infer a deviation compared to the expected service differentiation. The algorithm then adjusts service rate allocation and the drop rates to attenuate the difference between the service experienced and the service guaranteed. A prediction-based feedback control is used to achieve proportional delay differentiation. Absolute differentiation is expressed in terms of saturation constraints that limit the range of the controller. The control loop around an operating point is made stable through differential feedback, and a stability condition is derived on the linearized control loop. The stability condition gives useful guidelines for selecting the configuration parameter of the controller.

ISSUES AND SOLUTIONS

It is quite possible that the supply chains from the various producers to the consumers crisscross or intersect each other, calling for a kind of contention for the resources. The contention could be in various forms, in terms of financial investment or storage space.

The first step towards resolving this contention and optimizing the supply chains is to define service classes for each of the chains passing through the intermediate agents or the brokers. In addition, for each of the service classes, a set of quality parameters is defined. Both the absolute value and the relative value of these parameters are important for optimization. It is a requirement to keep the absolute parameters within a certain agreed limit and the relative parameters at a prespecified constant value. Various algorithms and implementation schemes exist considering the optimal utilization of resources.

In the REP method of meeting service quality parameters, a differentially fed artificial neural network is used as a system level controller.

The broker model, whereby the intermediate agents apparently shield the actual source from the destination and often act as virtual sources down the line, may be thought of as an extreme case of the supply chain. In such a scenario, the service quality constraints are to be met by all the agents in between.

The issues arising out of the transfer of commodity down the line and the solution based on shifted feedback were discussed separately in the previous section. The other issues in supply chain management (SCM) are highlighted here. Having a common goal among the players of the supply chain is a tough task. Each element down the line will have its own agenda. Appropriate common goals and interfaces need to be defined so that the individuals align themselves towards the goal. The interfacing can be meaningfully defined only if the units commit to adhere to some quality guideline. However, it requires some time.

Interoperability is a major issue in the communication along the supply line. It may be improved with a common protocol with a machine-independent language such as XML.

The language description would be bound to the commodity and would be interpreted by all the players along the line.

The SCM models are required to be scalable. The required scalability may be brought in with the help of a DANN. The model remains invariant with the inclusion of additional flows, the only change being that the loss rate would increase faster.

FUTURE TRENDS

The increased dimensions in the organization call for the usage of collaborative and Web-based technologies for data collection. The data handling and integration systems in a supply chain come with increased communication and quality capabilities. This happens through increased collaboration among the elements of the supply chain down the line.

Supply chain components make use of a variety of software. Integration of these components and software under one platform would gain momentum, paving a path for new software in the market.

The concept of distributed computing, multiagent software and technology is getting in to the supply chain. The elements of the supply chain are quite often located at distinct physical and geographical locations. The data or commodity exchange among them can happen through a shift-based protocol. The protocols of distributed computing are expected to bring some order into the data exchange within the supply chain.

Advanced prediction of end user behavior would continue to contribute to the success of the manufacturing supply chain: it reduces the overhead on inventory. Further, development and usage of the customized prediction software tools as a part of the SCM suit would gain momentum. The usage of prediction of the health of the supply line has been explained in the previous sections.

Supply chain automation would be a common call in the future. The usage of automation software would enter into all forms of the supply chain. With the SCM software, it would be possible to automatically route the commodities all along the line. A variant of the software is electronic shopping, where the end user can directly negotiate with the distributor over the Internet and bypass the supply chain. This results in faster movement of the commodities. The Web services are coming along the supply chain. With this, it is possible for all players of the supply chain to get into a common platform and instantly interact over the Internet.

With supply chains involving digital contents, it is possible to specify the distribution patterns and rights through the associated meta-languages. The contents would be sold as commodities involving various middlemen like distributors and resellers, each having a specific rights over the contents.

The nature of the supply chain gets complex with the inclusion of more players. Often the chains would contain branches or mergers down the line. Some of the chains could include parallel paths in between and increase the complexity further. The SCM software has to consider all these scenarios.

CONCLUSION

The timely management of an end-to-end supply chain has become a challenging task in large and medium enterprises with distributed units scattered across the globe. In this chapter, the supply chain has been treated in a generic way, and no assumption has been made on the nature of the chain. It could be the data transferred over the Internet or the supply of arms to the ground troop deployed in the war field.

The different issues of the supply chain including the secure and timely movement of the commodities are addressed, and a solution has been sought based on a type of feedback from the tail of the supply chain to the head. The feedback includes a time-shifted version of the extrapolated loss or delay parameter of the commodity as seen by the destination. The feedback signal controls the overall flow in the supply chain.

The problem of resource contention at the intermediate nodes in the supply chain as a result of multiple flows has been defined, and the solution in terms of relative quality parameters has been explored.

REFERENCES

Arntzen, B.C., Brown, G.G., Harrison, T.P., & Trafton, L. (1995, January-February). Global supply chain management at Digital Equipment Corporation. *Interfaces.*

Breitman, R.L., & Lucas, J.M. (1987, January-February). Planets: A modeling system for business planning. *Interfaces, 17*, 94-106.

Cohen, M.A., & Lee, H.L. (1989). Resource deployment analysis of global manufacturing and distribution networks. *Journal of Manufacturing and Operations Management, 2*, 81-104.

Cohen, M.A., & Lee, H.L. (1985). Manufacturing strategy concepts and methods. In P.R. Kleindorfer (Ed.), *The management of productivity and technology in manufacturing* (pp. 153-188), UK: Plenum Press.

Cohen, M.A., & Lee, H.L. (1988). Strategic analysis of integrated production-distribution systems: Models and methods. *Operations Research, 36*(2), 216-228.

Geoffrion, A., & Graves, G. (1974). Multicommodity distribution system design by benders decomposition. *Management Science, 29*(5), 822-844.

Geoffrion, A., & Powers, R. (1995). 20 years of strategic distribution system design: An evolutionary perspective. *Interfaces, 25*(5), 105-127.

Manjunath, R. (2006). *Compact architecture for the analysis and processing of subnet signals using differentiators as building blocks.* Unpublished doctoral dissertation, University of Bangalore, India.

Manjunath, R., & Gurumurthy, K.S. (2002). System design using differentially fed artificial neural networks. In *Proceedings of TENCON'02.*

Manjunath, R., & Gurumurthy, K.S. (2005a). Hyperplanes generation through convolution with Gaussian kernels. IICAI

Manjunath, R., & Gurumurthy, K.S. (2005b). Bayesian estimator with differential feedback. In *Proceedings of MWSCAS.*

Chapter XIV
Performance Management

Srikanth Srinivas
Opex Partners, Inc., USA

ABSTRACT

The purpose of this chapter is to help you design a performance management framework that will result in choosing, successfully implementing, and getting significant benefits from e-supply chain technologies. The framework is designed to stimulate action by pinpointing where the gaps are, and leveraging technology to bridge those gaps. This is done using a balanced scorecard revolving around five critical variables: value, variety, velocity, variability, and visibility. The maturity level of each of these critical variables is classified using a six-level capability maturity continuum: ignorance, awareness, understanding, approach, action, and culture. This integrated approach of combining critical variables, balanced scorecard, and capability maturity helps leverage technology for the right purposes, and significantly improves the performance and productivity of the supply chain.

LITERATURE REVIEW

Supply chain literature tends to either focus on a process view or a functional view. In the process view, the focus is on processes, such as source, make, and deliver (Bolstorff & Rosenbaum, 2003; Hugos, 2003). In the functional view, the focus is on functions such as manufacturing, distribution, warehousing, and transportation (Robeson & Copacino, 1994; Tompkins & Harmelink, 2004). While this is good to understand and communicate the state of an organization, it is not conducive to understanding what the critical variables are, what the high impact set of changes that can be made are, and leveraging technology to the right set of activities. Keeping the primary focus on critical variables provides a way of looking at the relative impact of leveraging technology across the different processes and functions.

In addition, it is critical to learn from change management literature to ensure technology implementations result in successful change and performance improvements. Current change management literature focuses on people and organizational aspects of change (Cameron & Green, 2004; Hiatt, 2003).

Tracking progress against a change program needs to be done with a carefully selected balanced scorecard (Kaplan & Norton, 1996).

I end by describing supply chain quotient (SQ) as a way to use the performance management framework to assess the SQ or supply chain performance quotient of an organization—to understand the current state (baseline) on a maturity level continuum and where the key gaps are (assessment), and put in a structured implementation plan to leverage e-supply chain technologies to bridge those gaps systematically and gain competitive advantage.

INTRODUCTION

This chapter takes an action-oriented view of the supply chain (as opposed to a process or functional view) and combines that with a capability view of change management (as opposed to a people or organizational view) to provide a performance management framework (with a supply chain balanced scorecard, as opposed to an organizational balanced scorecard) that will result in choosing, successfully implementing, and getting significant benefits from e-supply chain technologies.

The key theme of the chapter is: "E-Supply chain technologies create superior value by making focused changes to critical variables" (see Srinivas [2003, 2005] for another perspective on the theme0. I start by first defining what a critical variable is, and then defining and identifying the critical variables that can be improved by e-supply chain technologies.

What gets measured gets done. To get the right things done, we need to take the trouble to measure the right things. It is important to build a performance management framework around the critical variables. The measures associated with each of the critical variables are defined and discussed. For example, for cash flow velocity, measures like cash-to-cash cycle are discussed. For shareholder value, measures like economic surplus are discussed. As each of the framework elements are discussed, the relevant e-supply chain technologies that create a large impact on that measure are discussed.

CRITICAL VARIABLES

A *variable* is something that *can* be changed, as opposed to a constant that cannot be changed. A *critical* variable is one where small, focused changes can make a big impact on the results that matter to an organization.

In every company I visit, I find a large number of employees spending much of their time and energy on "If only", "I wish", "Why can't they"—things that they cannot change. It is therefore worth highlighting explicitly that it is important to focus on variables—things *within your control* and that *can* be changed, and more importantly, to focus on *critical* variables—those that are *worth changing,* because they make a big impact on the results that matter.

For example, by better serving the 20% of customers that give you 80% of margins, you can improve the penetration in the account and thereby increase your profitability even further.

My focus will be on providing a framework for performance management. The specific measures to be used for each of the critical variables will vary from organization to organization, and therefore what is described here will only be indicative of what can be used within the unique context of a specific organization. However, the overall framework described here applies to every organization.

Value

The results that matter to an organization are primarily delivering superior value to its stakeholders—its customers, shareholders, and employees. While the relative importance of the stakeholders varies from organization to organization and from time to time within an organization, leaning too far in favor of one stakeholder at the cost of another stakeholder invariably causes problems in the future. Every e-supply chain technology evaluation and selection should start by understanding its impact on *all* stakeholders.

Shareholder Value

Many organizations reduce shareholder value to earnings per share (EPS). This then gets translated into targets and goals that focus on quarterly increases in EPS, many times at the cost of long-run cash flow returns. The most significant damage an EPS focus causes is making decisions without taking the cost of capital into account—sharp discounts at the end of the quarter to meet increasing quarterly targets can increase capacity and capital requirements considerably, create uncontrolled variability in demand patterns, stress employees, and create overload on supplier infrastructure and their ability to meet requirements.

For example, if the average demand is 100 units, by giving a 20% discount for customers placing orders in the last week, demand in the last week shoots up to 150 units. The system cannot cope with such sharp spikes in demand. So one of two things happens: (a) there is overtime all around, employees get stressed, and immense pressure is applied on the supplier network; or (b) the capacity is increased to cope with 150 units, in which case there is a lot of spare capacity during the rest of the quarter. In reality most organizations end up somewhere in between the two extremes and end up with both problems—stress on the network and poor use of capital.

Economic surplus (ES) overcomes this limitation by accounting for the cost of capital, and helps focus investments on those opportunities that earn returns above the opportunity cost of capital.

Moreover, it is a myth that the share market focuses only on short-term earnings. Studies have shown that there is a high correlation between economic surplus and share market valuation (Copeland, Koller, & Murrin, 2000). Companies that earn returns less than their cost of capital trade at or below their book value. Companies that earn returns well above their cost of capital trade at many times their book value. In other words, using ES as a measure also aligns the organization with the way investors evaluate their performance.

- **Economic surplus (ES)** = (return on invested capital (roic) % – weighted average cost of capital (wacc) %) × invested capital (ic)
- **ROIC%** = net operating profits less adjusted taxes (NOPLAT)/invested capital
- **Invested Capital** = operating working capital + net property, plant & equipment + other operating assets
- **WACC** = % of debt × after tax cost of debt + % of equity × opportunity cost of equity

For further details about each of these terms, see Copeland et al. (2005).

Customer Value

It is critical to monitor the impact of e-supply chain technologies on the value provided to customers.

For example, retailers like Wal-Mart and Target use GMROI (Gross Margin Return On Investment) as a key indicator of performance. If you are supplying goods to them, it would be good to track your GMROI, how that compares to your competitions' GMROI, and how you can provide superior GMROI.

- **GMROI** = GM% × inventory turns

For example, if your product has a gross margin of 30% and turns over 12 times a year, the GMROI is 3.6. In other words, for every dollar the retailer invests in your product, they get back $3.60 each year.

If you can find ways to increase your customers' inventory turns, you can provide more value to your customer while maintaining your margins. This will also help you get into a virtuous circle of market expansion. By measuring GMROI and improving it constantly, your interests get aligned with your customers, you give them fresher product which moves faster, and because you make more money for the retailer, you get more shelf space and the increased shelf space gives you more visibility and increases sales...which gets you into a virtuous circle of expanding market share, revenues, and profitability.

Cash contribution ratio (CCR) is another good customer value measure (Srinivas, 2005). It measures the cash contribution.

For example, if your customer pays you in 30 days, and your products turn over every 10 days, your customer has had the opportunity to earn cash 3 times before they have paid you. In this case the CCR will be 3.

Providing superior CCR, and highlighting your superior performance to your customers will give you a significant competitive advantage.

In summary, you want to measure the value you create for your customers. Some examples of such measures are the payback period for investments in your goods and services, the return they get on the investments they make in your goods and services, the savings they have in the total cost of ownership, and the fixed costs they can avoid by buying from you. By comparing your performance on the appropriate metrics with your competitors, you can identify where you provide superior value to your customers, and communicate that to your customers to expand your market presence. By improving your performance on the appropriate metrics over time, you can improve your market presence over time.

Employee Value

One of the most important contributors to employee energy, enthusiasm, and excitement is being in a place where they are growing—financially, in terms of their capabilities; and organizationally, in terms of their responsibilities, the roles they play, and the titles they have. On the other hand, a company that is shrinking and reducing in size can be one of the greatest sappers of energy and morale.

In other words, a good way to measure employee value will be to check if the pool of funds available for employees is growing. The amount of value added by employees (VAE) is the difference between the revenues earned from customers and the cost of goods and services purchased from suppliers. value added productivity (VAP) is the VAE/number of employees. If this number is growing from year to year, the pool of funds available to employees is growing. If this number is shrinking—even if the organization is growing by other metrics like shareholder value, revenues, market share, and so forth—the morale of the employees will tend to decline. This will make increases in the other areas unsustainable. It is therefore critical to maintain and grow VAP.

Key Measures for Value

1. **Customer value:** What is the return we are providing to the customer on their investment? Measures can include gross margin return on investment (GMROI) and cash contribution ratio (CCR).
2. **Shareholder value**: Economic surplus.
3. **Employee value:** Value added productivity. This helps answer the question: "Is the pool of funds available for employees increasing with time?"

Key Concepts Associated with Value

1. **Measure value from multiple perspectives:** The value customers receive, the value shareholders receive, and whether the pool of funds available to employees is increasing.
2. **Ensure that an 'economic surplus' measure is used to measure shareholder value.**
3. **Ensure you provide better value than your competition and communicate your superior value creation to your customers.**

Key Technologies Contributing to Value

1. **There are a number of optimization solutions** available that use a combination of linear programming and mixed integer programming algorithms to optimize inventory, transportation costs, and total landed cost. There are solutions tailored to solve specific problems."
2. **Strategic questions:** Should I consolidate distribution centers (DCs)? What would be the best place to open a new DC?
3. **Near-term planning questions:** How much should I make? Where? Where should I source from?
4. **Execution questions:** How do I consolidate orders into truckloads?
5. **There are a few solutions** that claim to maximize revenues and margins. In my opinion, this is a gap that can be filled by new and innovative technologies.
6. **Very few solutions** focus on maximizing economic surplus.
7. **There are no solutions** to maximize customer and employee value.

Critical Variables That Contribute to Value

You cannot improve value by improving value or by wishing for an improvement in value. Value is an effect. In order to improve value, you need to change the underlying causes of value. You need to change the variables that create those effects. The critical variables that have a strong connection with value are:

1. **Variety**
2. **Velocity**
3. **Variability**
4. **Visibility**

Figure 1 provides an overview of the critical variables.

Subsequent sections get into the detail of each of these critical variables.

VARIETY

Variety is one of the most critical variables, and also the one least used in practice. Henry Ford was the master of *eliminating* variety. He said, "You can have any color car as long as it is black." He was so successful at eliminating variety that the black Ford Model T became the best selling model in its time. He also brought down the cost of the car manifold and made it affordable to the common man.

Figure 1. Critical variables

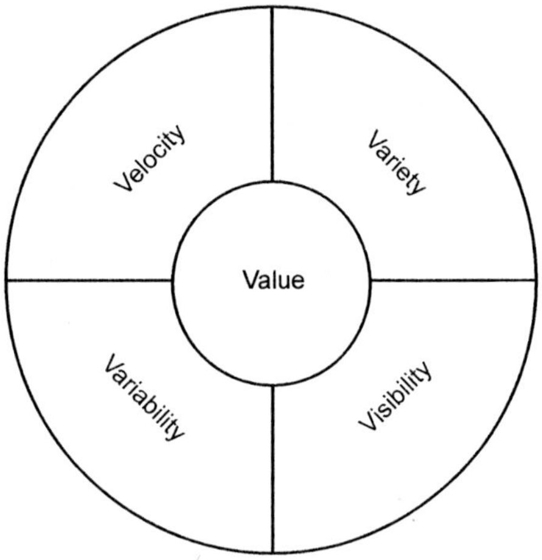

For example, a more contemporary example of a company that focuses on eliminating variety is Southwest Airlines. They operate only one type of aircraft—Boeing 737. That means they need to train their engineers, pilots, and flight attendants on only one type of aircraft; they need to keep only one set of spare parts; and they need only one FAA certification. This focus on eliminating variety is one of the key reasons for Southwest continuing to be the lowest cost airline.

Jet Blue is another example of a company that eliminates variety by operating only one type of aircraft.

All too often e-supply chain technologies are introduced when variety in operations makes it too complex to manage efficiently. On many of these occasions, effort should first be put into *eliminating* or *minimizing* variety *before* deploying technology. Any time you hear people saying the implementation failed because of performance problems or because the solution was too complex, variety is a good variable to check first before looking at improving the technology portion of the solution.

A key question to ask is, "Are the costs of differentiation and increased variety more than compensated for by increased revenues?" If not, eliminate it. The cost of variety is invisible and insidious. Most importantly, it drains management time and attention, and distracts them from what matters most.

On the other hand, customers demand more and more differentiated offerings. If there is a way you can deal with variety without its associated costs of complexity, you have got the best of both worlds—the variety that customers love, with the simplicity that employees and shareholders love.

For example, for Southwest Airlines to grow, they need to introduce more variety in the routes they offer. But at the same time, in order to eliminate the complexities associated with variety, they have to choose routes that have good synergy with the one aircraft they have chosen, and with the type of customers they have chosen to serve.

Wal-Mart has limited variety in its store formats. The Supercenter—which combines grocery along with their traditional product range—has been the reason for their astronomical growth in recent years. This meant providing more product variety at the shelves for the consumers shopping at Wal-Mart. At the same time, they have eliminated complexities associated with the increased variety by standardizing store formats and keeping the same distribution strategy that was the foundation of their success.

For most organizations it is more about *managing* variety than about eliminating variety. While Henry Ford focused on eliminating variety, Jack Welch focused on managing variety effectively. His primary focus was on distinguishing between good variety and bad variety. In his early days as CEO of General Electric, he distilled it down to a few words, "Number 1 or Number 2. Or Fix, Sell or Close the business." (Welch, 2001) Using market share as a measure of good variety, he identified the good businesses and nourished them. In turn, the businesses flourished with all that good nourishment. Rather than waste scarce management time and attention on the business with poor market share (bad variety), he instituted a policy of fix (if they were a close number 3 or 4, and it could be fixed in a defined timeframe), sell (if there was enough value in the business for someone else to be interested), or close the business altogether if it did not meet any of the criteria listed above. Just like a company is a portfolio of businesses, a business is a portfolio of customers, employees, processes, facilities, products, and suppliers. The same idea of good and bad variety can be applied in this context as well.

The 80/20 rule is one of the best ways to measure variety. What this rule states is that 20% of causes contribute to 80% of the results. The 20% of the businesses, customers, employees, processes, facilities, and products that contribute to 80% of the revenues, economic surplus, and cash flow represent good variety. The 20% of the business, customers, employees, processes, facilities, products, and suppliers that contribute to 80% of the economic losses and unproductive assets represent bad variety.

Good Variety

We need to have measures that identify how much of our products constitute good variety. Every product that is introduced needs to be designed, developed, and marketed. It also needs plant and equipment to manufacture it, and the infrastructure to distribute it. A good proportion of this is fixed costs that have to be recovered. A good way to measure the extent of good variety is to find the number of products that have earned money to recover all these fixed costs (over and above the variable costs incurred to sell each unit). This is the % of products that have crossed the fixed cost threshold.

Good Variety Differentiation

Good variety differentiation can come in many forms. For example, the 20% of customers contributing to 80% of revenues can be provided superior *Value* with better pricing and customer service; the 20% of products contributing to 80% of economic surplus can be nourished with superior *Velocity* with more frequent manufacturing and replenishment; the 20% of the facilities that contribute to 80% of shipments can be made more efficient by implementing technology that provides real-time inventory *Visibility*; the 20% of distributors that contribute to 80% of revenues can be supported by better forecasts that reduce *Variability* and improve forecast accuracy. In other words, good variety differentiation can be achieved by impacting the set of relevant critical variables and making them better for this 20% subset. By measuring the extent to which this is done, you can get in the habit of continuously nourishing the good variety and making it grow.

For example, airlines give preferential treatment to their frequent flyers. The Executive Platinum members get through lines faster (better Velocity), get free upgrades (better Value), get special phone numbers with more consistent service (less Variability), and get access to preferential information first (superior Visibility).

Bad Variety Management

Equally important, we need to make sure that bad variety does not drain away capital, and the energy, enthusiasm, and excitement of management talent. Bad variety management can come in many forms. For example, pricing for the 20% of customers contributing to 80% of economic losses can be increased to improve their *Value* contribution; *Velocity* of the 20% of products contributing to 80% of economic losses can be reduced by making less frequent manufacturing and replenishment so that they do not drag down the performance of the winners; the items that have shipped the least can be moved to the back of the Distribution Center so it does not clutter the *Visibility* of the big movers; the distributors that are small and with high *Variability* in demand do not drive the complexity of the forecasting technology. In other words, bad variety management can be achieved by impacting the set of relevant critical variables and making sure they do not come in the way of making good variety nourish and prosper. By measuring the extent to which this is done, you can get in the habit of continuously making sure bad variety does not come in the way of making good variety nourish and prosper.

For example, U.S. car manufacturers have a much greater variety in brands and models compared to the Japanese. While the Big 3 Japanese car firms have just two brands each—a basic brand and a luxury brand (Toyota & Lexus, Honda & Acura, Nissan & Infiniti), the U.S. car manufacturers have a much higher number of brands. General Motors has Chevrolet, Buick, Pontiac, GMC, Saturn, Hummer, Saab, Cadillac, Holden, Opel, and Vauxhall. Ford has Ford, Lincoln, Mercury, Mazda, Volvo, Jaguar, and Aston Martin. The American car manufacturers have done a poor job of managing their bad variety. As a result, it has dragged down their performance considerably, as opposed to the Japanese, who have managed their variety much better.

Key Measures for Variety

1. **Good variety:** Identifying it and communicating the winners to everyone. Keeping track of the percentage of products that have earned their keep (recovered their fixed costs invested in them).
2. **Good variety differentiation:** Nourishing and making this grow.
3. **Bad variety management:** Making sure this does not come in the way of the winners.

Key Concepts Associated with Variety

1. **Variety or complexity tends to slow down systems**, demand more monitoring and interventions from management, and create confusion and communication gaps. More importantly, all of this can be invisible and difficult to track down. It can also result in poorer quality as processes are tweaked to make things work. If we can resolve all this satisfactorily and add variety without increasing the complexity, then we have a good system in place.
2. **Distinguish between good and bad variety in terms of businesses**, and within the businesses, in terms of customers, employees, products, processes, facilities, and suppliers.
3. **Feed the good variety**, and make it grow and prosper.
4. **Starve the bad variety** and make it shrink. More importantly, prevent it from dragging the rest of the organization down, and draining the energy, enthusiasm, and excitement of scarce management talent.
5. **Are the costs of differentiation and increased variety more than compensated for by increased revenues?**
6. **Are the complexities and costs associated with increased variety worth it?**

Key Technologies Contributing to Variety

1. **Procurement:** A number of technology solutions have addressed eliminating variety by standardizing items and suppliers, consolidating volume of purchase, and reducing costs in strategic sourcing, and direct and indirect procurement.

2. **Planning:** Eliminating variety by standardizing processes, and creating common frameworks to plan, collect actual data, report variances, and analyze root causes.
3. **Good variety differentiation and bad variety management are not addressed adequately by e-supply chain technology solutions.** Most organizations currently rely on spreadsheets on an individual basis rather than as a corporate-wide initiative (if they do this at all).

VELOCITY

There are two fundamental ways to increase operational velocity:

1. **Reducing time**
2. **Increasing frequency**

The result of increasing operational velocity will translate into an increase in asset velocity—inventory and cash flow. Far too often, organizations try to increase asset velocity by reducing inventory without appropriate changes in policies and processes to reduce time and/or increase frequency. This results in poorer customer service. What you want to do is make underlying changes in operational velocity and see the flow through effect of the improvement in asset velocity.

Time

Reducing time and improving velocity has been the focus of attention for methods such as Lean Manufacturing (Womack & Jones, 1996). A number of e-supply chain technology solutions focus on understanding and compressing process time requirements.

We need to distinguish between the following time elements:

1. **Need time:** The time between when a customer requests a product or service, and when they need to get that product or service fulfilled.
2. **Lead time:** The time it takes for you to fulfill a customer request.
3. **Cycle time:** The time taken for each of the process elements.
4. **White space:** The time between process elements, spent waiting—for people, resources, assets, materials, cash, and so forth to start a process element.

The gap between need time and lead time is what creates the need for inventory. If you turn on the switch, the electricity gets made, transmitted, and powers your bulb—all in an instant. There is no gap between need time and lead time. There is therefore no need for inventory.

For example, companies like Dell have worked hard to reduce the lead time to less than five days by reducing cycle times, and more importantly, reducing the white space between process elements by synchronizing the various process elements both within its organization and with supplier organizations. At the same time, Dell has worked on your expectations to be OK with a need time of five days (to give up the instant gratification that comes from picking up the coolest gadget from the store the same instant you had the desire for it). As a result, Dell does not need to keep any finished goods inventory.

E-supply chain technologies have played a very critical role in making this possible by providing the visibility needed for effective synchronization and compressing the time requirements.

The process elements themselves may be value adding (i.e., contribute towards what the customer would regard as valuable), value supporting (i.e., the organization needs this to support customer value-added tasks), and waste (contributes neither to customer value nor to support a value-creating process). By eliminating processes that are "waste" and minimizing "value supporting" processes, cycle times can be improved significantly.

Frequency

While the Time element of Velocity has had a lot of attention, the Frequency aspect of velocity has been ignored largely. Frequency of sourcing, manufacturing, replenishment, and customer service has a critical role in improving velocity, and this has been largely untapped. Technology solutions available today also tend not to focus on this aspect of improving velocity. This aspect of improving velocity is ripe for streamlining. It is worth learning from the examples being set by the leaders in this area.

For example, retailers like 7-11 Japan are pioneers in this area. Their stores get replenished multiple times a day. They turn their inventory over 50 times a year, which is close to 10 times the industry average.

Retailers like Wal-Mart and Target have a streamlined frequency for replenishing their stores—ranging from daily for the high-volume stores, to weekly for the lower-volume stores.

Manufacturers like Proctor & Gamble and Unilever have consciously invested in improving the manufacturing frequency from monthly to weekly, and are working towards a daily frequency.

Improving frequency directly improves the velocity of operations and reduces cycle stock requirements dramatically. Since forecasts have to be made over a shorter duration, the safety stock requirements also decline.

If the number of products is large, you can also think in terms of a stratified manufacturing frequency, with good variety being made daily and the rest being made weekly. If 20% of the products contribute to 80% of the volume, by making that 20% subset daily, you create a significant improvement in asset velocity while managing far less complexity, as the weighted average asset velocity with a stratified approach comes to 0.8 * 1 (for the 80% that gets made daily) + 0.2 * 7 (for the 20% that gets made weekly) which is 2.2, compared to an average of 7, if everything was made weekly.

Similar ideas can be applied for how often:

1. **Vendors** replenish their inventories
2. **DCs** replenish their inventories from the plants
3. **Customer DCs** are replenished by your DCs
4. **Customer store locations** are replenished (DSD—direct store delivery).

While improving frequency, setup time and costs have to be taken into account. However, setup times are given more importance than necessary. Not enough time goes into questions such as:

1. **How can setup times be reduced to systematically increase the frequency?**
2. **Are we really using this to capacity?** Is this really a constraint? In other words, will we really lose productivity by incurring this setup time?
3. **What are the benefits of imposing such rigor on frequency?** Are they worth having? If so, how can we overcome the limitations of setup time to achieve those benefits?

Setup costs, including waste during the initial/setup portion of the run, can be more difficult to reduce compared to setup times, but can be achieved (Womack & Jones, 1996).

Just like manufacturing frequency needs to be traded off with setup time and costs, replenishment frequency will have to be traded off with truckload considerations. If truckload considerations come in the way of increasing frequency, multi-stop routes that together make a truckload can be another strategy to increase the replenishment frequency.

Asset Velocity

The important thing to understand is that asset velocity should be the result of making improvements in operational velocity—reducing time and increasing frequency. Without these underlying changes, inventory reduction will only result in lost sales and poorer customer service.

Asset velocity has two components:

1. **Inventory**
2. **Cash flow**

Inventory turns or the number of days of inventory are the two most popular ways to measure inventory velocity. Inventory turns measures the number of times the inventory turns over during a year. It is calculated as the annual Cost Of Goods Sold (COGS)/Average Inventory during the year. The number of days of inventory is the Average Inventory/Average Daily Cost Of Goods Sold.

- **Cash flow velocity** = accounts receivable days + inventory days - accounts payable days

For example, companies like Dell, McDonald's, and Wal-Mart have focused consciously on improving cash flow velocity and now have a negative cash flow velocity. They have reduced their inventory days and accounts receivable days to such an extent that it is less than their accounts payable days.

Key Measures for Velocity

1. **Frequency:** Manufacturing, Replenishment, Service frequency
2. **Time:** Need time, Lead time, Cycle time, White space
3. **Asset velocity:** Inventory turns, Cash flow velocity (also referred to as cash conversion cycle)

Key Concepts Associated with Velocity

1. **Asset velocity** is the result of improving operational velocity.
2. **The gap between need time and lead time** determines the amount of inventory needed.
3. **Frequency is a largely untapped way of increasing velocity**. Key questions to ask in relation to leveraging frequency include: Is it worth imposing rigor in frequency? What are the benefits of imposing such rigor? Will they be worth it? What are the risks in imposing such rigor? Are they worth taking?

Key Technologies Contributing to Velocity

1. **A number of technology solutions address the time element of velocity.** They have played a very critical role in providing the visibility needed for effective synchronization and compressing the time requirements.
2. **There are a number of technology solutions that are compliant with "Lean"** (Womack & Jones, 1996) and help you with value stream mapping, a process that helps classify the process elements, document cycle times, and white space.
3. **There are few technology solutions that address frequency.** This is an area that is ripe to be addressed, as it is a much simpler route to improving velocity compared to other methods.
4. **While there are a number of e-supply chain technology solutions available to reduce inventory**, technologies to optimize

all of the components of cash flow velocity are not as common. This is a gap that is ripe to be addressed.

VARIABILITY

Deming was one of the foremost thinkers on variability. He provided Japanese management with theories and methods that prepared the roadmap of Japanese economic success, which has since been expanded upon as TQM and Six Sigma implementations by organizations across the globe (Deming, 1986; Latzko & Saunders, 1995).

There will always be variability—in the inputs you receive, the outputs you produce, and the products and services you deliver. The key is to contain the variability such that it is well below limits of acceptability. So if your customer will accept weights to the nearest gram, and the variability of your processes is in milligrams, your product variability should not cause any problems to your customer.

In order to reach that level of sophistication, it is important to distinguish between common causes that cause random variability, and special causes. If there are no special causes, all the data points will be within upper and lower control limits. Such a process is said to be stable or in control. The limits will depend on the nature of distribution. For normal distribution, three standard deviations on either side of the mean form the upper and lower control limits. A number of technology solutions exist to calculate and map control limits.

For example, all too often the salesperson who exceeds quota is rewarded and courted, and the ones that do not are shunned or fired. By understanding the variability and the distribution pattern, it is possible to answer questions such as: (a) Was this just a random variation that he may not be able to repeat again? (b) Was this a common cause or was this an exception? Examples of exceptions could include poor training by the manager, narrow territory assignment, getting lucky with a large order, and so forth.

It is useful to divide variability into output variability, process variability, and input variability.

Output Variability

1. **Customer demand fluctuates:** Forecasts of customer demand can be compared against actual demand to calculate the forecast accuracy. mean absolute deviation (MAD) is one popular way to measure forecast accuracy.
2. **Product quality also fluctuates:** Product quality can be measured in terms of yield (% of good product/total product) or defect rates (% of bad product/total product).

Process Variability

1. **Process capability fluctuates:** Fill rate measures the percentage of orders that were delivered in full on time.
2. **Process compliance fluctuates:** Plan compliance measures the deviations between what was planned and what was actually produced, delivered, and sold. Understanding the root causes of these deviations will help plan better and execute the plan better.
3. **Process control:** It is important to understand whether the process is in control. The number of data points that are more than three standard deviations away from the mean is an indication of the extent to which the process is out of control. What we want is zero data points outside these limits. Companies that have made great strides in process control measure the number of data points that are outside six sigma limits. This can be used to truly understand variability

in quality, outputs (production, sales), and inputs (raw material arrivals, defects).

Input Variability

Supplier capabilities fluctuate.

1. **Lead time variability** measures the variability in lead time.
2. **Supplier defects and yields** measure the variability quality of goods and services provided by suppliers.

Key Measures for Variability

1. **Output variability:** Demand variability, forecast accuracy, yield.
2. **Process variability:** Fill rate, plan compliance.
3. **Supplier variability:** Supplier lead time variability, yield.

Key Concepts Associated with Variability

1. **All processes have variability:** There is variability in the inputs they receive, the outputs they produce, and in the resources, costs, and time they consume to produce those outputs.
2. **Understand variability:** Minimize it where possible; if not, minimize its impact by buffering against the variability where it matters most.
3. **Differentiate between common causes that do not need intervention** and special causes that can be improved.

Key Technologies Contributing to Variability

A number of mature technology solutions are available to understand variability, detect whether processes are stable, highlight the exceptions, create forecasts, and calculate buffers required to protect against a given level of variability.

VISIBILITY

The effects of visibility have been described effectively by Senge (1990). The beer game illustrates the distortions caused by poor visibility. The three participants in the game—the retailer, the wholesaler, and the marketer/manufacturer—share little data among themselves other than the orders placed. Each participant also tries to maximize his or her "patch." As a result, when there is a small change in demand at the retailer's end, it causes a "bullwhip" effect that results in bigger changes in "demand" for the wholesaler, and even bigger changes in "demand" for the marketer/manufacturer. First there is growing demand that cannot be met. Orders build throughout the system. Inventories get depleted. Backlogs grow. Then the beer arrives en masse while incoming orders suddenly decline, and everyone ends up with large inventories they cannot unload.

While the beer game describes visibility problems *between* organizations, there are equally prevalent visibility problems *within* organizations. Organizations create teams to ensure specialized competencies are created and nurtured. Over time, each of the teams starts to work within its silos, and the walls that get created distort visibility across the organization (the "fog" effect). Each team begins to create its own set of numbers (forecasts, inventory buffers) that result in a lot of local optimization, but at the cost of global optimization. This distorts "demand" and creates "bullwhip" effects within the organization.

A number of collaboration and workflow tools are available to solve visibility problems both within the organization and between organizations. Technologies like barcode, EDI, and enterprise resource planning (ERP) have played a critical role in improving visibility. Emerging technologies like RFID (Radio Frequency Identification) will result in an order of magnitude improvement in visibility at the individual case or pallet level, as opposed to the product level visibility that is currently prevalent, and create all the benefits that can come from such improved visibility.

For example, you know that the average time spent by an item in the DC is 5 days. With RFID technology, you can get fine-grained visibility of the movements of individual pallets and cases. With that you can find out how many cases spent less than 2 days, how many were around for more than 7 days, what the root causes of the differences are, and eliminate these root causes to improve velocity all around.

In addition, because of the automatic detection capabilities of RFID, system inventory will be more closely aligned with the real, physical inventory. People's faith in the inventory shown in the system will improve, and they will tend to keep less (rather, hide) just-in-case stock. It can also help trigger replenishment processes automatically.

For example, Wal-Mart has leveraged RFID's improved visibility to streamline processes and achieve a 16% reduction in stock-outs and two-thirds drop in replenishment times. The company used RFID to generate automatic pick-lists of the specific items needed to restock shelves. As customers go through checkout, they combine point-of-sale data on their purchases with RFID-generated data on what is available in the backroom to produce the pick lists. Basically, RFID enabled Wal-Mart to change its pick-list generation process from a reactive one that required associates to take the initiative to determine restocking needs, to a proactive one, in which lists are automatically created in real time, based on sales. (Johnson, 2006)

In creating visibility performance measures, it is useful to think in terms of internal visibility, customer visibility, and supplier visibility.

Customer Visibility

1. **%POS volume:** Point-of-sale data refers to the data pertaining to what actually sold at the store. Many retailers now provide POS data to their suppliers. This gives a true indication of what is selling at the store level, as opposed to what was bought by the retailer (which may still be sitting in a DC). Given our discussion about the "bullwhip" effects caused by multiple layers in the supply chain, as the %POS volume increases, the "bullwhip" effect should decrease. By measuring the %POS volume, you can look at where you are and what you need to do to improve it.
2. **%Collaboration volume:** There are a number of collaboration technologies available that help retailers, wholesalers, and manufacturers share their forecast, capacity, demand, inventory, and so forth. As conditions change, the forecasts can be changed, and the suppliers can be better prepared. By measuring the %Collaboration volume, you can look at where you are and what you need to do to improve.

Internal Visibility

1. **One number:** This measures the extent to which all the different organizations see and use the same numbers for decision making. ERP systems have this as their core value proposition—the ability for the entire organization to work off one set of numbers.
2. **Update frequency:** This can measure the frequency with which updates are made. For example, are inventory updates made in real time? Are they done by the end of the day?

How can this be improved? When do the books get closed after the period is over? Can you see monthly results one business day after the month has closed? After seven business days? How can this be improved? Can you get true visibility on what happened last week by Monday morning? Can you understand all the variances and root causes, and apply the lessons learned for the coming week?

Supplier Visibility

%VMI volume: Vendor-managed inventory (VMI), as the name implies, makes the vendor responsible for the management of the inventory. This helps foster improved visibility between the organizations. For suppliers to manage inventory well, they need visibility into forecasts and the accuracy of the forecasts. By combining this with the actual withdrawals, and their replenishment lead times and variability in lead times, they can manage their inventories efficiently. By measuring the %VMI volume, you can look at where you are and what you need to do to improve. There are a number of technology solutions available today that address this problem effectively. For manufacturers providing VMI services to retailers, POS data can serve as an effective foundation for improved visibility into what is actually selling at the stores.

For Example, Wal-Mart pioneered supplier visibility with its Retail Link. It continues to be the benchmark for supplier visibility and the power it provides for superior decision making by all participants in the supply chain. It provides visibility to suppliers on what has happened—POS (Point Of Sale), Inventory—and all of the factors the company needs to make smarter decisions about what to expect in the future in terms of demographics by store clusters, sales forecasts, and expected volume of business. For suppliers participating in the RFID pilot, they also provide visibility to every movement (DC to store, store backroom to floor, etc.), within hours of the movement happening.

Just like bar codes have become mainstream technology, RFID will mature and become mainstream technology in the years to come. When that happens, the percentage of volume tagged through RFID will serve as an effective measure of visibility at a granular level—visibility at the individual items, cases, and pallets, as opposed to the product level.

Key Measures for Visibility

1. **Supplier visibility:** Percentage of VMI, collaboration volume.
2. **Internal visibility:** Percentage of DCs with hourly/daily inventory updates, percentage of DSDs with daily updates, percentage of RFID volume, one number, time to close period.
3. **Customer visibility:** Percentage of VMI, POS, collaboration volume.

Key Concepts Associated with Visibility

1. **Improve visibility within the organization** by designing policies, processes, performance measures, and systems that breakdown the visibility barriers between marketing, sales, planning, manufacturing, distribution, and transportation.
2. **Gain visibility to customers' sales at the stores**, the events and promotions they are planning and their impact on forecasts, and the inventories they have at the stores and DCs.
3. **Provide visibility to suppliers**.

Key Technologies Contributing to Visibility

1. **E-supply chain technologies** have played a very critical role in improving visibility significantly.
2. **Bar code and EDI** have transformed the industry and provided visibility across organizations very effectively.
3. **ERP solutions** have greatly enhanced internal visibility by providing one view across the entire organization.
4. **A variety of e-commerce, workflow, and collaboration solutions and standards** have greatly contributed to visibility across the supply chain and its participants.
5. **Standards like XML and technologies like Web services** have greatly simplified the process of exchanging information between organizations, and therefore increased collaboration and visibility.
6. **Technologies like RFID** will revolutionize the granularity of visibility available by going from product level to case and pallet level visibility.

PERFORMANCE MANAGEMENT FRAMEWORK

It is now time to turn our attention to taking all of the individual elements we have discussed and putting them together in an overall framework. Figure 2 summarizes the performance management framework.

Below is a summary of the framework:

1. **The measures** in the framework are connected in a cause-effect relationship.

Figure 2. Performance management framework

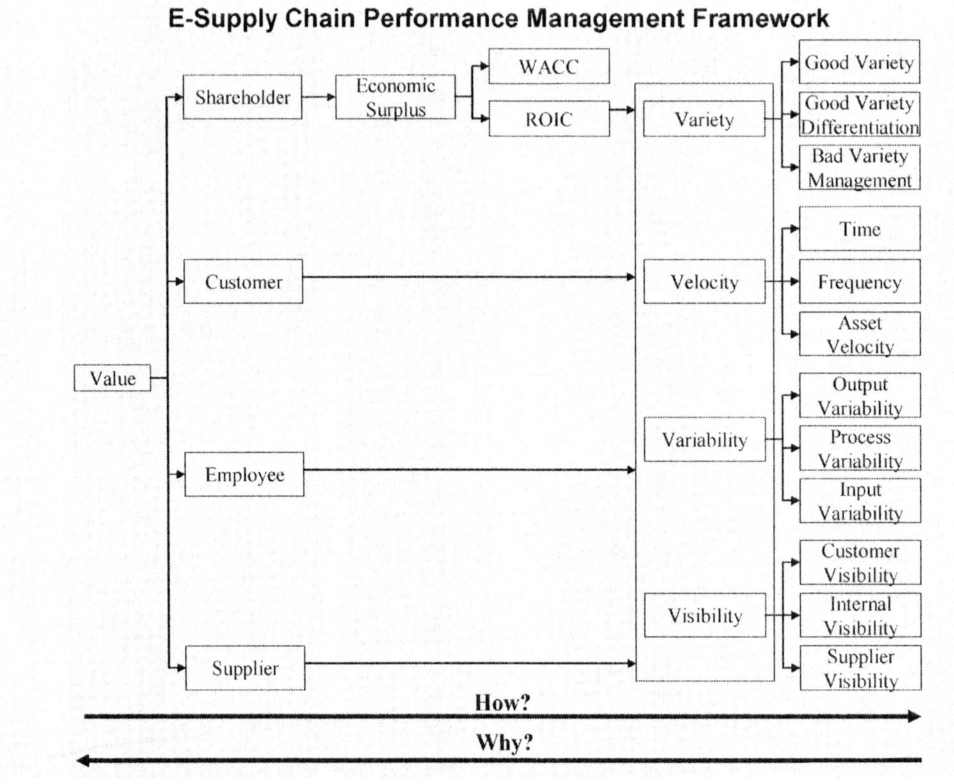

2. **The framework** describes goals—"what" should be measured. It does not describe the actual measures.
3. **The measures** should be designed with key principles in mind.

Cause-Effect Relationship

The measures in the framework are connected in a cause-effect relationship. As you go from left to right, you get the "How" question answered. As you go from right to left, you get the "Why" question answered. For example, to answer "How" to improve the critical variable velocity, you go to the right and you find that you can do that by working on time, frequency, and asset velocity.

When creating measures, it is important for every one (not just the person who created the measure) to clearly understand why that measure is important and what it contributes to. Otherwise, the measure will become just another number in a report. It will not change behavior or influence decision making. Laying it out in such a visual framework will also help you think through whether the cause-effect relationships are really true or not. We often make implicit assumptions, and laying them out explicitly will force us to examine those assumptions more carefully.

Goals

The framework describes goals—"what" should be measured. It does not describe the actual measures. This is because the framework is applicable across different contexts. The specific measures will be very specific to each organization's unique context, defined in terms of where improvements will result in competitive advantage. What gets measured gets done. So to get the right things done, we need to make sure that the right measures are in place. A number of measures have been discussed throughout this chapter. These can be used as starting points and then tailored to suit your unique situation.

For example, the framework highlights frequency. Whether it is manufacturing frequency, replenishment frequency, or sales call frequency will depend on what is currently constraining performance.

Principles

When designing the performance management framework, keep the following principles in mind:

1. Measures should be aligned with purpose.
2. Build the measures that highlight the right set of critical variables that will help you achieve your purpose.
3. While this framework applies to a wide range of companies, no two companies will have the same set of measures.
4. Take the trouble to make sure you measure what needs to get done.
5. Leverage this framework to align the entire organization.
6. Measure the value you are providing to your customers. This will serve as a constant reminder to make sure you provide superior value

SQ: SUPPLY CHAIN QUOTIENT

The performance management framework described in the previous section can be used to understand the current state (baseline) on a maturity level continuum, where the key gaps are (assessment), and put in a structured implementation plan to leverage e-supply chain technologies to bridge those gaps systematically and gain competitive advantage. Figure 3 describes this pictorially, and the text that follows explains the different elements of the picture. (The numbers in the picture are for illustrative purposes only)

In most organizations, each technology solution is evaluated independently. This framework

Figure 3. Supply chain quotient (SQ)

	Critical Variable	Goal	Maturity Level							CQ	Comments	Results	Effort
			Ignorance	Awareness	Understanding	Approach	Action	Culture	N/A				
			Why Bother?	Why Change?	What to Do?	How to Do?	Doing now	Will Continue Doing					
		Score->	0	1	2	3	4	5	5				
1	**Value**	Shareholder Value		0.3				0.7		**3.8**		Med	High
2		Customer Value		0.5		0.5				**2**		Low	Low
3		Employee Value		1						**1**		Med	Low
4	**Variety**	Good Variety		1						**1**		Low	Low
5		Good Variety Differentiation		1	(X)					**1**		Low	Low
6		Bad Variety Management		1						**1**		Low	Low
7	**Velocity**	Time					1			**4**		High	High
8		Frequency	0.3	0.3	0.4					**1.1**		Low	Low
9		Asset Velocity						1		**5**		High	Med
10	**Variability**	Output Variability					1			**4**		High	High
11		Process Variability						1		**5**		High	High
12		Input Variability			1	(Y)				**2**		High	High
13	**Visibility**	Customer Visibility		1						**1**		Low	Low
14		Internal Visibility		0.2			0.8			**3.4**		High	Med
15		Supplier Visibility							1	**5**		None	None
16	**Overall**	Continuous Improvement				1				**3**		High	High
17		Performance Focus	1							**0**		Low	Low
18		Synergy			1					**2**		Med	Low
19		Winner's Mindset		1						**1**		Low	Low
20		Agile	1							**0**		None	None
		Total Score	**2.3**	**7.3**	**2.4**	**1.5**	**2.8**	**2.7**	**1**	**46.3**	<-CQ		

serves to highlight where the gaps are, and the right technology solution can then be implemented to bridge those gaps. In other words, this framework helps evaluate the different technology solutions relative to each other and identifies the most relevant ones—the ones that will contribute most to improving competitive advantage.

Figure 3 succinctly summarizes the current state of an organization:

1. **The critical variables and the goals**
2. **The maturity level** of the organization
3. **A scoring mechanism** to quantify the current maturity level
4. **Current initiatives being undertaken** and their impact in terms of maturity improvement (the arrows can be used to depict what the current maturity level is and the maturity level that will be reached at the successful completion of the initiative).
5. **Initiatives undertaken in the past:** The effort and the return on the effort in terms of superior results, so we can learn from the past and not repeat the same mistakes. Since the primary purpose of this framework is to identify the best uses of technology, studying historical patterns of returns from technology initiatives will help guide decisions on the most successful applications of technology.

Critical Variables

In addition to the critical variables described in previous sections (value, variety, velocity, visibility, variability), there are five overall variables that need to be managed well in order for organizations to compete successfully and win.

For detailed illustrations, stories, and examples highlighting these five overall variables, see Srinivas (2005).

Continuous Improvement

Nothing stays still. In this world of fierce competition and fleeting opportunities, to stand still is to be left behind. In order to cope with these ever-evolving market dynamics, the organization has to sustain a culture of continuous improvement.

Performance Focus

Organizations tend to get carried away by fads and what is hot at the moment. They can get process centric and get all carried away trying to reengineer processes and perfecting them. They can get carried away by tools and techniques. TQM, Six Sigma, and Lean are all excellent tools, but they are merely means to an end. They can get carried away by technologies like RFID, Web, and optimization. To be performance focused, the organization must have a culture where the focus is on enhancing performance, and the right tools, technologies, and processes are deployed to sustain superior performance. In general, enhancing performance will entail balanced attention to a number of parameters. We started with a focus on performance measures. We then looked at designing and strengthening policies such as manufacturing and replenishment frequency. We looked at processes to reduce variability and bring them under control. It is important to take people along a maturity continuum—all the way from ignorance to embedding the right practices in the organization's culture. Finally, it is the passion that must pull it all together and drive performance. You have to pay attention to all the parameters needed to enhance performance. In other words, performance has to take center stage, and all the other parameters should be used as necessary to contribute to performance improvements.

Synergy

When the lead goose flaps its wings, it creates uplift for the one immediately following. By flying in a "V" formation, the whole flock flies at least 70% more distance than if each bird flew on its own. You find synergy all around you in nature. However, it is not so common within organizations. There are walls erected between functions and between business units. There is a lot of internal political competition between the different teams and within individuals in a team that destroys synergy. What is worse, it creates negative energy. To maximize performance, the organization must change its course and set itself on a path of synergy within the organization, as well as tap into the energy, enthusiasm, and excitement of every individual in the organization in a constructive and aligned manner.

Winner's Mindset

Organizations tend to look at problems rather than opportunities. They tend to reward the people who put out fires, and manage the many crises that all organizations inevitably face. Rarely does the individual who has taken all the proactive measures and completed his work smoothly without any news or noise get the attention and rewards. As a result, it takes effort to unlearn these habits and create a winner's mindset—where people want to be proactive, want to find answers to problems (rather than find problems with every answer), where they believe that it is possible even if it is difficult (rather than it may be possible but it is too difficult). Creating a winner's mindset is critical to competitive advantage.

Agility

There are many definitions of agility. The one I use is best described using an analogy. A plane starts in London and is headed for Argentina. If it is one degree off course, it will end up in Mexico instead. Most planes are off course by more than a degree 95% of the time, because of changes in wind conditions, the load patterns in the plane, and so forth. They still end up in Argentina. How do they manage to do that? By having constant course correction. Similarly, businesses will be buffeted about by market conditions. They should fully expect to be more than one degree off during the course of a week. An agile business is one that can make course corrections in time to make a difference. If figures are only reviewed monthly, and the monthly numbers only come out five days after a month is closed, it is too late to make course corrections. If figures are reviewed weekly, and the numbers are out the day after the week is closed, you get 52 opportunities to make course corrections to an annual plan. There is a reasonable chance of being an agile business.

Maturity Level

For each of the critical variables (e.g., velocity) and goals (e.g., frequency), the organization's maturity level can be classified into one of six categories:

1. **Ignorance:** There is no organizational knowledge of the importance of this goal. The key questions people ask in relation to this goal are: Why bother? Given everything else on my plate, why should I give this any attention? Why me?
2. **Awareness:** The organization is aware of the importance of this goal. It knows the answer to the question: Why we need to change?
3. **Understanding:** In addition to understanding the importance of the goal, the organization now knows "what" needs to be done.
4. **Approach:** Now the organization knows "how" to achieve this goal.
5. **Action:** This goal is already being achieved satisfactorily.
6. **Culture:** After the action is repeated many times, it becomes an integral way of doing business, an inherent part of the culture, and stands the test of time. In other words, goals continue to be met, even when people change and organization structures change, because it is deeply embedded in the culture of the organization. See Hellriegel, Slocum, and Woodman (2001) for a detailed discussion on culture, and the relationship between culture and an organization's performance.

Each maturity level builds on the previous one and extends the maturity of the organization. The arrow above maturity level highlights the fact that organizations have to progress from one level to the next in a staged manner.

Scores

The organization's maturity on each goal can be rated on a scale from 0 to 5 (Ignorance to Culture). By systematically looking at the current state of each goal, this framework helps establish the organization's supply chain quotient.

To account for the fact that some goals may be partially accomplished (replenishment frequency is being done, but manufacturing frequency is only at an awareness stage), the same one point could potentially be distributed across the different stages. The comments field can be used to document the reason for the same goal in multiple stages of the maturity continuum.

The overall score and the scores in the individual goals can be used to identify where the gaps are, what needs improvement most, and where attention should be directed in terms of implementing new technologies.

Note that we have a scoring scheme that uses explicit, tangible, and specific factors to do the scoring rather than a generic Poor-to-Excellent five-point scale. For example, if people understand the goal, they should be able to articulate it; if they are taking actions, it should be obvious. This takes subjectivity out of the scoring mechanism.

Current Initiatives

The impact of any current initiatives can be visually depicted, as highlighted by the arrows marked X and Y, which illustrate the improvements that can be expected from implementing initiatives X and Y.

Some current initiatives will not figure anywhere in the picture. The advantage with such a framework is that it makes the irrelevance explicit. The fact that they do not contribute to improved performance is visible and cannot be hidden. In that case, tough decisions must be made:

1. **Can the goal of the initiative** be changed so it fits in the picture?
2. **Can it be run in maintenance mode** so it is not draining the best talent?
3. **Should it be eliminated?**

Past Initiatives

This same framework can also be used to compare the return on investment of initiatives already completed in the last one to three years. Initiatives with "low effort" and "high results" are what we need to learn from and repeat. Initiatives with "high effort" and "low returns" are the ones we want to avoid repeating. What were the lessons learned?

You also want to make sure that you have a reasonable number of initiatives that have yielded good results for reasonable effort. If not, this can highlight a major weakness in the way initiatives are conceived, managed, implemented, and followed through.

CONCLUSION

Fundamentally, it is all about choosing the right race to run, and running faster than the competition by enhancing performance. Start with a balanced focus on *performance measures.* Then look at the right *policies* to grow the good variety and limit the drag effect of bad variety, and improve velocity by streamlining frequency and compressing lead times and strengthening policies that have become weak with time. Strengthen *processes* to reduce variability and lead times, and improve visibility by focusing on cross-functional processes. Structure the change in bite-sized phases so that the *people* can digest these capabilities, and *practice* them regularly until they become ingrained habits. Ensure that people have the *passion* for continuous improvement and sustaining operational excellence. Creating this *performance-focused* organization will result in choosing, successfully implementing, and getting significant benefits from e-supply chain technologies; and creating superior value for shareholders, customers, and employees.

Performance management is a synthesis of three key concepts:

1. **An action-oriented view of the supply chain** that focuses on what are the best areas to improve
2. **Creating a supply chain balanced scorecard** that is supply chain focused and tracks progress
3. **Having a capability framework** that leverages change management principles and practices

While the effect of applying the synthesis of these three concepts has been field tested in a dozen organizations, further research is needed to systematically study the impact of these concepts on improved performance on a broader basis.

REFERENCES

Bolstorff, P., & Rosenbaum, R. (2003). *Supply chain excellence: A handbook for dramatic improvement using the SCOR model.* New York: AMACOM.

Cameron, E., & Green, M. (2004). *Making sense of change management: A complete guide to the models, tools & techniques of organizational change.* VA: Kogan Page.

Copeland, T., Koller, T., & Murrin, J. (2000). *Valuation: Measuring and managing the value of companies.* New York: John Wiley & Sons.

Deming, W.E. (2000). *Out of the crisis.* Boston: MIT Press.

Hellriegel, D., Slocum, J.W. Jr., & Woodman, R.W. (2001). *Organizational behavior.* OH: South-Western College Publishing.

Hiatt, J.M., & Creasey, T.J. (2003). *Change management.* CO: Prosci Research.

Hugos, M. (2003). *Essentials of supply chain management.* New York: John Wiley & Sons.

Johnson, J. (2006, January). Transmissions from the RFID front lines. *RFID Watch.*

Kaplan , R.S., & Norton, D.P. (1996). *The balanced scorecard: Translating strategy into action.* Boston: Harvard Business School Press.

Latzko, W.J., & Saunders, D.M. (1995). *Four days with Dr. Deming: A strategy for modern methods of management.* Boston: Addison-Wesley.

Robeson, J.F., & Copacino, W.C. (1994). *The logistics handbook.* New York: The Free Press.

Senge, P. (1990). *The fifth discipline: The art & practice of the learning organization.* New York: Doubleday.

Srinivas, S. (2003, April). Leveraging technology to improve supply chain performance. In *Proceedings of the 2003 Supply Chain World Conference,* Atlanta, GA.

Srinivas, S. (2005). *Shocking velocity! Rapidly achieve more with less.* Greenwich, CT: Information Age Publishing.

Tompkins, J.A., & Harmelink, D. (2004). *The supply chain handbook.* NC: Tompkins Press.

Welch, J. (2001). *Jack: Straight from the gut.* New York: Warner Business Books.

Womack, J.P., & Jones, D.T. (1996). *Lean thinking: Banish waste and create wealth in your corporation.* New York: Simon & Schuster.

APPENDIX: ABBREVIATIONS USED

- **CCR:** cash contribution ratio
- **DC:** distribution center
- **DSD:** direct store delivery
- **ERP:** enterprise resource planning
- **ES:** economic surplus
- **GMROI:** gross margin return on investment
- **IQ:** intelligence quotient
- **POS:** point of sale
- **RFID:** radio frequency identification
- **ROA:** return on assets
- **SQ:** supply chain quotient
- **VAE:** value added by employees
- **VAP:** value added productivity
- **VMI:** vendor managed inventory

About the Authors

Qingyu Zhang is associate professor of decision sciences and MIS at Arkansas State University (USA). He has published in *Kybernetes: The International Journal of Systems and Cybernetics, Industrial Management & Data Systems, International Journal of Services Technology and Management, Supply Chain Management: An International Journal, Journal of Operations Management, International Journal of Operations and Production Management, International Journal of Production Research, International Journal of Production Economics, International Journal of Logistics Management, International Journal of Product Development, International Journal of Quality and Reliability Management, European Journal of Innovation Management*, and *APICS: The Performance Advantage*. Dr. Zhang's research interests are supply chain management, value chain flexibility, e-commerce/e-business, Web-based information systems, and product development.

***

Latif Al-Hakim is a senior lecturer of supply chain management in the Department of Economics and Resources Management, Faculty of Business at the University of Southern Queensland, (Australia). His experience spans 35 years in industry, research and development organizations, and universities. Dr. Al-Hakim received his first degree in mechanical engineering (1968). His MSc (1977) in industrial engineering and PhD (1983) in management science were awarded from University of Wales, (UK). He has held various academic appointments and lectured on a wide variety of interdisciplinary management and industrial engineering topics. He has published extensively on facilities planning, information management, and systems modeling. His research papers have appeared in various international journals, and have been cited in other research and postgraduate works. Dr. Al-Hakim is editor of the *International Journal of Information Quality* and associate editor of the *International Journal of Networking and Virtual Organizations*.

Ozlem Bak is a member of the Strategic Operations Management Center, and taught seminars in operations strategy and management at the University of East Anglia. She currently teaches as a lecturer in supply chain management, international operations, and e-logistics at the University of Greenwich, (UK). Her principal research interest is in the area of manufacturing operations management and especially on the value shifts within automotive supply chains. She also worked in multi-national automotive corporations and on project management for companies in professional sectors in Germany, the UK, and Turkey. Her research interests are supply chain management, value creation, marketspace, transformation, and the automotive industry.

Wade H. Baker is a PhD candidate in the Department of Business Information Technology at Virginia Tech (USA), and an information risk management consultant for Cybertrust. His academic and professional interests involve information security, risk modeling and management, business intelligence, and decision support systems. His work in these areas has been published in several academic journals and security magazines. He is a member of the Decision Sciences Institute, INFORMS, the Anti-Phishing Working Group, and recently served as a research and technical consultant for the President's Information Technology Advisory Council.

Patcharee Boonyathan is a PhD student in the Department of Management and Marketing at the University of Melbourne (Australia). She received her BEng (civil) degree from Kasetsart University, (Thailand) and her MEng (Industrial IT) from Swinburne University (Australia). She was a visiting scholar working with Dr. Latif Al-Hakim at the University of Southern Queensland (August—October 2003), where the research work in this book was done. She is particularly interested in the areas of supply chain strategies, supply chain collaboration, business process modeling, and business improvement. Her PhD research is looking at the empirical investigation of the relationship between strategic response to supply chain uncertainty, supply chain relationship, and firm performance.

Indranil Bose is associate professor of IS in the School of Business at the University of Hong Kong. His degrees include BTech from the Indian Institute of Technology, MS from the University of Iowa, and MS and PhD from Purdue University. He has research interests in telecommunications, data mining, electronic commerce, and supply chain management. His teaching interests are in telecommunications, database management, systems analysis and design, and data mining. His publications have appeared in *Communications of the ACM, Computers and Operations Research, Decision Support Systems and Electronic Commerce, Ergonomics, European Journal of Operational Research, Information and Management*, and *Operations Research Letters.*

Elizabeth Chang is professor in the School of Information Systems and director of the Center for Extended Enterprises and Business Intelligence at the Curtin University of Technology (Western Australia). Her research interests include information hiding, cryptography, multi-site software engineering, and ontologies.

Bintong Chen graduated from Shanghai Jiao Tong University of China with a BS in ship building and electrical engineering (1985). He obtained his PhD degree in operations research/management from the Wharton School of the University of Pennsylvania (1990). Since then he has been working for the Department of Management and Operations of Washington State University as assistant, associate, and full professor. He was recently named the Don and Mary Ann Parachini faculty fellow by the College of Business. He is currently a senior editor for *Production and Operations Management Journal.* His research interests include continuation methods for complementarity problems, optimization techniques, and their applications for business problems. More recently, he has been working with his students on optimization models for supply chain management.

Ron Craig is professor of business in the Operations and Decision Sciences area of the School of Business & Economics at Wilfrid Laurier University (Canada). His research interests cover small business and information systems; he has published several articles and cases in these areas.

Gavin Finnie is professor of IS and director of the Smart Enterprises Research Center at Bond University (Australia). His current research interests are primarily in the areas of AI/expert system applications in information systems, intelligent agents and electronic commerce with a specific focus on applications of artificial intelligence, and case-based reasoning in supply chain management and electronic bargaining. Dr. Finnie is a member of ACM, ACS, and AIS.

John Hamilton is the director of e-business at James Cook University (Australia). His extensive domestic business ownership and management experience includes: importing, exporting, mining, rural, wholesale, manufacturing, and several small-medium businesses (supermarket, video wholesale, fashion stores, florist/gifts, restaurants). His international business experience includes: sapphire mining, processing, and gemstone sales; plastics manufacturing; importing/exporting; and international finance. He has extensive consultant, business, management, and research experience. He is an active researcher, and his current specializations include: development of strategic Web-based instruments including QFD, strategic positioning, strategic e-marketing, logistics, strategic e-business models, and service value networks. He is currently engaged in developing smart business networks delivering industry-wide new technology solutions; and in the performance, value, and alignment of customer-business interfaces. He is manager and research director of a major CRC.

R. Manjunath is a research scholar from the Visveswaraiah College of Engineering, Bangalore University (India). His doctoral thesis spans signal processing, neural networks, data transfer over the network, and data integration. He has published about 55 papers in international conferences and journals in diverse areas involving the applications of signal processing. He has chaired many international conferences. His research interests include networking, signal processing, supply chain, and database architecture. He has industrial and academic experience over 11 years in various fields including signal processing, data transfers, data organization, and neural networks.

Charles L. Munson is associate dean for graduate programs in business at Washington State University (USA). His PhD and MSBA in operations management, as well as his BSBA, summa cum laude, in finance, are from Washington University's John M. Olin School of Business. He formerly worked as a financial analyst for Contel Corporation. He currently serves as vice chair of the board of directors of the WSU President's Teaching Academy. His primary research interests include supply chain management, quantity discounts, and international operations management. He has published articles in *IIE Transactions*, *Naval Research Logistics*, *Production and Operations Management*, *Decision Sciences*, *Journal of the Operational Research Society*, *Interfaces*, and *Business Horizons.*

Raktim Pal is assistant professor at James Madison University (USA). He holds a PhD in transportation systems from Purdue University. Also he has a BTech (Hons) in civil engineering from the Indian Institute of Technology, and MS degrees in civil engineering and industrial engineering from Purdue University. His research interests are in the areas of supply chain management and logistics, transportation systems modeling, electronic commerce, and applied operations research. His publications have appeared in *ASCE Journal of Transportation Engineering, Communications of the ACM, Computers and Operations Research, European Journal of Operational Research*, and *Transportation Research Record.*

Vidyasagar Potdar is a doctoral candidate working on information hiding techniques like steganography and watermarking. He is associated with the Center for Extended Enterprises and Business Intelligence, Curtin University of Technology (Western Australia).

Chunming (Victor) Shi is a PhD candidate at the College of Business, Washington State University (USA). He received the BEng degree from the Department of Automation and the BBA degree from the Department of Management Science, University of Science and Technology of China. His MEng degree is from the Department of Electrical and Computer Engineering, National University of Singapore. His research interests are in supply chain coordination, electronic commerce, price optimization, and other applications of operations research. His previous research has been published in the *Journal of the Operational Research Society* and *IEEE Transactions on Systems, Man, and Cybernetics.*

Gregory E. Smith is an assistant professor in the Department of Management Information Systems at Xavier University (USA). He received his PhD in business information technology from Virginia Tech. He also holds an MA in actuarial science from Ball State University and a BS in mathematics from the University of Scranton. Dr. Smith's research interests center on the integration of computers, mathematics, and artificial intelligence to solve business problems. He is a member of DSI, INFORMS, POMS, and APICS.

Srikanth Srinivas is the managing partner of Opex Partners—a U.S. firm that specializes in helping clients achieve breakthrough performance by creating a sustainable, actionable performance management framework that enhances organizational capability systematically. He has extensive experience in the areas of performance management, supply chain and information technology, and has added significant value to customers in the United States, Australia, China, India, Korea, Mexico, Singapore, and Taiwan. He is the author of *Shocking Velocity! Rapidly Achieve More with Less*, a book that has received rave reviews.

Zhaohao Sun is a lecturer in information systems at the University of Wollongong (Australia). He holds BSc, MSc, MSc, and PhD degrees from Hebei University, Brandenburg Technical University Cottbus, and Bond University. He has experience of working as a lecturer at Hebei University, a visiting scientist at RWTH Aachen, and a research assistant at both Technical University Cottbus and Bond University. He has more than 70 publications including a monograph published by Springer (2004). His current research interests are intelligent techniques in e-services, e-commerce, knowledge/experience management, and case-based reasoning. He is a member of IEEE and AIS.

Pierre F. Tiako is a faculty member of computer science and information systems, and the director of the Center of IT Research at Langston University (USA). Prior to his current position, he worked as a visiting professor at Oklahoma State University and as an expert engineer at INRIA, the French national institute for research in information technology. He also taught in several French research universities, including the University of Rennes and Nancy. He is currently a member of IEEE and chairman of the IEEE Oklahoma City Computer Society, as well as a member of the U.S. Association for Small Business and Entrepreneurship, the Association of Collegiate Business Schools and Programs, and the International Council for Small Business. He earned a PhD in software and information systems engineering from the French National Polytechnic Institute of Information Technology.

Kevin James Watson is an assistant professor in the Department of Management at the University of New Orleans (USA). His academic and professional interests involve supply chain management, process design/improvement, environmental management, and the theory of constraints. He has published a number of articles in academic journals including the *Journal of Operations Management*, *International Journal of Production Research*, and *Management of Environmental Quality*.

Chen Wu is a doctoral candidate working on distributed services architecture, service quality, and service mediation. He is associated with the Center for Extended Enterprises and Business Intelligence, Curtin University of Technology (Western Australia).

Shilei Yang is a PhD candidate in operations management at Washington State University (USA). His BS in management science and BE in computer science are from University of Science and Technology of China. Then he obtained his MA in economics and MS in mathematics from Middle Tennessee State University (USA). His primary research interests include supply chain coordination, inventory control, and optimization.

Alex Ye is currently pursuing his MBA at the University of Hong Kong. He holds an undergraduate degree in mechanical engineering from Zhejiang University of China. His interests are in the areas of supply chain management, information technology, and finance. He has extensive industry experience in the area of implementation of information systems.

Index

J

K

L

M

S

DATE DE RETOUR

23-11.12		
10/12/15		